The
World
Broke
in Two

The
World
Broke
in Two

Virginia Woolf, T. S. Eliot, D. H. Lawrence,
E. M. Forster and the Year that Changed Literature

Bill Goldstein

BLOOMSBURY CIRCUS
LONDON · OXFORD · NEW YORK · NEW DELHI · SYDNEY

Bloomsbury Circus
An imprint of Bloomsbury Publishing Plc

50 Bedford Square   1385 Broadway
London   New York
WC1B 3DP   NY 10018
UK   USA

www.bloomsbury.com

BLOOMSBURY and the Diana logo are trademarks of Bloomsbury Publishing Plc

First published in 2017 in the United States by Henry Holt and Company, New York
First published in Great Britain 2017

© Bill Goldstein, 2017

British Library Cataloguing-in-Publication Data
A catalogue record for this book is available from the British Library.

ISBN: HB: 978-1-4088-9458-3
EPUB: 978-1-4088-9457-6

2 4 6 8 10 9 7 5 3 1

Typeset by
Printed and bound in Great Britain by CPI Group (UK) Ltd, Croydon CR0 4YY

For Joanne Goldstein,
who was born in 1922,
and for Blake West,
who lived through it with me.

CONTENTS

INTRODUCTION

The world broke in two in 1922 or thereabouts.

Willa Cather, *Not Under Forty*

SOME YEARS ARE UNDERSTOOD AS PIVotal in history—1492, 1776, 1865, 1914, 1945, 1968. Nineteen twenty-two is a dividing line in literary history. *The World Broke in Two* tells the story of 1922 by focusing on four legendary writers: Virginia Woolf, T. S. Eliot, E. M. Forster, and D. H. Lawrence, who were all similarly and serendipitously moved during that remarkable year to invent the language of the future.

Willa Cather began her 1936 book of essays, *Not Under Forty*, with the melancholy remark about changes in literary fashion: "The world broke in two in 1922 or thereabouts." Cather was thinking of the publication of *Ulysses* in February and of *The Waste Land* in October of 1922, and the ways in which those works seemed, all at once, to herald a new modernist era in which the form of storytelling she prized, and had excelled at, was no longer of signal importance. Her own novel of the war, *One of Ours*, was published in 1922 and won the Pulitzer Prize in 1923. But Joyce's novel and

Eliot's poem, and the coincidence of their publication dates, had very quickly given 1922 a privileged place in the history of literary modernism in which she and her work seemed to have no share. She was a relic of an old literature the value of which had not been preserved against the new literature that Joyce and Eliot represented.

For Woolf, Eliot, Lawrence, and Forster, the literary apocalypse of 1922 had less to do with publication dates than with the personal and creative challenges that indeed broke the world in two for them in 1922. Woolf, Forster, Eliot, and Lawrence were, at the start of 1922, writers in deep despair, privately confronting an uncertain creative future; each of them felt literally at a loss for words. None of these essential pillars of twentieth-century literature could foresee the work just ahead that was about to transform them as writers. *The Waste Land* was published in 1922—but the drama of the year for Eliot had less to do with the poem's appearance than with how close he had come to not finishing it or having it published at all.

Renewal came as each in turn experienced a sudden, if still tentative, spark of vision. In early spring, Woolf thought to write again of a character who had appeared in her first novel, *The Voyage Out*, published in 1915: this was Clarissa Dalloway. Forster, picking up the abandoned manuscript of what was to become *A Passage to India,* made his first significant progress on a work of fiction in eight years. Both of them began to read the first volume of Proust's *À la recherche du temps perdu*, in French, which inspired their work, and on which both drew as they continued to work through 1922 and beyond. Lawrence started *Kangaroo*, his neglected but perhaps most autobiographical novel, written at light speed during his hundred-day sojourn in Australia that spring and summer. And Eliot, stopping in Paris for two weeks with Ezra Pound, began editing his poem into a 450-line distillation of his years of intermittent and sometimes aimless work. By the end of the year, the blank pages facing them in January were filled: they'd found the words, or were making new words, new forms, new styles, reworking the words into new shapes.

Rivalries and jealousy—including with James Joyce and the specter of his *Ulysses*—had a role in these writers' renewed creativity, as did the various ways each of them gained fresh publicity, and increasing renown, as 1922 progressed. Reviving the joy at the heart of their endeavors in 1922 is one of the goals of *The World Broke in Two*. In February 1922, Virginia Woolf looked over her shoulder at her friends and rivals and remarked in her diary with a mix of admiration and awful surprise, "How these writers live in their works—How ambition consumes them!" How right she was.

* * *

"It is after all a grrrreat litttterary period," Ezra Pound wrote to T. S. Eliot in January 1922.

This was a prophetic sentiment Eliot, or Virginia Woolf, E. M. Forster, or D. H. Lawrence, was unlikely to have shared at that moment. Most people begin a new year with a sense of resolution, a glimmering hope that by this time next year dreams will have come true, or plans been achieved, or nascent ideas become novels or poems. For these four authors, all among the major writers of the twentieth century, the year 1922 began, frighteningly, with a blank page even more starkly empty than usual because of personal travails and the open questions of form, style, and subject that haunted them all. Their shared questions were based in a shared fear: that a great (in plain English) literary period Pound foretold might be approaching, but it would pass them by.

Virginia Woolf turned forty on January 25, 1922. It was an unhappy milestone. For weeks before and after the dreaded birthday, she was stranded in bed, "apparently the favourite breeding ground of the influenza germ," and alternately preoccupied by a lingering fever and her equally persistent failure to have yet written a novel that commanded the precise quality of literary esteem she aspired to.

After years spent strenuously avoiding writing fiction, her friend E. M. Forster had likewise become painfully conscious of past and impending failures of his own, and of his evaporating prominence. "So here I am with 3 unfinished novels on my hands. Even mother must notice I'm played out soon," he had written in his diary as long ago as December 1913. One of these was his Indian fragment—seventy-five pages of which he abandoned the next year, before the world war. Born on New Year's Day, 1879, Forster celebrated his forty-third birthday on the first day of 1922, and as January got under way he was literally at sea, on his way home after having spent most of 1921 in India, more time abroad that he had hoped would offer some direction for the latest of his incomplete novels. But when he returned to England in March 1922 from the Indian sojourn that was meant to inspire him, he was no less adrift than before. As a writer and as a man, he was trapped, having struggled with an unrequited love for Mohammed el Adl, the married Egyptian tram conductor whom he'd met in Alexandria during the war, as laboriously as he'd wrestled with his continuing failure in fiction. That he was well into middle age and living with his mother was lost on no one, least of all himself.

T. S. Eliot—"That strange young man Eliot," as Virginia once called him—was as uncertain of himself and his work, as adrift, as Forster and Woolf were. He marked the start of 1922 in Lausanne, Switzerland, recovering from a nervous breakdown so severe he had left his job at Lloyds Bank for a three-month rest cure in October 1921. Eliot's distress, in part, was rooted in the sense of failure he shared with Woolf and Forster. Eliot, during his Lausanne treatment and in London before and after it, had to face down his inability to make any real headway on a long poem he had been contemplating for years. The many disparate pieces of what would become *The Waste Land* consisted in part of lines and fragments written during the war and before, including some bits from his undergraduate days at Harvard. For many years, the poem existed only in the future tense. Eliot could not put it together in a coherent way, and the frustrations and collapse that shadowed him as 1922 began were the culmination of years of attenuated effort.

"I am trying to finish a poem," Eliot wrote from Lausanne to a friend shortly before Christmas. It was "about 800 or 1000 lines . . . *Je ne sais pas si ça tient.*" I do not know whether it will work. It was as if he could not express his doubts in English, hiding his fear of failure in a whispered aside in French.

D. H. Lawrence might have been speaking for them all when as the new year began he wrote his friend Earl Brewster from Taormina.

> More and more I feel that meditation and the inner life are not my aim, but some sort of action and strenuousness and pain and frustration and struggling through. Men have to fight a way for the new incarnation. And the fight and the sorrow and the loss of blood, and even the influenzas and the headache are part of the fight and the fulfillment. Let nobody try to filch from me even my influenza.—I've got influenza at the moment.

As ill himself as Woolf and Eliot, who came down with influenza just as Woolf became sick, he was also as much at odds with domestic life as Eliot and Forster, anxious for change, restless with routine, almost allergic to his surroundings, and as eager as Woolf, Forster, and Eliot to start on new work. Lawrence and his wife, Frieda, living in self-exile in Sicily since 1919, were longingly and persistently in search of what Lawrence called "naked liberty"—the freedom to write, but also, simply, to live without prejudice and without the moral straitjacket England represented. A year and a half in Taormina, absorbed in the "carelessness of the South which dispelled like an unconscious benison the harsh and petty carefulness" of his English roots, living in a big house with a big garden, "beautiful and green, green, and full of flowers . . . on a steep slope at some distance above the sea—looking East," had not, after all, put enough distance between Lawrence and the England he had fled.

In late 1921, vacillating about where he might "live apart and out of the usual pattern," he received an invitation from the wealthy patron of the arts Mabel Dodge Sterne, who hoped he would come to Taos, New Mexico, to live near her in a house she had ready for him and write a novel about the ancient land and the persisting spirit of the Taos Pueblo. He agreed, impulsively, yes. He would come. But, as he recognized, "my compass-needle is a shifty devil," he wrote, and he put America on hold.

Lawrence, in 1922, was years away from publishing his most notorious novel, *Lady Chatterley's Lover*. The novel, published privately in 1928, spans the years 1917 to 1924. Yet Constance Chatterley first meets her lover, the gamekeeper Oliver Mellors, at the beginning of 1922, on a "frosty morning with a little February sun," as if finally, after five years of reliving the horror of the war that had crippled her husband and made him impotent, Lady Chatterley at last feels the frozen core of her own life beginning to melt. Her existence, she muses, is "either a dream or frenzy, inside an enclosure," a glass bubble of domestic ennui from which sex will deliver her. As 1922 began, Woolf, Forster, Eliot, and Lawrence himself were similarly impatient to break free—but from the stifling enclosure of literary tradition.

Just before Lady Chatterley meets her lover, she is talking with her husband, surveying together the dwindling forests that surround their estate. "One *must* preserve some of the old England!" Clifford Chatterley says from his wheelchair.

"Must one!" Constance replies. "If it has to be preserved, and preserved against the new England?"

Lady Chatterley poses the question almost to herself, but it was precisely what Lawrence, Eliot, Woolf, and Forster were asking themselves, on the page and at home, with their friends, or in their diaries and letters. It was the question of their lives at the start of 1922, when the ice of the postwar hangover they shared with Lady Chatterley was finally on the verge of thawing, although they didn't know it yet.

I do not know whether it will work, Eliot had written. In fact, 1922 would be a crucial year of change and outstanding creative renaissance for Woolf, Lawrence, Forster, and himself.

* * *

Behind these four writers' creative struggles and triumphs and private dramas—nervous breakdowns, chronic illness, intense loneliness, isolation, and depression, not to mention the difficulties of love and marriage and legal and financial troubles—lay a common spectral ghost: the cataclysm of World War I that each of them, in 1922, almost four years after the Armistice, was at last able to deal with creatively.

In 1922, Eliot, Forster, Lawrence, and Woolf each discovered a private literary way to recapture and to bridge the lost time that the war represented. The gap itself—the distance of the past that had been made more unrecoverable by the trauma of the war—now became the theme of their work. "Under the brown fog of a winter dawn, / A crowd flowed over London Bridge, so many, / I had not thought death had undone so many," Eliot writes in *The Waste Land*. One consequence of the unprecedented scale of killing during World War I was a new awareness that the past became a piece of the present through the experience of memory.

"Big Ben was striking as she stepped out in the street," Virginia Woolf wrote at the start of "Mrs. Dalloway in Bond Street," the 1922 story that became her 1925 novel *Mrs. Dalloway*. "The war was over," Clarissa will think. But the sound Virginia Woolf conjured signaled at the same time that the war was present everywhere. It had been three and a half years since the Armistice, but in small ways and large England was unable to escape the war or its long aftermath. Church bells did not chime in England until after the war was over, forbidden by the Defense of the Realm Act in 1914. And though each year on November 11, the anniversary of the

Armistice, the nation observed a two-minute silence in honor of the fallen, this did not seem to sanctify their sacrifice enough. In November 1921, the Royal British Legion had begun Poppy Day, a new way to mark the anniversary that Field Marshal Haig asked the nation to join. His plan was that to support ex-servicemen, people should buy a "Flanders poppy" to wear that day as a "sign of remembrance and reverence" for the thousands of "our heroes who lie beneath this flower in Flanders field." The idea for the silk flowers came from the wartime poem by the Canadian lieutenant colonel John McCrae that began "In Flanders fields the poppies blow / Between the crosses row on row." This was to be the third Remembrance Day, but Haig's idea, and his call that "November 11 shall be a real Remembrance Day," suggested that the solemnity of the day had been ebbing year by year and must be reconsecrated in a way visible to all (and a rebuke to those who did not buy or wear a poppy). The response was so great—eight million sold on that one day, not enough to satisfy demand, and more than £105,000 raised—that on Remembrance Day 1922, another real Remembrance Day, more than thirty million would be sold. Remembrance was now a national effort even as individuals were, in their own daily lives, moving farther and farther away from it.

The English translation of the first volume of Proust's *À la recherche du temps perdu* was published in September 1922, only six weeks before the fourth anniversary of the Armistice. The title the translator C. K. Scott Moncrieff chose for the volume was *Swann's Way*, an apt English counterpart to the French original, *Du côté de chez Swann*. The title of the seven-volume work he translated more freely as *Remembrance of Things Past*. It was an allusion to Shakespeare's Sonnet 30: "When to the sessions of sweet silent thought / I summon up remembrance of things past / I sigh the lack of many a thing I sought." But Scott Moncrieff was a veteran and had been injured in the war. Remembrance of things, including the war, was very much on his mind, and on England's. Remembrance Day—Poppy Day—endures nearly one hundred years later. The design of the flowers, and their manufacture, has changed, as have the wars the nation remembers.

* * *

Autumn 1921 brought remembrance of the war back in another way. At almost the same time as Poppy Day was announced, Parliament was debating a return to the prewar licensing hours that would allow people to eat and drink at both earlier and later hours than wartime restrictions mandated by the Defense of the Realm Act. The effort would mean that people could return, as the *Times* reported, to their prewar "liberties" (Lawrence's "naked liberty" in a different guise). But not everyone was pleased with this idea, and the issue was debated—not only in Parliament but vociferously among groups opposed to and in favor of the return. It was a question of morality for some—akin to the idea for Prohibition in the United States—but for others it was a question of business. Hotels and restaurants were eager for the change, and their customers, they argued, were, too. It was not to be simple. Parliament voted to change the hours, but local resistance led to confusion across the country. In London the difference was felt borough by borough, where different boards oversaw different districts and wished for different times (an extra hour before lunch, to cater to visiting tourists, or a later hour at night, to satisfy theatergoers and others). On one side of the street in the West End of London the rules were one way, on the other side another.

Some of the most famous lines in *The Waste Land* take on a new meaning in the context of England's awkward embrace of its onetime liberties. A conversation is overheard in a pub, the snippet as unmoored from clarity (and clarifying punctuation) as such conversations usually are.

> *When Lil's husband got demobbed, I said—*
> *I didn't mince my words, I said to her myself,*
> *HURRY UP PLEASE IT'S TIME*
> ... .
> *And if you don't give it him, there's others will, I said.*
> *Oh is there, she said. Something o' that, I said.*
> *Then I'll know who to thank, she said, and give me a straight*
>   *look.*
> *HURRY UP PLEASE IT'S TIME*

The interjections were the familiar cry of the pub owner asking for last orders. It is repeated five times in the poem. Eliot had written this section during or just after the war, and later said the exchange was recounted to him by his maid. By the time he published *The Waste Land* in October 1922, it had become the slogan for a changing London. The narrator of the poem, walking through postwar London, had not known that death had undone so many. The narrator might have been equally surprised by where and when he might drink.

One consequence of the unprecedented scale of killing during World War I was a world haunted by the palpable absence the death of so many created: the past made indelibly present by loss that could not be forgotten. The techniques these writers experimented with in 1922 were an attempt to make personal and artistic sense of a dislocation in time and consciousness between the country England had been before the war and what it was now, and between the artists they had been then and the pioneers they were becoming. Looking back at their work before the war and just afterward—and at the work that Joyce and Proust were doing—impelled them to confront and pin down on paper the texture and vitality of a new landscape of the mind. In formulating a new equation of experience and memory, in reinventing the literary depiction of the past and its persistence in the present, Eliot, Forster, Lawrence, and Woolf conspired to make the modern happen. Memories of the war were inescapable on the streets of London, and across the nation and Europe, a misery compounded by the start, during the winter of 1921–22, of an influenza epidemic unlike any seen in Europe since the pandemic of 1918–19. It was not clear, as 1921 ended and as 1922 began, how much worse it would become.

Virginia Woolf became extremely ill with influenza the first week of January. She was one of the homebound casualties and she did not know whether her various ideas for new books would also be.

VIRGINIA WOOLF
NEARS FORTY

Even WHEN VIRGINIA WOOLF WAS FEELING well, winter took a toll.

"Oh but the cold was too great at Rodmell. I was frozen like a small sparrow," she wrote one January. At a happy time, the perennial cold might be no bar to writing with pleasure, whether in London or at Monk's House, in Rodmell, their country home in Sussex. Even "a few staggering sentences" were enough satisfaction for a morning's work, the frigid weather almost enlivening her mood, especially when the recompense was the icy beauty of Monk's House at Christmas time or New Year's.

"Oh its [sic] so lovely on the downs now . . . I lie on the ground and look; and then the bells tinkle, and then the horses plough; and then, forgetting all the days to come and days past and this day and tomorrow,—well, you know the mood."

New Year's Eve, December 31, 1921, a Saturday, had been spent at Monk's House, but eager to be back at work early in the new year, Virginia and her husband, Leonard, returned by a Monday afternoon train to Hogarth House, 40 Paradise Road, in Richmond upon Thames, a suburb southwest of London.

Tuesday was to be her first day of work, and Virginia, as if to prepare, wrote a long entry in her diary, which for the sake of "parsimony" she wrote in the "odd leaves at the end of poor Jacob," in the notebook she was using for her third novel, *Jacob's Room*. She was looking forward to being busy again—writing, reading, printing.

Her apology to herself for not writing in her diary as often as she liked was "quite truthfully, the Hogarth Press," she wrote after a gap of ten days. The press would mark its fifth anniversary in 1922, and a number of its recent books had sold surprisingly well for Christmas, including an edition of Roger Fry's woodcuts that had been reprinted twice, and which she had hand-stitched herself in December. In October, they had bought a larger secondhand printing press for £70 and decided to use their Paradise Road basement for a print shop. More important, in November she had finished the draft of *Jacob's Room*. She had already begun revising it so that they would be able to publish it in the spring—the first full-length work of hers that Hogarth would issue.

Virginia also had a book of essays, about reading, in mind. Once those were under way, in January, "I shall think of another novel, I daresay." Looking ahead to her work in 1922, she had wondered, "Will my fingers stand so much scribbling?"

But almost as soon as she and Leonard were back at Hogarth House, Virginia came down with influenza. On the night of the fifth, "I was shivering over the fire & had to tumble into bed." Sentences, staggering or otherwise, were not forthcoming.

Winter had settled unseasonably over London as early as November— "Winter is upon us; fog, frost, every horror," Virginia wrote to her sister Vanessa Bell—and remained extremely bad. "We go to bed under red blankets, quilts, fur coats," she had written, worried all through the autumn and into the winter that she would become sick with influenza. She had escaped, until the new year. This was to be one of those long Januaries that Leonard found dispiriting, particularly at Monk's House: "a north east wind sweeping on to the croft . . . and a grim grey sky hanging not more than two feet above the elms and rain, sleet or snow banging on the windows." Sunset was at only shortly after three in the afternoon, so it was unsurprising that "one creeps about the house longing only for bed. Even without a cold, one's nose drips perpetually." Whatever the weather Virginia would have worked in the mornings, and even in January, whether in the country or in town, she would have walked in the afternoon—if influenza didn't mean she wasn't allowed out.

To walk was, to Virginia, also to write, for she worked out sentences in her head as she walked, settling them in her mind in order to write them down the next day. In London's winter cold, or in Sussex's summer splendor, Virginia walked after tea at four p.m., loping her own "delicate" way "a little unevenly, one foot turning very slightly inwards," through the countryside or city and going through the sentences she'd composed that morning, writing and rewriting in her head to seal that day's work and—observing people, hearing their talk—to anticipate her next day's adventure. "I keep thinking of different ways to manage my scenes; conceiving endless possibilities; seeing life, as I walk about the streets, an immense opaque block of material to be conveyed by me into its equivalent in language," she had written while working on her second novel, *Night and Day*, published in 1919. She had not—and would never—change.

Virginia had come to London resolved to start work on the essays on reading she was thinking through. "Tomorrow my reading begins!" she had written in her diary. But her reading did not begin the next day.

Leonard Woolf's pocket appointment diary recorded the sudden change in Virginia's health: "Work morn Walk w V aftn V. unwell even Went disp. Saw Fergusson," meaning he had done his own writing in the morning and took a walk with Virginia in the afternoon, and then in the evening she was ill. Leonard went to the dispensary, and they saw Dr. D. J. Fergusson, the local doctor, whose office was a short walk from Paradise Road.

Leonard's pocket diaries are filled with abbreviations, written quickly to save time, to jog his memory about daily and weekly events, and even, perhaps, as parsimonious as he was, to save money on ink. His entries recorded their daily routines, his careful inscription of the same activities day after day—work and printing usually in the afternoon—itself a routine, the main variations across the year consisting only of the names of visitors for tea or dinner, or an overnight stay. Leonard and Virginia made no distinction between weekdays and weekends, at Hogarth House or Monk's. "We should have felt it to be not merely wrong but unpleasant not to work every morning for seven days a week and for about eleven months a year," Leonard later recalled.

* * *

"Its [sic] foul," Virginia wrote of influenza, "it leaves one like a watch that doesn't tick." And unable to scribble. Her days were instead spent bedridden, largely without visitors, one of the usual compensations for her morning's work, and she was conscious only of waste. Not writing her reading essay—not revising *Jacob*—these were losses enough. But every day of January that passed meant that the twenty-fifth, and her fortieth birthday, were one day closer.

On Thursday the twelfth, a week after she first became ill, it was a major step that "V came down for tea," Leonard noted in his diary. A few days later, on Sunday, the fifteenth, "Vanessa came dinner," Leonard wrote. Vanessa was just back from a three-month painting trip in France and would soon be gone again. The hurried meetings before she went away again were painful for both sisters. Virginia feared that Vanessa's travels, and her children, left her, by contrast, seeming "settled & unadventurous," in her own eyes, and in Vanessa's. Virginia, childless, felt constitutionally "less normal" than her sister. Vanessa, in turn, pursuing her art in France, felt that Virginia and Leonard had something "binding" in their marriage as they approached their tenth anniversary that she, despite her three children, and her husband, Clive, and her lover, Duncan Grant, lacked in her own life. In London her work and Duncan's went for virtually nothing, she thought, whereas in France it could be at the center of their lives—just as in London, writing and books were at the center of Virginia and Leonard's and their circle of friends.

In London Vanessa felt invisible—in the shadows in Bloomsbury and in the larger world of the arts. "I have seen all the cleverest people," she complained to Virginia, "and not one has asked me about the South of France. Nobody mentioned painting." She had even hung two of her own and Duncan's latest paintings in Maynard Keynes's apartment, and he never noticed them, Vanessa said. Virginia tried to feel sympathy, but the way in which Vanessa seized independence—"only sixpence a year—lovers—Paris—life—love—art—excitement—God! I must be off!" left her "rather depressed," Virginia wrote in a letter to her "Dearest Dolphin," after another of Vanessa's visits, that her own life seemed to her a "dull respectable absurd" one in Vanessa's judgmental eyes. "This leaves me in tears."

Her sense of difference from Vanessa unsettled her, "donkey that I am . . . susceptible to the faintest chord of dissonance twelve fields away," she wrote in her diary after one visit. It was transitory and would pass, she knew—except that this time, ill as she was, and unable to write, her own life "did not very vigorously rush in," the usual recompense, her work, forbidden her by her doctor, who proscribed writing as too much of a strain. This meant it was impossible for her to write for her two hours every morning, "the sacred morning hours," she called them. "Phrase tossing can only be done then." When she was well, the afternoon was set aside for printing; then she would write letters and in her diary, usually for a half hour after tea. Her diary served the same purpose as her walks, and she kept to both as regularly as possible, believing, as she put it in 1919, "the habit of writing thus for my own eye only is good practice. It loosens the ligaments. Never mind the misses and the stumbles. Going at such a pace as I do I must make the most direct and instant shots at my object, and thus have to lay hands on words, choose them and shoot them with no more pause than is needed to put my pen in the ink."

* * *

Life, she wondered, "consists of how many months? That's what I begin to say to myself, as I near my 40th birthday," she wrote in January, the day almost ominously without light: illness and the weather had turned her inward upon her "exacting brain," isolated in her solitude rather than liberated from social obligations. "The machinery for seeing friends is too primitive: one should be able to see them by telephone—ring up, & be in the same room," she wished, for even when she was well, too many visitors often left her "in tatters," a state in which "my mind vibrates uncomfortably," and she might feel consumed by the failures of the encounters: "One's talked nonsense; one's ashamed; they've been uncomfortable; the contact of one with the other was difficult."

Yet she didn't like to be away from people too long, either. Too much isolation seemed a proof of illness and frailty and brought uncomfortable vibrations of a different kind. An "endless rain of visitors" brought frustrations but also reminded her of childhood, and of summer vacations in St. Ives, Cornwall, where family life "was rather shabby and casual" and Talland House "untidy and overrun with people," her nephew Quentin Bell would write.

Turning forty was to be an unhappy milestone for Virginia Woolf. "I feel time racing like a film at the Cinema. I try to stop it. I prod it with my pen. I try to pin it down."

* * *

Virginia's influenza was an inconvenience to her ambition, but it was not only that. The morning she became ill, the *Times* reported that there had been 151 deaths from influenza in London that week, nearly triple the number—54—in the preceding week. This was the start of what would soon be recognized as an epidemic. The *Times* had reported on a steep rise in "Winter sickness" as early as November, with the medical correspondent warning that "persons with weak hearts or chests must . . . avoid rapid changes of temperature, which severely tax the circulation and which lower bodily resistance to infection," among other nostrums.

Virginia had been worried she would become ill because she had very good reason to: she was among those warned to take particular care. She had been so eager to begin work early in 1922 because she had lost so much time to serious illness in 1921.

Seven months before, Leonard had noted an ominous change on June 10, 1921: "V went concert[.] Could not sleep." It had been years since Leonard had recorded Virginia's insomnia—or had the need to monitor her health so minutely. As the weekend and the following week proceeded, the situation worsened: Monday, "V still unwell"; Tuesday, "V not well." On Wednesday and Thursday Leonard's entries collapsed economically to "Ditto." Even his usual shorthand was too much to write out. The last time he had used his diary to track Virginia's failing health in this way had been six and a half years before, in February 1915, and his abbreviations were similar to those he used then, a replay of the familiar and the foreboding. For most of 1915 Woolf had been given sedatives liberally, as she had also been in 1913, when she had been ill for nearly a year and had attempted suicide with an overdose of Veronal, the sleeping medication she was once again using, time folding in upon itself.

The summer of 1921 set a cascade of "plagues" upon her, she wrote to Lytton Strachey. She had endured "days spent in wearisome headache, jumping pulse, aching back, frets, fidgets, lying awake, sleeping draughts, sedatives, digitalis, going for a little walk, & plunging back into bed again," she wrote in her diary. Only in August was she sleeping well without medication.

"What a gap!" Virginia had exclaimed in her diary on August 8, "two whole months rubbed out—These, this morning, the first words I have written—to call writing—for 60 days." She had lost weight, despite oppressive milk cures that she hated, but by autumn, recovering despite the unpalatable regimen, she was more sanguine. "Oh what a damned bore!" she had written a friend, making light of the severity of a crisis in order to be entertaining. She spent much of the fall "scribbling away" to make up for lost time. She had felt better in the autumn for that reason, closer to finishing *Jacob's Room*—and because September at Rodmell had brought gorgeous weather and long walks after summer rains. To be bedridden again so soon, after only four months in the autumn and winter, and with her revisions of her novel only partially done, was as dispiriting—and as debilitating—as the second bout of illness itself. The consequences to her work would be too great. She had wanted to publish *Jacob's Room* in the spring of 1922. Now it would have to be postponed until the autumn. It seemed too long to wait.

* * *

She had been incapacitated for long spells of her life, because of either mental illness or physical illness. To become ill, even not very seriously, was never free of apprehension for Virginia. The gap of summer had meant, as she had written in her diary, "all the horrors of the dark cupboard of illness once more displayed for my diversion." Among the particular symptoms of the epidemic of 1922, the *Times* reported, was a "tendency to 'feel the heart'—i.e., to palpitation," the breathlessness, nervousness, and muscular pains that were typical leading to a "marked depression" that was generally likely to occur along with heart trouble— and the threat of which exacerbated the disturbances of even minor illness for Virginia. The dark cupboard seemed to be opening again, and far too soon. She had had such a short time in which to catch up, to return to the necessary order of her days.

* * *

Leonard monitored Virginia's habits, and their finances, very carefully, noting their daily, weekly, monthly, and annual expenses, minuscule or large, ever more rigorously as the years went by after their marriage in August 1912. In 1921, he bought socks on July 29 and razors on August 5; a year later, on August 28, 1922, he replenished his supply, six razors for 3 shillings. Virginia bought a comb on January 5, just before falling ill. They bought a mousetrap, at 2 shillings and 6, on May 9. He would note his purchase of a toothbrush and a nail brush in 1923 but seems to have bought neither in 1922, an actuality more likely than that he would have omitted to record the purchase. Observing Leonard at work on the ledgers of the Hogarth Press, Clive Bell, Virginia's brother-in-law, called him "the inexorable Jew."

Virginia was not always happy about Leonard's supervision, which could seem punitive, and Leonard knew that it was not always wise to exert the control over her daily schedule that he wished to, for her own good. He was careful on Virginia's behalf partly because she was not, and because he knew that there was never, as Willa Cather would write about Katherine Mansfield, "an interval in which she did not have to drive herself beyond her strength." But Leonard was also careful because he knew that if he managed Virginia well, then she was at greater liberty to write, and to do her work with greater freedom of mind. He had learned that the "continual nagging which that kind of shepherding always involves" would "do no good & only spoil things"—so he knew he must be as unobtrusive a monitor as he could be, aware at the same time that "it was mad" to be too unmindful, even when nothing appeared to be wrong. Now, as the two months' gap that had hobbled her in 1921 seemed to reappear to mar 1922, his task was more delicate than ever. After one examination that winter, Virginia wrote in her diary that the doctor was worried about her heart. He "pronounced my eccentric pulse had passed the limits of reason & was in fact insane." They spoke in metaphors of mental illness even when trying hardest to avoid the precipice.

"V has relapse w temperature," Leonard wrote just before her birthday. She went back to bed, with a second attack "more wearisome than the first." Wearisome and worrisome. At the start of the epidemic the *Times* had reported that the course of the influenza was usually about ten days— but that in weakened patients, there was a tendency to relapse that was worse than the first incident. The nationwide pattern was worsening, and Virginia's recovery continued to be slow. The *Times* and Fergusson concurred on the "best advice": to keep working and to maintain a normal schedule as long as one felt well "and not meet trouble halfway by brooding on the possibility of attack"; but at the first sign of illness one "should go to bed at once, for their own and their neighbours' sake."

Three years after the Armistice, the war was receding in time, but new reports of illness and rising death tolls brought the memory of it closer again: the influenza epidemic of 1918–19 had brought more death than the war itself. The idea of a new national epidemic took increasing hold through January, as Virginia's second attack continued to worsen. The pope died, of influenza that became pneumonia, on Sunday, January 22. Virginia recorded his dying in her diary. The death of explorer Sir Ernest Shackleton, from heart failure caused by complications of influenza, was reported in the *Times* on January 30. He had died, in South America, on January 5, at the beginning of a new voyage to the Antarctic, the same day Virginia herself became ill. The epidemic was also spreading across the Continent. Vanessa's children came down with it, though this did not prevent Vanessa from returning to Paris after only a fortnight at home.

* * *

January 25 was Virginia's birthday. She saw uncomfortable truths weighing on her present and future, and thought with some confusion about her own achievements. Something ought to be settled about a writer at forty. In an essay about Laurence Sterne in the *New York Herald Tribune*, she would observe that he published *Tristram Shandy*, his first novel, "at a time when many have written their twentieth, that is, when he was forty-five years old." The hyperbole touched on a truth about her own slow start. Virginia Woolf, nearing forty in January 1922, was not quite the writer she had imagined she would be by now.

In December 1920 she had toted up, "Nearing the end of the year. . . . Here we sit over the fire, expecting Roger—whose book is out; as everyone's book is out—Katherine's, Murry's, Eliot's. None have I read so far." These were Katherine Mansfield; her husband, John Middleton Murry, editor of the *Athenaeum* literary magazine and a critic and novelist; and T. S. Eliot, whose poetry the Hogarth Press had published in 1919, and whose first book of criticism, *The Sacred Wood*, had just been published by Methuen. As the winter of 1922 deepened, and the twenty-fifth approached, January seemed to Virginia not the auspicious beginning to a new year she had confidently looked forward to returning to from Rodmell, but rather the demoralizing continuation, the lowest end point, of a year of writing that had not, she despaired, gone well.

Postponing the publication of *Jacob's Room* demoralized her: "K. M. bursts upon the world in glory next week," she wrote in January, when another book of Mansfield's, a collection of stories, was about to be published. Virginia had hoped, the first week of November, to finish *Jacob's Room* "in two days [*sic*] time—during the weekend at any rate." She had done it, and had put the loss of summer behind her, knowing that what lay ahead was "to furbish up Jacob." But the plan that seemed feasible as she and Leonard were at Monk's House at Christmas was very far from possible a month later. The delay until autumn left her worrying that by then "it will appear to me sterile acrobatics." To herself—and to others.

The unwelcome prospect of a birthday left Virginia ever more conscious that her achievements in the art of fiction were beginning to seem very distant in time, merely anachronistic relics of a prewar England that had been summarily swept away.

Her first novel, *The Voyage Out*, had been published in 1915, during the first year of World War I. Her second, *Night and Day*, appeared in 1919, roughly a year after the Armistice. The two novels hardly looked to her, nor could they to anyone else, she was sure, like precursors of an imminent literary breakthrough. *The Voyage Out* had actually been finished, at great emotional and psychological cost, a full decade ago—in 1912. She had spent her twenties writing one version or another of it, but a nervous breakdown, and then the start of the war, had delayed its publication. As for its successor, *Night and Day*, it had been received with praise for its formal elegance but was criticized, too. Gently if unmistakably, by E. M. Forster, who admired *The Voyage Out* as fresh and innovative and thought *Night and Day* a step backward, less decorously by Katherine Mansfield.

"We had thought that this world had vanished for ever," Mansfield wrote in the *Athenaeum*, "that it was impossible to find on the great ocean of literature a ship that was unaware of what had been happening. Yet here is *Night and Day*, fresh, new and exquisite, a novel in the tradition of the English novel. In the midst of our admiration it makes us feel old and chill. We had never thought to look upon its like again!"

In private, Mansfield was more scathing, writing to Middleton Murry in terms that she could not print: the novel was "a lie in the soul"; "so long and so tahsome"; contemptible for its "boundless vanity and conceit." But Virginia had read between Mansfield's published lines, and even as she savored the praise of other reviewers and friends, she questioned the favorable judgments: *Night and Day* was a novel of manners, apparently written in a social and political vacuum, and what good was that? Meanwhile, everywhere in London, other (often younger) writers were writing, publishing, rising in popularity and fame.

The opinionated Virginia was the doyenne of a remarkable literary circle that her contemporaries regarded, and either admired or ridiculed, as almost unnaturally set apart. It was "a kind of glittering village with no doors," Enid Bagnold, the author of *National Velvet*, would remember. "It hovered ungeographically and had to my mind, only one inhabitant—a woman with a magnet." Bloomsbury—so specific as a place but so elusive to pinpoint or define—was, in its earliest beginnings, the London outgrowth of a coterie of friends from Cambridge, among them Leonard Woolf, Virginia's brother Thoby Stephen, Lytton Strachey, Maynard Keynes, Roger Fry, and E. M. Forster, who, with some others, moved to, or at least in and out of, London between 1900 and the start of World War I. "Bloomsbury" was an urban version of the university world in which, with varying degrees of separation, they had met, in groups like the Cambridge Apostles, a society of skeptics willing to question every accepted idea, including, in later years, whether "Bloomsbury" itself had ever existed.

A hallmark of Bloomsbury was "the cultured attitude" painter and critic Roger Fry thought could not be acquired by study; the common ground of those opposing Bloomsbury, whether from critical conviction or dismay about its perceived social or cultural pretensions, was, Fry thought, "envy and a hatred of intellectual freedom." Yet the intellectual rectitude of Bloomsbury bordered on, and blurred into, what others saw as self-satisfaction, a dead end. Virginia Woolf's magnetic pull had little allure to those who, publicly and privately, deplored the group's snobbery and claustrophobia, what one writer called its "central heating." Eliot himself had once despaired over the "Bloomsburial" of Aldous Huxley—worrying, not a little, that he might be similarly tarred by too close an association.

"La belle Virginia," as Clive Bell called her, tongue only partly in cheek, had long since taken her place as a prolific arbiter of taste, a woman among the great conversationalists of her day, a secular priestess in a coterie where conversation was near to religion.

When, after Lytton Strachey's death, Dora Carrington read through his correspondence with his old Cambridge friends, she "suddenly felt the quintessence" of the undergraduate bond that gave rise to Bloomsbury: "a

marvellous combination of the higher intelligence and appreciation of literature with a lean humour and tremendous affection." They drew around
them those like them—sisters (Virginia and Vanessa Stephen); returning
civil service administrators (Leonard, who returned from Ceylon in 1911
and married Virginia the next year); husbands and lovers (Clive Bell,
Duncan Grant, Dora Carrington herself); and in circles expanding out-
ward, the lovers of those people, too (Mary Hutchinson, Clive's mistress,
and Mary's husband, Jack), and artists, writers, socialites, among them
Ottoline Morrell and T. S. Eliot and his wife, Vivien. What they prized, and
honed, was an ability, in conversation, to give it "backwards and forwards to
each other like shuttlecocks, only the shuttlecocks multiplied as they flew in
the air," Carrington wrote. Yet the volley itself was not enough. Eliot wrote
once of a woman he met who had a "remarkable flow" of talk, but who, he
realized, fell beneath the uniquely high Bloomsbury standards of conversation that had won his admiration and raised his own game. Bloomsbury
people had mastered the deployment of silences, pauses offered, and recognized as an essential part of what was at its best a theatrical dialogue—
"opportunities for the other person to show his wit."

Remembering a later period, novelist Christopher Isherwood evoked the
scene: "We are at the tea table. Virginia is sparkling with gaiety, delicate
malice, and gossip—the gossip which . . . made her the best hostess in
London." The gifts that made her an attractive hostess were deployed somewhat differently as a critic—but to no lesser scintillating or withering effect.
From a very young age, beginning in the nursery, "speech became the
deadliest weapon as used by her," Vanessa was to say; later, Virginia perfected the art of putting "her living presence" into her work: "When one had
spent half an hour in a room with her one could easily believe that it was she
who . . . had scribbled quickly in purple ink in the summer house at Rodmell that fresh and sparkling article that had just appeared in the *Nation*."

Even her warmest enthusiasm couldn't (and wasn't meant to) entirely
conceal a devastating, often wounding, capacity for judgment of writers who
were friends, rivals, or frequently both. "I see she is very beautiful & very
distinguished—but she is so full of mockery & contempt & sees people
entirely wrong . . . because having no *humanity* she really cannot see what is
human," wrote Ottoline Morrell, who fell into both categories, in her diary.
Educated, entertaining, aristocratic, generous, Morrell oversaw the salon

that was Garsington; she had admirers as well as detractors—the writer Sieg-fried Sassoon lovingly hailed her in 1922 as "O Philosophress of Garsington"—and her ego was as fragile as Virginia's. Morrell continued to worry over Virginia's judgment of her and in her diary added to her first thought in a different, darker ink: "Her contempt is not balanced by her heart."

Virginia voiced her verdicts publicly in print and rather more regularly in private—in her diary or in frank letters to friends, among them Eliot and Forster, to Vanessa, to Clive Bell, and an array of others. Clive, variously "the Yellow Cockatoo" and "the Yellow Bird of Bloomsbury," played a particular role in the "orchestral concerts" of conversation that the regular Bloomsbury evenings usually became: to "keep up a general roar of animation" and "to egg on and provoke Virginia to one of her famous sallies."

During a trip to America in 1920, Sassoon wrote to Ottoline Morrell about the sense of waste that London, and the Bloomsberries, kindled in him. "From this distance," he wrote from Lake Forest, Illinois, "I look back on it with something like despair—all those clever people saying ill-natured things about one another—cackle, cackle . . . [ellipses in original]." Forster, separating himself from Bloomsbury idolatry even as he remained close to Leonard in particular, and Strachey, and Keynes—the "old" Bloomsbury—was always wary of what its insularity crystallized: "The London intellect, so pert and shallow, like a stream that never reaches the ocean."

* * *

And of course there were also the confidences offered to Leonard, her husband, partner in the Hogarth Press, and first reader (though he did not read her work in progress—he only read it once she had completed her revisions). Leonard and Virginia, echoing the humor of their friends, often referred to themselves in the third person—they were "the Woolves," together forming a pair different—in name and character—from the usual plural. Virginia, or Fate, had chosen her husband well—her married name, together with her own, Adeline Virginia, encompassed the contradictions of her personality with an inevitability that was as accidental as it was apt. "Tenuousness and purity were in her baptismal name, and a hint of the fang in the other," Vita Sackville-West wrote.

Virginia was quick to fault most of her contemporaries' otherwise lauded accomplishments, often with her own good reasons, and she claimed, repeatedly, to be deeply suspicious of the idea of literary celebrity itself. She acknowledged her jealousy—of Katherine Mansfield, of James Joyce, of T. S. Eliot—in her diary and letters, and disclaimed it in alternate paragraphs (or even phrases). Once she was even "momentarily" jealous of Leonard, after a good review of a short story of his appeared in the *Daily Mail*: "But the odd thing is—the idiotic thing—is that I immediately think myself a failure—imagine myself peculiarly lacking in the qualities L. has," she wrote in her diary. (Leonard published two acclaimed novels before her own first novel was published but did not write another. The first Hogarth book, *Two Stories*, contained one each by Leonard and Virginia.) When her own work was going well, then the jealousy passed as quickly as it came. When it was going badly, the jealousy lingered.

This winter, her doubts about her position sharpened by her impending birthday, she protested in her diary that she wasn't concerned with fame, that she had other achievements in mind. This went hand in hand with her disillusion about her past accomplishments and the slackened pace of her current work—but her sense of imminent failure was amplified by the fact that she was confined to home and had time, not writing, to ruminate.

"I have made up my mind that I'm not going to be popular, & so genuinely that I look upon disregard or abuse as part of my bargain," she claimed to herself. "I'm to write what I like; & they're to say what they like. My only interest as a writer lies, I begin to see, in some queer individuality; not in strength, or passion, or anything startling; but then I say to myself, is not 'some queer individuality' precisely the quality I respect?" Not writing had brought, at least temporarily, a kind of clarity about the ends she sought, or would seek, when, eventually, she was writing again.

* * *

Just before her birthday, on the twenty-first, Virginia wrote to E. M. Forster, who she and Leonard had learned at dinner with Forster's mother would soon be returning to England after nearly a year in India. In March 1921, she had wondered whether she would ever see him again. The prospect of his arrival was a happy surprise, and her letter, a long one, would reach him at Port Said on his journey home. She confided to Morgan the disquiet she had also described in her diary. Time was running short, she wrote him.

> ... I was stricken with the influenza, and here I am, a fortnight later, still in bed, though privileged to take a stroll in the sun for half an hour—after lunch.
>
> But it is not going to be sunny today.

* * *

> Writing is still like heaving bricks over a wall; so you must interpret with your usual sympathy. I should like to growl to you about all this damned lying in bed and doing nothing, and getting up and writing half a page and going to bed again. I've wasted 5 whole years (I count) doing it; so you must call me 35—not 40—and expect rather less from me. Not that I haven't picked up something from my insanities and all the rest. Indeed, I suspect they've done instead of religion. But this is a difficult point.

Her letter, with its cheerfully grim, self-deprecatory confession, found an apt recipient in Forster—the "evanescent, piping, elusive" Morgan, "timid, touching, infinitely charming" and "whimsical & vagulous," as Virginia variously attempted to encapsulate him during their long friendship. This "vaguely rambling butterfly" would interpret with his usual sympathy because Virginia had chosen her correspondent carefully.

The evocative monotony of her heaving of bricks, whether it was to write the letter itself that he must interpret sympathetically or a novel, would resound with him, and the totting up of wasted years would, too. Here was a friend, and one with a more august reputation all around, who had last published a novel far longer ago than she had. Virginia's playful calculation of her real age as a writer barely concealed a despondency she understood Morgan, too, knew well. He had recently published an anonymous article in the *Nation*—" 'Too Late in India' occurs on the front page in the largest letters"—that she recognized as his by the "neckties and the grammar." Nevertheless, she added, "But I won't bother you about your writing." That would be a relief to him. He was bothering himself enough about it, and writing no fiction at all.

The agony of perhaps having to expect less from yourself and asking your friends to do the same, of being found wanting in your own estimation and in others' eyes—these were subjects Woolf and Forster had gingerly broached between them before the bleak, cold beginning of 1922. Now, the damned lying in bed left her surveying her achievements and her prospects with what Joseph Conrad, sick with influenza that winter, too, confided to a friend was "the peculiar invalid's acuteness of emotion."

* * *

The news in the *Times* on Saturday, February 4, 1922, was grim: "There have been 13,000 deaths from influenza in England and Wales since Christmas."

Virginia was still in bed that day, very slowly—too slowly—recovering from the second attack. She had now been in bed for a month. Her heart had become "naturally abnormal" and she worried about death. "I have taken it into my head that I shan't live till 70," she wrote in her diary. "Suppose, I said to myself the other day this pain over my heart wrung me out like a dish cloth & left me dead?"

Fergusson enforced bed rest for another two or three weeks. She was nearing the "two whole months rubbed out" that had undermined her in the summer. She could not concentrate and she had the lethargy of an alligator at the zoo, she wrote Lytton Strachey. As the end of February approached, she was already "furious, speechless, beyond words indignant with this miserable puling existence which has now lasted over 6 weeks, and doesn't really pay," she wrote to Vanessa. It was as if she were being held prisoner, and she resolved that at Fergusson's next visit she was "going to make him let me out." She hoped that "a little air, seeing the buses go by, lounging by the river, will, please God, send the sparks flying again." But it was not to be, not quite yet.

* * *

Virginia's illnesses had tried Dr. Fergusson's skill, or his patience, or both. He came twice in two days the last weekend in February. Leonard kept to his habits, recording in his diary the facts of the situation: "Work morn Fergusson came & saw V. shd see heart specialist Print aftn." Roger came for tea and "stayed dinner played chess." An appointment was made for Monday the twenty-seventh with Dr. Harrington Sainsbury, in Wimpole Street. Leonard worked in the morning as usual. They "motored" to the appointment,

Leonard noted in his pocket diary, having ordered a car to take them to Sainsbury's office, despite the expense. The doctor examined her for an hour and prescribed more bed rest, as well as a cancellation of their planned trip to Italy in the spring. She could go out for brief walks, Sainsbury said, but for only ten minutes—"The cat lets this mouse run a few steps once more"—and not uphill, which would be too much of a strain.

As writing would be, though in the case of this prohibition the treatment was worse than the disease, as the passing weeks had proved. Her mind, and perhaps her career, was atrophying while her body rested, for bed rest had not left her mind at ease. Her constant temperature, over 99.5, as well as the slackening tensity of her brain at work, left her feeling "all dissipated & invalidish," as she put in her diary for February 14, a most unromantic day that year. Exasperated at her lack of progress in writing anything substantial, she listed in her diary the books she had been reading, a catalog of fiction and "an occasional bite" of biography that she hoped "like dead leaves" would fertilize her brain—*Moby-Dick*, Walter Scott's *Old Mortality*, a life of Lord Salisbury, and "anything else I can find handy"—but which left her bloodlessly uninspired as far as her own delayed prospects were concerned, and demoralized about both past and future: "what a 12 months it has been for writing!—& I at the prime of life, with little creatures in my head which won't exist if I don't let them out!"

* * *

Clive Bell, writing to Vanessa, gave the view from outside, as if describing a still life of Vanessa's. He had been seeing Virginia. Her bed had been moved downstairs, for everyone's convenience and to make her convalescence less lonely. He found her reclined "exquisitely on a bed in the drawing-room (banked up with bits of card board & odd scraps of stuff—to make the light fall right I suppose)—I hope I shan't fall more deeply in love. However it's a great compliment for a woman of forty don't you think."

In fact, now that Virginia was forty, she was aware of how crucial the right lighting was, and how precisely, if unconsciously, women of a certain age, now her own, moved to find it. One afternoon, "the fire dying out," she realized sitting there, all in shadow, that it was "the best light for women's nerves once they're passed 40. I observe that my women guests of that age . . . move to have their backs to the window, on some excuse or other."

Clive was only part of a spring resurgence of people she wanted to see.

In March two people who had been away returned to her: Forster and Tom Eliot.

* * *

Virginia and Tom met in November 1918, though he was not yet Tom to her but only Mr. Eliot—"That strange young man Eliot," as she called him in writing to Roger Fry, who had first mentioned T. S. Eliot to them and suggested he might have some poetry they could publish. Leonard wrote him that he and Virginia "both very much liked your book, *Prufrock*; and I wonder whether you would care to let us look at the poems with a view to printing them." He came to tea on Friday, November 15, at the end of the week that began with the Armistice.

The end of the war and the last page of Virginia's diary for the year came simultaneously, and as she wrote in the last entry of the book, on the twelfth: "Peace is rapidly dissolving into the light of common day," she wrote, describing the mental change that peace quickly brought. "Instead of feeling all day & going home through dark streets that the whole people, willing or not, were concentrated on a single point, one feels now that the whole bunch has burst asunder & flown off with the utmost vigour in different directions. We are once more a nation of individuals." Part of the change she allowed herself to feel—or at least to express—was a kind of loneliness. As she wrote to Vanessa on the thirteenth, "There's practically no one in London now whom I can talk to either about my own writing or Shakespeares [*sic*]."

Into this world, into this need, walked T. S. Eliot.

She was writing in her diary—in order to save money, she was now using a notebook in which she usually made notes on books she was reading—when he arrived, and was "interrupted somewhere on this page" by his visit. Eliot wished so much always to be properly courteous, to be so carefully mannered, it is perhaps ironic that his arrival at Woolf's home was an interruption of anything. They talked about his poetry—but also of the end of the war. The question of peace was an interesting one, she wrote to Vanessa. "We literary people have been comparing our feelings a good deal," she told her the day after his visit. With Eliot there was some difficulty, however, as she reported to Roger Fry. "His sentences take such an enormous time to spread themselves out that we didn't get very far."

Her first comments on Eliot foretold the ensuing two decades of their friendship. She noted immediately the disparity between who he appeared to be and who, "beneath the surface," as she put it, he might really be. Nothing about him was casual or seemed to be spontaneous; as if in reaction to this, Woolf, too, was guarded. Once, after a visit from him, she wrote, "To go on with Eliot, as if one were making out a scientific observation," and in this spirit of experimentation, she would never be satisfied she had understood him. Early on she questioned the six-year gap in their ages—"What happens with friendships undertaken at the age of 40?"—but in the next two or three years felt herself drawn increasingly into a friendship based on what she knew they shared, "our damned self conscious susceptibility." Yet on her side this meant there was always some new aspect revealed, an eccentricity of his or characteristic to test or break or stretch her theory and discomfort her. From the start she was dubious of many of his literary ideas, and more intrigued by the persona he adopted in announcing them—his manner, she thought, was variously comic and effete, almost unbearably formal and pretentious.

One of her rituals was to offer a January accounting of her friendships, a gallery of portraits of those she knew and what she felt about them. In January 1919 she wrote of Eliot that she liked him "on the strength of one visit & shall probably see more" of him, too, "owing to his poems which we began today to set up." The book was published later that year. As they got to know each other better she realized that intimacy did not increase. "I plunge more than he does: perhaps I could learn him to be a frog," she wrote in her diary.

Chapter 2

ELIOT IN JANUARY

T. S. ELIOT MARKED THE END OF 1921 IN Lausanne, Switzerland, continuing to recover from a nervous breakdown so severe that in October he had taken a three months' leave of absence from his job at Lloyds Bank. The new year looked to be an improvement on the one very soon to be behind him. It seemed unlikely it could be worse.

Tom had stayed overnight with Virginia and Leonard at Monk's House on Saturday, September 24. Leonard's date book records, simply, "Eliot." Virginia didn't seem to be looking forward to the visit. She wrote to Vanessa with a less than thrilling invitation: "I suppose you wdn't come for the 24th? When Eliot will be here?" But the visit "passed off successfully," Virginia wrote in her diary, "& yet I am so disappointed to find that I am no longer afraid of him—." She punctuated it with a long dash and left her reflection on him incomplete. It was a new era in their friendship, whatever it might mean.

Thomas Stearns Eliot, born in Saint Louis, Missouri, in 1888. "What a big white face he has . . . a mouth twisted & shut; not a single line free & easy; all caught, pressed, inhibited," Virginia wrote, his outsized head a symbol of his imperious intellect, and of the literary talent, and ambition, that had won him a place among both the Bloomsbury set, including Virginia and Leonard, and the anti-Bloomsburians, too, led by Ezra Pound, Wyndham Lewis, and others. But his big white face and his mouth twisted shut were elements of a mask, a facade, that had, by the summer of 1921, become less and less effective in hiding the depression, and hopelessness, beneath.

Financial uncertainty, an unhappy marriage, and a stultifying anxiety over the lack of time his job at Lloyds left to write had sculpted what Virginia called the "grim marble" of Eliot's face into puffy hollows. Sagging cheeks deepened the lines around his nose, and dark circles shadowed his eyes. The strain of his private disappointments, including his own ill health and, more significantly, the fragility of his wife's, had been growing more evident for some time. In 1919, he was able to assure his mother that he was establishing himself as a significant critic, perhaps the most influential American in England since Henry James. But his responsibilities at the bank grew alongside his reputation, and he had once explained to Lytton Strachey that poetry had been pushed aside and that he was preoccupied instead by questions of "*why* it is cheaper to buy steel bars from America than from Middlesbrough, and the probable effect—the exchange difficulties with Poland—and the appreciation of the rupee." This was making light of it, but when Eliot wrote this to Strachey, in the summer of 1919, he was still able to make light of it. The effect of all this business, he told Strachey, was to make him look at London with "disdain" and to see mankind divided into "supermen, termites and wireworms." He himself, "sufficiently specialized," was "sojourning among the termites." Strachey expected raillery, and Eliot, happy to oblige the more famous author and to prove his wit, rose to the occasion. But by the summer of 1921, he no longer was able to. His life in the previous two years had revealed his bleak metaphor as very far from funny. He had proved himself a termite eating away at his own foundations. There was very little humor left in his letters, or himself, enmeshed as he was in a depression that became more crippling as the astonishing career he had so recently foreseen—and

which so many others, including Ezra Pound and Virginia Woolf, had foreseen too—slipped farther and farther away.

"Have you ever been in such incessant and extreme pain that you felt
your sanity going, and that you no longer knew reality from delusion?" he
wrote a friend in March 1921. "That's the way she is," he wrote, referring to
his wife's agony, and to another recent diagnosis of her series of illnesses,
neuritis. But it was more and more the way Eliot himself was, undone not
only by worry over Vivien's health but by the expense of her recuperation,
first at a nursing home and, when the cost of that became too great, at
home, a situation that inevitably trapped him in a flat turned hospital
ward, where the patient, Vivien, and her attendant, Tom, came to alternate their roles amid a medley of symptoms—nervous exhaustion, colitis,
and other digestive troubles—that only seemed to get worse with treatments
that in Vivien's case were more severe and debilitating than her ailments.
What had been "very anxious moments" over Vivien's health gave way to
very anxious days and months, which then became indistinguishable from
anxious days and months about Tom's health and his career, the toll taken
on him increasingly too dangerous and perhaps too selfish to acknowledge
as long as Vivien was so ill.

In April 1921, in the wake of Vivien's most serious crisis yet, he wrote to
a friend that he could not yet let anyone see the poem he was trying to finish, a mix of typed and handwritten drafts that he had been working on
slowly and intermittently almost from the time he'd arrived in England,
seven and a half years before. It was a "hoard of fragments" he had not had
"the freedom of mind" to put into a final and as yet unforeseen form. At
one time, freedom of mind had meant the free time in which to write. But
more recently he had been losing his ability to concentrate; his mind was
itself no longer free, and he had become a "prey to habitual worry and
dread of the future."

* * *

Tom had come to England in 1914 to study at Oxford, and to complete the
Ph.D. in philosophy he had been working on at Harvard. But he had also
come to write poetry, as he had done in Europe before arriving in England,
where, liberated from family strictures, he might pursue the literary—and
not academic—career that he preferred. By the end of that school year, he

was married to Vivien Haigh-Wood, the daughter of Charles Haigh-Wood, a modestly successful painter who had studied at the Royal Academy, and whose inheritance of his mother's properties, and their rentals, supported a comfortable life for him, his wife, Rose, their son, Maurice, and Vivien, who continued to receive a small allowance after her marriage. Six months after their June 1915 wedding Eliot wrote to the poet Conrad Aiken that he had "lived through material for a score of long poems in the last six months." Some of the hoard of fragments evidently preceded his marriage, and there were pieces that had been written before Eliot left Harvard in 1914, or earlier. The six months Eliot had mentioned to Aiken had now stretched into years, and the longer it took Eliot to write the poem he had in mind, the more and more material he lived through that might be a part of it.

* * *

In the spring of 1921, Tom had looked forward to finishing the poem, still untitled, still unfocused, before October. Then he would spend an autumn holiday in Paris, working on it with Ezra Pound. He outlined his plans to friends in letters throughout the year, but his assurances that he was near to finishing whatever *it* was did perhaps more to convince himself that an end was in sight than it did others. In the winter Wyndham Lewis wrote to a mutual friend, the art patron Violet Schiff, that Eliot had told him he was "engaged in some obscure & intricate task of late: though what *his* task has been I cannot say."

Lewis and Pound were familiar with Eliot's overly optimistic prognostications about delivery of his assignments to the magazines they had edited. "Eliot can not be depended on to have stuff *in* at a given date," Pound had written to Margaret Anderson, the editor of the *Little Review*, years before, in 1917. The long poem was at the forefront of his mind through 1920 and 1921, but between Lloyds Bank, which occupied him five and a half days a week (with a half-day Saturday, and a full day on Saturday every fourth week)—about fifty hours a week including his commute—and the distractions of "Mrs. E" and her many illnesses, he could not actually write it or even think about it very much.

The "chief drawback to my present mode of life," he wrote a friend, "is the lack of *continuous* time, not getting more than a few hours together for myself, which breaks the concentration required for turning out a poem of any length." This straightforward accounting concealed a more dire mathematics of incalculable loss. After Tom finished his days at Lloyds, Vivien wrote to a friend, he then had to tend to her, filling water bottles for her, making "invalid food for his wretchedly unhealthy wife, in between writing!" But, really, he did his writing in between these and other responsibilities. Eliot published forty-nine reviews and essays in the *Times Literary Supplement* and elsewhere between 1919 and the end of 1921, and was in despair about his inability to concentrate on the creative work he knew he ought to be doing. Tom for his part could seize only "a moment's breathing space" for his poetry after work, preoccupied as he was by "private worries," mainly about Vivien and the financial necessity that kept him at Lloyds and also drove him to undertake so much journalism that further distracted him.

Tom's brother Henry described Vivien's illnesses as her "migraines and malaises," writing to their mother, Charlotte, with a condescension Vivien did not deserve. Vivien liked "the role of invalid," Henry Eliot thought. If only she had "more of 'the Will to be Well' she would have less suffering." But this Eliot credo was an inconveniently ineffective one, as Tom's own case was proving.

Henry and the rest of Tom's family did not meet Vivien until the summer of 1921, by which time Tom had not seen his mother or his brother for six years. Charlotte and Tom's sister Marian arrived in early June for a two-month visit, and then Henry joined them separately. The reunion was "another anxiety as well as a joy" and added to the strain on Tom, and Vivien, too, who moved into a borrowed flat in order to accommodate Tom's mother and sister. Whatever "in between" time Tom might have hoped to devote to the poem was now given over to his family's entertainment. He could, of course, not quite admit that his family's presence disturbed him even as it brought pleasure, though it revealed a lot that he had called it an anxiety first and a joy second. "These new and yet old relationships involve immense tact and innumerable adjustments," he wrote a friend. "One sees a lot of things one never saw before etc."

Not only did he see things about his mother, sister, and brother he had not seen before, he saw his marriage anew; their fresh scrutiny of Vivien brought unbearable exposure of both of them. Vivien, then most recently diagnosed with neuritis and digestive troubles, was to have been out of town at least during part of her in-laws' visit, but rather than recuperate, she returned to London against her doctor's (and, it seems, her husband's) wishes. "So I shall not rest until I have got her away again," Tom wrote to one friend. But was it that he wouldn't be at ease until Vivien did what she ought to do to recover; or was it that he wouldn't be able to rest until they were apart?

* * *

Vivien Haigh-Wood met Tom Eliot in Oxford, at a luncheon party at Magdalen College, in March 1915. Tom, awarded a Sheldon Traveling Fellowship in philosophy at Merton College for the academic year, was twenty-six and nearing the end of his fellowship. That spring he was reading Plotinus and once a week writing short papers he hoped would form part of his Ph.D. thesis at Harvard. Vivien, also twenty-six, was one of the "emancipated Londoners" who entranced him, a group of English girls over twenty-five who, he wrote a friend, were very different from other women he had met in America or even in England, "charmingly sophisticated (even 'disillusioned') without being hardened." Any younger, and the girls were completely managed by their mothers, he'd decided. He had gone to tea or dinner on several occasions with these girls who had "such amusing names" and whose flouting of convention Tom found intoxicating. He took great pleasure in seeing women smoke. If that wasn't shocking enough, he had even danced.

Perhaps Vivien was drawn by the oblique allure of the "sleek, tall, attractive transatlantic apparition" that Tom seemed to Wyndham Lewis, who met him at this time in London and noticed his "sort of Gioconda smile," into which the transfixed admirer poured meanings of her own. Vivien was beautiful and flirtatious, and there was something elemental in her frank allure that was utterly new to the inexperienced Tom.

* * *

The host of the Magdalen College party was Scofield Thayer, whom Eliot had met at Milton Academy, and whom he also knew at Harvard. Thayer would later become the editor of the *Dial*, the New York literary magazine for which Eliot began writing a "London Letter" in 1921. Thayer was himself attracted to Vivien and wrote in a notebook at about the time Tom and Vivien met in his rooms, "Vivien's smell peculiarly feline." Aldous Huxley, observing the Eliots early in their marriage, wrote to Ottoline Morrell of the erotic charge between them, "one sees it in the way he looks at her . . . she's an incarnate provocation."

The Gioconda Tom, Lewis saw upon meeting him, was "the author of Prufrock" to the life—"indeed, it was Prufrock himself: but a Prufrock to whom the mermaids would decidedly have sung." Eliot may have been an indecisive J. Alfred Prufrock, the title character of his most important early poem—constitutionally hesitant and uncertain about anything apart from the intellectual life—but he was also "a handsome young United States President," Lewis later recalled, praising Eliot's beauty but under-scoring the hard lesson he had by then learned from their long associa-tion, that Eliot was an adept politician, too. For Vivien, Tom was an exotic outsider who, under the sway of Ezra Pound, was staking his life on London as the only place where a literary career meant something. A poet's reputation established in England might spread to America, and worldwide. It would not work the other way around. His career as a poet and his marriage began at the same time—"The Love Song of J. Alfred Pru-frock," his first published poem, appeared in the June 1915 issue of *Poetry*; Vivien and Tom were married on June 26, 1915—but they would not be equally satisfying.

The reasons for Tom and Vivien's haste in marrying are unclear; per-haps there was no reason. Eliot's own explanations varied through the years. He told one friend decades later that he was too busy courting Vivien to "be fully conscious of" why he was doing it. At the time, writing to J. H. Woods, his philosophy professor and thesis adviser at Harvard, he was cryptic. "Our marriage was hastened by events connected with the war," he wrote, offering a decorous justification to a person in whose eyes he would not willingly appear impulsive. This was, perhaps, an oblique reference to the death of his friend Jean Verdenal on May 2, 1915, a suggestion of Tom's desire to solidify an emotional relationship in the wake of unexpected loss, and to overcome his Prufrock indecisiveness at a time of uncontrollable change. He would dedicate "Prufrock" to Verdenal.

The marriage was also a bid to be, at last, an adult, free of his parents' control, if not completely from their purse strings or his family's expecta-tions that he would return to America and pursue an academic career. A week after the wedding he wrote to his brother, Henry, "The only really surprising thing is that I should have had the force to attempt it," his marriage a breakthrough that had left him more confident "and much less suppressed" than he had ever been, perhaps an allusion to sex, or simply to the elation of having acted on his own without any consultation or warning to his family. It was as if he married in order to say he was mature enough to be responsible for himself, though the price of his action was that now he was also responsible for Vivien, too. He welcomed this enlargement of self through duty; his ability to make Vivien happy depended on his being himself "infinitely more fully" than before. In his letter to Henry, Tom mentioned nothing of romantic attachment or love. They were attracted to each other, as others had observed, but there had barely been time for anything beyond first impressions, and each was far more fragile emotionally and physically than the other understood. The happiest moments of the relationship were all before the wedding.

The mistakes were shared equally between them. He had married the wrong woman and made a complete mess of his personal life, he would much later confide to a friend whose marriage was failing. He had sought relief in Vivien's admiration from "a maddening feeling of failure and inferiority" that had accompanied his desire to abandon academia. He had only wanted a distraction, a "flirtation or mild affair" with Vivien, one of the girls who had such amusing names. Unfortunately, he had been "too shy and unpractised to achieve either with anybody," even at twenty-six, he realized near the end of his life, "very immature for my age, very timid, very inexperienced" when he met Vivien. Vivien had been a means to an end; looking back, he thought it might simply have been a matter of persuading himself he was in love with her "because I wanted to burn my boats and commit myself to staying in England."

He committed himself, and became anchored by marriage in a country that he had wanted to live in for the good of his career. Vivien, too, was thinking of the poet Tom was and would become. Her faith in his career had persuaded her, he later thought, to marry him—to "save the poet" by keeping him in England where his work might really matter. Tom and Vivien's impulsiveness had helped to make a mess of Vivien's life, too, he knew, but he seemed, facing her unhappiness and in judging his own role, to both accept responsibility and deny it. Perhaps this was why he felt such a heavy burden of guilt in addition to regret and helplessness. Decades later, he would write in his play *The Cocktail Party* of the disastrous marriage between "A man who finds himself incapable of loving / And a woman who finds that no man can love her." This put the husband's fault first, then the wife's. The couplet was unsparing of the failure in the man, who was congenitally incapable. But it rendered a harsher judgment of the woman, who was unloved by all men. Eliot might be responsible for the emotional sterility of the marriage, he might admit that much, but he was not to blame.

During rehearsals for the play, produced in 1949, the actress Irene Worth recalled that Eliot sat silently at the back of the theater, making notes and smoking. At only one moment did he intervene. It was during a scene in which Worth, as the wife, was arguing with her husband, played by Alec Guinness. Something was missing, and Eliot "bolted up to the stage" from his place in the shadows. "The wife," he insisted, "must be fierce. *Much more fierce.* The audience must understand that she is impossible."

It was their sad lot to be yoked to each other. Tom put it all in the poem he was trying to finish in 1921.

"My nerves are bad tonight," an unknown "she" said in one passage amid the fragments. "Yes, bad. Stay with me. / Speak to me. Why do you never speak? Speak. / What are you thinking of? What thinking? What? / I never know what you are thinking." Reading these lines in Eliot's typescript, Ezra Pound wrote the word "photography" next to them. He thought it was perhaps too realistic a reproduction of an actual conversation. Except that it was not a conversation. There were two people, but only one spoke. The silence of the man sparked another anxious volley, and once again the woman, her need rising into vituperation, was confronted by silence: "Do / You know nothing? Do you see nothing? Do you remember / Nothing? . . . Are you alive, or not? Is there nothing in your head?" she said. Pound wrote again, "photo."

In the margin of the draft, Vivien wrote twice that all of this was "wonderful," praising the poetry even as she despaired, and Tom did, too, about the married life that had led him to write it. He could not, as a husband, answer her questions, but as a poet, at least, he had heard them and used them.

"To her the marriage brought no happiness," Tom was to write when he was in his seventies, adding that "to me it brought the state of mind out of which came *The Waste Land.*" The making of his career had come at a very great price for both of them.

* * *

Tom's tact hadn't hidden that state of mind, or that price, from his family after all. Henry saw the difficulties. So did his mother Charlotte, who worried that in addition to Tom's other problems, or certainly as a result of them, his work "has deteriorated." Henry tried to smooth over her fear that this marked an irreversible decline, but he agreed that Tom's more recent poems were "much less inspired" than his earlier ones. One of the problems was Tom's living in London, he thought, the old disappointment, which the family had never come to terms with, revived. Seeing Tom again after so long a gap, Henry told her, "to me he seemed a man playing a part" among foreigners for whom he "always must be an American—even Henry James never became a complete Englishman."

Tom had confided to his brother that having to be "keyed up, alert to the importance of appearances, always wearing a mask among people," had taken a toll on him. The mask was visible to all his friends (and enemies) in London, too, and Tom remained, after more than seven years in England, a divided man who spoke with a "still-trailing Bostonian voice"; even two decades later his accent would seem neither "recognizably English" nor similar to that of "the general run of Americans who came to England." And as if to confirm his foreignness, at the very moment in 1921 that his life was in most precarious balance, there were new tensions related to his living in England at all. Amid his other woes, he had been "further exasperated by insults from the American Consulate"—attempts to collect income tax from him—which only left him more anxious about money. He was also worried about the status of his naturalization papers, which languished in bureaucracy and required "some prominent person in the Home Office to press it forward," a connection he did not have and which underscored that he was an outsider in the place he most wanted to call home.

After meeting Eliot for the first time, Ottoline Morrell had written in her diary about what appeared to her Eliot's willed opacity. Their conversation had turned to Ezra Pound's true gift as a poet. "He only really *expressed* himself when he hid behind the mask of some Antique Writer[.]—Then he was at ease," Eliot told her. But Ottoline took this as a revelation, unintentional though it may have been, of Eliot himself, as a poet and as a man, who could not speak in his own voice. Ottoline was awed by Eliot's intelligence and charmed by his interest in her, but she had been warned by Aldous Huxley to be wary: "Aldous says that Eliot has created a character for himself—a sort of wooden artificial armour."

Vivien had belatedly discerned what Huxley described. Tom in his tactful armor had become impervious to her, more and more so as the years passed and his obligations to her increased. Writing a long letter to Henry after he left England in the autumn of 1921, Vivien added a postscript that revealed her loneliness. She feared, and no doubt knew, that her husband was no longer in love with her, however dutifully preoccupied he was by tending to her illnesses. "Good-bye Henry," she wrote. "And *be personal*, you must be personal, or else it's no good. Nothing's any good."

Almost immediately after his family's departure, Tom found a new way to add to his portfolio of burdens. Lady Rothermere, Mary Lilian Harmsworth, the wife of the publisher Harold Harmsworth, agreed to subsidize a literary magazine he would edit. This was to be the *Criterion*. Taking it on fulfilled one ambition, at the same time as it severely limited any time he might have to write poetry or, perhaps even more urgently, to earn any extra money from his own journalistic work. Lady Rothermere promised a subsidy of £600 a year for three years, including £100 he could take as his annual salary if he wished. But Tom did not want to risk that Lloyds would object to his being on salary elsewhere.

As his commitment to Lady Rothermere and what was as yet a "Hypothetical Review" got under way, his evenings became an extension of his day at Lloyds: "Therefore I am immersed in calculations and estimates, and problems of business management," he wrote to Mary Hutchinson, a cousin of Lytton Strachey in addition to being Clive Bell's mistress, who was one of his closer confidantes. He apologized to her for the exhaustion that had left him "little time . . . for the amenities of society or even the pleasures of friendship." The prospect of the quarterly made Vivien nervous; work on the review would mean Tom also had little time left for the amenities—or simply the realities—of marriage. Here was another distraction, another willfully added division, a particularly obvious one given that Tom would work on the review in the evenings from their flat. Vivien's pride in Tom's ambition, and her sacrifice to it, led her to some degree to see the review as a shared endeavor on which she might advise him. But she saw more clearly than he could, or than he would admit, the over-whelming new burden it would be for him and for both of them. "It *is* going to be the most awful affair, so difficult and tiresome," she wrote to Henry, carefully adding, "all the business I mean . . . I see rocks ahead."

* * *

Tom had reached such a nadir in the wake of his family's visit, lost in dread of a future that appeared darker because of the work he could not accomplish on his poem, that his mind had virtually ceased to function. Even his typewriter was worn out. Henry, in fact, had left behind his own typewriter to replace his brother's old one, along with a gift of some money. He did it silently, and left it to be noticed after he was gone. Vivien urged Tom to see a "nerve specialist," made the appointment, and accompanied him, during the last week of September, even joking to Scofield Thayer, "Look at *my* position. I have not nearly finished my own nervous breakdown yet."

Vivien might have expected Thayer to be particularly sympathetic to Tom and to her. He had left New York in July 1921 and arrived in Vienna to begin treatment with Freud in September, just as Tom's condition worsened. His divorce from his wife of five years became final in the second week of October, not long after his sessions with "the Professor himself" had started.

* * *

On Wednesday the twenty-eighth, Tom reported to a friend of his upcoming visit to the doctor he called "the most celebrated specialist in London." The doctor examined him "thoroughly," Tom wrote his brother, and described the poet's malady in financial terms the Lloyds banker might understand, telling Eliot that he had, as he relayed to Henry, "greatly overdrawn my nervous energy." The doctor, alarmed and decisive, advised action—two or three months away, immediately.

Eliot saw Wyndham Lewis on the afternoon of Friday, September 30, and, after confiding in him, added that he didn't know whether he would take the doctor's advice. His planned Paris holiday, visiting Ezra Pound, might be enough, he thought; he might "feel quite different after," he told Lewis. No doubt aware that Lewis would feel no compunction in sharing Eliot's confidences with any number of mutual friends and literary acquaintances, he added a warning: "As nobody knows anything about it whatever except the specialist, my wife and yourself, it can go no further if you don't speak of it."

By the next morning, Tom had made his decision. He spoke to Lloyds, and invoking his doctor's "great name, which I knew would bear weight with my employers," obtained its agreement to a three-month leave, with full salary. It was relief from an unexpected quarter. He had managed it "without any difficulty at all," he wrote to Henry, and was to depart in little more than a week, "as soon as I have trained another man to my work." Eliot dreaded the doctor's dire regimen—"enforced rest and solitude"; "strict rules for every hour of the day"; he must "not exert [his] mind at all." It was to be a total withdrawal, and the first phase of the treatment was likely to be the most difficult: a period of great depression would come in reaction to Tom's release from the pressure and tension of the last few months. The rebound promised to be equally great, but Tom went away trying not "to think of the future" until after New Year's. He confided to Henry the extent of his breakdown, his forthright account an acknowledgment that this was no more than the culmination of what Henry had already seen for himself. But he asked Henry not to let their mother know the gravity of his situation. Writing to Charlotte, Tom cast his leave from the bank more mildly as a "fortunate opportunity to rest and recuperate."

"I have not described to her at all how I feel," he wrote to Henry, "and indeed it is almost impossible to describe these feelings even if one wants to."

That was what poetry was for.

* * *

The doctor's plan called for Tom to be "quite alone and away from anyone," including his wife. Instead, against their original plan, Vivien accompanied Tom, and they took rooms at the Albemarle Hotel, in the Cliftonville district on the eastern end of Margate. Standard treatment called for the isolation of patients "from nervous stimuli," and overfeeding in order to "'fatten' and 'redden' them until they could return to active life."

Within days, partly because this was, in essence, his first vacation in a very long time, and partly because they dined well, and too expensively for their strained finances, Tom was "getting on *amazingly*," Vivien thought, already looking "younger, and fatter and nicer."

But as he rested, he saw more clearly that rest itself was not the cure. Writing had been forbidden, as it had been frequently forbidden to Virginia at times of crisis. Yet it had a salutary effect on him when he began to write, recognizing—and seizing—his freedom from Lloyds as the first time in years he had the continuous time that had eluded him. He went daily to a wooden shelter, ornately Victorian, built only a few feet from shore, a location that by late October and early November was largely deserted and therefore even more thoroughly private than a seaside hotel in the off-season. The spot he chose was at some distance from the Albemare, and he traveled there by tram, along the Canterbury Road, as if the regimen of a daily commute, as in London, was itself restorative, a habit he enjoyed. At Margate, he was unconfined, freed not only from his office below grade at Lloyds but also from the noise of London, which he often found intolerable, and from the pressure of the confinement of their Clarence Gate Gardens flat. At the shelter, which resembled a railway station waiting room built upon the sand, he wrote some fifty lines of his long poem—the first he had added in many months. Though he usually wrote at the typewriter, these he wrote in pencil.

> *My feet are at Moorgate, and my heart*
> *Under my feet. After the event*
> *He wept. He promised "a new start."*
> *I made no comment. What should I resent?*

Moorgate was the underground station Eliot used when working at Lloyds.

The rhythm and the brevity of the next six lines resemble the postcards he sent friends from Margate. The first line was itself a postmark, on a "postcard to himself."

> *On Margate Sands.*
> *I can connect*
> *Nothing with nothing.*
> *The broken fingernails of dirty hands.*
> *My people humble people who expect*
> *Nothing.*

But at Margate he did connect things. He had not only written the first lines of poetry in a long time, but while resting—and writing—he began to wonder whether the specialist in London who had proposed the draconian regimen was, despite his celebrated reputation, "quite the best man for me." He had not suffered the great depression at the start that the doctor had warned about. His trouble, he decided, was "not solely due to overwork and anxieties," he explained to his brother. The cure could not be found in a kind of deprivation of stimulation, or a banker's replenishment of his overdrawn physical energies. He had begun to see that his troubles were more than "nerves." A "nerve man" like his London specialist saw his problem as a physical one. His suffering was, he saw, "largely due to the kink in my brain which makes life at all an unremitting strain for me."

It was the way his mind, not his body, worked. The insight that this was not something that rest or willpower could cure offered hope and a new direction. The prescribed rest, and eating heartily, would not restore him. He wanted a specialist in "psychological troubles."

The kink was why he could connect nothing with nothing. Traveling from Moorgate to Margate, he had made the "new start" the lines he had written suggest the doctor had promised. But it was to be in a new direction of treatment that neither the specialist nor Tom himself had envisioned.

*　*　*

In fact, despite the Eliot family's inclination against it, perhaps there would be something in what Henry had condescended to see in Vivien—that it "is a relief to talk about one's pains." Realizing he needed a different approach, Eliot asked the advice of Ottoline Morrell, in whom both he and Vivien had confided about their illnesses, and who had discussed with them the depression that often left her feeling "utterly dead & empty & it is like being in a cold fog—or a pond." This was one of the bonds of sympathy that drew her to both Eliots across a chasm of what she often felt, in close contact with Tom, was the inadequacy of her own intellect. Ottoline recommended the Swiss doctor Roger Vittoz, who had treated her before the war. Julian Huxley had also seen him, she said. Eliot—relieved to learn of an alternative to English doctors, who seemed only to diagnose "nerves or insanity!"—wrote to Huxley, who replied immediately with an endorsement. "I shall go to Vittoz," Eliot told him.

To seek out Vittoz, as he did, was to see the source of his problem in the mind. To see a kink in his brain was to apprehend a condition akin to what Freud had labeled neurosis, though Eliot never subscribed to Freud's theories. Vittoz's approach was similarly akin to, but different from Freud's. Vittoz was not a psychoanalyst and because of that "more useful for my purpose," Eliot was to explain to a friend in London while in treatment in Switzerland. But aspects of Vittoz's procedures—regular daily sessions, for example, that were, in part, a talking cure—were like Freud's.

* * *

Lausanne was "a dull place" in a *carte postale colorée* country," high in the mountains of Switzerland, on the shores of Lake Geneva with an expansive view of the Alps rising across the lake. It was a quiet town, "except when the children come downhill on scooters over the cobbles," filled with banks and chocolate shops, and his accommodations, at the Hôtel Ste. Luce, recommended to him as Vittoz was by Ottoline Morrell, were ideal—"the food is *excellent*, and the people make everything easy for one—ordering milk etc." He was even staying in what he'd been told was Ottoline's room, he wrote her shortly after his arrival in late November.

Roger Vittoz had treated Morrell and Huxley, and also William James and Joseph Conrad. His 1911 book *Traitement des psychonévroses par la ré-éducation du contrôle cérébral* had been published in an English translation in 1913 as *Treatment of Neurasthenia by Means of Brain Control*, a 1921 French edition of which Eliot owned, but which it seems he obtained either at Vittoz's clinic or after his return to London. Ottoline saw Vittoz in 1913 and recalled that his method—he taught his patients a "system of mental control and concentration, and a kind of organisation of mind"—had a great effect "steadying and developing" her. A few years later, she urged Bertrand Russell to see him, telling him that one might see Vittoz for only two weeks in order to become proficient in his system. Even more in his favor was the fact that he charged only a modest fee. Vittoz, a devout Christian, was a benevolent figure of "extraordinary poise and goodness," Morrell recalled, a quality that immediately impressed Eliot, who wrote to Morrell that from the first Vittoz inspired him with confidence. He liked him very much personally, he wrote, and "in short he is, I am sure[,] much more what I want than the man in London."

Eliot's description of the "kink" in his brain was an echo of Vittoz's overarching contention that "every form of neurasthenia is due to the brain working abnormally." It was only possible to cure the condition by accepting that, and therefore rejecting the usual diagnosis that it was either a matter of willpower or a physical ailment that required a physical cure, either through diet or rest, as the celebrated specialist of London had claimed. The cure relied on self-control, but not, as Eliot might have previously understood it, as a moral issue. It was necessary to learn new tools for clear thinking, for overcoming "imperfections of that [brain] control." Vittoz's was a hopeful, expansive treatment based on what would later come to be known as cognitive therapy, one designed to overcome self-judgment rather than finding a way forward in asceticism, either moral or physical.

Vittoz argued that the duality of the brain—between what he called the objective and the subjective brains—was invisible when an individual was functioning normally. It was the tragedy of the "uncurbed brain" that, without the controlling power of the objective faculty, it gave rise to a "state of anarchy" in which the suffering person was "prey to every impulse, subject to all fears, unable to reason or weigh an idea." As the insufficiency of control increased, so did the patient's symptoms; vague feelings of discomfort grew into a "painful confusion . . . a whirl of unconnected and uncontrolled ideas."

Vittoz's technique involved holding the patient's head, in the belief that he could read the brain waves this way and work with the patient to alter them. Effective or not as a diagnostic tool, his laying on of hands worked also as a manifestation of his benevolent presence and was a method by which the patient might relax under his care. Vittoz's touch physically encouraged the patient to recalibrate his mind through exercises that involved seizing upon images and words that brought happiness and repeating them in order to intensify focus.

Eliot would be in treatment for about a month. His plan was to leave Lausanne on Christmas Eve. Not long after arriving, he wrote to Ottoline that Vittoz's diagnosis was a good one, though he did not say what it was. The treatment was all-involving from the start. "I seem to have no time for any *continuous* application to anything else," he told her. This was a fulfilling breakthrough in itself—he had wanted, earlier in the year, to have continuous time enough to finish his long poem; now Vittoz was keeping him so busy that he had no time for anything but the treatment, focus on which was the effort of concentration he must later apply to finishing his poem or any substantial work.

From the start, he wrote Ottoline, he had felt moments of "more calm than I have for many years—since childhood." He hoped his initial optimism would not prove illusory.

THE WORLD BROKE IN TWO 47

* * *

The calm that Eliot experienced continued and deepened. He wrote at the shore, overlooking Lake Geneva, and, as he had at Margate, he wrote the moment into his poem, beginning in penciled lines drafted on the reverse of a section he had typed out long before, and which the new lines replaced. He described the flight of "City directors; / Departed, have left no addresses," who had left London behind, as he had done, and told almost no one where they were going.

> *. . . By the waters of Leman I sat down and wept . . .*
> *Sweet Thames, run softly till I end my song,*
> *Sweet Thames, run softly, for I speak not loud or long.*

Lac Leman is the name of Lake Geneva in French. And as he had traveled from Moorgate to Margate, soon he must travel from Lausanne and Lac Leman back to London and the River Thames. Tom had originally planned to leave Lausanne on Christmas Eve, a Saturday, but even at the beginning of that week he wasn't sure whether he would go to Paris, where he would rejoin Vivien, or to take an additional few days in the South of France first. "Apparently all of Western Europe is equally expensive," though any time on the Continent was cheaper than London. He decided to prolong his treatment and stayed on with Vittoz for an extra week.

* * *

Tom and Vivien had stopped in Paris on the way to Lausanne, staying at the Hôtel Pas de Calais, at 59 rue des Saints-Pères, only a few doors away from Ezra Pound. During his few days in Paris, Tom was able to show Pound the disorganized pages of the poem that he had at last added to at Margate. Then he was gone. Vivien was lonely in Paris by herself and, like Tom, was also anxious about the "awful expense" of the city. "I live in a high up little room," she wrote Mary Hutchinson, one of the few in Bloomsbury, or seemingly in all London, unreservedly kind to her. A Rapunzel awaiting her prince, she felt herself shunned by the English people she knew who were also in Paris. When she saw Roger Fry in the post office, for example, he "did not seem at ease, or pleased to see me," she thought, "and escaped hastily." She saved money by having her meals "*en pension* which I loathe," unable to afford restaurants. Hotel living, even on a modest scale, and in a city far less expensive than London, was "too incredibly dear. It costs *fortunes.*"

But it would be an ideal home for herself and Tom, if they could actually live there and he could write. The Pounds had a "most exquisite Studio (with two rooms)," Vivien wrote. It was only £75 a year, and they had only just moved in, after having lived themselves at the Hôtel Pas de Calais. "Now if I could secure such a thing, I would certainly take them," Vivien wrote Mary. She would prefer Paris and seemed to think that her own income might be enough to support the two of them. "For Tom, I am *convinced, Paris!*" Fresh in her mind was the last night they'd spent in London before leaving for Margate in October, an evening at the Huxleys'. "*What* a last impression of London. . . . The monotony, the *drivel* of the whole stupid round."

* * *

The extra week Tom devoted to treatment was also extra time that might help with his poem. He wrote to a friend that he was trying to finish a poem, "about 800 or 1000 lines. *Je ne sais pas si ça tient.*" I do not know if it will work. He would find out in Paris, where he was to meet Vivien, and Pound.

He had written another six pages of poetry, drafting them rapidly in pencil as if "in a trance—unconsciously," he told Virginia Woolf, though he was usually skeptical of the automatic writing this last burst of poetry represented. As at Margate, the newest lines suggested his mood, but now a very different one, of gratitude and hope revived during his sessions with Vittoz to which the lines alluded.

> *The sea was calm, and your heart responded*
> *Gaily, when invited, beating responsive*
> *To controlling hands. I left without you*
> *Clasping empty hands. I sat upon a shore*
> *Fishing, with a desolate sunset behind me*
> *Shall I at last set my kingdom in order?*

Immediately after the new year, he left Lausanne for Paris with that question in mind. He also had a larger sheaf of manuscripts ready to show, again, to Pound.

In mid-October, Vivien had written to Scofield Thayer about Tom's unfinished assignments, "Everything is now postponed until January." Now January was here. The train from Lausanne to Paris took more than half a day, a very uncomfortable ride on an overcrowded train.

Pound, in Paris, had begun a new calendar. "The Christian Era ended at midnight on Oct. 29–30 of last year," he wrote to H. L. Mencken early in 1922. This was the night that James Joyce finished *Ulysses*. They were now living, and writing, "in the year 1 p.s.U," he told Mencken, post scriptum *Ulysses*. Eliot arrived in Paris near the start of the month Pound called Saturnus An I—year one. Eliot had marked the start of the new era without festivities at Margate, uncertain of his prospects. His long poem would be finished, and published, before An I would end.

* * *

Tom's arrival in Paris from Lausanne coincided with New York publisher Horace Liveright's "furiously busy six days" there under Ezra Pound's helpful management. Liveright had "sailed for YURUP," as Ezra Pound put it, at the end of 1921, and, eager to sign up the best European books, planned to stay abroad for the month of January, meeting with publishers and authors. Liveright had published Pound with enthusiasm and regularly sought his advice on what and whom to publish. Pound was to be Liveright's "guide and mentor" in Paris, "the last of the human cities," according to Joyce, where scale and intimacy (and the cost of living, as Vivien had calculated) were still in balance. Liveright and Pound had never met, but Liveright's hunch—that he'd enjoy his time in Paris with Pound "best of all," he wrote his wife—was to prove correct.

Liveright, whose father-in-law was owner of International Paper, had founded his firm, Boni & Liveright, in 1917, the same year that Leonard and Virginia Woolf published their first Hogarth Press books. He saw his buying trip to Europe as a way to expand the adventuresome scope of what the company might do. And if Liveright met with no writers other than the two Pound introduced him to in the first week of the new year, it would have been a historic trip. Pound took advantage of serendipity and brought Liveright and Eliot and Joyce together for dinner. Joyce was in typically dire straits, even as the publication of *Ulysses* approached. In his Christmas letter to his father, Homer, Pound gave him the news that "Joyce nearly killed by motor bus last week. Caught between it an [*sic*] lamp post, but nothing apparently broken."

Liveright, in Pound's view, was "much more of a man than most publishers." He was a man "going toward the light not from it." Pound's father was also an admirer: "Glad Liveright is to see you," he wrote his son. "I met him last year—seems like a 'live wire.'"

Liveright was two years younger than the literary jack-of-all-trades Ezra Pound, poet, critic, translator, editor, publisher, matchmaker, and "a great 'fan.'" For Liveright, and for Scofield Thayer, of the *Dial*, Pound acted as literary concierge and go-between to dozens of literary figures, from W. B. Yeats to Robert Frost to James Joyce, a range of writers who comprised what Lewis, a sometime member, called the "Pound circus." Pound worked at what Lewis called "Ezra's boyscoutery" with unrelenting diligence but resented that his own work was being undermined. "Point I can never seem to get you to take," he wrote to one editor, "is that I have done more log rolling and attending to other people's affairs, Joyce, Lewis, Gaudier, etc. (don't regret it). But I am in my own small way, a writer myself, and as before stated I shd. like (and won't in any case get) the chance of being considered as the author of my own poems rather than as a literary politician and a very active stage manager of rising talent."

Liveright had a distinguished if not patrician bearing that marked him as different from the old-line publishers with names like Harcourt or Scribner or Harper: he "had an unforgettable look: graying hair, a beaked nose, and piercing black eyes; a face so riveting as to obscure his body, which it seems to me was lean and fairly tall," a young employee of the firm recalled. He was "always dressed as Beau Brummel himself, a New York boulevardier," and was "quite aware of his dandified appearance." Walking in Bryant Park one afternoon, a friend remembered, Liveright was seen "in a well-fitted Chesterfield topcoat . . . a smart pearl grey fedora hat . . . a carnation in the lapel of his coat and he sported a cane with a silver knob. . . . He resembled a wedding guest in search of a wedding."

Liveright's habits at work were less formal than his clothes, as an employee later remembered. "Horace's hangovers" were obvious at the office, and "discipline was about as out of place as at one of the then brand-new progressive schools." One morning, having breakfast a little before noon at a nearby drugstore, the employee encountered Liveright, who arrived for a similarly late breakfast, and "with a well-trained smile" exclaimed, "This is a hell of a time for me to be coming to work!"

* * *

A dinner with Liveright, Joyce, Eliot, and Pound would have involved heavy drinking, if the men kept to their usual habits. Eliot was at the time mainly a gin man, though his taste would change. Liveright was so distinguished a drinker that back in his New York office, "Authors in the waiting room were often outnumbered by bootleggers," as his employee Bennett Cerf, later the cofounder of Random House, remembered it. Pound, too, became even more voluble and opinionated "after he had begun to get into his cups, which was fairly soon," one poet remembered of a Paris dinner that year. And Joyce's wit and charm were founded on "the agreeable humanity of which he possessed such great stores," liberally mixed with "his unaffected love of alcohol, and all good things to eat and drink."

The previous summer Joyce's patron Harriet Weaver, anxious that Joyce finish *Ulysses* at last, had been worried about his progress and his health after hearing reports from Wyndham Lewis and Robert McAlmon, a younger American writer of substantial means and promising but modest talent. Joyce replied to her letter of concern with a long letter of his own and told her, "A nice collection could be made of legends about me. . . . I suppose I now have the reputation of being an incurable dipsomaniac," adding that, among other rumors he had heard, he had supposedly enriched himself in wartime Switzerland "by espionage work for one or both combatants," or was "a cocaine victim," or "I could write no more, had broken down and was dying in New York."

Joyce was still relatively anonymous a month before the publication of *Ulysses* by Sylvia Beach's Shakespeare and Co. Soon enough he would claim he had to avoid the restaurants "he was in the habit of frequenting because people crowded to look at him." For all the likely conviviality at the dinner, it would not have been a dinner of equals, at least to Joyce's mind. He "made no pretense of being indulgent towards other writers" and once asked Robert McAlmon whether he thought "Eliot or Pound has any real importance?" But Joyce's egotism was wavering, and McAlmon's response to the rhetorical question was to sidestep it. "Now, Joyce, is that a question for you to ask, who can doubt anything, even yourself?"

Liveright, not surprisingly, was enamored with Joyce, and was probably intoxicated as much by the conversation of his companions as by the liquor. The evidence of what Joyce thought of Eliot is equivocal at best. He commented, later, after reading *The Waste Land*, "I had never realized that Eliot was a poet," but at least until that revelation saw Eliot, whatever his or Pound's "real importance," as a useful publicist, a persuadable critic, a journalist who, cultivated with proper assiduousness, could write about him. Joyce sent him advance copies of episodes of *Ulysses* in the spring of 1921, ingratiating himself and perhaps sensing Eliot's resistance to his own arrogance, which Eliot thought a "burdensome" trait mitigated only partially by what Eliot decided was a calculated courtesy. "Oh yes. He is polite, he is polite enough," Eliot complained to Wyndham Lewis. "But he is exceedingly arrogant. Underneath. That is why he is so polite. I should be better pleased if he were less polite."

* * *

Liveright was a "pearl" among "U.S. publicators," in Pound's eyes, but he was a pornographer and a Jew given to "impertinence" and worse, according to the New York lawyer John Quinn, a patron of Eliot's and Pound's (and Joyce's, though increasingly unhappy with him). Liveright was a "firebrand" at the very least, which is the title of a biography of Liveright by Tom Dardis. On that inebriated evening he did his best to sign up all three writers. This was his way—to mix cocktails with contracts, as Sherwood Anderson, whom Liveright successfully wooed, recalled of an evening in New Orleans in which the two met in a speakeasy, and over absinthes Liveright offered Anderson $500 a month for five years, an advance-cum-salary, if he would switch to Liveright from Viking.

Pound reported to Quinn that Liveright had "offered to bring out *Ulysses* in the U.S. and hand over 1000 bones to J. J." But Joyce was not receptive, to Pound's angry astonishment. "Why the hell he didn't nail it AT once I don't know. The terms were O. K. 1000 dollars for first edition . . . However, Joyce is off my hands, free, white, 21, etc."

Joyce demurred because it was not the first time Liveright said he wanted to publish the book, as Quinn well knew, having negotiated with Liveright about it in the spring of 1921, after Ben Huebsch, the publisher of *A Portrait of the Artist as a Young Man* and *Dubliners*, had decided he could go ahead with *Ulysses* only if Joyce cut the book, which as it stood was unpublishable.

After Quinn could not come to terms with Huebsch, who wanted what Quinn called a *Ulysses* "slightly draped," he then offered Liveright *Ulysses* with a warning that he should not publish the book unless he wanted to face "the certainty of prosecution and conviction." At first Liveright agreed to publish it. But then he backed down, Quinn reported to Joyce. "He said he did not want to be convicted and so he dropped the matter. And that ends Liveright." Following these disappointments, Sylvia Beach proposed publishing the book herself, and as soon as possible, before the end of 1921. But there had been delays on Joyce's part, and more than two months after he had finished writing, the memorable date that was a new epoch to Pound, he was still rewriting and making further corrections on page proofs that he would continue with until the very end of January.

Quinn, replying to Pound's news of Liveright's offer, was as angry and as astonished as Pound had been. But he was enraged by Liveright's "Jew impertinence." He had flourished a lucrative contract as if it were a kind of dessert? And had no doubt drunkenly proposed to publish *Ulysses* after having not had the nerve to do so before? It would not come to anything, Quinn predicted. And it didn't.

Liveright made a similar kind of offer to Eliot after talking about the poem at dinner. Liveright expressed interest in publishing it. But following the dinner Liveright became worried that the poem Pound and Eliot described would be too short for a book on its own. Could Eliot add any poems to make the book longer? he wrote to Pound from London the next week. And he was concerned about Knopf's option on Eliot's next book— Knopf had published a book of Eliot's poems, in 1920, and another of his criticism, in 1921. Liveright would consider the poem if Knopf were out of the picture. Eliot and Pound continued to edit the loose pages of the manuscript.

* * *

The winter of 1922 was far milder in Paris than in London, and Pound's two-room studio near the Luxembourg Gardens became an oasis where Eliot and Pound could work together, the third stop on Eliot's recovery from his breakdown. The Pounds lived in a flat up a hill from the Seine, where the air was good, and the studio quiet, protected from the street by a buffer of two gardens. There were little shops nearby with "meat, cake, breads, etc. just at hand, so life is very convenient . . . much more like Kensington" than he had expected, Pound wrote to his grandmother. But the similarities with London went only so far. Daily life was not only far cheaper. In Paris, working on the poem, Tom seemed to Pound "so mountany gay." The London Tom had not been, and would not be, nearly so happy.

For Pound, Eliot had appeared as a second coming of himself, a poet whose advances and innovations the visionary Pound had himself predicted, or even summoned, into being, in his "Prolegomena," published in 1912.

> As to Twentieth century poetry, and the poetry which I expect to see written during the next decade or so, it will, I think, move against poppy-cock, it will be harder and saner, it will be what Mr Hewlett calls "nearer the bone". It will be as much like granite as it can be, its force will lie in its truth. . . . I mean it will not try to seem forcible by rhetorical din, and luxurious riot. We will have fewer painted adjectives impeding the shock and stroke of it. At least for myself, I want it so, austere, direct, free from emotional slither.

Pound and Eliot met two years later, in September 1914, and when Eliot gave his poem "The Love Song of J. Alfred Prufrock" to Pound, it seemed to the master that he had found the protégé who justified his prophecy and the poetry he had foreseen. "The Love Song . . ." was "a portrait of failure, or of a character which fails," and with it Eliot had made such a stark recoil from sentimental uplift that it stood as an uncompromising rebuke to the "false art" of others, who might have contrived to end the poem "on a note of triumph." Pound hailed Eliot as "the last intelligent man I've found . . . worth watching," and "Prufrock" as the best poem "I have yet had or seen from an American," not excepting himself. But Eliot's faith in the poem, or in himself, was not as extravagant as Pound's. He wanted to join Pound's "move against poppy-cock," but the "devil of it" for Eliot, even as early as 1914, was his certainty that he had written "nothing good" since he had completed "Prufrock." The anxiety that he might not write another poem equal to it—and had not yet—was what had led him, seven years later, to Margate and then to Lausanne.

Eliot had left Vittoz's care unsure of whether the now larger manuscript of the poem could be made to work, but his two weeks in Paris with Ezra Pound—more *continuous* time—changed that to certainty that it would. Working through the guts of the poem was exhilarating, all the cutting away of "superfluities," a "caesarean operation" bringing out the "nearer the bone" poetry that Pound had prophesied in his "Prolegomena." In 1912 he had projected the poetry he expected would be written in the next decade or so, and now it was, precisely. And Eliot thrived on collaboration. It fit his temperament as an artist and was why, very soon, he began to think of writing plays. It was also why, after 1930, he focused almost exclusively, and very successfully, on verse drama. Eliot wanted to be done with editing the manuscript as soon as possible because he wanted it to be published as soon as possible, as he and Liveright had discussed at dinner, no later than the autumn of 1922. Because Vivien was not accompanying Tom back home to London—she was going to Lyons for a week and then would spend a few more days in Paris—his time alone at home in the evening was to be a further "period of tranquility" of work on the poem he had become confident, after his time with Pound, was his best. Vivien's absence from home, she recognized, could help the poet in a way that might preserve their marriage in the end.

* * *

On January 22, 1922, a week after Tom had returned from Paris, Wyndham Lewis wrote to Ottoline Morrell that he had seen him. "He has written a particularly fine poem." Tom had evidently begun to circulate it. That week, working at home in the evenings while Vivien was still in France, Tom prepared a new version. He sent it to Pound at about the same time Lewis wrote to Ottoline with his good news about Eliot.

"MUCH improved," Pound wrote on January 24. "The thing now runs from April . . . to shantih without a break," Pound wrote, referring to the first line of the latest draft, "April is the cruellest month," and the last, "Shantih shantih shantih," the Sanskrit word for "the peace which passeth understanding," though this was "a feeble translation of the content of this word," Eliot was to write, the repetition of the word perhaps a way of finishing the poem with a tribute to one of Vittoz's exercises, which was to seize upon a calming word and repeat it three times. "That is nineteen pages," Pound calculated, "and let us say the longest poem in the English langwidge. . . . Complimenti, you bitch. I am wracked by the seven jealousies."

The "hoard of fragments" had become a poem. Getting it published was now the question. Seeing Pound in Paris during the summer of 1921, John Quinn had warned him that "he had done enough, or almost enough, for others," and that instead Pound should now "begin to do for himself and play his own game." But Pound went to work again on Eliot's behalf.

Chapter 3

EDWARD MORGAN FORSTER.

EDWARD MORGAN FORSTER—EDWARD FOR his father and Morgan for a maternal grandmother—was born on New Year's Day 1879. He was an only child, but not his parents' first. His mother, Alice Clara Whichelo, had miscarried, shortly after her January 1877 wedding day. Theirs was a family known by nicknames. Edward Morgan, the father, was Eddie, Alice Clara was Lily, and Edward Morgan, the second-born and surviving son, was always and to everyone Morgan. The little group of Forsters was shaped by loss. Eddie died when Morgan was a year old. Lily and Morgan were the only two left, and they lived together, amid a "haze of elderly ladies," until Lily's death, at age ninety, in 1945.

Morgan marked the end of 1921, and the approach of his forty-third birthday the next day, with the ritual he followed all his life, writing in his diary about the year just past and recording his mood as his birthday arrived. This annual rite, adding a few birthday lines, sometimes a lengthy entry, continued into his eighties. In his most autobiographical novel, *The*

Longest Journey, published in 1907, when Forster was twenty-eight, he wrote of his protagonist, and confessed about himself, "The boy grew up in great loneliness," his childhood spent conducting "solitary conversations, in which one part of him asked and another part answered." Morgan's diary, begun not long after the novel was published, arose from that boyish impulse, though even as he undertook it, talking to himself had long since ceased to be the "exciting game" it had been for the boy. Morgan's inward glance was unforgiving in its self-appraisal, and, perhaps for this reason, intermittent. Unlike Virginia Woolf, he kept the diary lackadaisically, at best, through the rest of the year.

The end of one year, the beginning of another, the burden of his birthday a double reminder of the passage of time. For all the hope Morgan seemed to want to have about the future, it was his temperament to pause and look back rather than forward, to hesitate and ruminate. "Will review the year, eat an orange, read, and go to bed," he wrote the winter he was thirty. Finishing his novel *Maurice*, his fantasy of an intimate, fulfilling, and enduring sexual and romantic love between two men, before the First World War, he had dedicated it to a "Happier Year." His birthday entries repeated his realization, and disillusion, that the happier year was always a long way off. Here was an essential paradox: Morgan perennially looked forward to a happier year but was usually unhappy about his accomplishments in the year just past, and very rarely expressed satisfaction with the present or confidence about his immediate prospects for happiness.

It was this way on December 31, 1921. Morgan was unsparing in his assessment as usual, and frank. The situation was as dire as any he'd faced. He had written very little, really nothing, in the past year. *Maurice* apart, he had written only journalism in the past ten years. Now, to his surprise and to the surprise of his friends and family, he was not at home but in India. He had started an Indian novel after a first trip to India in 1911–12. After several years of intermittent work, he deceived himself enough to wonder whether he had faltered because it had already been too long since he'd been immersed in the landscape and among the people. That had been in 1916.

To make progress on the novel, left unfinished since before the war, had been chief among the reasons he'd come to India, a decade's bleak lack of achievement looming behind him. But as the months in India passed, he acknowledged to himself that progress had proved impossible. And might always be. He was as downhearted as he'd been a year before, when he had reached what he recorded as a dramatic low. "I may shrink from summarising this sinister year," he'd written as 1920 ended.

Now he wrote, "India not yet a success, dare not look at my unfinished novel, can neither assimilate, remember, or arrange." Morgan had published his previous novel, *Howards End*, almost a dozen years ago. "Am grinding out my novel into a contrast between money and death," he wrote in his diary as he was completing it. At the time, a neighbor asked him, "In your novels which takes you longest—the writing or the thinking?" He recorded the question, an example of all the silly things people asked an author about his work, but not his response, if he made one. *Howards End* was published in the autumn of 1910. It was a great success. Forster published a collection of six stories, *The Celestial Omnibus*, the next spring. Then, nothing. He wrote *Maurice* but did not think of publishing it, and circulated it privately among his friends. The passage of more than a decade suggested the belated answer to his neighbor's question was *both*. He thought too much and had written too little.

Morgan was only three years older than Virginia but seemed almost to be of another generation. (He was of the generation before Eliot, who was nine years younger.) He had early on been a productive and esteemed writer, publishing his first novel, *Where Angels Fear to Tread*, in 1905, when he was twenty-six. Three more novels followed in the next five years. When *Howards End* appeared in October 1910, it was widely called the year's best. "There is no doubt about it whatever. Mr. E. M. Forster is one of the great novelists," wrote the critic for the *Daily Telegraph*. The acclaim was echoed everywhere, and in the *Standard* it came was this extravagant fillip: "With this book, Mr. Forster seems to us to have arrived, and if he never writes another line, his niche should be secure." The book sold extremely well—7,662 copies by the end of 1910—and references to it in *Punch* delighted Morgan. He wrote in his diary, "Let me not be distracted by the world. It is so difficult." Though he thought he was "not vain of my overpraised book," he wished he would be "obscure again." The superlative in the *Standard* had soon become more prophecy than praise, and his publisher, Edward Arnold, eventually gave up hoping that there would be another. Forster did, too. "I should satisfy myself as well as my admirers if I produced another novel. I will let you know if ever I do," he wrote to Arnold at the end of January 1921. A few weeks later, he was gone to India.

In March 1921, he left England, escaping the burden of his literary silence and the routine of his domestic life with Lily that he treasured and resented in equal measure. During the war, when he had made a previous break and gone off to do war work for the Red Cross in Alexandria in 1915, he had confided to a friend, "One 'oughtn't to leave one's mother when she has no one else' I know[,] yet the question is complicated when filial piety finds compensation in an arm chair and four meals a day served regularly." The three months of his wartime stint became three years, in which he'd found the freedom to, among other liberties, lose his virginity, at the age of thirty-seven. He came home in early 1919. His return was the occasion for one of the few outwardly emotional moments between mother and son. Lily was so moved, "she unexpectedly read family prayers which she hadn't done in my presence since I was a boy." Morgan was surprised by the show of sentiment and remembered it all his life. Then months and years began to pile up once more, and with them no novel.

"You see, I too have no news," he wrote to his friend Forrest Reid in February 1921. It was a familiar refrain. Reid, a Belfast writer a few years older than Forster (and consistently prolific) had tried again to fortify Forster, whom he regarded as a master, and certainly superior to himself. Forster replied, "As you say, I shall go [on] some long and fantastic journey; but we do not yet know whither or when. I am so sad at the bottom of my mind—but I've told you this before and it's useless saddening a letter."

Wither or when—wherever he must go must be far from Weybridge, the hideous "sububurban" [sic] town so near London and yet so far, where he and Lily lived. The house he shared with his mother there was "a little builder's house," as undistinguished as its setting could require, "very fully over furnished" with the relics of Lily's long life. She would be seventy-seven in January 1922, though Morgan would not be at home to celebrate with her, and she had been a widow for more than four decades. In the house's favor was the fact that it was a freehold and, though small, was for that reason "easy to run," since Morgan and Lily had two maids, Ruth and Agnes, and there was only one other inhabitant, a cat, Verouka, who was as placid and as overstuffed as the house he shared with the two servants and his two masters. "The house is littered with manuscripts," Morgan wrote a friend, "to the great discomfort of every one except the kitten," who moved from the piles of papers to the backs of chairs, leaping from one to the other with increasing levels of clawful enthusiasm, "until its destructions . . . [are] so appalling that I have to play a chord on the piano. The chord of C is enough. It stops in the middle of a bound and slinks under a book case, no more to be seen."

The piles of manuscripts were evidence to Morgan of a shallow prodigality he despised in himself. He wrote sixty-eight articles in 1919–20 alone and the number depressed him. His situation and his prospects were much like T. S. Eliot's. "I am happiest when busy," Forster wrote in his diary. "How fatuous! . . . Always working never creating." Too sensitive, he thought, to both praise and blame, he worried he had failed himself and was "just the aimiable [*sic*] journalist—who can't even write as soon as he looks into his own mind." He was prolific, but to no meaningful or satisfying end, a distraction from the work he ought to be doing—until it was too obvious to him that it was no distraction at all from his larger failure.

One of his 1919 articles was a review of Virginia's second novel, *Night and Day*. Not long after the book was published that autumn, Morgan visited Virginia and Leonard at Hogarth House. Virginia was preoccupied by some of Morgan's guarded criticisms of the book. Forster, attentive to Virginia's brilliance on the one hand and to her insecurity on the other, alleviated her worry about what was otherwise a very favorable review by offering additional praise and a fuller explanation of what he'd meant to convey about the importance of her overall achievement. He wanted to encourage her; he knew how fragile a writer's ego, and creative spark, could be. As they walked together along the Thames for an hour after dinner, they talked "very easily," Virginia noted in her diary, "the proof being that we (I anyhow) did not mind silences." In between silences, Morgan confided to her that he was "in trouble with a novel of his own." He was "fingering the keys but only producing discords so far," she wrote.

This was the "Indian M.S." he had begun before the war. He had written seventy-five pages then—and had not added to them. A few months before his November 1919 dinner at Hogarth House he wrote the poet Siegfried Sassoon, "While trying to write my novel, I wanted to scream aloud like a maniac, and it is not in such a mood that one's noblest work is penned." After a while he was no longer even trying, and wrote more articles instead.

Shortly after writing Reid in February 1921, Forster received a providential cable that offered a reprieve from his armchair life. He was summoned by the Maharaja of Dewas, an old friend, to "go for six months and be a Prime Minister or something." The request, to step in for another Englishman, Colonel Leslie, an aide who would be on leave, fulfilled Reid's prophecy. The whither and when of Morgan's long and fantastic journey became clear, but not what he would do there or, really, why he should bother to go. The maharaja wrote to Morgan in an infectious burst of childlike enthusiasm to see him once again, yet it was as fantastical that the maharaja would ask Morgan of all people to be the substitute as it was for Morgan to say yes. Morgan, accepting with an anxious sense of a last chance at a grand, if vague, adventure, rushed to "get a passport and passage" and left within two weeks, at the beginning of March. He was going away to serve a cause, as he had done in going to Alexandria, and once again hoping to find a camaraderie, and a purpose, missing from his constricted domestic life. He also hoped to summon, through an engagement with the outside world, the drive he had once felt for writing fiction.

Still, at least to those who'd known him the longest, the university friends he'd met at Cambridge who formed the nucleus of the amorphous Bloomsbury set, it seemed that at forty-two Forster was simply running away from home.

"Morgan goes to India, & I think for ever," Virginia wrote in her diary of his hasty departure. "He will become a mystic, sit by the roadside, & forget Europe, which I think he half despises." When she heard the surprising news from Bob Trevelyan, one of Forster's companions on his first trip to India in 1911–12, that Forster was leaving England in a few days, and without a farewell, she thought "Trevy" made it "all seem very reasonable & desirable"—but also very clear that it wasn't only Europe Morgan half despised, but his life at Weybridge. It would be, Trevy told her, "just the thing for him—a relief after his . . . well, his mother is trying sometimes—very fond of him, of course; devoted to him & he . . ."

The ellipses are Woolf's, and in trying, as she often did in her diary, to capture the rhythms and curlicues of a person's way of talking, she suggested a trailing off on Trevy's part into a knowing silence. For Virginia Woolf rarely abbreviated gossip, savoring, exaggerating, or even inventing detail rather than eliding anything of real or imaginary substance from an account, in conversation or in her diary, of what she had been told, in confidence or otherwise. She added without self-awareness, "This is in the usual Bob style, hinting little defects & mysteries with one corner of his mouth, praising with the other." Their shared innuendo was one Morgan might have echoed, acknowledging as he did to himself what his friends saw plainly: in still living with Lily, he was "too submissive and deferential," the very words Morgan used when thinking back, at the age of eighty, on his mother and her unwonted influence on his life. Lily, like the mother in his autobiographical *The Longest Journey*, "was dignified and reticent, and pathos, like tattle, was disgusting to her. She was afraid of intimacy, in case it led to confidences and tears, and so all her life she held her son at a little distance." In life, the distance was carefully managed on both sides. Morgan wrote in his diary of a morning when he "broke down at breakfast—very unwise as it puts me into mother's power. She is *very* sweet but it is never safe to be seen in pieces." In *The Longest Journey*, Morgan consigned Mrs. Elliot, like Lily a young widow with a son, to an early death, when her son is fifteen. Lily, whatever the fate of her fictional counterpart, lived until Morgan was sixty-six.

Morgan could no more acknowledge aloud that the maharaja's invitation had presented itself as a fortuitous call away from his mother's dominance than Virginia Woolf or Trevy could. Having noticed long before that "the sudden business of my life only makes her feel the emptiness of her own," he left his escape to stand as a kind of unspoken reprimand to Lily, who was angered by his sudden departure and whose "naughtiness" at being abandoned marred the usual studied calm of their close quarters in the days before he sailed.

But he had gone farther to find less satisfaction. His first trip to India had inspired the pages he abandoned within a couple of years. The vastness of India had, on his trip a decade before, made him "careless of this suburban life." He had hoped it would again. But in Dewas he was doing a job he was unprepared for, and one he knew almost immediately upon arrival that he was unsuited for. It had been willful blindness that an administrative job might be right for him. Or any job at all.

He was "treated with great kindness by" the maharaja—"H.H.," as he was called, short for His Highness—but employment as a so-called private secretary was an even starker reminder of his failure to write than being at home, not writing, had been. He had come in order to revive his novel, and now he had more leisure than ever to do so. One of his proposed tasks was to read aloud once a day to H.H.—but in practice he did this only once a month at best. He started a literary society, to be focused on "noble writings of the past and present," but attendance at the Wednesday meetings was "slight and the enthusiasm slighter." The solicitous H.H. was undemanding of little more than Morgan's companionship at his own royal whim, and the court was overrun with underlings and servants (and spies) who better understood its mysterious operations in any case. Morgan had more spacious quarters than Weybridge afforded—a suite, "decently furnished in the European style," including a bedroom, sitting room, anteroom, bathroom, and veranda. Here was room to write in, if he could set himself to write more than the voluminous correspondence he built up with Lily, his aunt Laura, and various friends. Instead he spent evenings looking at the little pile of his abandoned pages, feeling "only distaste and despair."

Forster tried, from a sense of duty, to impose some order in Colonel Leslie's absence, the once acclaimed novelist now immersed in trying to stabilize the state's catastrophic finances, and occupied with mundane tasks, overseeing the palace gardens and garages as well as the "electric house" and power supply. But Leslie planned to return, and Morgan would shortly have to decide what to do, though he was constitutionally unable to make wise decisions in circumstances like this. His impulsive leap to take the job in Dewas had been a great error, and he recoiled from further action, sapped by the heat and the mosquitoes, and bound as he was by ties of affection and obligation to H.H. Shortly became months.

"Perhaps it is the heat, but I feel so stupid, almost senile," he confided to a friend. "I cannot concentrate and I cannot remember." He was lonelier than ever. "The very fact that I have friends will be absent from my mind for hours."

It was hardly surprising that his job, such as it was, "does not use in me what there is to use," as he put it. But it was also true that he was not using in himself what there was to use, and had not for many years. "My Indian M.S. is with me," he wrote to a friend, "but I dare not open it, and I have even lost the desire and the capacity for journalism. I read very little. In fact I think I'm losing more ground."

The reacquaintance with India that he thought was necessary had not been a key to renewal of work on his novel; in fact, it had the opposite effect. He was disappointed to find that in Dewas the "silliness of Indian life is presented to me in too large a beaker." The pages he'd written "seemed to wilt and go dead," almost as if they, too, had been undone by the humidity. He ultimately decided he had "struck a dull piece of India," where the people were "unattractive for the most part" and even spiritual beauty was "mainly confined to H.H."

One night in August 1921, amid the cacophony of an elaborate religious festival marking the birthday of Lord Krishna, Morgan had a bad dream. Because he had wanted to be closer to the celebrations, and to have a better view, he had moved from his usual suite into rooms in the Old Palace, where among other inconveniences shoes were prohibited. In the dream, Morgan was at home in Weybridge, with his cat, Verouka. "I thought I had shown him a mechanical doll that frightened him so that he was mad and raced round and round in a room overhead," he recounted in a letter. Morgan awakened, relieved to discover the sound was really the rhythmic noise made by the steam engine that had been brought in at extravagant cost to run the special electric lights required for the festivities.

At home, the room overhead was the attic, where Morgan went to write. Morgan was the frightened one and had been racing round and round in circles in a room overhead for years.

* * *

In his birthday retrospective on the year 1921, he wrote, "how unsuitable were my wanderings at Dewas, where everyone laughed at my incompetence." He had been defeated by yet another sinister year. "My desire for self-expression has slackened along every line," he wrote, looking inward without vanity but also without hope. It was a bleak encapsulation of exhaustion at middle age but also a lapsed novelist's lament for all the lines he had not written.

In the early pages of the long-stalled fragment, there was a description of one of his Indian characters, who in thinking about the British is frustrated that he "felt caught in their meshes." The character, "Dr Aziz," knows that his life is shaped by their demands rather than by his own will. Morgan understood the trap on a domestic scale, and had given Aziz his own dilemma. Weybridge was Lily's domain, Morgan was in her power there, and as his protagonist did he wanted "to escape from the net." For Aziz, this would mean leaving British India. Morgan had left Weybridge but had not escaped at all. The seventy-five pages of his Indian manuscript were the meshes in which Morgan was caught.

"Slowness and apathy increase," he wrote in his birthday entry. "I can't go on any more here." He had not gone "for ever," as Virginia had perhaps fancifully believed. He had not become a mystic. He had also not become a novelist at work again. The next escape was to go home. He would sail on January 14, 1922.

* * *

Life with Lily at Weybridge had been a retreat from the social engagement of his years at Cambridge and a too early abandonment of the possibility of an independent life and romantic companionship. His desires were homosexual, and the promise of sexual satisfaction and emotional contentment seemed unattainable. Once again isolated in the suburbs after the war, he had worried that in middle age, "My mind is now obsessed by sexual fancies and hopes: wasting much time." During his most prolific years, beginning long before he lost his virginity, he had begun to write "indecent" stories "to excite myself." It was stimulating to write them and to be able to fantasize about "indecent acts" when a partner, casual or otherwise, was unobtainable. Because the impulse behind the stories had nothing to do with artistic expression, he felt a thrill in doing "something positively dangerous" to his career as a novelist, then in full flight. That he was not ashamed of the stories or of his desires did not mitigate what seemed to be his fear—that the discovery of the cache of stories (as he was also to fear the discovery of his diary), or any kind of open discussion of his sexuality, would be fatal to domestic peace or even to his career, though anything short of a public scandal would mean a vast personal relief. Yet it turned out that the danger was somewhat different. The freedom with which he wrote his private stories convinced him of the sterility of the writing he was doing for publication. In 1910, the same year that *Howards End* was published, he fell in love with Syed Ross Masood, an Indian who had come to England to study. Morgan had been recommended as a tutor in Latin. The year was a watershed. Forster's popularity reached its height, and at the peak of his literary success, a few days before his thirty-second birthday, he found the courage to confess his feelings to Masood. They were sitting together talking. The conversation was inconsequential. Masood praised Morgan's "insight into Oriental things." Morgan, impatient with the formulaic emptiness of the compliment and overwhelmed by suppressed emotion, spoke without forethought. "I could bear no more: He answered 'I know.'" Masood was less surprised to hear the truth than Morgan was to hear himself express it.

Morgan sent Masood a note the next day, but by New Year's Eve, he wrote in his diary, "Non respondit, and though I do believe it is all right, my breast burns suddenly & I have felt ill." Morgan had awaited his birthday, and a response from Masood, burdened with the knowledge that the inauspicious silence meant what he knew it meant, even as he tried to convince himself otherwise. Shortly after the new year, Masood replied. He loved Morgan deeply, but as an affectionate friend. The fame that *Howards End* brought him, and Masood's demurral, marked the beginning of an era of decline and withdrawal that was to reach its nadir in India.

Perhaps inevitably, Forster after *Howards End* felt "weariness of the only subject that I both can and may treat—the love of men for women & vice versa." Four novels had exhausted that well. But it was not only a question of the subject conventionally open to him. More insidious was the creative self-doubt—and personal despair—that arose from the fact that anything related to the sexual love of one person for another, "men for women & vice versa," but also the love of men for men, was unknown to him. After four novels, and after his erotic stories, he did not feel able to write in the abstract any longer. The real Morgan Forster wasn't to be found in the novels but in the "indecent thoughts and acts" that those novels couldn't address openly—and that aside from some aborted fumblings, long before, he had never experienced. After the publication of *Howards End*, and only ten days before he spoke to Masood, he wrote in his diary, "Desire for a book." It was a sexual longing, and one destined to remain as unfulfilled as his desire for romantic and sexual companionship.

The pile of erotic stories grew. *Maurice* had arisen from a similar impulse, in the hope that in the novel he would connect "lustful thoughts and glances" with "the personal," as he longed to do in life and as he had seen other men do it. The inspiration for *Maurice*, which Forster had written quickly, had been a September 1913 visit with the writer Edward Carpenter, "a believer in the Love of Comrades, whom he sometimes called

Uranians." Carpenter, then sixty-nine, lived openly with his working-class companion George Merrill, more than two decades younger. Their intimacy was a revelation to Forster, as was the casual ease with which Merrill had touched Morgan's backside, "gently and just above the buttocks. I believe he touched most people's," Morgan recalled a half century later. The sensation Morgan felt was unusual and intense, "as much psychological as physical. It seemed to go straight through the small of my back into my ideas, without involving my thoughts."

But nothing of what he had seen, or imagined in his stories or in the novel that he knew was unpublishable, had ever happened to him.

* * *

That had changed in Alexandria. He had arrived near the end of 1915 and, almost a year later, was able to confide the news that on October 15, 1916, "for the first time in my life I parted with respectability"—the phrase with which he reported the information to his friend Florence Barger—on a beach, with a soldier. The hurried encounter had left him feeling "curiously sad," and he thought he would have felt differently, more exultant, if he had taken "the step . . . at the usual age."

He had become even more attuned to male beauty because there was so much of it to see in Alexandria, where his work was to "do the motherly to Tommies," the British soldiers there, and where he had been exposed to a parade of them, "all these young gods . . . the beauty of a crest of a wave." Soon after arriving in Alexandria he had also noticed a tram conductor working on a line he used frequently. Forster had looked up as the young Egyptian man walked past him and was attracted. "Nice," he remembered thinking. "That boy has some African-Negro blood," Forster and a friend agreed. Over the course of the next year, Forster and the young man had spoken intermittently as Forster continued to ride the route. He was soon waiting as long as three-quarters of an hour for the conductor to appear at the terminus at the end of a shift. The young man was so beautiful, "in the prime of . . . physical glory," that for a long time Morgan did not want to "intervene or speak," but only to look at him. The flirtatious dance had culminated, in the late spring of 1917, in what Morgan knew was "one great piece of good luck—the sort of thing that comes to most men as a matter of course when they are 18 or 20"—the conductor had agreed to meet Morgan, in a public garden on the outskirts of town. They still did not know each other's names. The conductor's, he'd soon learn, was Mohammed el Adl.

At first Morgan had been drawn by differences in "age, race, rank." As they had become better acquainted, he had discovered he had "hit on things of objective worth" in Mohammed, including "romantic curiosity . . . on both sides." Eventually they had "adventures" in each other's rooms; but love and proximity, love and reciprocated desire, seemed destined never to mix for Morgan. First there had been the misconnection with Masood. Mohammed went further but responded to Morgan's sexual overtures from "a gracious generosity rather than upon a nature exactly like mine," Morgan wrote Florence Barger. Morgan recorded Mohammed's remark, "my damned prick always stands up whoever it is, it means nothing," as no more than his own self-abnegating due, and though he had no choice but to believe the explanation, Morgan had worked on Mohammed's somewhat playacted inhibitions for many fruitless months. Eventually, he found that a "sudden placidness" was more effective than anything more aggressive. "R has been parted with," Morgan wrote to Florence in October 1917—R meaning respectability—"I am so happy—not for the actual pleasure but because the last barrier has fallen." Morgan's tactics apart, Mohammed was leaving Alexandria in a few days for Cairo, for war work, at double his present pay, that Morgan had arranged. Mohammed may simply have been aware of his debt to his friend.

* * *

Morgan claimed he had been content with caresses: the ruffling of each other's hair; the feeling of Mohammed's arm under his head as they lay on Morgan's bed after a game of chess more vivid in his memory than their first kiss; his fondling of Mohammed's thighs when, after an obligatory "gruff demur," the younger man would loosen his linen underclothes "and lean back a little." But he was deeply hurt by the limits of their physical relationship and did his best to ignore Mohammed's "frequent coldness." They saw each other occasionally when Mohammed could visit Alexandria. Mohammed married in the autumn of 1918, and not long afterward it was time for Morgan to return to Weybridge. He continued to correspond with Mohammed, helped him financially as much as he could, and intervened as far as he was able when Mohammed was imprisoned on trumped-up charges.

"If the letters cease it will only mean one thing—that I have died," Mohammed told him. When Mohammed had a son, he gave him an Egyptian name, but called him Morgan.

* * *

As soon as Morgan made arrangements to leave for Dewas, in 1921, he wrote to Mohammed with the news, hoping that they would be able to "snatch a meeting" as his ship passed through Port Said. In fact, the opportunity to take a sea route through Egypt was likely one of the incentives to accept the maharaja's offer. Now, as 1922 began and he planned his journey back, he looked forward to another, longer visit with Mohammed.

During Morgan's stop at Port Said on the way out in 1921, Mohammed had been so eager to see his friend, he had pushed his way on board and escorted him to land. They had "four perfect hours together," having sex on a deserted beach, despite the cold, under a vaporous cover of fog, Mohammed in a "great coat and blue knitted gloves with which he repeatedly clasped my hands, saying how are you friend, how are you." The echo of the repeated question sustained Morgan for nearly a year. Now Morgan anticipated a month rather than four hours, and in order to prolong his stay he chose a sea voyage for the second leg rather than a quicker, more expensive trip that would have taken him across Europe by land. That would bring him home too soon. He could save money, a convenient excuse he used in explaining his delay to Lily, and indulge his heart.

* * *

A couple of days after his birthday, Morgan wrote his mother with New Year's greetings for 1922 and an account of the elaborate birthday celebration that had been given to him at Hyderabad, where he was visiting with Masood before he was to sail from Bombay. Amid the public festivities for New Year's Day, there was a toast to Morgan's "health, which was drunk in sherbet flavoured with rose water." But his "flowery day" did not end there, he told Lily. His bedroom had been festooned "like a bridal chamber," he wrote, and was filled with flowering shrubs pinned to the curtains, vases full of roses on the dressing table, and ropes of rose leaves around the bed. More rose leaves were strewn on it, this last decoration more beautiful than practical, as they ended up "feeling rather like crumbs in the night." He emphasized to Lily, as he always did, his happiness. "It was roses all the way," he wrote and signed his letter with another of their nicknames, "Pop."

It was roses all the way, except that it was not. He wrote the same day to his friend Goldsworthy Lowes Dickinson, a fellow at King's who was also a member of the Apostles, and informed "Goldie," too, of his sailing in two weeks. "Let us wish one another a Happy New Year," he wrote, "though this is to prepare you for my sad and inglorious return."

* * *

The last two weeks of his Indian adventure were as one with the previous nine months: disheartening. Morgan had to travel about 435 miles from Hyderabad, in the interior, to Bombay, on the western coast, from where he would set sail. On his way, he wanted to see the Ajanta caves, a group of thirty cliffside caves, some from as early as 200–100 BC, with elaborate murals and carvings, depicting the life of the Buddha, that represent the beginning of classical Indian art. The caves ringed a cliff above a tributary to a larger river. He planned to travel there on the seventh and to arrive in Bombay on the twelfth, in time for the sailing two days later.

But Morgan didn't make it to the caves. He fell and injured his left elbow and right wrist, badly enough that he couldn't feed himself, no less make the walk. The caves were about twenty-five miles from the nearest train station, and the "elaborate arrangements" that had been made for the visit were now canceled. He quickly regretted his "foolish abandonment" of the plan: his decisions large and small went equally wrong.

When, later in the 1920s, Virginia was preparing an article on Forster's novels, she made notes to herself on what was impressive and what was lacking in his books. She copied out some lines Forster gave to one of the protagonists of his first novel, *Where Angels Fear to Tread*, published in 1905: "I seem fated to pass through the world without colliding with it or moving it—I don't die—I don't fall in love," and added, "True of M: but he has moments of vision."

But Morgan, as he was leaving India, felt that he had not had a moment of vision in a long time. He had missed the caves. He was passing through the world without moving it. He did some last sightseeing before sailing two days later, on the RMS *Kaisar-i-Hind*.

* * *

It had been ten months since he had seen Mohammed, and Morgan was more eager to get to Egypt again than he was to return to Weybridge. Planning his stay, he wrote his mother disingenuously but obligingly that after mid-January his address would be "C/o Messrs T. Cook Cairo, which seems nearer Mummy." Nearer the truth, however, is that Cairo was nearer to Mohammed. Economizing on his return passage, as he had told her he would be doing, also meant he had money "for a splash in Upper Egypt" with Mohammed. Morgan was lonelier than ever in middle age—"inclined to a pot belly, a red nose, and baldness," he soon complained. Worried that he was long since too old to "make another great friend," he was, he had confided to Goldie, relieved that he'd "pulled in Mohammed only just before the gate shut."

His expectations for the visit, already high, rose further as its likelihood became more fragile. By December, Egypt, occupied by the British since 1882 and under martial law since November 1914, had come closer and closer to open rebellion. The country might be too dangerous to stop in, and he worried: "I shall be carried past not 100 yds. from my goal," meaning Mohammed. His own "frustration & wretchedness" could hardly weigh against "the misery of an entire nation," he knew, but it was hard work to balance his conscience against thwarted desire. Egypt, however, was under control by the time of his arrival on January 24.

But fair political weather did not make for the triumphant reunion he hoped to have. He had worried that his arrival a day ahead of schedule would mean that Mohammed would be unable to get there in time, as he had promised. And he wasn't there to greet the boat. A messenger gave Morgan a letter. Mohammed was too ill to make the roughly eighty-mile trip from Mansourah, the town in the Nile delta where he lived. Morgan would have to go to him.

Only a few days into the new year, Mohammed had suffered a recurrence of his tuberculosis first diagnosed years before. Once in Mansourah, Morgan knew immediately he would "not see him alive again." Mohammed had all the worst symptoms of consumption: "haemorrage, night-sweats, exhaustion—he cannot live," Morgan wrote to Masood. The local doctor was "a robber and probably a quack" and in the interest of higher fees had refused to make the proper diagnosis, instead inoculating Mohammed pointlessly and pumping "tubes of useless stuff into his poor little arm." Mohammed rallied a bit after Morgan's arrival, but even so was mostly too weak to walk far.

Shocked by Mohammed's condition, Morgan thought, initially, that he must leave Egypt as quickly as possible. He could not simply "sit attempting to nurse in Mansourah," he told Masood. Mohammed had become "irritable and hard—it is an unhappy time for me in the local daily sense." Morgan recognized, though, that his money could be of use both now and in the future, and he made arrangements through friends who might pay out monthly allowances for Mohammed on Morgan's behalf.

But two days with Mohammed softened Morgan's resolve. Indecision, usually Morgan's weakness, here became a strength. Illness had also made Mohammed "sombre and beautiful, no longer responsive, which last I have to face." The end might be very soon, and if Mohammed's case were as dire as it seemed, Morgan would not be a nurse but a final companion, his own desires, in every sense, set aside.

"I am very ill so my roughness must be excused," Mohammed said quietly one day. He, too, had been making plans for Morgan's arrival, and Morgan was moved by the fact that Mohammed, who for all the bravado of his greeting the year before was usually unsentimental, had been looking forward to seeing him, too. Morgan would go to Alexandria to visit friends there and would return to Mansourah for another week or two with Mohammed before then leaving for England.

Morgan became nurse, concierge, and companion, able to attend to practical details, a happy contrast, amid unhappy events, to the incompetence he had felt at Dewas. Mohammed's illness had been exacerbated by his doctor's inept treatment and by unsanitary living conditions. Morgan was able to pay for a visit to a Cairo specialist, a trip of about seventy-five miles that would otherwise have been beyond el Adl. They went in early February, and it was as he feared. "The leading doctor in Cairo confirms my worst suspicions—no shadow of hope, only doesn't know whether it will be weeks or months." Morgan did not want Mohammed to return to Mansourah, and certainly did not want to go there himself. Now that they were in Cairo, perhaps at least part of the "splash" might still be possible. Morgan found them a comfortable home in the "rheumatic and consumptive resort" of Helouan, about twenty miles south of Cairo on the Nile, opposite the ruins of Memphis.

In the end he was in Egypt, and with Mohammed, for almost the full month he had anticipated.

* * *

In ancient times the town was known as Ain-An, its sacred therapeutic springs legendary in the time of the pharaohs. Morgan and Mohammed lived together but not alone: they lived with Mohammed's wife and child and others of Mohammed's extended family.

Mohammed briefly rallied; "perked up by this good desert air, he announced he should get well." The town was less expensive than Morgan had thought, and together they were "oddly tranquil considering the circumstances." Some days were even "merry and happy."

Though he had capital enough to live on, Morgan was always worried about money, particularly since royalties from his books were now negligible. Only sixty-six copies of A Room with a View had been sold in 1921; and only thirty-two of Howards End. Still, he was enormously wealthy by Mohammed's, and Egyptian, standards. "How wonderful money is, I said to myself, when the mid-day train drew up," he wrote, even though husbanding his resources was as much on his mind in Egypt as it was in Weybridge, where he had occasionally been in debt to his mother for his yearly contribution to the housekeeping. "I wish I knew how long he would live, since I could spread my spare cash accordingly," he wrote to Florence. He thought that once he was back in England, he could continue to support Mohammed for about six months "without difficulty."

Morgan's sadness at Mohammed's condition was complicated by his disappointment that they would not have sex. In Dewas, sex had been one of the very few bright spots, though he was not pleased in an unmixed way. H.H. had provided him with a concubine. He was uneasy about the boy at first, though H.H. was frank with him about the management of the relationship with Kanaya: he must not take the passive role, for this would lead to shame at court if it were talked about, as it inevitably would be, H.H. knew. For Morgan, this was a time, he was to remember, of "very violent" sexual desire. Only a few years later he was to look back and note a "great loss of sexual power" in only a relatively short period of time. The intensity of his desire for the concubine surprised Morgan and saddened him. It did not seem comradely, in the Carpenter way, to have a concubine at his disposal, or simply to make use of him with what Morgan took to be cruelty. He remained uneasy that he had found the encounters deeply satisfying, and he looked forward to sex with Mohammed, perhaps partly to redeem the fact that their own sexual relationship had been satisfying to neither of them, and had never been consummated as Morgan had hoped it would be.

But the tuberculosis had apparently left Mohammed impotent, or he "rather believed himself to be," as Morgan put it, so that it amounted to the same thing. "I had been looking forward for months," he admitted to Florence. But he was distracted from Mohammed's lack of interest, at least briefly. A "half hour's stroll along the sea front solved one of my difficulties," he told Masood. He had, to his own, and Mohammed's, relief, "parted with r.—!" he wrote Florence. The phrase was no longer code for virginity itself. Every encounter was a delightful and newsworthy parting from respectability.

Yet the two weeks they spent in Helouan were largely happy. Mohammed's rally meant that they were able to take donkey rides in the desert "and we sit about at cafés, and the weather has turned delicious, and he is stronger and cheerful." But Mohammed's cough worsened as Morgan's departure neared. He had strength enough to accompany Morgan to the port of Cairo and was determined to do so despite the fact that he was "little more than bones now." Morgan's ship, the SS *Delta*, departed on February 20. The awkwardness of their failed physical intimacy was behind them now, irrelevant, as they said good-bye for the last time. "He sat by me in the Railway carriage and said 'My love to you, there is nothing else to say,' which is exactly the truth," Morgan wrote to Florence. The face of his "poor dear little fellow" was unchanged. It was still "a very nice one" despite illness. Morgan focused on that as he departed, and on the sight of Mohammed, in a yellow velvet cap, his body folded up "as only an Oriental can, so that his intelligent beautiful face seems to be resting on a pyramid of clothes." At the last instant Mohammed nudged Morgan twice with his right elbow, "out of love."

As they parted it was evident to Morgan that the "collapse may come any minute," he wrote Masood. He only hoped it would come without more suffering. Morgan had done all he could, and lamented to Florence, "Ah me—but everything is bearable, it is the betrayal from within that wears away one's soul and I have been spared that."

* * *

He would be home by March 3. His cabinmate was uninteresting, a man "who has been the usual 25 years of his life in India, and treats me, unasked, to the usual fine fruits of such an experience." Eventually the man became tired of talking, or of Morgan's lack of interest in India, "for now he is silent, having apparently no other topic of conversation." The silence was a relief.

To his aunt Laura he wrote, "We passengers are a dull company, or perhaps it is that each of us has his own thoughts: it is natural that he should, returning from the East in such times as this." He was referring to the political situation, in India and in Egypt, but the phrase encompassed the other subject he privately dwelled upon. He had been buoyed on the voyage from Bombay to Egypt by the thought of Mohammed's awaiting him. He had little to hope for as he got closer and closer to home and to his former life with Lily.

"The public tragedy seems an extension of my private trouble," he wrote to Masood. He was expert at encoding secrets, writing to his aunt Laura from the *Delta* that his month in Egypt had "passed very pleasantly, among old friends, but not altogether among old places." He had spent the last fortnight, he told her, at Helouan, near Cairo, "with a friend who is ill—Mohammed el Adl is his name: I must not forget to mention it."

He felt obliged to name him, even if he could not tell his aunt or his mother why.

* * *

"The knack of a double life grows."

Morgan confided this to Florence Barger about real estate difficulties, whether, in 1924, he and his mother would move from their longtime home in Weybridge, as they eventually did, to West Hackhurst, the house in the village of Abinger Hammer inherited from Aunt Laura. At the moment they had both houses. "I am here alone for two nights, rather to mother's distress," Morgan wrote to Florence from West Hackhurst. "I thought I would like to feel what it is to be in my own house, for a minute, and

I cannot do that while she is in command!" The question of what to do preoccupied Lily in particular. His own consolation, Morgan wrote, was "that as soon as I leave either of our abodes my mind becomes perfectly free; the knack of a double life grows."

It had been growing for a long time. An uncle of Morgan's, Willie Forster, had noticed around the time of Morgan's twenty-first birthday that Lily treated her son "as if still a child." He thought it spelled trouble that Morgan was "invariably" the only man around, "and if there were any they wd. be quite as bad as the women." Morgan needed "country air and pursuits with genial pals," Willie advised, rather than living in the closed domestic world of women "swapping lies and making mischief." It was having an emasculating effect on him: "His descriptions of the teas are very nice, being always in Jane Austin [*sic*] fashion."

Not quite a year after *Howards End* had been published, Morgan wrote in his diary, "Depressing & enervating surroundings. My life's work, if I have any, is to live with a person who thinks nothing worth while."

He had gone to India to see whether he might finish another novel. He had failed. Nostalgic and melancholy for a career he was powerless to resume, he returned instead to his "life's work" in Weybridge.

Chapter 4

"SOMEWHERE AWAY BY MYSELF"

As A BOY HE WAS BERT, AND WAS ALWAYS Bert to his family, including the older brother and two sisters, George, Emily, and Lettice Ada, who outlived David Herbert Lawrence by several decades. When his mother, Lydia, was dying, in December 1910, she hoped to live long enough to see "our Bert's first book." He sent "message after message, telegrams to the publishers" for an early copy of *The White Peacock*, which was to be published in 1911, that he could give to her. Lawrence's first novel was put into her hands on her deathbed, but it was no use—"no sign was given that she knew what it was." The publication of almost every one of his novels would be accompanied by similar disappointment, and difficulties, legal and otherwise.

As a boy, Bert had "a genius for inventing games," his sister Ada remembered. He hated football and cricket, and played mainly indoors. Outdoors to him meant gathering "the girls together to go blackberrying" and talking to the flowers that filled the meadows beyond yards paved with red brick that were the landscape of Eastwood, where he was born on September 11, 1885, a place filled with "hundreds of niggardly houses" that covered the valleys of Nottinghamshire. Bert's face was white as chalk, and the red of his ginger hair only made his skin seem paler in comparison. The contrasts only intensified with age: seen in bathing trunks, at a hot springs near Taos, New Mexico, where he arrived in 1922, his body "was as white as lard," the skin translucent over his shoulder blades, ribs, and even the striations of the thin muscles.

Mabel Dodge, who invited him to Taos, wrote in her memoirs of the startling impact of the sight of Lawrence with his "tousled head and red beard and eyes like blue stars." They were disappointed with each other almost immediately upon actual acquaintance, but Mabel paid posthumous tribute to Lawrence's startling physical presence, his body "indomitable, with a will to endure as ivory endures." D. H. Lawrence, she wrote, had stood out from the contemporary landscape of humanity like a work of art or an allegory, "a fleshly Word" that she and the rest of the world had not understood.

He had been misunderstood since childhood. In Eastwood, he was called "Bertie," which he hated, and teased for his clinging and babyish ways. He was effeminate, and his squeaky voice "girlish." And because all of his friends were girls, the boys would crowd around him singing, "Dicky Dicky Denches plays with the Wenches." He may have played with girls, but "he had not much use for the Plain Janes." His playmates were only the town's good-looking and vivacious girls.

As a child, his voice would rise in pitch when he was even the least excited. It was the same when he grew up. An unkind witness remembered that Lawrence "perpetually squeaked or squealed in a ridiculous manner, like a eunuch." He seemed to people either childlike, exultant in his reaction to the world, or childish in the extreme, moody and given to tantrums.

There was very little about Lawrence that wasn't irritating to someone. Edmund Wilson, meeting him in New York in 1923, at a tea given for Lawrence by Thomas Seltzer, his publisher, thought him "ill-bred and hysterical," and wrote in his diary that Lawrence's appearance was disconcerting. He was lean, and his head "disproportionately small," Wilson wrote. "One saw that he belonged to an inferior caste—some bred-down unripening race of the collieries. Against this inferiority—fundamental and physical—he must have had to fight all his life: his passionate spirit had made up for it by exaggerated self-assertion." Wilson, seemingly unaware that Lawrence might have intuited this reaction and been fighting against it that very afternoon, added that when the conversation veered away from whatever it was that Lawrence himself was interested in, he "burst out in childish rudeness, and in a high-pitched screaming voice with something like: 'I'm not enjoying this! Why are we sitting here having tea? I don't want your tea! I don't want to be doing this!'"

Lawrence had faced condescension all his life and, in large and small ways, had all his life resisted doing what he did not want to do. His conversation, like his work, was a rebellion against mere gentility. What Wilson might scorn as childish rudeness, Lawrence saw, self-righteously, in grander terms, as a resistance to the way others said the world, or he, must be. The teas that found him chatting with Wilson and others like him, whether in New York, or in London, or in Eastwood or Nottingham, where only the scale was different, were no more interesting to him than football or cricket had been to him years before. He did not care when others thought him—or his work—rude, or at least did not when their judgment, literary or personal, arose, as Wilson's did, from a more elemental disdain that riled Lawrence in pride and anger.

Lawrence did not like the world of people as he found it and, as a child and as a man, preferred to immerse himself in nature or in worlds of his own creation. This was one reason he so frequently wrote outdoors, off for the morning in a forest, in whatever place he happened to be, under a particular tree that, once discovered, seemed to him the unique and necessary shelter for whichever thing, a poem or novel or article, he was working on at the time. This was also one reason so much of his writing, his poetry and his travel essays in particular, forms a vast and exultant celebration of the natural world, which man did not make; and why, in his novels, poems, and stories, he reimagined man, and the totality of the world of human relationships that man did make, as defiantly, as sincerely, and with as much genius as he had invented games in childhood. He could not waste self-discipline at a tea party. It was reserved for his work alone.

"It seemed inevitable that Bert should spend his life creating things," his sister Ada remembered after Lawrence's death. "We had to create our own happiness," she recalled of their childhood. "There was little ready made about us."

* * *

Bert turned thirty-six on September 11, 1921. He was also Lorenzo, was also Lawrence, was also David, was also Lawr, known by different acquaintances and friends by different names. On September 19, he renewed his passport at the consulate in Florence. Soon to come to an end was an unusually lengthy era, for him, of stability. He lived at Fontana Vecchia, his house in Taormina, Sicily, for more than two years, as long as he would live in any one place after eloping with the already married Frieda Weekley, née von Richtofen, in 1912, whom he married in 1914. He was ready for 1922. The new year would bring an end to an interregnum of relative permanence in more than a decade of nomadic travel until he died, in 1930. Every flight, all his life, was a bid for happiness. In every place he found happiness only briefly.

The consular official's handwritten description in the passport records that D. H. Lawrence was an "Author" from "Eastwood, Notts," short for Nottingham. Here was a fact, as was his height, which was five feet nine inches. But recollections of what he really looked like are as various as the nicknames by which he was known. Officially he had blue-gray eyes and light brown hair. It was left to friends to redeem the mundane and to recall the hypnotic power of Lawrence's eyes and the dark red of his beard and hair that glowed "like flames from the intensity of his life." The official saw nothing of this posthumous glamour. In the space under the heading "Special peculiarities" there is only the word "None." An earlier more elaborate passport, issued in London by the Foreign Office in September 1919, included a more detailed physical description of the Lawrence then identified as "Novelist." His height, eye color, and hair color were all the same. His forehead and mouth were "normal"; his nose "short"; his face "long"; his complexion "pale." His chin was "normal," too, the passport records, or perhaps it was as one friend recalled, a chin "out of proportion" to Lawrence's slender face, a defect Lawrence had artfully concealed by the "dainty decoration" of his beard.

The official photograph does not capture Lawrence's frequently "sardonic" smile, which was endearing and charming, or the "funny little cackle of a laugh" that with a "rising inflection" was "like a little scream."

* * *

For Lawrence and Frieda, the year 1922 began with a fantasy he had in the fall of 1921. "I wish I could find a ship that would carry me round the world and land me somewhere in the West—New Mexico or California— and I could have a little house and two goats, somewhere away by myself in the Rocky Mountains," Lawrence wrote to his publisher, Thomas Seltzer.

Lawrence was vague on geography—the Rockies do not extend as far west as California—and what he wanted, then as always, was as contradictory as it was temporary. But now he had reached a crisis, one punctuated by the expiry of his and Frieda's passports and the sense this gave that time had run out. Three years after the end of the war, he had still found no mental peace.

The Lawrences had spent the spring and summer traveling, nearly three months in Germany, a month in Florence, Siena, Rome, and Capri. Visiting his mother-in-law in Germany, he felt that the country, and the continent for which it became a symbol, was "so empty—as if uninhabited." It did not matter that in a nation devastated by war, every house might be crowded from the coal cellars to the attics. It felt empty—"life-empty; no young men," Lawrence wrote.

In Taormina, on the eastern shore of Sicily, at his house on an idyllic hilltop, he could stand looking through "the great window of the eastern sky, seaward," away from the scars of the war still visible on the continent behind him. He and Frieda had come here in self-exile, driven out of England in 1917, suspected as spies, but also dangerous because he was a writer of supposedly obscene books. He had come to Sicily in search of what he called "naked liberty"—to write, but also, simply, to live. He was almost as far south from the "bog" that was England as one could go and still be in Europe at all.

D. H. Lawrence's fifth novel, *Women in Love*, was published in England in June 1921. The reviews were very negative, led by an attack in the *Times*. The book did not sell well. That it was published in England at all was in large part a miracle. His earlier novel, *The Rainbow*, to which the new novel was a sequel, had been published in 1915 and was almost immediately withdrawn by its publisher after it was banned under the Obscene Publications Act of

1857. Lawrence, who had conceived *Women in Love* before *The Rainbow*, wrote the new novel in defiance. "You will hate it and nobody will publish it. But there, these things are beyond us," he wrote his literary agent. The reception of *Women in Love* was predictable. As was the stubborn drive to write what he must, as he had always had to create his own happiness. Lawrence had the self-possession that book by book fortified him to court, and to face, critical and personal enmity. And yet he was naive enough, and optimistic enough, that when the enmity, in its many forms, came he was outraged, disappointed, and hurt. Then his childlike enthusiasm, a combination of hopefulness and curiosity, turned to childish rage.

The reviews of *Women in Love* were only one problem. The threat of a libel action, brought by Philip Heseltine, an acquaintance of Lawrence's, was a further nuisance. Lawrence had caricatured Heseltine, a composer, but thought he had covered his portrait in enough veils—including changing the character's profession to painter—to distract attention. Heseltine was no more than "a half imbecile fool" who only wanted publicity, and Lawrence advised his publisher that resistance was the surest way to defuse the threat.

But news of the libel suit was only part of the problem that awaited him when he returned to Taormina. In addition to a copy of *Women in Love* marked with the passages Heseltine objected to, Martin Secker, his publisher, had sent Lawrence a copy of the reactionary newspaper *John Bull* that included a denunciation of *Women in Love* under the headline "A Book the Police Should Ban."

To the editor of *John Bull*, Lawrence's *Women in Love*—the story of the sisters Ursula and Gudrun Brangwen and the men with whom they are involved—was not a novel at all but was, rather, a "neurotic production exposed for sale on the bookstalls as a 'novel' . . . an analytic study of sexual depravity, the more repulsive from the fact that he seems to gloat over its production. . . . It is ugly, repellent, vile." On the one hand, Lawrence was used to the vituperation, and even welcomed it, taking *John Bull* as calmly as he did Heseltine's threat of prosecution. As the attack reminded people, Lawrence was "an old offender," suspect as both citizen and writer. Lawrence professed amusement, at least from afar, because "to disapprove of me . . . is so unoriginal." The *John Bull* publicity could not even improve sales. To satisfy Heseltine's solicitors, Secker had already suspended the

circulation of the book "at considerable pecuniary loss" to both himself
and Lawrence.

But Lawrence's indifference to the legal problems and the bad reviews
actually cloaked the "rare, pure innocence" with which he had trusted
that his work would find an audience. *Women in Love* was "the best of my
books," he thought, and this new repudiation aggravated the displacement he had felt in Germany. He had "come loose from all moorings." He
saw as if with new eyes that Taormina had become crowded with the post-
war wealth of English and American people drawn to what was now like a
"continual Mad-Hatters tea-party." Everybody had at least £500 a year, and
"it feels so empty," as "life-empty" as Germany, but in a new, more festive
form, perhaps more insidious and soul-killing. "What isn't empty," he
wondered, "as far as the world of man goes."

* * *

He'd had the same fantasy for years—an escape from that bog of England,
to a new world. During the war, he had had visions of establishing himself in Florida, on a farm, a commune to be called Rananim. He was "a
Columbus who can see a shadowy America before him," but for lack of
followers with devotion enough, among other more practical reasons,
Rananim had never come to pass. There were never followers devoted
enough. All his "companion adventurers" failed him, recalled one, who
counted herself among those who had disappointed him, and regretted
it. He needed friends, she thought, "if only to leave behind." Only Frieda
never fell away.

Lawrence was an amalgam of such extreme contradictions that the tru-
est thing about him was that the opposite was also true. His fantasy of
America was as long-standing as his horror of it. "America, being so much
worse, falser, further gone than England, is nearer to freedom," he had written to his friend the novelist Catherine Carswell in 1916. The fate of nations
had its own logic, perceptible to Lawrence and perhaps no others. America,
as corroded as it was new, as hospitable as it was hostile to this new Columbus, was fertile ground for his communitarian vision because its commer-
cialism and its imperialistic tendencies had already left it "dryrotted to a
point where the final *seed* of the new is almost left ready to sprout."

In October 1921, he knew only that he wanted to go "really away." If he were to leave Europe, as he knew he must, could America be the right next place?

Where he would go, and how soon, also depended on money. He had only "forty-odd pounds in the bank," and his English money was "at the last crumbs." There was a larger balance in American accounts—he awaited an accounting from his American agent, Robert Mountsier—but because he had misplaced the checks Mountsier had sent him, he could not use the American money he might have.

He began to look into ships. A tramp steamer was more in his budget than a passenger ship, and it did not seem to matter what the destination was. His friends Earl and Achsah Brewster were soon moving to Ceylon, from Capri, where Earl was to study Buddhism. The proposal to join them was attractive, the camaraderie it offered a bit like the Rananim of old at last come to fruition. But the meditative life seemed only more emptiness, as worn as the Old World itself, and "without new possibilities" for him. Buddha was *vollendet*, he wrote, "consummated."

The news from England, his indecision, and the slow drain of his bank accounts left him "in a hell of a temper" all through the autumn. He did no writing, avoided all visitors, and was so disagreeable a presence that their maid, he thought, did her work "as if a dagger was at her neck." At the beginning of November he wrote Brewster that he was again considering Ceylon. It seemed as good a place as any, if only because the people there were as likely to be as "beshitten" as they were everywhere else on "this slippery ball of quick-silver of a dissolving world."

Then, three days later, a letter from a stranger arrived. To a writer preoccupied by destiny, the invitation it brought seemed providential. Lawrence answered it the same evening.

* * *

It was a little over half a mile, no more than a twenty-minute walk, from Fontana Vecchia to the Ufficio Postale di Taormina, where Lawrence picked up his mail. When, and if, it arrived. The Italian post was as beshitten as everything else, though the stories about it at least still had a rough charm. One train had recently fallen into a river in Calabria, he wrote a friend that autumn. All the luggage, and all the mail, had been lost, "stolen, of course." Strikes then paralyzed the railways all through November. The fascists under Mussolini were fighting in the streets.

An American woman he didn't know, Mabel Dodge Sterne, had written to invite him to live in Taos, New Mexico. She had read an excerpt from *Sea and Sardinia*, his forthcoming travel book about Italy, in the October issue of the *Dial* magazine, and sensing the "queer way" in which he uniquely gave "the feel and touch and smell of places," she hoped Lawrence would want to write about Taos in the same spirit and with the same sure hand.

She had a house for him, an adobe cottage, to live in while he did it. There was a tribe of Indians in Taos, "there since the Flood."

Her letter was not a letter but rather a strange missive "so long that it was rolled like papyrus," one she had worked hard to endow with magical powers of allurement, personal and spiritual. She put in with her scroll a few leaves of desachey, "the perfume the Indians say makes the heart light," and also a bit of osha, a medicinal root. Lawrence was as enchanted as she'd hoped and read it on his way home, unfurling the letter to its full length as he walked the Corso Umberto. He was entranced by the "Indian scent" Mrs. Sterne had effectively wafted in his direction, and decided, "*There* is glamour and magic for me. Not Buddha." Taos was six thousand feet up on a mountain in the desert, and twenty-five miles from the nearest railway. He had "nibbled" at the osha, which tasted like licorice root, and it had transported him far from the Corso, which, like Europe in microcosm, was "just one long arcade of junk shops now." Taos, not Ceylon, now seemed his fate.

Lawrence rarely saved his correspondence. The papyrus is lost. But the force and beauty of Mabel Dodge Sterne's prose are evident in her memoirs, and the incantatory potency of the glimpse she gave of Taos was irresistible to Lawrence. Whatever she proposed, what she said of Taos, the future she envisioned—his, hers, the prospect for humanity itself, she blended it all—touched him. She had tried to "tell him every single thing I could think of that I felt would draw him—simple things as well as strange ones." The land she described was "full of time and ease," and his house was at one with it, newly built in the old way, with furniture "carpentered right there in the house," and spacious enough, at five rooms, for the children she didn't seem to know he didn't have.

His immediate yes was an impulsive response, full of hope and trust and his instinctual curiosity.

"I believe what you say—one must somehow bring together the two ends of humanity, our own thin end, and the last dark strand from the previous, pre-white era. I verily believe that." It would be quite feasible, he told her. There were logistical details to work out, but nothing seemed to be standing in his way. In *Sea and Sardinia* he had called Frieda the "Queen Bee." Now he wrote Mabel in the same convivial spirit. "Truly, the q-b and I would like to come to Taos—there are no little bees," he told her. Whether it was desirable to travel halfway around the world at the behest of a stranger he did not seem to consider at all.

But neither Mabel Dodge Sterne nor D. H. Lawrence was as she or he appeared.

He acted impulsively but was, paradoxically, practical: he and his wife, "the q-b and I," were, he told Mabel, "*very* practical, do all our own work, even the washing, cooking, floor-cleaning and everything." But the Lawrence Mabel Dodge wrote to in the fall of 1921 was the Lawrence she thought she knew from his writing, not that one. When the parts of *Sea and Sardinia* were published in the *Dial*, Lawrence complained to his agent that the book had been unfortunately "very much cut up" and pieced together again in an unrepresentative way. "Damn them for that." Lawrence might have cursed himself as well as the *Dial* editors for the idea that *Sea and Sardinia* gave to Mabel Dodge Sterne. The whole of it is not representative of the "real" Lawrence, either. His ingratiating and fanciful self-portrait transforms Frieda and Lawrence into comic characters. What in life was "annoying and uncomfortable" about them was dramatized in the book into "vivacity, or made material for comedy." Mabel later wrote of Lawrence that he was a "mass of contradictions and shocks." She didn't yet know— but would learn—that one of the crucial contradictions was that he portrayed himself and Frieda far more realistically in the conflicts of his novels than in his nonfiction accounts of their actual travels. It did not help that Lawrence continued the jocular tone about himself in his first letter to her. He had been summoned as the Lawrence of *Sea and Sardinia*, and he was writing as that character.

Lawrence decided important things first—"he made a fetish of spontaneity and used it as an excuse for yielding to any impulse which came to him"—and to his (and often everyone else's) regret learned the facts of the matter, and the real character of a person, only later. Like Mabel, he saw the world selectively. Mabel was wealthy enough to afford (or indulge) this failing. Lawrence, in contrast, paid a high price for this tendency to errors of judgment. In this he made Anna Brangwen, the heroine of his novel *The Rainbow*, like himself: "Still she thought the people she did not *know* were wonderful. Those she knew seemed always to be limiting her, tying her up in little falsities that irritated her beyond bearing." This could be hard on friends, family, a wife, one's patron. And oneself.

* * *

Mabel had a commission in mind and hoped that Lawrence, in a book about Taos, would "give a voice to this speechless land." But what she hoped he would do might be impossible for a white writer in any case, a fact she did not consider. Taos was not like Italy, the Indians in New Mexico were not like the Italians, and Lawrence could not be the same among them. Mabel excluded herself and Lawrence from the general sanction offered by Tony Luhan, the Pueblo man who was her lover and would become her fourth husband: "The white people like Taos and call it 'climate.' Do they know what *climate* is? Do they know why the sun is better in Taos and why they feel happy in it?" She knew, she thought, and Lawrence, whom she believed to have "more consciousness than anyone alive," would also know what climate is.

But, in fact, he didn't. Mabel, dreaming of a Lawrence who existed only in the *Dial*'s potpourri from *Sea and Sardinia*, had not understood the Lawrence of the novels, if she had read them carefully (which it seems she had not, though she sent a copy of *Sons and Lovers* to her former psychiatrist, in New York, who diagnosed Lawrence has having a "severe homosexual fixation" for which he was trying to compensate). She did not seem disturbed by Lawrence's first, mundane, and very practical questions—which were about the climate. "Are there any trees? Is there any water?—stream, river, lake?" he asked. "How warm must the clothing be? How cold, and how hot is Taos?"

He wanted to leave Europe, Lawrence wrote her. "I want to take the next step. Shall it be Taos?—I like the *word*. It's a bit like Taormina." As a move it was a long leap, but there was a symbolic continuity in the sound of the two names that he took as another sign of destiny. He had heard of Taos, he thought, from Leo Stein, in 1919. It was vague in his mind, but all the more alluring for that. That was enough for him.

At least one significant unknown remained, and even a writer, who survives by words, is liable to be led astray by the sound and promise of *a* word seductively spoken. Charmed by Mabel and the Indian scent of her scroll, he wondered in a postscript where he might really be going. "How far are you from El Paso or from Santa Fe. I don't see Taos on the map."

* * *

But Lawrence's next step was more an escape than it was a journey. He was, as always, in search of the perennially elsewhere, as in a 1917 poem he originally called "Terranova" and published as "New Heaven and Earth." "I was so weary of this world, / I was so sick of it, / everything was tainted with myself, / skies, trees, flowers, birds, water, / people, houses, streets, vehicles, machines, / nations, armies, war, peace-talking, / work, recreation, governing, anarchy, / it was all tainted with myself."

Such a place was, of course, impossible to find, and it was one of Lawrence's most admirable—and frustrating—characteristics that he all his life lighted out with the "secret and absurd hope" that one day he would find himself landing in the Garden of Eden. This desire peeked out in all his writing. But in Taos there was another significant unknown, not of where but of whom.

He wrote to his New York agent the next day and asked a question he might more wisely have waited to have answered. "I had a letter yesterday from Mabel Dodge Sterne—do you know who she is?—from *Taos, New Mexico*: do you know anything about that? She says she can give us a *house* there, and everything we need. And I think it is there I should like to go."

* * *

Mabel talked of consciousness but her income was $14,000 a year, much of it in the form of an allowance from her mother. Her life with Tony was a lazy one. They had no need "to earn our bread & meat. And I am not so rightly energized that I move without having to," she wrote. She was bored doing nothing in Taos, bored by "having to do nothing," and this was one reason she had invited Lawrence, and why she had sought to lure other artists and writers to New Mexico. "A round of unimpeded pleasure ceases to be amusing."

Her patronage was founded in an awe of artists, but it was compromised by an envy that became a desire for control and regard. She could be the only "q-b" in her world. Surrounding herself with artists and writers gave her purpose and engagement. Writing of an artist she knew, she exclaimed, "I envy Mary Austin her ambition & her economic pressure!" This was envy as only the rich could feel it.

Mabel was inordinately wealthy and generously philanthropic. But the royal, eccentrically peremptory, summons of her scrolling papyrus was an ornamentally masked financial transaction. She had sought her latest idol on a whim, and because her art was charm, it seemed to her that her *noblesse* came without *oblige* on his part. But Lawrence knew the value of money, having had so little of it. Mabel had described the house she had for him, a house in which the roof was supported by twisted columns, the ceiling supported by glistening beams. She had repeated the word too often, and Lawrence immediately understood that in this house that Mabel offered as a gift he would be supported by her. From a strictly financial point of view, Lawrence needed a patron. He was too proud and practical to accept one.

Her own house on the property was the Big House. The Lawrences would live in the Pink House. It would be dependency and ruin if he were to live there without paying his way. Lawrence had from childhood known "the terrible indignity" of poverty and had learned to see life, and his life as a writer, as the business it was. He kept track of his productivity carefully and kept more detailed accounts of money owed or owing than his agent or his publishers ever would.

Lawrence's response to Mabel's grand gesture represented continuity in another, unspoken way. He was attracted to her as he had always, from early on, been drawn into the orbit of older women of position. Frieda had been the first, and before Mabel there had been Ottoline Morrell and Cynthia Asquith. The *first* had really been his high school sweetheart Jessie Chambers, the "Miriam" of *Sons and Lovers*, and before her there had hung over the family the lost dream of his mother Lydia's elegance, literally dirtied by the roughness of his coal miner father and by the waste of his father's alcoholism. All the entanglements followed the same course of attraction and disappointment, usually followed by rapprochement, and often then by a later break. Of course this was also true of his friendships with men, and, as Mabel would write with only some exaggeration, "he threw everyone over sooner or later, and not once, but as often as they rejoined his turbulent and intractable spirit." The only possible permanent reconciliation with Lawrence was a posthumous one.

* * *

He had told Mabel, "I want to take the next step." The next step, though, was not only a place but a step forward into new writing. He had finished a novel, *Aaron's Rod*, in early June 1921. He had written nothing other than two poems all summer. He had reached the end of something, he thought, with *Aaron's Rod*, about an English musician who abandons his wife and children to pursue his art in Italy. A new place to write would mean new things to write, new ways of writing, that he could not achieve "till I have crossed another border," he told Mabel.

The New World was a place where a new form might be found, just as he had imagined for years that Rananim could be built there. Almost a decade before, he had sent his editor Edward Garnett the typescript of *Sons and Lovers*. It is a great novel, Lawrence told him with confidence. But its greatness could be found in the fact that "it has got form—*form*." Frieda, in a postscript of her own to Garnett, seconded Lawrence and added, "any new thing must find a new shape, then afterwards one can call it 'art.'"

She had written that in 1912. It was true for Lawrence nine years later, in Taormina. He was in search of a new shape. As a writer he must evolve, book by book, poem by poem, story by story—continent by continent, too, if necessary—completely away from what he had formerly been.

Sons and Lovers had been published in 1913, when Lawrence was twenty-seven. It was his third and most highly praised novel. It had brought him literary renown and had shaped the expectations, and corresponding disappointments, that had marked Lawrence's career since then. An American journalist, Henry James Forman, met Lawrence through mutual friends in Taormina in the winter of 1921–22. He expressed his admiration for *Sons and Lovers* and asked, "Why don't you write more books like that one?"

It was the question nearly everyone asked him, Lawrence replied with a smile that was probably more impatient than his overawed American interlocutor could perceive. He didn't want to write more books like that, Lawrence told Forman. He wrote his books three times, not just "copying and revising as I go along, but literally." He wrote a first draft, put it aside, wrote a second draft, and then put that aside, too. He published the third draft. The first draft was generally somewhat like *Sons and Lovers*, he said. Forman, whom Lawrence thought "dull but nice," then advised him, "Very well, then in the next novel write one draft only and see how your sales will mount."

This was not new advice. Lawrence "murmured half to himself" that he didn't want to be rich. "But I do want to be able to do absolutely as I please."

To do as he pleased. He did not want to write another book like *Sons and Lovers*, and he did not want to make small talk with Edmund Wilson at a publisher's tea party. Yet how and where to do it all in his own way? Lawrence was a traveler between destinations, an artist between forms. As 1922 began he was looking again for an answer to the question one of his characters posed in *Women in Love*, "For where was life to be found?" This had been the central question for him even in childhood. "What do you think life is?" a childhood friend recalled his asking. She retained a sense "he had been waiting anxiously to ask it." He was happiest far away from wherever he had most recently been. The lure of Taos was that it was twenty-five miles from any railroad. Writing to friends about his decision to go to Taos, he repeated that magical distance in letter after letter, giving the altitude of the town variously as either six thousand or seven thousand feet. Inaccessibility was vital. The only road to Fontana Vecchia was a mule track. The claustrophobia of a house crowded with children, and of a town like Eastwood, haunted him. All his life he was drawn to people and yet just as quickly resisted the trap of "all this intimacy and neighbouring" that left one "caught like a fly on a flypaper, in one mess with all the other buzzers. How I hate it!" He could not be happy with a life made up of the "common emotion like treacle" that seemed to satisfy most people, including Frieda, who to his frustration sometimes seemed content to settle anywhere. But where was the life of *uncommon* emotion, and the new form of art that would arise from it, to be found? He was as anxious as ever to discover the answer. Maybe Taos would reveal it.

* * *

Lawrence announced his terms for the future in the first letter he wrote in 1922, a New Year's greeting to his friend Earl Brewster, who had by now arrived in Ceylon and was still hoping the Lawrences would join him there. He had decided he must go to Taos, Lawrence wrote, offering his manifesto for the new year. The East was not his destiny, he told his friend, invoking that favorite word that suggested he was obeying an inner call, a word he used whenever it might be necessary to quiet any disagreement his course of action might provoke. It was just as he had thought when they had first talked of Ceylon and Buddhism in the autumn. Meditation and the "inner life" were not for him. He sought "action and strenuousness and pain and frustration and struggling through," though how this would be accomplished in the isolation of Taos was not clear. He was as dismissive of serenity as he was of common emotion and thought that a "new incarnation" awaited him in the land of the ancient sun worshippers. He must be a man in battle, struggling through toward the new writing he would do, and which would be his contribution to the larger fight.

Lawrence was restless with routine, almost allergic to his surroundings by now. In December, he had come down with a fairly mild but naggingly persistent case of the influenza that Virginia Woolf and Tom Eliot both had and which was spreading across Europe. It seemed almost a victory to have caught it, and he was relieved to be sick enough to spend Christmas in bed. "I hate Christmas anyhow," he wrote one friend. His illness was a purification rite in the struggle toward a rebirth "through the blood and psyche. . . . Let nobody try to filch from me even my influenza," he wrote.

But his flu meant he and Frieda missed the early boat he'd hoped they would be able to take. They couldn't leave on January 15, and he would have to find another passage they could afford. He would be in Taormina at least until the first week of February. Destiny, and Mabel Sterne, would have to wait a little longer.

Lawrence's life would probably have been a lot easier if he'd caught that first boat. The decision to go would then at least have been made for him. He had prepared for departure, and at the beginning of December he had sent off the revisions of nine stories he hoped would make for two separate volumes to be published by Seltzer. He had sent a similar package to his London agent, Curtis Brown, who was to arrange for English publication by Secker. It was his way of tying up the loose ends of what he'd written in the years during and after the war, so that he could travel light. The titles told their own story. One was called "Tickets, Please." Another he changed to "The Last Straw." For Lawrence, it was. He was ready for 1922.

* * *

But then, at the end of January, he changed his mind again. Brewster's happiness in Ceylon had persuaded him that he would find "rest, peace, inside one" there. He would "postpone the evil day" and go to America later.

He wrote to Mabel about his detour. "I feel it is my destiny to go east before coming west." He would stay only a short time there, he thought, "perhaps a year." He invited her to join *him* in Ceylon, via San Francisco and China, as soon as she could. They could then go on to Taos and the "later Onslaught" together.

Six months after eloping with Lawrence in 1912, Frieda had written to a friend, "Lawrence *is* wear and tear." His plans for 1922 had changed yet again, but he had not.

Chapter 5

"THE GREATEST WASTE NOW GOING ON IN LETTERS"

TOM RETURNED TO LONDON, DUE BACK AT
Lloyds the week of Monday, January 16. A few days before, Vivien wrote to
Mary Hutchinson that he was much better, looking forward to seeing her
and "not very many others." He had many reasons to regret the end of his
three months' leave, and not all of them had to do with Lloyds. The confined domestic life of Clarence Gate Gardens—the "wife obsession" that
Wyndham Lewis deplored but that Eliot saw as his duty—was another
routine he had not missed.

Tom would be back, this particularly cold January, to the unlovely
London that he evoked with a sense of personal horror in the opening section of the poem he and Pound were editing together in Paris.

> *Unreal City I have sometimes seen and see,*
> *Under the brown fog of your winter dawn,*

A crowd flow over London Bridge, so many,
I had not thought death had undone so many.

Eliot had in an earlier version called London the "Terrible City," but so great was his horror of the place, where he had thought he must make his career, but where his great work had been delayed, it was not real but *unreal.* The "crowd" included the morning commuters whose ranks he was about to reenter, described in a passage that evoked Dante and in doing so made arrival at Lloyds into a kind of death itself.

. . . And each man fixed his eyes before his feet.
Flowed up the hill and down King William Street,
To where Saint Mary Woolnoth kept the hours,
With a dead sound on the final stroke of nine.

It was the daily death of a typical London morning "crush hour," and on Eliot's way to nearby Lloyds—the entrance to the bank was on King William Street, which ran from the north side of London Bridge into the city—he could hear Saint Mary's clock toll the time by which city workers were to arrive at their offices. But it was not only the commute. London, Tom wrote, was a kind of death, too: "London, the swarming life you kill and breed, / Huddled between the concrete and the sky; / Responsive to the momentary need, / Vibrates unconscious to its formal destiny." Pound cut these lines, and scrawled "B—ll—S" (Bullshit) alongside them. Eliot could only be weighed down by so much despair, for the poem was proof that Eliot's destiny as a poet, and Pound's prophecy of it, *had* been fulfilled at last. Pound soon had a plan that would free Eliot from the bank that trapped him between the concrete and the sky.

* * *

Tom was saved from Lloyds by influenza: he was sick for more than ten days, another casualty of the rising epidemic that was keeping Virginia confined to bed and that had also affected but been less debilitating to Lawrence. Whatever mental respite he had found in the writing he'd done at Margate and then Lausanne, and in the collaborative work he did with Pound in Paris, quickly evaporated. He was very soon "excessively depressed," he told Pound, though in a change perhaps made possible by practicing Vittoz's mental exercises for calm, he did not let this, or his influenza, stop him from continuing to revise the poem at top speed. The improved concentration that he had felt in Lausanne seemed to hold, helped by the unanticipated postponement of his return to Lloyds and the fact that Vivien was not a distraction.

At their dinner in Paris with Liveright, Pound and Eliot seemed to take for granted that the *Dial* would publish the poem, even though he had not yet sent it to Scofield Thayer. But if it were to be published in the *Dial*, then the length of the poem would not be Liveright's only concern. If the entire poem were to appear in a magazine, its publication in book form might only be an afterthought. From London Liveright wrote to Pound asking for clarification. Eliot had been home only a few days when, on January 20, he wrote to Thayer that he would soon be able to send him a poem of about 450 lines, in four parts, half the length it had been when he left Lausanne. He hoped Thayer would be able to let him know quickly whether the *Dial* would want to publish it, and also "approximately what the *Dial* would offer." A day or two after that, he sent further revisions to Pound in Paris.

Eliot told Thayer it would not be published in an English periodical, perhaps in the hope that the *Dial* would in that case pay more for the poem. Perhaps for the same reason, he did not inform him of Liveright's interest in publishing the poem in book form. Tom was deferential, but not forthright, telling Thayer he would "postpone all arrangements for publication" until he heard from him. And in a further sign of deference, he left it up to Thayer to decide how the poem might appear, assuring him it could be divided to go into four issues, if he liked, "but not more." He also wanted to assure Thayer that it would be ready soon, and that it came with an imprimatur, so that Thayer need not accept Eliot's own word for its excellence: "It will have been three times through the sieve by Pound as well as myself so should be in final form." The poem was still in flux, however. In its final form the poem would be in five parts, not four.

Thayer acted as quickly as Eliot had hoped: at the top of Eliot's letter is the arithmetic he did to calculate Eliot's fee. Thayer divided the estimated 450 lines of the poem by both 35 and 40, the number of lines of poetry that usually appeared on a *Dial* page. It had been a founding principle of Thayer's that the *Dial* would pay all writers a standard rate—$10 a page for unpublished poetry, double the rate for prose—and writers were paid upon acceptance rather than publication. The uniform fee displeased some well-known writers but gave fair pay without a long wait to less established writers in need of income. Whether Eliot's poem would appear in one issue or in several did not affect the price. It might run to a little over 11 pages: "12pp. 120," Thayer noted in the margin of Eliot's letter. He revised upward and made Eliot an offer of $150, which he thought very generous.

Thayer was eager to publish a poem by Eliot, who had by now not published a new poem in a periodical in two years. He had cultivated Eliot as soon as he became the owner and editor of the *Dial* in 1920. There was no one whose verse or prose he admired more, he told Eliot. "I only wish I could give you carte blanche." But all of Eliot's contributions to the *Dial*, beginning in November 1920, had been prose. Despite promises of poetry to come, Eliot had written no poetry to show Thayer. In February 1921, he had written Eliot, "Why no verse? I serve notice that I do not consider it seemly for the editor of *The Dial* ever again to repeat this question." It was the same question Eliot had been repeatedly asking himself, eventually to the point of breakdown.

Tom finally wrote to Thayer in January, the first time Thayer had heard directly from Tom for eight months, since May 1921. It was not a matter of simply having been out of touch. Eliot had avoided Thayer, evidently concluding that it was easier to say nothing about overdue work than to continue to make excuses for habitual delinquency. In the fall of 1920, Tom had agreed to write a bimonthly London Letter, about English literary life. But he missed even his first deadline, apologizing in due course for the lateness of the "puny" result (Thayer thought it distinguished). In July 1921 Vivien had written to Thayer on her husband's behalf, "You must excuse Tom for any dilatoriness in writing," an umbrella apology that seemed to cover both his delay in responding to Thayer's letters and the failure to deliver a London Letter and other promised contributions to the *Dial*, including a review of Marianne Moore's poems. Despite these delinquencies, Vivien wrote, Tom would be delighted to review Joyce's *Ulysses*. "That at least is definite," she added, accepting with alacrity a new assignment as if to share in the illusion that Thayer himself promoted, that Tom would be able to complete them all soon enough.

Tom had also left it to Vivien to inform Thayer of his illness and leave and to tell him that because Tom would not be able to do his usual London Letter, he had helpfully arranged for someone else—St. John

Hutchinson, Mary's husband—to do it instead. But neither Thayer nor Gilbert Seldes, the managing editor of the *Dial*, liked the letter Hutchinson eventually wrote. They rejected it, and the "embarrassing situation," as Tom discreetly called it, was a separate discord that created an undercurrent of ill will on both sides as negotiations to publish Tom's poem began and then quickly stalled. Thayer felt he was owed something, if only for his loyalty and forbearance. And the *Dial*, by this point, needed no defense as a literary journal of stature and relatively large circulation, compared to the *Little Review* and other similar publications. Tom, on the other hand, knew he had written his best poem and, believing gossip he'd heard that in some cases Thayer had paid other writers extravagantly, wanted a high price, distrusting Thayer on what Thayer assured Eliot, against this accusation, was a point of honor.

Despite this Eliot and Pound—and Thayer—knew that the *Dial* was the natural place for a new poem by Eliot, even if it was not the only place in which it could be published. Rarely can there have been such a protracted negotiation to publish a poem that was never seriously offered to any other magazine—and for which, as with its publication in book form, there was only ever one bidder. Neither Thayer nor Liveright would know for eight months—until September—whether or when he might publish the poem. Or at what price.

Thayer made his offer but in his reply was clear that he thought it took some gall for Tom to ask him to do anything quickly. His last letter to Tom, written in December to explain their disappointment in Hutchinson's piece, had betrayed another, more personal, grievance. "I was glad to hear from Pound that you looked not badly when he saw you in Paris," he began. Having heard nothing of Tom's condition since Vivien's letter announcing his "serious breakdown," Thayer now seemed to doubt whether Tom had been ill at all. Thayer closed with the fulsome New Year's hope that "howsoever good your next London Letter may be the best thing about it will for me at least be that it will indicate you are well again." Despite the offer of the poem, this did not seem to be the case. The poem might be nearly ready, but Eliot had also to explain a new delay in the next London Letter: his influenza meant that he was behind and his article could not appear before the April issue. That would mean a gap of seven months, which he knew was intolerable for Thayer.

Even with the prospect of the poem in view, Thayer could not conceal his contempt for Tom's ingratiating nonchalance. He was glad to see that influenza, having kept Tom at home, had led his old friend to have "again taken up the old-fashioned custom of answering letters." He hoped he would not have to "await another case of influenza" before receiving another. Thayer also asked Tom to send him a copy of the poem in Vienna. But Tom, whether out of pique or a more elemental procrastination, did not write another letter in reply, nor did he send the poem.

* * *

"My feet are at Moorgate, and my heart / Under my feet," he had written at Margate. Now, as he prepared the poem for Pound's third review, the lines had a different resonance: he was to be back at Lloyds and would be at the Moorgate tube station every day, walking past St. Mary Woolnoth and hearing its bell toll nine times every morning. Vivien was soon at home, too, and in conveying this news to Pound Eliot reported her complaint "that if she had realised how bloody England is she would not have returned," as if to say he regretted his own return, and perhaps hers as well, not only to bloody England but to their marriage.

But no one regretted Eliot's return to London and Lloyds more than Pound, who had wanted Eliot out of the bank from the moment he went into it during the war. "Three months off and he got that poem done," Pound wrote Thayer, suggesting to the editor just how high a price literature was paying for Eliot's servitude, and how necessary it was for Thayer to publish it, if he took his role as editor seriously. He was playing the diplomatic intermediary for Thayer and the *Dial* and for Eliot—and for literature itself. Though his formal role with the *Dial*, as foreign agent, had ended the previous year, he tried to salvage Thayer's interest in the poem as a way of liberating Eliot from Lloyds. But it was to be very hard work on both counts for Eliot's "Cher Maître," who was that winter and spring constantly making excuses for, and begging Thayer to overlook, Eliot's consistently "undiplomatic" behavior.

Pound knew that Thayer had little patience left, and he knew, too, that his defense of Eliot must encompass the fact that Eliot was an inveterate offender, who repented as frequently as he disappointed. Still, Pound was messianic in pushing Eliot's case. He wrote Thayer on February 8, to echo, and verify, Eliot's own enthusiasm about his poem—"almost enough to make everyone else shut up shop," he wrote, though he was quick to add,

"I haven't done so," and told Thayer he had, by the way, sent a new poem of his own to the *Dial* editors in New York.

But then Eliot's penchant for what Pound had once called "incommodious delay" got in Pound's—and Eliot's—way again. He was confident it was his best work, and Pound had ratified that to him and to those who would likely publish it. But now he seemed unable to do the easier work of actually getting it to those who were eager to read it and publish it, namely Liveright and Thayer. Thayer took Eliot's silence as tantamount to an intemperate rejection of his blind, but good-faith, offer.

* * *

"Some minds aberrant from the natural equipose / London! your population is bound upon the wheel!" Eliot had written not long after he began working at the bank the first time. Now, after his leave, he was bound again. The "solemnly smiling transatlantic reticence" that Wyndham Lewis thought one of Tom's most enduring masks began quickly to crack again as winter turned to spring. Vivien was confined again to bed, Eliot was again tired and depressed, and, he confided to Lewis two months after his return, "life has been horrible generally." The Eliots were again what they had always been: "two highly nervous people shut up in grinding proximity," as the novelist Elizabeth Bowen described them. The time with Vittoz, and his techniques, seems to have been forgotten.

Thayer's offer of $150 (about £35) did not satisfy Eliot, but it was not only a question of money. Eliot noticed every bit of the condescension Thayer had intended him to see in his letter, and he was offended. He complained to Pound that the offer did not strike him "as good pay for a year's work," but he also resented that Thayer had not "offered the 150 [dollars] with more graciousness." He would have "felt more yielding" if Thayer hadn't made it seem he was doing Tom a great favor. And yet Thayer was doing him a favor. Because he had not read the poem, he was, in effect, giving Tom the carte blanche he had warned him he couldn't.

Eliot did not send the poem to Thayer, or to Knopf, who likely had the option on it, though before his dinner in Paris with Liveright they had corresponded about other terms of their 1919 contract that John Quinn had negotiated. Eliot had not realized that Knopf had the right to sell Eliot's verse for use in anthologies in Great Britain without notifying Eliot or seeking his approval and was annoyed by this. Knopf, in his reply, was offended at Eliot's suggestion that he had behaved badly, and in a second letter to Knopf on the subject, written on Christmas Day from Lausanne, Eliot had apologized that he'd been away from home for nearly three months and said he would look at the contract when he returned to London. Liveright's interest, and his caveat about Knopf's option, would have given Eliot a reason to do so promptly in January. But even if the question of the anthology slipped his mind, it seems unlikely that the question of Knopf's option did. Yet Eliot did not write to Knopf again until March, a nearly three-month delay. He was then warmly accommodating about Knopf's interpretation of their contract regarding anthologies—"I have no disposition to interfere with any arrangement you may have made"—but still said nothing about his new poem, even though any progress he might make with Liveright, who had now been waiting two months, was dependent on clarifying what Knopf would want to do.

This went beyond forgetfulness. Eliot often dealt in very narrow, very selective truth. Many of those who knew Eliot well—and liked him or even loved him—did not trust him. His reserve seemed to others a form of deception, a mask, rather than a retreat into privacy. Rumors began to circulate in London that spring that Lady Rothermere had withdrawn her promised support for the literary magazine Eliot would edit under her patronage. It had seemed to be moving forward before Eliot's breakdown. Now it seemed to be dead. Or was it? Wyndham Lewis decided to ask Eliot directly.

"I have just got through to Eliot on the telephone," Lewis wrote their mutual friend Violet Schiff. "The Rothermere review he says is *not* finished. It continues. But (greatly as I hesitate to say this of such a man as Eliot) that may be a lie."

* * *

At lunch on February 14, Eliot complained to Conrad Aiken about the obstacles to getting his poem published. Aiken recommended an alternative: Maurice Firuski, a Cambridge, Massachusetts, publisher of lucrative limited editions. Firuski had paid a $100 royalty in advance to other poets, Aiken told his friend. Eliot's eyes "glowed with a tawny light like fierce doubloons" when he outlined the arrangement. Aiken wrote to Firuski the next day, though why Eliot would be so greedily interested in a price lower than anything Liveright or Knopf would likely offer for book publication is not clear. Aiken had not read the poem—"it may not be good, or intelligible," he wrote—but assured Firuski of what Thayer, grudgingly, knew, too, that given Eliot's reputation a long poem by him would be "a real curiosity, even perhaps an event."

But once again, Eliot put off writing to Firuski for two more weeks. When he did, he asked for his terms at the publisher's earliest convenience, he wrote, because "the other offers for it cannot be held in suspense very long," a finessing of the truth. Firuski's reply indicated that Aiken had outlined the terms correctly. While waiting to hear from Firuski, Eliot replied, at last, to Thayer with a telegram that confused and angered Thayer:

CANNOT ACCEPT UNDER !8!56 POUNDS = ELIOT +

Now it was Thayer's turn to be offended. He was appalled at Eliot's high-handed demand of an absurd amount of money and waited several days to reply, which he did, drily concealing his outrage by repeating the words of the telegram and adding that he assumed this was an error on the part of the telegraphic service. In fact, it was—Eliot had meant that he could not accept less than £50, or about $250—but Thayer was past the point of thinking Eliot would cooperate with him in any way, or that he could deliver anything, poetry or prose, that he promised. He outlined again the "general rule" of the *Dial*'s policy on rates and asked Eliot to let him know *why* an exception should be made in his case, in a tone that made it clear that no reason seemed possible, particularly given the personal sacrifices he and his co-owner, James Sibley Watson Jr., had made to keep the magazine running, at a large deficit but still paying "all contributors famous and unknown at the same rates," a position with which he thought Eliot would be sympathetic. "I have had to notify *The Dial*"—meaning his colleagues back in New York—"that we are apparently not to receive the poem," Thayer continued, closing with only slightly veiled contempt that whatever the fate of the poem, "I trust your review of Miss Moore and your London Letter are now arriving in New York."

Writers are more usually swayed by pay rather than an editor's rectitude, and when Eliot replied to Thayer, as he did unusually promptly, he told him that he simply did not think the equivalent of £30 or £35 was enough for a poem that he said had taken him a year to write (though this was not true) and would be his "biggest" work yet (which was). He had not wanted to publish it in a journal first, in any case, Eliot added, though this, too, was not true. Thayer would of course remember Eliot having offered it to him, supposedly exclusively, in January, even though he'd withheld that he'd already talked with Liveright about publishing it.

* * *

Pound had not foreseen such protracted negotiations or such ill will, and as much as he did not want to play the broker, he saw that he must do what he could if the poem was to be published at all. He tried to arouse sympathy in Thayer and urged continued forbearance. Eliot "has merely gone to pieces again," Pound wrote. It was a case of *abuleia*, "simply the physical impossibility of correlating his muscles sufficiently to write a letter or get up and move across the room." This also explained Eliot's not having sent Thayer the poem itself. "Damn him for not sending you the mss. And curse his family," Pound added for good measure, "they are the absolute punk of punk<mother brother sister>."

Pound's sense of mission meant his salesmanship was as sincere as his intervention was necessary. He had also thought, after the dinner with Liveright in Paris and his endorsement to Thayer, that his task would be done quickly and he could resume his own work. He was in league with Thayer, he seemed to say to the editor, though of course his effort was all on Eliot's behalf. "I dare say you and I have more reasons for wanting to wring his neck than any one else has; I mean we wd. have, or wd. have had, if it were not definitely a pathological state," he wrote, begging Thayer to think instead of Eliot's supreme importance and assuring him Eliot's poem—neither he nor Eliot had shared its title yet—"is as good in its way as Ulysses in its way—and there is so DAMN little genius, so DAMN little work that one can take hold of and say 'this at any rate stands['], and make a definite part of literature."

It was not only the poem but an entire career at stake, Pound suggested. Robert Frost had a sinecure as a poet in residence at the University of Michigan. Joyce had his patrons, and "two offspring, which I can't see that he has any business to have." But Joyce, like Pound himself, was "tougher than Thomas," Pound added. It was nothing less than duty, Pound seemed to urge Thayer. What else was there for a forward-thinking magazine editor to do but help Eliot through: "Three months off and he got that poem done. I think he is being in that bank is [*sic*] the greatest waste now going on in letters, ANYWHERE."

Quinn, in New York, was concerned about Eliot, too, when he heard of the situation, but angry at Pound's efforts to persuade Thayer and Liveright to publish the poem. This was too much of a distraction from his own poetry—just what Pound usually complained about. Why did Pound continue to waste his time on the *Dial*, even on Eliot's behalf, now that his own contract had not been renewed and he was not being paid to do it? "Let The Dial stew in its own Simian juice," Quinn wrote, his anti-Semitic objections to Liveright now entangling the Christian Thayer, who, among other imagined crimes and insults, published too many Jewish writers and artists in the *Dial* for Quinn's taste. Quinn was personally affronted by Pound's mediation. "Don't be a legal adviser without pay, a liaison officer without commission," he wrote.

In the meantime, Eliot went to tea with Virginia and Leonard Woolf on Sunday, March 5. It had been nearly six months since he had last seen the Woolves, at Monk's House in September, the weekend before he saw the specialist who had proposed a leave from Lloyds.

When visitors arrived, Virginia "was much given to drawing them out," remembered the writer Gerald Brenan, who met her in 1922. Virginia would sit in her chair, he recalled, "leaning sideways and a little stiffly" toward her companion, whom she addressed "in a bantering tone, and she liked to be answered in the same manner." She took a "lightly ironical tone" that was "personal and took on a feminine, and one might almost say flirtatious, form." Virginia leaning in, the more guarded Tom leaping away—it might have been almost a kind of physical distrust, one revealed also in their manner of talk. With a "little encouragement" Virginia was likely to "throw off a cascade of words like the notes of a great pianist improvising," her voice vivacious, so that nothing she said "was ever bookish. She talked easily and naturally in a pure and idiomatic English," her conversation seeming to "preen itself with self-confidence in its own powers" given the right interlocutor. This was the grounds of her distrust of Eliot. She could not feel always self-confident in his presence, brought up short by the profound stare of his eyes and his tendency toward oracular statements.

Virginia, in conversation, was opinionated but not domineering. She sought, and inspired, a grand architectural effect of total engagement. If Virginia was, in Brenan's view, a great pianist improvising, a talk over tea or dinner was not a recital but was meant to be a piece for four hands, or six, or eight—a concerto, at least, and with Virginia most at ease, most scintillating and glittering, as one instrument among many.

Back from Paris, Tom was, Virginia recorded, more relaxed, was "yes, grown positively familiar & jocular & friendly, though retaining some shreds of authority. I mustn't lick all the paint off my Gods," she wrote about his visit, though there was a vestige, as always, of suspicion, in her and in him. He was "grown supple as an eel," she thought.

Supple and able to put on a good show (or a brave front) for the Woolves, before whom his mask was firmly in place. For he was "irritable and exhausted" at that moment, as he confided to another friend, and "overwhelmed with the labours of moving," which had consumed him for the past two weeks, "having let my flat for two or three months." The Woolves saw none of this.

"What, then, did we discuss?" Virginia wrote in her diary. Nothing apparently about Margate, Lausanne, or his breakdown and treatment. He told them he was starting a magazine. This was to be the *Criterion*. He also had news about his own work.

"He has written a poem of 40 pages, which we are to print in the autumn." It was set for England. But there was no immediate money in that for the financially desperate Eliot, who knew, as Lawrence did, that the American market was more lucrative than the English, in any case.

"This is his best work, he says. He is pleased with it; takes heart, I think from the thought of that safe in his desk," she wrote, content for him and satisfied as his publisher, even though she had been able to do no revisions of *Jacob* for two months.

But the next day was momentous for Virginia for two reasons, and Leonard recorded one triumph: "V. went for short walk," the ten minutes that Dr. Sainsbury had allowed. Virginia recorded the other, once again writing in her diary later in the day, and not in the morning, instead of work.

"I am back again, after 2 months this very day, sitting in my chair after tea, writing; & I wrote Jacob this morning, & though my temperature is not normal, my habits are: & that is all I care for." The thought of what Eliot had safe in his desk seemed to spark in her the sense of rivalry with other writers that she had denied earlier in the year. She was hopeful she could continue—to walk and to write, and because she no longer felt "very trustful" of doctors' prognostications, she felt she must ignore them and return to "my habits."

As for Tom, all seemed well, at least as far as Virginia could tell. In so easily settling with the Woolves about their publishing the poem, he hid from them any immediate anxieties about money. But even when Eliot seemed at ease with her, as he did at this visit, Virginia detected a pose. For that was what it most likely was, she decided. "Clive, via Mary, says he uses violet powder to make him look cadaverous," she wrote in her diary. That spring, the writer Osbert Sitwell gossiped gleefully with Virginia about Eliot and recalled a party at Eliot's flat that coincided with Virginia's astonishment at the poet's penchant for cosmetics. "I sat next to Tom. . . . . Noticing how tired my host looked, I regarded him more closely, and was amazed to notice on his cheeks a dusting of green powder—pale but distinctly green, the color of a forced lily-of-the-valley. I was hardly willing, any more than if I had seen a ghost, to credit the evidence of my senses."

When Sitwell met Virginia for tea shortly thereafter, "She asked me, rather pointedly, if I had seen Tom lately, and when I said 'Yes' asked me—because she too was anxious for someone to confirm or rebut what she thought she had seen—whether I had observed the green powder on his face—so there was corroboration!" Woolf and Sitwell decided that "this extraordinary and fantastical pretense" meant "the great poet wished to stress his look of strain and that this must express a craving for sympathy in his unhappiness."

Were his poetic and marital travails themselves another in a multiplying sequence of disguises, played for sympathy when occasion demanded it? He might wear a mask, it seemed, even to appear ill. Virginia was not able to forget the cosmetics worn by her "penniless" friend with an "invalid wife" who unfortunately had to "work all day in a Bank," as she put it. Later in the year, she was to write in her diary about Tom, "He still remains something of the schoolmaster, but I am not sure he does not paint his lips."

* * *

In not writing to Knopf about the new poem, Eliot may have been thinking of Quinn's assurance, in 1919, that the clause in the contract guaranteeing Knopf the right of "first refusal" of his next books meant nothing and that "Knopf knows that it means nothing." Eliot could easily fulfill his obligation to Knopf by making impossible conditions, Quinn had explained to him, demanding from his "dear publisher," for example, a royalty of 30 or 40 percent. To Liveright, too, it would have been obvious that Knopf's option clause was a legal nicety that could easily be circumvented. Yet Liveright's interest in the poem would have been all the more reason for Eliot to state his impossible conditions to Knopf as quickly as possible if he wanted to free himself.

Quinn felt about Knopf as he did about Liveright: he was an "Israelite" publisher, in business only since the war (Knopf had founded his own firm in 1915), a relative newcomer forced, for lack of old-line heritage, to take on risky writers like Pound or Joyce, as Huebsch had done in publishing *A Portrait of the Artist as a Young Man*. (Quinn did not seem to think they could simply share his taste for the modern.) When Knopf, in 1922, had, like Liveright, expressed interest in publishing *Ulysses*, Quinn castigated him as even more "timorous" than Liveright and as unlikely as Liveright or Huebsch to publish it "unexpurgated and undiluted," which Knopf, of course, did not. Quinn marveled at the persistence of these "three New York Jewish publishers re: Ulysses," and their "apparently enormous insatiable perennial appetite . . . for slaughter," as he told them time and again that the book, at Joyce's insistence, must be published unchanged. It was something unique about their race that had them cajoling him anyway. They "apparently loved to be skinned and come back again," he told Harriet Weaver, even though it would do no good and only wasted his time.

But Eliot still did not write Knopf. In this he was procrastinating, or playing a "game of chess"—the title he gave to the second section of the poem—against himself. He wanted the poem published as quickly as possible. But the longer he waited to let Knopf know that the poem existed, the less possible it would be for Knopf to publish it in the autumn of 1922, which was to be one of Eliot's conditions. Forestalling Knopf in that way might free Eliot to go to Liveright. But the longer and longer into the spring Eliot waited, the more difficult it would become for Liveright to publish in the autumn. Eliot was also losing the chance to find out whether Knopf might offer an even higher price. Or whether Liveright, in turn, might, too.

He still sent no one a copy of the poem. He had the version he and Pound had edited. But despite Thayer's request, and Liveright's, he did not type another one. Months had gone by. No one in a position to publish the poem, including those who had already made offers to do so, had read it. Eliot closed his March letter to Thayer declining the $150 offer with a reminder-cum-threat, "You have asked me several times to give you the first refusal of any new work of mine, and I gave you the first refusal of this poem." Thayer wrote a note in the margin, "Not submitted."

* * *

Eliot gave the title "Death by Water" to one section of the long poem, as if at Lloyds he experienced a kind of drowning every day. The crowd flowed over London Bridge, and many of them came to rest, as he did, underground. In the bank, his office was a room below grade—"my cave," he called it, his heart under his feet at Moorgate and his desk under foot. A visitor remembered the distorted view, as if underwater, up through the thick squares of green glass of pavement that filtered in a watery light, and upon which "hammered all but incessantly the heels of the passers-by." Eliot sat on a perch above the other clerks at their desks, his tall frame stooping "very like a dark bird in a feeder," one friend remembered. His lunch hour was strictly from noon to one, and because he could not be ten minutes overtime, he did what he could to avoid lunches any distance from the bank and asked people to meet him at Lloyds so that they would have time to talk while walking to the restaurant.

Eliot was as jovial as possible in describing the requirement to those who were to visit him, but Ottoline Morrell apprehended the horror of the city and had a vision of it that matched Eliot's in the poem he had completed, but which she had not yet read. She and Eliot agreed to have lunch one day in 1922, but she was late and missed him. She went directly to the restaurant, Simpsons, hoping to find him there. She wrote in her diary that she had "hunted round like a ghost—it was like Hell to me—Seeing the men standing at the bars—and upstairs sitting in that impossible atmosphere of heat & whiskey & decomposed humanity . . . no wonder Tom's view of life is mournful." Eventually she went back to Lloyds, where she waited at the bottom of the stairs for half an hour. It was as dispiriting outdoors as it had been inside the restaurant. She watched the passersby and despaired that she saw in none of them "*any* beauty of soul. . . . But perhaps one may be too careless," she feared. The horror was outside, but also within. "I have become desperately unloving—so easily disgusted."

It was the same for Tom. He saw the decomposed humanity around him stripped to their unlovely souls, himself among those whom life, not death, had undone. Negotiations for his poem reached an impasse. He fell into a deeper depression, perhaps made worse than last year's by the recognition that the rest at Margate, and the treatment in Lausanne, and the completion of the poem, had not had the lasting effect he'd hoped. Not if his biggest and best work were not published.

Very soon, Ottoline conceived that she must help get Tom out of the bank. It was a commission she undertook on her own because she saw Tom and Vivien continuing to suffer much the same psychological and spiritual predicaments she herself did. Not long after meeting them, she had written in her diary that she had enjoyed herself "enormously" at a dinner that revealed there might be as much darkness as light in the camaraderie. Vivien had seemed to her "so spontaneous & affectionate," and yet the bond lay elsewhere. "We are all lonely wanderers—in a very barren land," Ottoline had written in 1919, when Tom's long poem was barely formed, their friendship, for her, based in a shared feeling of desolation that Eliot's poem, with its eventual title an echo of her diary, would express.

Ottoline would soon get Virginia Woolf to help her in what became the "Eliot Fellowship Fund." But Ottoline was not the first to have the idea that Eliot must be rescued from Lloyds. Ezra Pound had a plan, too. He called his "Bel Esprit."

* * *

Two days after Eliot married in June 1915, Pound had sent to Henry Eliot a "sort of apologia for the literary life in general" he had written at Tom's request, affirming his belief in Tom's preeminence, even though only "Prufrock" had so far been published. Pound stressed to Henry Eliot the importance of Tom's remaining in London to pursue a literary career rather than return to academia in America, as his family wished. Building his life in England was the only way for Eliot to go "the whole hog or he had better take to selling soap and gents furnishings." Despite the timing of the letter, Pound made no mention of Tom's marriage, and only in the postscript did he come to the real point, which was financial. "As to the exact sum, or the amount a man actually needs to begin on, I should think that if a fellow had five hundred dollars for the first year and two hundred and fifty for the second he ought to be able to make the rest of his keep and get decently started."

Seven years later, in the winter of 1922, Pound was once again canvassing for a way for Eliot to make his keep. Tom had long since started on his career, and he had not done it decently, at least by Pound's reckoning, having gone to work at Lloyds within eighteen months of Pound's letter to Henry. Eliot must now free himself, or be freed, from what Pound took to be nothing less than indentured servitude. If, in consequence, Eliot could not earn a living, then one must be provided for him. For Pound, the long poem proved his point, that, as he had written to Quinn in 1920, "No use blinking the fact that it is a crime against literature to let him waste eight hours vitality per diem in that bank." He had told Thayer as much, three months off from the bank and Eliot had gotten the poem done, Pound had written it. To Eliot, however, it proved the exact opposite point. Working at Lloyds had not prevented him from the poetic accomplishment Pound so long ago had predicted of him.

As John Quinn was to write to Pound in the summer, "Eliot is worth saving."

But neither Quinn—nor Eliot—thought Pound had found the right way to do it.

Pound proposed Bel Esprit in an obliquely titled manifesto, "Credit and the Fine Arts: A Practical Application," published in the *New Age* on March 30, 1922. The artist at work was a part of an economic system, a political system, Pound wrote, and it was a failure of civilization that writers of the greatest talent were inevitably the writers who would starve. Democracy, he wrote, "has signally failed to provide for its best writers," who were not surprisingly rewarded in inverse order of merit: "That is to say, the worst work usually brings the greatest financial reward." The rise of democracy meant there was no "coordinated civilisation" left in Europe, and that aristocratic patronage existed "neither in noun nor in adjective." The valuable function of the old aristocracy, in Pound's view, had been to select. By contrast, today, the world was filled with "illiterate motorcar owners . . . incapable of that function."

This was not a new cry. Pound had railed against this reality for a long time, his new broadside in effect a bookend to his "Prolegomena," written ten years earlier. Then Pound had foreseen a new kind of poetry. He now foresaw a new kind of patron. Civilization must be restarted somehow, and Bel Esprit was a plan simply to *"release more energy for invention and design."* The practical way Pound proposed to do it was through modest subscriptions of £10 each, solicited broadly, guaranteeing an income of, say, £100 a year to twenty or thirty artists "who have definitely proved they have something in them, and are capable of its expression," either for life or perhaps for shorter periods if that were all the support a particular artist might need. The only possible gift to an artist "is leisure in which to work," Pound wrote, and to provide that is "actually to take part in his creation." Bel Esprit would make free men of artists and was "definitely and defiantly" not a charity. His plan was not based on pity for the "human recipient" of the funds it would raise. But most of the manifesto was a rhetorical gambit to present what became clear only near the end. Pound was not, for the moment, concerned with twenty or thirty artists or writers, or with finding patrons for all of them. Civilization could be restarted later. He was concerned with only one writer and what might become of him.

"Rightly or wrongly some of us consider Eliot's employment in a bank the worst waste in contemporary literature," Pound wrote. He then referred, almost in passing, to what most people would not have known. "During his recent three-months' absence due to complete physical breakdown he produced a very important sequence of poems: one of the few things in contemporary literature to which one can ascribe permanent value."

There was the crucial word. *Value.* The value of art and the value of money. Pound was providing for a new exchange of value in a marketplace that had no room for commodity. But, at least for the present, he did have only one human recipient in mind.

The completion of *The Waste Land*, not named yet and also still referred to as a "sequence of poems," was "a fairly clear proof of restriction of output, due to enforced waste of his time and energy in banking." That Eliot was a banker seemed almost too pointed an indictment of the whole system of capitalist economics and the poverty of the artist. The poet wasted his energy in service of the very machine that denied him his place as an artist. And Pound twice used the word "waste."

Only Pound and Vivien, and perhaps a very few others, had read the poem. But among those who either read or heard about Bel Esprit were the critics who would shape the poem's reception whenever it did appear. Pound had guaranteed that long before they read *The Waste Land*, they knew of the *waste*, and of Eliot's breakdown.

The wishes of Mr. Eliot, he stated, "have *not* been consulted."

* * *

That was not true. "I had not intended to say anything to you about the scheme until I had got it working," Pound wrote Eliot on March 14, enclosing a detailed overview of his plan for ensuring his friend's *"complete* liberty." But Pound's public disclosure of Eliot's breakdown, so pointed and yet so casual at the same time, was as near the bone as the poetry Pound had prophesied in his 1912 "Prolegomena." It certainly was for Eliot. His poem was no closer to publication, but the disarray of his private life was now on public display. Pound had also made a bold claim that gave public notice to the small circles interested in such things that Eliot had an important work forthcoming. But who would publish it and when was anything but settled. In fact, more parties seemed to be balking than to be proceeding.

Quinn was outraged by Pound's publication of the scheme. He was worried that it would hurt Eliot's feelings to be exposed in this way and was inclined to think Pound was at best naive about the practicalities involved and the impact on Eliot's reputation. "These things should be done privately. There should be no publicity about them," he wrote. It was also not enough to solicit contributions. "If you really mean business," and Quinn felt that *he* did and that Pound did not, there must be written agreements with people, obligating them to specific amounts for a given period of years.

Quinn soon learned that Pound had solicited Liveright's participation, which was an even worse mistake. "For Gawd's sake, keep Liveright out of it. He is vulgarity personified. He would advertise it all over the place. I would rather make my guaranty $350 a year, that is, I would rather add $50 to my $300 a year guaranty, than have Liveright in it. I do this out of pride in Eliot's name."

Chapter 6

"WITHOUT A NOVEL & WITH NO POWER TO WRITE ONE"

M ORGAN HAD DREADED THE APPROACH to Plymouth. It might be impossible to hide from Lily the effect of what he had passed through in passing through Egypt. As he had written to Florence Barger of an earlier crisis of Mohammed's, "part of my trouble must be that no one knows of it: this makes me frightfully irritable—I can scarcely bear to be in the room with anyone." It was to be worse this time.

On the last night of the trip that had begun more than six weeks before in Bombay came what was either a final humiliation or a gateway into a new series of calamities. He was robbed of nearly £30. "A nice state of affairs," he wrote to Masood. Someone had come into his cabin while he was asleep and "pinched it out of my pocket book. . . . The Purser and his minions were detestable over it, and if one of the passengers had not lent me £2 I couldn't have got home." The amount was also equal to almost two months of the stipend he had promised to Mohammed, a sum which, depending on how long Mohammed lived, he might be less able to spare.

This was the way in which Morgan Forster, famous novelist of the Edwardian age, made his way back to England after a year away.

* * *

"I felt no enthusiasm at seeing my native cliffs again," he told Virginia and Leonard when he came to tea at Hogarth House on March 7, two days after Eliot's visit. "That was obvious," Virginia remarked in her diary. It had been almost precisely a year since he had sailed from Tilbury on March 4, 1921. His departure the year before had left her "melancholy. I like him, & like having him about," and the prospect of his absence had then reminded her, "I suppose I value Morgan's opinion as much as anybodies [sic]."

She was not expecting that she would feel melancholy when seeing him again, but the first sight of him was a shocking one, and a dispiriting conversation followed. Virginia and Leonard had visited Lily for dinner the previous October, and she had shared with them Morgan's deceptively cheerful letters. There had been no hint to Lily of any unhappiness. Now he confided the range of his disappointments—"told us as much as we could get out"—but it was all immediately clear, and words were almost unnecessary between them. He was, they thought, "depressed to the point of inanition," Virginia wrote in her diary, summarizing later in the week the substance of his unsentimental confidences to her and Leonard that afternoon: "To come back to Weybridge, to come back to an ugly house a mile from the station, an old, fussy exacting mother, to come back having lost your Rajah, without a novel, & with no power to write one—this is dismal, I expect, at the age of 43."

Here was one of Virginia's "devilish, shrewd, psychological pounces" that Vita Sackville-West found unnerving and also acutely revelatory. "Damn the woman, she has put her finger on it," she wrote after one letter from Virginia. Woolf could see Forster baldly, in stark relief, but she was unsettled. Her last confidence to him, in her letter of January 21, had been that she was herself, at forty, heaving bricks over a wall, without a new, finished novel herself and perhaps, too, without the power to write one. His visit came only one day after she had returned to writing.

Five days later, she had not quite exorcised the vision of her friend and "best critic" at low ebb. He was "charming, transparent"—he had stories to tell of "the sparrows that fly about the Palace—no one troubles about them"; he was pointed, too, in his analysis of politics and empire. She had recently despaired "what a 12 months it has been for writing!" For him, it had been twelve years. She saw in him, and feared in herself, a dilemma she was to describe in *Orlando*: "Ransack the language, as he might, words failed him."

Amid the talk of sparrows and native states, Virginia noticed something else that afternoon. "The middle age of buggers is not to be contemplated without horror." She discerned in him a loneliness that was elemental to him.

* * *

Despite his inanition, Morgan was talkative on a variety of subjects. As afternoon gave way to evening, "Off he went, carrying a very heavy plate, to dine with Aunt Rosalie at Putney." This was Rosalie Alford, his favorite aunt. Leonard walked with him to the bus for the short trip to Putney, four miles away. The plate was actually a small round tray—one piece in a set of plates and vases that had been a farewell present from Masood. He wrote to Masood upon arriving home: "It was such a happiness seeing all these things in England, indeed my chief happiness, and they all remind me of you."

The inanition Virginia had discerned was not new. In February 1915, when Morgan met D. H. Lawrence for the first time, Lawrence had used that same word to describe him: Forster's life "is so ridiculously inane, the man is dying of inanition."

Seven years—and more—dying of inanition. This was a slower death than Mohammed's, and one without as clear an ending. Two weeks after his visit to the Woolves in Richmond, Forster paid a visit to the poet Siegfried Sassoon at the Reform Club, on Pall Mall.

"This evening, E. M. Forster came to dine with me," Sassoon wrote in his diary on Tuesday, March 21. In a bad mood exacerbated by the sight of Forster's aimlessness, he described the paradoxical feelings of frustration and enthusiasm he inspired.

Forster, eight years older, was singular, one of the few "people who think for themselves," a man whose "delicate and sympathetic" mind left Sassoon seeking Forster's approval all his life. But sitting before him now, Morgan was "a disappointing (and disappointed) creature," an exhausted artist despite his "extraordinarily interesting and brilliant qualities." Forster was indisputably a great writer, "one of the very few who signify anything in our wilderness of bestsellers," and far more important than Sassoon himself was or ever would be. Sassoon could not make sense of it. "Anyhow he causes me to explode."

At the Reform Club it became obvious to both of them that, as Sassoon put it, "*something* deters him from writing the good stuff of which he is surely capable." But it was not only as a novelist that Forster was diminished. He stated as a fact that his "'memory and power of observation' are not as good as they used to be," but he also complained, vaguely, that he had become "'dissatisfied with' his character." Here before Sassoon was the inanition Lawrence and Woolf had also described.

Sassoon's italicized *something* suggests that Sassoon, who was also homosexual, understood a truth Forster did not state openly—that if Morgan feared his powers as a novelist had declined, or atrophied completely, he was equally debilitated by Mohammed's impending death, and perhaps also by the sexual embarrassment of their last visit. "I judge him to be over-sensitive and sexually thwarted. (He once told me he believed in sexual austerity. But he gives an impression of being sexually starved.)" Forster was, or had been, a great artist, but he lacked a "driving force," it seemed. Sassoon was unnerved. "I wish he would get really angry with the world. Or fall passionately in love with an Idea."

But the problem was that for Forster, the idea of love, the ideal Mohammed had represented from afar while he was in India anticipating their reunion, had died even while Mohammed still lingered. He continued to receive letters in which Mohammed declared his love for Morgan, but each was a reminder of the fact that it was not a romantic love and that Mohammed invoked a supposedly higher ideal that for Morgan was incomplete.

Mohammed had, in fact, written Morgan a letter dated March 10, which, in the normal course of things, he might have seen just before he dined with Sassoon. The letter from Egypt confirmed the inevitable slow demise and contained nothing that Morgan didn't already expect. The specific details were horrifying but almost irrelevant, and added to Morgan's guilt at having begun to wish that Mohammed's death would come quickly, for both their sakes. It had taken several weeks for a letter of Morgan's from the boat to reach Mohammed, and it had "buoyed" him to see Morgan's handwriting.

"I think we shall meet each other if not in the world it will be in heaven," Mohammed wrote. "I am sure you are remembering me. I think always of you without exception. I am trying to be good in order to meet again either in Egypt or in England." He sent "compliments to mother" and closed as he usually did, "My love to you, my love to you." The scrawl of his signature, "Your ever friend / Moh el Adl," conveyed its own message of death. But expressions of affection like this, promising a reunion in an afterlife in which Morgan did not believe, only exacerbated Morgan's loneliness, and his resentment that Mohammed had not, and could not, reciprocate the love and desire he had inspired—and perhaps played upon—in Morgan.

The night before he went to dinner with Sassoon at the Reform Club, Morgan wrote for the first time in five years in a commonplace book he had begun during the war, in Alexandria, the year he had met Mohammed. In it, he had transcribed unidentified passages of poetry and prose into what became a little anthology of writings he divided into three parts, one on war itself; another on "external life: beauty, fun, inevitable death, old age"; and the last one dealing with "hopes, fears, desires." Looking through the old notebook, he added a note at the front that he dated "Weybridge / 20-3-22." He had turned to the quotations with the hope that the writers whose words had once been meaningful to him would, he wrote, give "direction to my thoughts."

The passages about war were irrelevant now. But the excerpts he had culled on death and old age, fears and desires, had become less abstract with time. Writing in the book during the war, he had described a universal anxiety of the human mind, the desire to be "otherwise than it is." ("I have transcribed to fill up my own emptiness," he was to write once about his lifelong habit.) He had once thought he was condemned to a life of unfulfilled longing. He had then met Mohammed. Now, unfulfilled longing, for romantic love and for the will to create, left him sure that at least one way to be otherwise would simply be to be elsewhere than he was at home with Lily. He went to London the next day, a small respite, and saw Sassoon that night.

* * *

Writing in the notebook, hoping to give direction to his thoughts, he was as bad off in Weybridge at the end of March as he had been in India. But on the last leg of his long sail home from Egypt, he had found a glimmer of inspiration. His boat had stopped in Marseilles at the end of February. There he bought a copy of Marcel Proust's *Du côté de chez Swann.*

"I plunged into Proust on the boat," he wrote to Masood a week after he arrived home. "He certainly is very good though 5 parts, each consisting of two volumes, make one pause." (In this, Morgan unknowingly echoed the private reaction of Ezra Pound, initially a champion of Proust, later a harsh, almost demented critic, who upon first reading him, in the summer of 1920, had written to Scofield Thayer, "it's great stuff . . . The book will be 50 000000000000000 [*sic*] pages long. . . . Some stretches are indubitably boring=but he is a gt. writer. I have been slow to discover it=perhaps=perhaps not.")

Proust's *Swann* hit him with great force aboard the SS *Delta* as it moved north through the Atlantic toward home. He wrote in his diary on March 1, on board ship, that he was particularly surprised by "how cleverly Proust uses his memories to illustrate his state of mind." Forster was awestruck. "His work impresses me by its weight and length, and sometimes touches me by its truth to my feelings. Would that I had the knack of unrolling such an embroidered ribbon. Yet even then I should not be content. The little sip of pure creation that I have been granted has spoilt me."

In Virginia's letter to Forster just before her fortieth birthday, she had written about Proust: "Everyone is reading Proust. I sit silent and hear their reports. It seems to be a tremendous experience, but I'm shivering on the brink, & waiting to be submerged with a horrid sort of notion that I shall go down—down & down & perhaps never come up again."

"Everyone" was presumably at least Clive and Roger, from whom she had first heard of Proust during the war. She had feared being "spoilt" in just the way Forster thought he had been. Even their metaphor of Proust as a kind of watery depth was the same—she wrote of being submerged; he had plunged.

Two days later, as the ship neared England, Morgan wrote in his diary as if his own submersion in Proust had at least in a small way already transformed him. Perhaps he had not been spoiled. Perhaps he could find some new freedom after all. "Plymouth Sound: filled with memories of my quaint and not very nice relatives: seen from a new altitude."

* * *

À la recherche was no mere novel. The writer André Gide, in a remark that especially moved Proust, compared reading the sequential volumes as they appeared to "entering an enchanted forest; a forest in which you are lost from the first page, but happily lost; soon, you have forgotten where you came in, or how far it is to the next clearing." One might be lost in a forest, as Gide was, or be filled with memories and therefore see things from a new altitude, as had happened to Forster. Proust disoriented you, and that was the liberating point.

The shock of *Swann* for Morgan in particular would have been evident in only the first dozen pages of Proust's embroidered ribbon. As the novel begins, the narrator conjures himself as a traveler waking in the middle of the night in an unfamiliar hotel room, trying to bring order to his sense of time and space. Realizing he is far from home, he tries to regain a fixity of mind by recalling other bedrooms, particularly his childhood bedroom. Soon enough, all the details of that long-ago sanctuary arise in his mind, together with memories of his mother, his grandmother, and, even more consequentially, his great-aunt Léonie, who serves him the cup of tea and the famous madeleine, the scent of which gives rise to his memories and the rest of the book.

It was as if the solitary traveler and the triumvirate of women had been selected for their resemblance to Morgan's own isolation on the *Delta* and to the dominating trio of his own life: his mother, his aunt Laura, and his great-aunt Marianne Thornton, whose nickname, Aunt Monie, was even a rhyming cousin to the elderly great-aunt who dominates Proust's narrator's recollections of the town of Combray.

From Léonie came the cup of tea that gave rise to *À la recherche*. From Monie had come a legacy to Morgan of £8,000 that made possible Morgan's books and his relative freedom.

Aunt Monie, the sister of Forster's paternal grandfather, was known as a woman with a "formidable tongue" who often quarreled with her brothers and sisters, to whom she never hesitated to say why and how they'd arranged their lives ineffectively. The "haze of elderly ladies" Forster had recalled from his childhood included his grandmother Louisa and a farther-flung set of aunts, great-aunts—among them Monie—and cousins in a family expanded by second or previous marriages and resulting rings of half- and step-relations. "There have always been aunts in my family," Morgan was to announce to the Memoir Club, the group of Bloomsbury friends who met to share frank, often intimate, essays read aloud and then discussed. In the spring of 1922, this memoir vignette was the first thing he wrote in England after his plunge into Proust. The sentence might easily have replaced "For a long time, I went to bed early" as the first sentence of Proust's long novel, or been recovered from an early draft of it.

These elderly women were not just spectral presences of Morgan's childhood. Many of them were as long-lived as Lily would prove to be, and they were part of his life still. He had written voluminous letters to his aunt Laura from India, and shortly after his return to England he would take a vacation to visit other aunts on the Isle of Wight. In *Howards End*, Forster's protagonist Margaret Schlegel said, "I suppose that ours is a female house, and one must accept it." She did not mean that their house was simply "full of women." It was that their house was "irrevocably feminine, even in father's time." As Weybridge had been, and was.

It added to Morgan's susceptibility to Proust that he was returning from Mohammed's deathbed. It was not only that the French novelist conjured the past from sensory impressions taking place in the present. Morgan discerned immediately in Proust what Edmund Wilson described as one of Proust's "favorite formulas . . . that of an abject and agonizing love on the part of a superior for an inferior person, or at least on the part of a gentle person for a person who behaves toward him with cruelty." In *Swann*, this is the complication of Charles Swann's love for Odette de Crécy. The truth of this to Forster's own romantic predicament was bracingly clear. Morgan had perhaps not thought Mohammed intentionally cruel, but as his distance from Egypt increased, and he saw Mohammed from a new altitude, he could not be sure just what Mohammed's feelings had ever been. As Proust revealed, to know the intentions of another was impossible in any case. This was a realization that might lead either to freedom or to greater depths of suffering; or, as Forster discovered in Proust's novel—and in his own life that spring—to alternating doubts and fits of sentimental attachment and desire, a paralyzing blend that was another sensation entirely.

But reading Proust on board ship did not only kindle in Morgan thoughts of what lay behind him. The more devastating echo of his own life was of what certainly lay ahead. The opening pages of *Swann* are memorable for being devoted to the narrator's recollection of the night, many summers before, when he waited in agony for his mother's good night kiss. Eventually she bestows it, and the narrator's mind is put at ease. Morgan would soon be arriving back at home to live with a mother whose good night kiss, or morning greeting, or daily conversation he did not anticipate with pleasure.

* * *

Writing about Proust years later, Morgan described him as "introspective and morbid and unhappy and limited." This also described Morgan at the time he first read Proust. But Morgan saw that Proust the artist had transcended the limitations of his nature. This was the sip of pure creation he had tasted. Proust had vitality—"he couldn't have written a million words if he hadn't."

Morgan at one time had vitality, too. Inanition had come upon him later. The inspiration of Proust seemed to be that he remained "imaginative about tomorrow" in a way that Forster had for a very long time not felt himself capable of being. To Forster it seemed as if the unspooling of the embroidered ribbon came naturally to Proust. By contrast, his own powers of observation had been willed, and he no longer seemed to have that will. As Morgan saw it, Proust's characters reflected this elemental vitality that Proust himself uniquely must have had. Like their creator, he thought from the evidence of Proust's million words, they kept an eye open—even when dragged down by disease, and even if sometimes it might only be "half an eye"—on a "sort of adventure" of life that Proust had bravely explored and that Forster found thrilling and redemptive. The adventure, though, was not a swashbuckling one. The modern twist of Proust was that it was interior and encompassed nothing less, Morgan saw, than the entire "adventure of the disillusioned post-war world, when the whole man moves forward to encounter he does not know what: certainly not any good."

Morgan first read Proust with the dead weight of the unfinished pages of his India novel in his luggage and amid the trailing sadness of his last weeks with Mohammed. He tried to move forward. He had no faith that he would encounter anything good.

* * *

Returning to England more than three years after the Armistice, Morgan saw that a spirit was missing. Something had been killed in the war, but this may have only been Forster extrapolating from his sense of personal and artistic defeat. To a friend in Egypt, Morgan described England in the spring of 1922 as "a sad person who has folded her hands and stands waiting," much as Lily had waited for him for almost a year. The "smallness quietness and greyness" of the countryside depressed him, almost as if

Lily, with her continuing complaints about her worsening rheumatism, a reminder of her age—and his—were all he could see. He saw friends, too, from a "new altitude" and with decidedly less sentimentality, drawing what he called a "hardish line" between those who mattered to him and those who didn't, he wrote to Masood. Florence Barger bored him when she visited Weybridge. She was long-winded and self-satisfied, he thought. Another friend's "feeble but authentic light" shined for two unsatisfying days and left Morgan feeling that his friends' minds were surprisingly undistinguished and that too much contact might lead him into the trap of an "inferior accommodating outlook." Those in whom he could confide, including Leonard and Virginia and Sassoon, were so shocked at his low ebb that their reaction only intensified his sadness.

* * *

That spring Forster also visited Cambridge, and he recounted to his mother a conversation he had at a Sunday lunch. A man he had not seen in many years said that Morgan "had totally disappeared from every one's view." Morgan replied he had "never been more famous," and added that if the man thought otherwise, Morgan "feared it meant he wasn't moving among important people." But the man was as adamant as Morgan was defensive: "some one had seen my obituary notice—some one whom he knew quite well," though it was also someone whose name the man diplomatically forgot when Morgan pressed him for it. A little later, Siegfried Sassoon asked T. E. Lawrence's permission to share with Forster the private, as yet unpublished, edition of Lawrence's autobiography, *Seven Pillars of Wisdom*. Lawrence agreed because he recalled admiring *Howards End*, "and it was the real thing." But Lawrence was doubtful: "was not the author long since dead?"

Morgan was living a posthumous life.

On Saturday, March 25, he wrote to Leonard, asking to meet. "I want to talk over my situation with you. There is no one whom I would so willingly consult, and I know you will help me if you can. . . . Would you be in town Friday, and if so could we lunch?"

Leonard recorded among his activities for Friday, March 31: "Work morn Lunch w Morgan talk his writing."

Leonard offered Morgan two pieces of advice: to give up journalism and to read over his "Indian fragment with a view to continuing it."

Chapter 7

"THE USUAL FABULOUS ZEST"

"**S**UMMER TIME"—THE CHANGING OF THE clocks—began on Sunday, March 26. The evening sky was prolonged, Virginia wrote in her diary, but that did not mean that summer, or even a hint of spring, had arrived. At the end of April she would be able to calculate that, far from enjoying any good weather they had had, "27 days of bitter wind, blinding rain, gusts, snowstorms, storms every day," as if winter, like her influenza, would never end. More significant than the arrival of "summer time" was that Virginia had been regularly at work in the three weeks since Eliot's and Forster's visits.

Attempting to erase the "12 months" it had been for writing, she returned to an idea she'd had a year before, in the spring of 1921, "my Reading book," her hopes for which grew out of her dissatisfaction with the limitations of other people's criticism, and her own. A year ago, writing *Jacob's Room* with an eye toward finishing it in the autumn, she had felt "too scatterbrained" to get her thoughts in order to write about reading, too. Now, approaching how to think about the state of reading in contemporary England, she began an essay that soon became a flight of fancy. She started the piece conveniently enough with a weather report, drawing herself "up to the fire (for it was cold in March, 1922)," to read an invented first novel, *The Flame of Youth* by the fictitious "E. K. Sanders," that its publisher had sent to the newspapers with intemperate fanfare. The Sanders novel promised to be "the talk of the season" and, padded out as it had been to "four hundred pages of sufficiently large type," would be easy enough for Virginia to read quickly "between tea & dinner." The next morning, "perhaps with labour, perhaps without," she would then write a review to fit precisely into the space the commissioning editor had allotted it. Virginia's piece, like the novel itself and the publisher's claims for it, were all part of the usual machinery.

But the conceit of the essay was now revealed. Virginia was not able to finish the assignment. The novel sparked nothing but rather snuffed out "my career as a reviewer." This was liberation, a fulfillment of one of her hopes for 1922, which was to do what Leonard was at the very same moment urging Morgan to do—to give up the unnecessary distraction that reviewing had become. It wasn't only a compromise of her time anymore, she feared. In December 1921, Bruce Richmond, the editor of the *Times Literary Supplement*, had called her on the telephone to discuss her review of a collection of Henry James stories. He had objected to her use of the word "lewd" and told her "surely that is rather a strong expression to apply to anything by Henry James." Virginia didn't agree with him but decided she could accept "obscene" instead, though she was firmly resolved that in the new year she would not compromise again. She must not be too eager for editorial approval. The growing success of the Hogarth Press meant that she was earning, as a publisher, enough to forgo some of what she might earn, as a writer, from reviewing. And in writing an essay on not being able to write a review, she found another way of striking out on her own.

She called the essay "Byron and Mr. Briggs" and in it imagined what a fictitious Mr. Briggs might think of Byron's letters, which she had been reading in a new edition published that spring. Through Mr. Briggs, born 1795; died 1859, Woolf began to sketch out an idea that was to become an essential part of her thinking: that, as Dr. Johnson had written, the fate of literature depended on "the common sense of readers, uncorrupted with literary prejudice." As Woolf put it in her new essay, "Milton is alive in the year 1922 & of a certain size & shape only because some thousands of unimportant people are holding his page at this moment before their eyes." To Mr. Briggs she playfully gave the name "Tom," the name of the most uncommon reader she knew. But if critics like Tom Eliot (and possibly herself) were irrelevant to literature, as Johnson had suggested more than a century before, was there any way to approach the question of what and who made literature alive this year? What kind of critical voice was necessary? Could that voice be hers?

Her own solution evolved as she wrote more about the fictional Briggs, a nineteenth-century burgher who thought the "new book by Mr Keats was trash" and who did not know of, and would not have cared about, the immortal Coleridge's reverence for him. She leaped with a novelist's freedom into the mind of Mr. Briggs, and, in giving him decided opinions of his own, she found the way to use herself as the protagonist of her work. In the dozens of reviews Woolf had written in the years after the Armistice, she had used the first person only two or three times, and only incidentally. More than a decade of unsigned reviews in the *Times Literary Supplement* required an oracular anonymity she had perfected, and the conventions of these and other assignments had until now precluded anything other than "we," "one," "the reader," and "you." Woolf had once written of the novelist George Meredith, "But if the sense of the writer stepping out from behind his books and delivering his message in person is abrupt and disturbing in some instances, it is singularly refreshing in others." In drafting "Byron and Mr. Briggs," "Virginia Woolf" delivered her message in person for the first time.

Within days of this breakthrough, she was writing "with the usual fabulous zest. I have never enjoyed writing more. How often have I said this? Does the pleasure last? I forget," she wrote in her diary. Virginia may have made Mr. Briggs a contemporary of Byron and Keats, but she was a twentieth-century woman writing in 1922, and, as a chronicle of her own progress, she put specific dates throughout the essay and gave the publication date of *The Flame of Youth* as March 26, the day the clocks were changed.

"In England at the present moment," Woolf wrote, "books are published every day of the week and every week of the year. The stream sometimes dribbles and sometimes gushes. But it is continuous and many waters of all salts and savours go to make it." She was writing not only as a critic but also as a publisher, parodying the commercial pressures and idiocies of publishing; and of course she was a writer herself. Hogarth would add her own *Jacob's Room* to the "stream" later in the year, and also, it seemed, Tom's new poem, which he'd promised them for autumn a few weeks before. Would some Mr. Briggs of today think Tom's poem, like Keats's, was "trash"? Would *Jacob's Room* be the talk of the season? Would it matter if it were? What about a posterity for her own books? Would there be more or less of one now that she felt free to write what she liked?

These questions came to the fore as Virginia moved through the generations to Briggs's grandchildren, characters she made her common readers of 1922. She set a scene in which she found them arguing about books for pleasure, speaking to one another with ease and, as she put it, a "sort of shrug of the shoulders as if to say 'That's what I think. But who am I?'"

This was Virginia's question as a critic, as a reader, and as a writer, and imagining an answer to it led her back to thoughts of her own fiction. As she continued with the essay, she described "a little party of ordinary people, sitting round the dinner table, & talking." And making up this little party was a cavalcade of her own characters, among them Terence Hewet and Mr. Pepper from *The Voyage Out*, and Rose Shaw and Julia Hedge, two characters in *Jacob's Room*. Virginia set them talking with each other about Milton and Shakespeare, Hardy and Tolstoy, and other authors. Terence and Rose and Julia, characters from separate books written almost a decade apart, joined by virtue of Virginia Woolf's having created them, chat about literature and life, gossiping among themselves about "who will marry who; what the Prime Minister said, have you read Byron's letters?"

One of those at the dinner table was Clarissa Dalloway.

* * *

Clarissa had been a minor but memorable character in *The Voyage Out*. The voyage out is a trip from England to South America on the *Euphrosyne*, a cargo boat, owned by the father of Virginia's heroine Rachel Vinrace. The boat takes passengers only by arrangement. Rachel is traveling with her aunt and uncle, and there is a gallery of other characters, including a love interest for Rachel. Clarissa Dalloway and her husband, Richard, are not part of this group. They have become stranded in Lisbon, and because "Mrs Dalloway was so-and-so, and he had been something or other else, and what they wanted was such and such a thing," it is fixed that the *Euphrosyne* will rescue them, and they come aboard for the short distance they have to travel. Clarissa is the daughter of a peer and Richard is a former member of Parliament who, unable "for a season, by one of the accidents of political life, to serve his country in Parliament," has been touring Europe in order "to serve it out of Parliament." Mrs. Dalloway, "a tall slight woman, her body wrapped in furs, her head in veils," boards the ship carrying a dressing case "suggestive of a diamond necklace and bottles with silver tops." Clarissa and "Dick" become part of a drawing-room comedy at sea, dropped into the novel as shipboard acquaintances would be in life, and plucked out again when, a few days and a few chapters later, the ship arrives at the Dalloways' destination. When they disembark—Richard Dalloway having pressed himself upon Rachel during a moment alone and given her her first kiss—Clarissa gives Rachel a copy of *Persuasion* as a memento and writes her name and address in the flyleaf as proof of her conviction that she and Rachel will become friends upon Rachel's return to London. Once they have disappeared from view, one character says, "Well, that's over. We shall never see *them* again." Relieved they are gone, Rachel's aunt Helen thinks Clarissa "was quite nice, but a thimble-pated creature" and advises her niece to be discriminating about friendships. "It's a pity to be intimate with people who are—well, rather second-rate, like the Dalloways, and to find it out later."

Second-rate in Helen's opinion. When Lytton Strachey read *The Voyage Out*, he wrote to Virginia with high praise for the novel, but singled out, "And the Dalloways—oh!—."

By 1922, when Virginia did see Mrs. Dalloway again, it had been almost a decade since she had written about her. But she had thought of her much more recently. In February 1920, she reread *The Voyage Out*. It had been almost seven years since she had read it, in the summer of 1913, and she wrote in her diary that she could not fix upon what she thought of it now—"such a harlequinade as it is—such an assortment of patches—here simple & severe—here frivolous & shallow—here like God's truth—here strong & free flowing as I could wish." Virginia made some cuts for the forthcoming American edition and removed an entire chapter late in the book. For copyright reasons, "the more alterations the better," she had written Lytton, asking him to be "so angelic as to tell me if any special misprints, obscurities or vulgarities" occurred to him. He offered one minor correction. "I have put it in," she wrote him. Undoubtedly there were hundreds more that ought to be made, she added, "but it can't be helped." She changed nothing about the Dalloways. Then, in September 1920, Lytton visited Monk's House for a weekend. During one of their talks, he praised *The Voyage Out* "voluntarily," Virginia wrote in her diary, perhaps remembering that his earlier enthusiasm had been effusive but rather belated, coming a year after the novel's publication, and therefore perhaps received by her as only obligatory. He had reread the novel, Lytton told Virginia, and had seen that it was "*extremely* good, especially the satire of the Dalloways."

From the start of her career she'd been worried that, as she had early on told Clive Bell, she had "so few of the gifts that make novels amusing." *Jacob's Room* was built around the absence of a central character. Jacob's room is empty. He is dead, killed in the war. Even Leonard, who would praise the novel as her best work so far and "amazingly well written," told her that in it "my people are puppets, moved hither & thither by fate. He doesn't agree that fate works this way."

If she had *few* of the gifts that made novels amusing, what were those few and what were others she might discover? What might she do that would please the common reader and herself? She gathered her puppets into the essay, gave them brief histories, and listened to them speak. Terence Hewet, in *The Voyage Out* an aspiring novelist, now became a descendant "on his mother's side" of Tom Briggs of Cornwall. The thimble-pated Clarissa, now set chattering with the other characters, praises the poetry of Donne and speaks as if she had inscribed Rachel Vinrace's copy of *Persuasion* only moments before: "Mrs Dalloway confessed to a passion for Donne on the strength of his portrait chiefly 'and some of the poems if you read them aloud—alas! my husband never has time to read to me now—though so difficult are extraordinarily moving.'" Virginia wrote the dinner party as if with Lytton over her shoulder, doing what she could to keep the satire of the Dalloways extremely good.

When Hewet praises *War and Peace* as the "most sincere book in the world," Clarissa, as self-assured as ever (and perhaps not quite so thimble-pated), thinks this is "a little too serious for life." She keeps silent—"she had an Englishwoman's respect for litrature [*sic*]"—even as her smile threatens to give her secret judgment away. But Clarissa has no interest in considering it any more deeply. Nor, as it happens, does she have the time. She must "fetch her husband from the House at ten," because they are going to an evening party being given by Clara Durrant, a character in *Jacob's Room* who in that novel actually is the hostess of a large evening party. In Leonard's opinion this was perhaps the only "lapse" in the otherwise "very interesting, & beautiful" book. Richard and Clarissa are taking Rose Shaw with them, and Mrs. Dalloway, "sitting up," almost as if she'd dozed as she prepared her excuses, says they must leave. "Come," Clarissa says to Rose. It was time for them to go to "Mrs D's party."

In February, Virginia had eyed Katherine Mansfield's popularity— "So what does it matter if K. M. soars in the newspapers, & runs up sales skyhigh?"—and, disclaiming any jealousy, framed her own future against her rival's. She herself was after "some queer individuality" and had made up her mind, she wrote in her diary, "that I'm not going to be popular, and so genuinely that I look upon disregard or abuse as part of my bargain." She came to a firm conclusion: "I'm to write what I like; & they're to say what they like."

"Byron and Mr. Briggs" was the first thing she wrote in this new state of mind. Woolf's typescript eventually reached thirty-eight pages. She revised it so heavily that in places it became "almost impenetrably overgrown" with alterations. Then she abandoned it. Leonard did not include it among the many previously unpublished essays he printed in several posthumous collections. It was unseen for almost six decades.

But the essay had been a crucial step. With her dinner party she had written her characters and herself into a conversation about—and with— some writers and some masterpieces of the past. Donne was alive in 1922 because there were women like Clarissa Dalloway either reading him or recalling the romance of their husbands' former habit of reading poetry aloud to them. Donne and Tolstoy lived in the minds of people, whether or not they were able to, or cared to, have a sustained intellectual—and perhaps bloodless—discussion about them. It was not just satire that Clarissa had given Rachel a copy of Persuasion. Virginia's dinner party of her own common readers was a way of revealing that anew. Here, in their table talk, was at least a part of what posterity must mean for a writer.

Soon Virginia was writing not only with zest, but according to her regular daily habits, including word counts calculated in the margins. The hybrid form of her draft became a preferred mode for her criticism, and when she came, the next year, to write an incisive exploration of character in fiction that perfected her new method, she imagined not a dinner party but a train car, and envisioned a woman, Mrs. Brown, sitting in it. Woolf argued that writers like John Galsworthy, H. G. Wells, and Arnold Bennett, sitting opposite Mrs. Brown, would be so absorbed in describing externals that they would miss the "solid, living, flesh-and-blood Mrs Brown." It was not a coincidence that she faulted male writers for what they would fail to see about a woman. But it was also a more substantive issue about modern fiction. In fact a living character could be revealed only if she were seen from within, Woolf was to write. She adapted the title of the new essay, "Mr. Bennett and Mrs. Brown," from the alliterative title of its unpublished predecessor and made it immediately contemporary. Bennett was still prolific as a novelist and critic—and with her new title she gave prominence to the novelist's way of seeing a woman as the modern standard by which he or, more to the point, she must be judged. The male writers she named had not yet achieved the necessary perspective, but neither had she herself. "Mrs Brown will not always escape. One of these days Mrs Brown will be caught," Woolf prophesied. "The capture of Mrs Brown is the title of the next chapter in the history of literature."

By the time she published "Mr. Bennett and Mrs. Brown" in November 1923, in the *New-York Tribune*, she was already well on her way in that chapter. Almost immediately after setting aside "Byron and Mr. Briggs," Virginia began a story in which the resurrected Clarissa Dalloway was the main character. She wrote quickly and, by mid-April, was able to tell Tom Eliot, who had asked her for a story for an early issue of his forthcoming London magazine, that though she thought "Mrs. Dalloway in Bond Street" might be finished in three more weeks, by early May, it would more likely take her six. And he had asked her for a story of fewer than five thousand words. "Mrs. Dalloway in Bond Street" would be too long, she told him, so after it was done she would try to write something else for him, however "ticklish" a thing it would be to write to order for him. "When one wants to write, one cant [sic]." He would have to be both sincere and severe with her. "I can never tell whether I'm good or bad," she wrote, and she would respect him all the more, she wrote, for "tearing me up and throwing me into the wastebasket." And what about his poem?, she asked. When would they see it? Then she could "have a fling at you."

Virginia began "Mrs. Dalloway in Bond Street" just as she had begun "Byron and Mr. Briggs," as an experiment. But she grew more confident as she worked on it. She had only recently been lamenting the "little creatures in my head which won't exist if I don't let them out." Then another month passed and she had devised the dinner party in "Byron and Mr. Briggs."

After a year of disappointment, she found a further way forward by writing about a little creature who already did exist. Virginia continued to revise and expand her story about Clarissa Dalloway long past May, into the summer. And even once the story was finished, and she was at Monk's House in August, she did not seem to be finished with this character who had been dispatched so easily so many years before. Woolf continued to think about Clarissa and what more might be done with her and through her. Mrs. Dalloway was her own Mrs. Brown, and when, in autumn 1922, Woolf began to see that "Mrs. Dalloway in Bond Street" was growing into a novel, it occurred to her that the "Mrs D." giving the party would be not Clara Durrant but Clarissa herself.

* * *

Virginia had begun "Mrs. Dalloway in Bond Street" when her days were still largely proscribed by uncertain health and by her doctors' limitations. And so she wrote a story that begins with a woman doing what Virginia wished she could do, simply leaving her house, and on a happy errand: "Mrs Dalloway said she would buy the silk herself." Woolf wrote her first drafts by hand and later typed them. In the typescript of "Mrs. Dalloway in Bond Street" she changed "silk" to "gloves," and the story continued:

> Big Ben was striking as she stepped out in to the street. It was eleven o'clock and the unused hour was fresh as if issued to children on a beach. But there was something solemn in the deliberate swing of the strokes; some[t]hing stirring in the murmur of footsteps.

Time gave a structure—and immediacy—to the story, more effectively and more subtly than specific dates had done in "Byron and Mr. Briggs." Sounds ordered the day, the implacable authority of Big Ben ringing in the air, and against that, the murmur of footsteps, including Clarissa's own, all of the sounds, from one extreme to the other, contributing to the noisy metropolitan flow.

Clarissa's leaving her house at eleven to buy gloves suggested a leisurely start to a June day for a "charming woman, poised, eager, strangely white-haired for her pink cheeks," older than when last seen in *The Voyage Out*. She was a woman who had no reason to rise early; eleven o'clock was as unused as most or all of her hours could be, if Mrs. Dalloway preferred. But the gaiety of her errand was quickly clouded. Once she is outside, Clarissa becomes aware, but as if only from a great distance, that in the bustle around her not everyone is "bound on errands of happiness." A passerby notices that Clarissa seems prematurely aged. Perhaps not all of her own errands have been happy ones. The hour of eleven might be an "unused" hour. But it also was a sacred one, as the "something solemn" in the strokes suggested. Even on a glorious June morning, the striking of eleven o'clock would have registered for Clarissa and the entire city as an echo of the war, of the Armistice that began at the eleventh hour of the eleventh day of the eleventh month, in 1918. On Remembrance Day, inaugurated in November 1919, a two-minute silence was observed at eleven o'clock. The first stroke of eleven "produced a magical effect," the *Manchester Guardian* reported.

> The tram cars glided into stillness, motors ceased to cough and fume, and stopped dead, and the mighty-limbed dray horses hunched back upon their loads and stopped also, seeming to do it of their own volition.
>
> Someone took off his hat. . . . Here and there an old soldier could be detected slipping unconsciously into the posture of "attention". An elderly woman, not far away, wiped her eyes. . . . Everyone stood very still. . . . The hush deepened. It had spread over the whole city and become so pronounced as to impress one with a sense of audibility. It was a silence which was almost pain. . . . And the spirit of memory brooded over it all.

At the end of "Mrs. Dalloway in Bond Street," Clarissa is paying for the gloves that she set out to buy. The shopgirl, who has been slow in bringing Clarissa's change, makes small talk. "Gloves have never been quite so reliable since the war," she says, rousing Clarissa to reproach herself for having been annoyed by the girl's "snail" pace. "Thousands of young men had died that things might go on," she thinks.

It had occurred to Virginia in 1920 that she would like to write a story set in June because "one has more pleasure from it than all other months." Now she was doing it. Virginia had had so little pleasure for so long, and now she set Clarissa on foot through a London that she herself had seen mainly on doctors' visits all year. Even as Virginia worked on the story, taking the extra weeks she had told Tom would likely be necessary, Leonard noted the rare occasions when he "walked with V.," who otherwise was still usually at home. "V. ill with temp over 101. Fergusson came," Leonard noted on May 6, the same day she wrote to Roger Fry that she had "the most violent cold in the whole parish." A week later, on the thirteenth, Virginia had her first lengthy exercise in months. "Walk Kingston w V.," Leonard jotted in his pocket diary. It was about four miles from Hogarth House, along the Thames. Whether it might be a sustained improvement was hard to predict. As Virginia worked on the story, the long-delayed spring arrived, even if she could not share in it. The warm weather was novel enough and had been so anticipated that the *Times* ran a long article under the headline "Sunshine and Happiness" describing the joy the first days of beautiful weather brought to London and "the intensity of the desire for liberty that the state of the weather creates." The end of the usual influenza season was in sight, Virginia's own condition apart, it seemed, but the effects of the epidemic had become clearer. In the first three months of 1922, there had been a total of 16,388 deaths in England and Wales in which influenza was the primary or contributing factor. But that number was misleading, the *Times* cautioned. The deaths of chronically ill people with influenza were often erroneously ascribed to other causes. In fact, it was not "improbable," the *Times* reported, that about 30,000 people had died "as the direct result of this plague," and not during three months but in a shorter, more devastating period of time, only five or six weeks. By contrast, there had been 36,204 deaths in all of 1921.

The *Times* reported another distinctive fact about the influenza epidemics of 1922 and the earlier wartime one of which it was a reminder. These were the only two times during the previous fifteen years in which the deaths of women had exceeded those of men. Virginia had been in greater danger—her doctors' fears less exaggerated—than it had appeared in her diary or letters, or as Leonard was to recall years later in his autobiography about their varying diagnoses. And Virginia was still at risk in April and May, even as she sent Clarissa Dalloway out on her errand and she herself ventured out tentatively with Leonard for exercise. Later in May there was to be yet another relapse, bringing a new cascade of symptoms, and, along with them, familiar and resented limitations. Virginia had walked to Kingston, but that freedom was short-lived. The recurrence of her infection in late May meant "my heart has gone rather queer," she wrote to Vanessa Bell, apologizing for having to cancel a visit. There was her heart, and also her teeth—"they said there must be germs at the root of your mouth," she told a friend, skeptical of the latest theory. Three teeth were extracted, "3 I could ill spare," but the temperature lingered anyway. At Monk's House a week after her visit to the dentist, she was able to take their dog for walks. But that was about all she could do. Her influenza, she wrote, "goes on like a very respectable grandfather clock."

Virginia gave her experience to Clarissa, who, anticipating the sound of Big Ben at the start of "Mrs. Dalloway in Bond Street," felt "an indescribable pause; a suspense (but that might be her heart, affected, they said, by influenza)."

* * *

Virginia's story was a flight of fancy, just as "Byron and Mr. Briggs" had been. Clarissa, purposefully walking through London's familiar streets, absorbing the sounds of omnibuses and motor cars, noticing the flowers, trees, passersby, meeting people she knew well in the park, window-shopping—this was Virginia's way of being in London, out of bed, and out of Richmond.

Richmond was too quiet, removed from the city and social pressures (and excitement), more conducive to work, perhaps, and to mental health and equilibrium. That had been Leonard's view of its advantages, and moving to Hogarth House had been one way of putting into practice the advice he had received from the Bell family physician in February 1914, when Virginia had recovered from the breakdown that had culminated in her suicide attempt five months before. "She must rejoice in her recovery and her entry into happier conditions of living," Dr. S. Henning Belfrage wrote to Leonard, emphasizing the importance of "ordering her life in the most careful & thorough fashion—the all important regularity of habits—the hours of rest, immutability of meal times & of going to bed." His prescription was that Virginia must "take life very quietly" in the morning and must be in bed "no less than 10 hours out of the 24."

The regularity of habits she understood, and prized, too, but the slower pace and lack of stimulation in Richmond were disappointing at the start and had become almost intolerable by 1922, particularly after her winter, and much of her spring, too, in bed. Virginia's first impression of their new neighborhood, in January 1915, had been, "Somehow, one can't take Richmond seriously." And when one wanted "serious life," as she often did, she had to go to London to find it, "for the sake of hearing the Strand roar, which I think one does want, after a day or two of Richmond." Writing "Mrs. Dalloway in Bond Street" seven years after this diary entry, she continued the thought as if without interruption. "Omnibuses joined motor cars; motor cars vans; vans taxicabs, taxicabs motor cars—here was an open motor car with a girl, alone," she wrote.

This was the unexpected thrill of urban—serious—life, longed for in 1915 and even more so in 1922. In "Mrs. Dalloway in Bond Street," the sounds of the city intrude even into the quiet confines of the glove shop, and as the story ends there is a violent explosion outside that makes the shop-women cower behind their counters. What is it? No one knows, but it is a counterpoint to the chimes that started the story, a sound that amid other associations is a sound of war, a scar that even full-length gloves cannot hide. Clarissa, however, is not afraid, and she smiles at another customer.

In the first sentence of the story Clarissa proposed to buy the gloves herself. In the next she was out in the street, on her errand. This was the essence of life in London, for Clarissa and Virginia—impulse, the immediate fulfillment of desire. The first thought Mrs. Dalloway had may be about buying her gloves. But the first thing she actually says in the story, when she runs into a friend, is, "I love walking in London. Really it's better than walking in the country." Was it Clarissa or Virginia speaking? Writing itself gave Virginia a feeling of happiness she once compared to "a strip of pavement over an abyss," an image she used again two weeks later when, to express contentment at some early progress in *Jacob's Room*, she wrote in her diary that she had gone "some way further along the strip of pavement without falling in."

* * *

It was a question of looking at an old character with a new method. And in trying to find the "solid, living, flesh-and-blood" of a character from within, as she would later put it in "Mr. Bennett and Mrs. Brown," she was continuing the development of techniques she had tried in earlier stories. But in her newest experiment she was also influenced by Proust, a writer who had not been on the list of books she was reading in the hope they would "fertilise" her brain, and whom, she had told Forster, she had been biding her time in avoiding. Perhaps Virginia's January letter to him had been in Morgan's mind when he bought his copy of *Swann* in Marseilles. Perhaps during his March visit to Hogarth House they had talked of Proust. But at some point in the spring, Virginia began to read Proust. And like Forster, she was immediately enthralled. Working on "Mrs. Dalloway in Bond Street," she attempted for herself what Forster noted as Proust's breakthrough: to use memory and experience to illustrate a character's state of mind. In Virginia's story, the chime of Big Ben announced that the present and the past were happening simultaneously in Clarissa's mind and also on the page, in the space of a single paragraph or even sentence, just as Proust was able to do in the first sentences of *Du côté de chez Swann*. The eleven solemn strokes of Big Ben bring back an entire national past, including the war. Yet the murmur of footsteps around Clarissa are quiet enough that it is as if she is able to hear her own thoughts, too—of eleven o'clock as an "unused hour fresh as if issued to children on a beach," which in the course of a few phrases leads her to thoughts of her own happy childhood, repeating the seamless movement of the narrator's thoughts in the first section of *Swann* she had read.

In *The Voyage Out*, Clarissa is described by the narrator, or by other characters, who see the same glossy surface Lytton Strachey did. That technique suited a novelist at work on her first book, but Virginia worried, even when the book was published, that it was already outmoded. In "Mrs. Dalloway in Bond Street" her experiment became to have Clarissa think everything we need to know about her. The warm day is not only leading Clarissa through London, it is leading her back to her childhood as the daughter of Justin Parry, who had "seemed a fine fellow (weak of course on the Bench)." It occurs to Clarissa, "there is nothing to take the place of childhood. A leaf of mint brings it back: or a cup with a blue ring."

Here was Proust's discovery of the whole of Combray in the cup of tea that the narrator's Aunt Léonie offers him. For Virginia, too, a cup and mint unexpectedly lead back to a buried and supposedly irretrievable past. The echo is so explicit. Perhaps this was the effect she had feared when she wrote to Morgan before her birthday, months before—to be submerged in Proust and never to come up again. Four months later, she wrote to Roger Fry that she had changed her mind about what submersion in Proust might mean. She might, as she wrote him on May 6, have the worst cold in the parish, and she might be "sweating out streams of rheumish matter." But the wonderful news, she told him, was that she didn't mind. It was, for once, a relief to be confined to bed, and perhaps because Fry had been the first person from whom she had heard praise of Proust, it was to him that she exulted that, sick as she was, "Proust's fat volume comes in very handy." Far from dreading submersion, she now longed for it as the ideal distraction, proposing "to sink myself in it all day."

> Proust so titillates my own desire for expression that I can hardly set out the sentence. Oh if I could write like that! I cry. And at the moment such is the astonishing vibration and saturation and inten-sification that he procures—theres [sic] something sexual in it—that I feel I *can* write like that, and seize my pen and then I *can't* write like that. Scarcely anyone so stimulates the nerves of language in me: it becomes an obsession. But I must return to Swann.

Virginia couldn't write like Proust, but soon enough, she was writing like herself again.

Woolf, who did not subscribe to the *Dial*, was unlikely to have seen Ezra Pound's Paris Letters in spring issues of the magazine praising Joyce and *Ulysses*. But she might have been surprised to see that he was largely in agreement with her about how a writer like Joyce or, in her case, Proust inspired the next writer's "desire for expression"—and what happened when she seized her pen.

"No 'method' is justified until it has been carried too far," Pound wrote, "and perhaps only great authors dare this." But in another sense, Pound argued, it was not possible to go too far, as Joyce, and Proust, had perhaps done. A "great author has some share in the work of his students and disciples," Pound wrote, "and only sound work will stand a continua-tion and further development."

Virginia had begun the further development.

* * *

Beginning to read Proust affected her as beginning to read *Ulysses* had not. In April, having decided despite her influenza to spend two weeks, including Easter, at Monk's House, Virginia wrote to her bookseller to order *Ulysses*, reluctantly and almost against her will. "I see it is necessary to read Mr Joyce," she wrote, as if the literary world were conspiring against her, "so please send Ulysses to the above address," meaning Monk's. She ordered it from London on Sunday, and it arrived a few days later. On Thursday, she spent two or three hours cutting the pages—but it was Leonard who began to read it, she wrote to Tom on Good Friday, April 14. She would begin, she wrote, "if it goes on raining," warning Tom that then, "your critical reputation will be at stake." She wrote to Clive the next day that Leonard had started reading. But she had other plans. "Now Mr Joyce . . . I have him on the table. . . . Leonard is already 30 pages deep. I look, and sip, and shudder."

Leaving it for Leonard was not a surprise, least of all to Clive, with whom she had first discussed Joyce after she read *A Portrait of the Artist as a Young Man* in 1917, and to whom she confessed her "unutterable boredom" with the book. "I can't see what he's after . . . I did my level best." Her anxiety about Joyce after that was similar to the low-grade fever that lingered through the spring: present, nagging, not in itself debilitating, but worrisome and persistent. Her jealousy of Katherine Mansfield was personal. They knew each other and had been confidantes. Her feelings about Joyce were more abstract. Joyce's ability to command attention—and the respect of those whose respect she desired—undermined her own sense of her powers. In September 1920, when she had not been far into *Jacob's Room,* Tom stayed with the Woolves and talked with them about *Ulysses.*

Tom told her that what he'd seen of the book—"the life of a man in 16 incidents, all taking place (I think) in one day," she wrote in her diary—was brilliant. But it was not simply his praise of the book that was a threat. It was that Tom's praise of Joyce (and his regard for Wyndham Lewis and Ezra Pound) was inseparable from what she felt was Eliot's complete neglect of her own "claims to be a writer." He was on *their* side, and she was able to resist being overpowered by him by recognizing that his opinions, including his effective dismissal of her, were liberally mixed with his own "concealed vanity & even anxiety" about his own work. "I suppose a good mind endures, and one is drawn to it & sticks to it, owing to having a good mind myself," she wrote in her diary, trying to understand the strength of her feelings. "Not that Tom admires my writing, damn him." Writing in January to Forster about why she was avoiding Proust, she had written of her fear of going down and down and never coming up again. She used the same metaphor in her diary when describing this weekend encounter with Eliot. She felt the "waters rise once or twice" and wondered whether, had she been more meek about pressing her own claims as a writer, "I should have gone under—felt him & his views dominant & subversive." But Eliot's dominance—and her fear of Joyce's—had persisted after his departure. Reflecting on Eliot's enthusiasm for Joyce the next day, which she was unable to shake from her mind, she feared that what she was trying to do "is probably being better done by Mr Joyce." She could not think of him, except as a rival: "Then I began to wonder what it is that I am doing: to suspect, as is usual in such cases, that I have not thought my plan out plainly enough—so to dwindle, niggle, hesitate—which means that one's lost."

The sense of inadequacy was made more intense by the praise she did receive. In the *British Weekly* of April 23, 1921, she was acclaimed as "in the opinion of some good judges" to be "the ablest of living women novelists," an accolade she quoted in her diary but meant little—she was not a writer, but a woman writer. As one of her characters in *To the Lighthouse* would put it, "women can't paint, women can't write."

Ulysses had been "published" on February 2, in Paris, the day of Joyce's fortieth birthday—if the appearance early that Thursday morning of two copies in Paris, rushed by train by the printer, could be called its official publication. The first copy went to Joyce, the second copy to the window of Sylvia Beach's bookshop.

Virginia had turned forty only the week before Joyce did. It was not a happy point of comparison that they were the same age and that he had this novel out in the world, a massive—expensive—box of a book. She had not published a novel in more than two and a half years and had had the fear eighteen months ago that perhaps what she was attempting to do in the novel that still had not been published was being done better by Mr. Joyce. Even in an unfinished state, appearing in pieces, *Ulysses* had become a fearsome presence in the landscape of her own literary prospects, seeming, in its style, its subject, its fame (and its notoriety), the unwavering conviction of Joyce's adherents, to mock her aims, her capacities, her sex, her invention, and her talent all this time. Despite her doubts about Joyce's *Portrait of the Artist*, she saw, as early as 1918, the importance of *Ulysses* as it was published in installments—aware of its interest and yet distrustful of its influence. In April of that year, Harriet Weaver, Joyce's publisher at the Egoist Press, had come to see Leonard and Virginia about whether the Hogarth Press might be willing to publish *Ulysses* as a book. Virginia was struck by the contrast between the prim Miss Weaver and the text of the first four chapters of the novel she brought with her. And though Virginia described some mild shock at some explicit passages, her displeasure with Joyce's work was that its unpolished surface betrayed, she thought, a lack of artistry. "First there's a dog that p's—then there's man that forths, and one can be monotonous even on that subject," she wrote to Lytton, referring to Leopold Bloom's reading a newspaper while defecating. The chapters were "interesting as an experiment," she wrote to Roger Fry, "he leaves out the narrative, and even tries to give the thoughts," but she did not think Joyce had "anything very interesting to say. . . . Three hundred pages of it might be boring." The decision whether to publish *Ulysses* as a book was made for them by the limited capacity of the Hogarth Press. They had not published a book even half as long as the manuscript of *Ulysses* as it stood, then, in its far-from-finished state, and Virginia wrote to Miss Weaver that it would be an "insuperable difficulty." She had escaped publishing *Ulysses* but could not escape thinking about it.

Eventually she put a little joke about Joyce into the novel that grew from "Mrs. Dalloway in Bond Street." One of her characters is sitting in the park, thinking about how much London has changed in the five years since he has been there.

"These five years—from 1918 to 1923 had been, he suspected, somehow very important. People looked different. Newspapers seemed different. Now, for instance, there was a man writing quite openly in one of the respectable weeklies about water closets. That you couldn't have done ten years ago—written quite openly about water closets in a respectable weekly."

Chapter 8

"ENGLISH IN THE TEETH OF ALL THE WORLD"

BY SPRING, LAWRENCE'S CIRCUITOUS, improvised route out of Sicily would take him and Frieda ten thousand miles from Eastwood, each stop farther away from England, from his childhood home, and from the nearby town, Nottingham, where as a young teacher he had met Frieda. Their 1922 journey to Ceylon, and next to Australia, was a remarkably timed reenactment of the hasty escape that had marked the start of their relationship exactly a decade before. Lawrence met Frieda the first week of March 1912, when he visited her husband, Ernest Weekley, a professor of philology at the University of Nottingham, with whom he had studied. Within weeks, in May 1912, they eloped for Metz, the start of what would be more than a year away, in Germany, Austria, and Italy, before they returned, for a brief six weeks, to England. After another year traveling in Europe, they were married in London in July 1914. Ten years later, another spring, Frieda and "Lawr" were again on the move.

Whatever their other disagreements and battles, the Lawrences had in common a feeling of perpetual displacement, exacerbated in Frieda's case by the fact that in 1912 she had left her three children behind her and had chosen Lawrence over them. Their search for a peace forever elsewhere was a permanent condition of their marriage, and of their lives. They settled first in England, but then the war made the unlikely pairing of the older—and German-born—Frieda and the younger David dangerous rather than eccentric. They had been driven from Cornwall as suspected spies during the war. Another five years on and their search for a sanctuary was impelled from within. They arrived in Ceylon, and Lawrence was just as disappointed in it as he had expected to be when Brewster had first invited him. He had changed his mind about going, but as with so many other places to which he would travel in coming years, the perfection it promised proved illusory as soon as he got there.

The mosquitoes and the humidity made Ceylon inhospitable, but, more fundamentally, Lawrence was convinced he would never be able to work there. The six weeks he spent there proved him correct, though at the start of 1922 he had been relieved not to be writing—it had been a respite "for a bit, thank God. I am sick of the sight and thought of manuscripts." As a distraction, he had undertaken translations of the Italian writer Giovanni Verga, author, most famously, of "Cavalleria Rusticana." The translations had been a lark, a way to clear his mind on the ship east from Italy. He was a writer at luxurious rest, and even traveling second class at an extravagant price, £140 for both of them, was like living in a deluxe hotel, with the decided social advantage over first class that "the people are so quiet and simple and nobody shows off at all." Their steward came at seven a.m., serving tea and offering to draw a bath. The only decisions the days required were how hot the Lawrences would like the water to be and what they would like to eat. The vast menu for breakfast, at eight a.m., included stewed pears, porridge, fish, bacon, eggs, fried sausages, beefsteak, kidneys, and marmalade. Lunch, at one p.m., tea at four, dinner at seven were equally elaborate, "always much too much." On their way east, they stopped for a few hours in Port Said, their short jaunt ashore the delightful respite it had also been for Forster in 1921, when he'd had his four-hour reunion with Mohammed. The Lawrences wandered among sights that Forster, in Mohammed's thrall, had not cared to notice: the water carriers and the scribes, amid Koran readers and a "yelling crowd" of "handsome Turks, Niggers, Greeks, Levantines, fellaheen, three bedouins from the desert, like animals, Arabs—wonderful." The brief adventure was like an immersion in the *Arabian Nights*, and their being spat upon as "hateful Christians" only added to the exoticism of the interlude. Later the same day, they passed through the eighty-eight miles of the Suez Canal in eighteen hours, and Lawrence loved the way the slow movement of the ship through the narrow channel—at only five miles an hour it felt to him more like walking than sailing—allowed a lingering view of the red-yellow Sahara, and of the Arabs and their camels on the banks, so near "one can easily throw an orange."

Yet for all the luxury and beauty of the trip, it became no more clear for what purpose he had been recouping his energies than why he had come to Ceylon in the first place. He had made "a strange exit" from the West, on his way, he hoped, to recovering a "lost Paradise." But he was as much "on thorns, can't settle" as ever, and this was as true of what he might write as of where he might live. Ceylon was too hot and sticky, it made him irritable, but as much as he wanted to leave, he was still repulsed by the thought of America. More fundamentally, he quickly discovered what he had already known, though he had tried to persuade himself otherwise: the Buddhistic teachings were not for him. Camaraderie with the Brewsters would not be enough to make Ceylon his home for the year he had told Mabel they would stay there.

The Brewsters had taken a large bungalow, high on a hill and isolated on sixty acres of forest. The house had a wide veranda, where, despite the weather, and his mood, Lawrence continued the translations of Verga, "curled up with a school-boy's copy book in his hand, writing away" in his neat, small hand, "as legible as print." This kept him occupied while he complained about the weather, and the fact that he was not writing any fiction, always the gauge in his mind of his creativity, no matter how productively he might write anything else. One friend, the Scot writer Catherine Carswell, would later say that Lawrence's continual complaints that he wasn't writing were usually the best indication that he was working—but in Ceylon he really wasn't.

Lawrence looked at his physical discomfort and creative discontent in typically grand terms. This was true anywhere, but the challenges of acclimation he found in Ceylon gave vivid life to one of his long-held theories. He had always believed that racial differences were based in the very makeup of the blood, which in his estimation "affected consciousness." Transplanted to another hemisphere and climate, Lawrence now elevated his own difficulties into a racial truth. He admired the beauty and indus-triousness of the "good-looking, more-or-less naked, dark bluet-brown natives," but the white man, Lawrence said, was not suited to the region, which was for those with dark skin, "whose flow of blood consciousness is vitally attuned to these different rays of the sun." Lawrence could not admit that his own constitution was not necessarily representative of any-thing larger than himself, conveniently overlooking the contradiction that Earl Brewster, his American host, was perfectly happy in the Ceylon for-est. For Brewster, Ceylon felt like home and even looked like it, the hills covered in exotic flowers that, for all their differences, he thought were as "colourful as a New England autumnal wood." To Brewster it seemed natural that, when walking with Lawrence on the narrow paths, they saw monkeys hiding in the trees, and they often had to step aside so that the tall, dark elephants they encountered could pass. Lawrence enjoyed little of it, though again, typically, once he had moved on, he missed the "glam-our" of Ceylon and wrote to Brewster with a kind of longing for what he'd left behind there.

Lawrence's time in Ceylon coincided with a visit by the Prince of Wales, later Edward VIII and then the Duke of Windsor, on a tour of Asia. It was a show of imperial power and grandeur intended also to make silent amends for the violence of a colonial past that was actually still very much alive, and which the tour did its own work to extend. Lawrence observed the ceremonial procession arranged in the prince's honor, a *perahera*, in which dozens of elephants paraded over white cloth laid down so the feet of the sacred animals "need never tread the earth," accompanied by fire-works, "strange, pulsating" music, and "devil dancers," some on stilts.

The festival made Lawrence unusually sentimental. At the center of it he saw the prince "sad and forlorn," marooned as the guest of honor and as "the *butt* of everybody, white and black alike," and perhaps even of the elephants, which Lawrence saw as salaaming before the prince in venera-tion—or mockery—of his royal state. The bruised dignity that the prince must bear silently aroused Lawrence's sympathy for a lonely man on dis-play, hated by all, "for being a prince . . . and he knows it," as if he, like Lawrence, had also been driven out of England for his virtues and was also being punished amid the heat and the flies. Now Lawrence became misty-eyed about England, wondering whether he had made a mistake "forsaking" a country he now became homesick for. In the prince, isolated amid the chaos of the *perahera*, Lawrence saw an Englishman akin to himself, an exile. Had he moved too precipitously out "into the periphery of life," first in Taormina and now in Ceylon? What about the even more dramatic departure for America he had contemplated? It unexpectedly occurred to him that "the most living clue of life" might actually be found among Englishmen in England, where he had not lived in nearly three years. If he were to return, he might be among those who, uniting together, would carry "the vital spark through." That was what he had hoped to do, all along, with his novels. Must he go back? Yet this patriotic fantasy was just that, a revelation that could not be sustained against what he inevitably remembered of his experience of the war, of the last five years, and even the anger he had felt the previous summer at the condemnation of *Women in Love*. Soon enough reawakened to the difficulty of earning a living in England, where his sales were negligible and his prospects worse, he came to his senses about what life, and a professional life, in England would be, even as he remained, as a matter of pride and defiance, "English in the teeth of all the world, even in the teeth of England."

Ceylon, however, was poisonous, too, and could not be a solution. Once again had come the urge to *move*, the desire to go incontrovertible, even if, once again, the where was harder to pinpoint. America loomed, but he still rejected it for the present. The next ship out would take him to Australia, and so he decided they must go. "Heaven knows why: because it will be cooler, and the sea is wide," he wrote a friend. What would he do there? He didn't care. "I think Frieda feels like me, a bit dazed and indifferent—reckless."

It was ten days' journey from Ceylon to Western Australia, and they arrived, on May 4, as aimless as they were reckless; he might *think* Frieda felt like him, but in fact he rarely minded what she did feel they ought to do, where they ought to go, or where they ought to settle, her own aim to follow him, given that his was not a rational choice of destination or even subject to discussion. In Western Australia they were taken under the wing of Anna Jenkins, a kind, elderly woman whom they'd met on the voyage to Ceylon, and who found them accommodations in a guesthouse sixteen miles outside of Perth, the capital of Western Australia, "bush all around . . . strange, vast empty country . . . with a pre-primeval ghost in it." A land to lose oneself in, "if one wanted to *withdraw* from the world," Lawrence thought. But the scale of the emptiness was too great for

Lawrence to fathom or to chart. It terrified him. He had wanted to be away from people, from the Mad Hatter's Tea Party of Taormina, but apparently, once true isolation presented itself, not as far from them as he had claimed to wish. He always dreaded too much of a social life, he said, but in fact he thrived on it, if only for the conflict the contact inevitably provoked, whether with friends, who were used to his mercurial shifts and outbursts, or strangers, who were not. Perth itself seemed to him only a "raw hole" amid the scrub, and so he was surprised to see some of his own books for sale at the Booklovers' Library. He and Frieda took pleasure in buying a rare copy of the withdrawn *Rainbow* of 1915 that had made its way there, and gave no hint that he was the author. He was safely incognito anyway. Most of the residents of "unhewn" Western Australia, one was later to recall, rarely read novels and had never heard of D. H. Lawrence, only Lawrence of Arabia.

* * *

Lawrence had hurried from Ceylon, and he was soon to hurry from Perth, having so far found no answer to the question he posed to himself about Australia: "Why had he come? Why, oh why? What was he looking for?" Within days he decided they must leave again, "but—but—BUT—well, it's always an anticlimax of buts. I just don't want to stay." There was a boat in two weeks to Sydney, which hardly seemed soon enough. He would have to be relatively patient, against his will.

The Lawrences had now spent as much time at sea as on land since leaving Italy, and Lawrence had discovered that aboard ship he could feel the pleasure of being "an outsider . . . off the map." But questions about the future could be suspended only temporarily. And might never be resolved if, as was the case with Lawrence, questions led only to paradoxes rather than answers. They were moving east in order to go west, for example, though in doing so, and in putting off a decision about America, he and Frieda were also going farther and farther south, south, in Lawrence's formulation, being the direction to go in order "to be one step removed." Once removed, however, loneliness came over him, and he quickly became unhappy. He did not want to be with people, and he did not want to be away from them.

Once again at sea, they sailed the southern route, through the Great Australian Bight, past Melbourne, past Tasmania, up to the Coral Sea, arriving in Sydney harbor, which he found as awe-inspiring as his first sight of a new place usually was. A day or two in "Sydney town" dashed his illusions of its suitability, however, and proved that the city was too expensive to live in. They had only £50, which would not go far in a country where many living costs were almost equal to those in England, Lawrence was disappointed to discover. Meat, however, "is so cheap," he wrote his mother-in-law, and "you get huge joints thrown at you."

Houses would be affordable only far from town, and in search of where to live they went by train another forty miles south, to Thirroul, which had been established as a seaside resort for Sydney industrialists in the twilight of the Victorian era. It was now a faded spot, population 2,587 in the 1921 census, though local newspapers continued, unavailingly, to do what they could to promote the seaside dancing pavilion, "Thirroul's Gay Arena," which had opened in 1919 to stave off further decline. But there would be no seaside dancing for the Lawrences. Spring had come to London, but they arrived in Thirroul just as the Australian autumn was to become winter.

Having traveled so far, Frieda and Lawrence were not quite so removed as they might have anticipated. Thirroul, small and remote as it was, was the third-largest town in the coal-mining region of Illawarra. The wealthy and the tourists had largely disappeared, and though the town still attracted some artists and intellectuals, the district was populated by coal miners and factory workers, so that two very different classes of people were living "under the brooding, rock-capped coastal range." Heritage and tempera-ment might link Lawrence to both groups—he wrote cheerily to his sister-in-law, "the men here are mostly coalminers, so I feel quite at home!"—but his confession to a friend was probably nearer the truth. "I feel awfully foreign with the people," he wrote, "although they are all English by origin. It is rather like the Midlands of England, the life, very familiar and rough—and I just shrink away from it." Not that he was intrigued into any kind of acquaintance. The working people, he decided, were "very discontented—always threaten more strikes—always more socialism," and on the other end of the spectrum, the Australian gentry, made up of those who owned large stores, and who cared only for commerce, repulsed him. That he had no interest in the artists and so-called intellectuals he need hardly waste a breath in proclaiming. It is not clear that he and Frieda actually met many people; they certainly spent little time with any they did meet. What he knew of the people and of Australian life and politics he likely learned from the newspaper, which he read every day.

The houses in Thirroul were as uncongenial as the people, "indescribably weary and dreary," and no more than "so many forlorn chicken-houses." The to-let advertisements in the *Sydney Morning Herald* had included one offering, "Sup. Acc. for visitors"—the superior accommodations of a beachfront house—available at a lower winter rate. The house was a three-bedroom brick bungalow as far as possible from the cheap development of the petered-out resort, an architectural showplace built in 1910 by a wealthy engineer who gave the commission to his architect son. The "holiday cottage," the first Australian house to show the influence of the Californian bungalow style, was covered by red roof tiles that, together with the brick facade, stood out in panoramic views of the town. There was a distinctively wide veranda for shade, as well as a lawn spreading out from the house to a cliff overlooking the Pacific. In a town where nobody wanted to live too near the ocean, this was not an obvious advantage, and Lawrence wrote his sister-in-law that "only we are on the brink," a remark encompassing more than geography.

Living so far from town, Lawrence did all he could to disappear. In Thirroul, those who saw him most frequently did not even know a writer had been among them until after he had left. The barber, whom he visited every week for a trim of his beard, remembered Lawrence as a "morose-looking fellow" who "ignored the normal give-and-take of conversation" and whose only unusual characteristic was that he seemed preternaturally curious. ("It doesn't pay to ignore the barber's chit-chat, even if you're D. H. Lawrence," an Australian journalist later wrote.) When Frieda and David left Australia, months later, the estate agent who had arranged their rental of the bungalow paid a visit to the house and found a number of discarded English magazines left behind. She noticed that some pages had been torn out. Glancing at the indexes she saw that D. H. Lawrence was listed as the author of the missing pages and only then realized he was a writer.

* * *

Continuous travel, at least, offered a respite from writing, the Verga translations apart. As they had sailed from Perth to Sydney, Lawrence wrote a friend that he was content to let his muse, "dear hussy, repent her ways."

He claimed to be relieved to be rid of her: "'Get thee to a nunnery' I said to her. Heaven knows if we shall ever see her face again, unveiled, uncoiffed." But even as he dismissed his muse, in fact he longed to write fiction again, and the settled feelings he might confess to in a letter were definitive only until the next letter. As he traveled, his dissatisfaction with each place had as much to do with the work he was not doing as it did with the places themselves. Aboard ship it had been enough to do the translations. In Thirroul, he was back on land and must be back at work.

But what would he write? He did not know when he arrived in Thirroul, even as the house itself posed the question, which may have been one of its devilish attractions. The man who built it at first called it "Idle Here" but it now was known as "Wyewurk," renamed probably because its next-door neighbor was called "Wyewurrie." "It is one of those places that fits its name as the hand fits into an old glove," ran an advertisement for the house. "'Why work' indeed when one has a retreat like this to tempt from the turmoil of city life to its restful murmur of the beach?" For Lawrence, the question was more elemental—*what* work would he do—and it had been nagging at him since before he'd left Taormina. He did not want to idle there. The bungalow was spacious and comfortable, allowing Lawrence and Frieda plenty of room to be apart from each other as he tried to write, but they brought their own turmoil with them, and Lawrence was alternatively expansive and miserable, if only to contradict his wife.

Frieda, for example, would say that she loved the sea. Lawrence did, too, and, savoring the privacy being so far from town allowed them, they took nude "bathes" every afternoon, and afterward would "stand under the shower-bath" to wash off the "very seaey water." But rather than admit to sharing Frieda's feeling, Lawrence instead told Frieda he wished for a wave fifty feet high to wipe out the whole coast of Australia.

"You are so bad-tempered. Why don't you see the lovely things?" Frieda asked.

"I do," Lawrence replied, though he admitted he saw them only "by contrast" with the darker things he usually concentrated on.

It had the sound of an old argument, and an endless one—he *was* wear and tear—but daily life provoked him, and he did not wait for a mood to pass.

The darkened skies of the Australian winter, and the proximity of the "boomingly crashingly noisy" ocean—there could be no "restful murmur" for Lawrence—brought to mind the landscape familiar from their time on the coast in Cornwall, which had seemed an escape at first but turned out to be far otherwise. Memories of wartime England, so far away in both distance and time, seemed nevertheless immediately present, for there was another reminder of that dark time, and of their persecution. Thirroul not only had its coal mines and its miners. That was surprise enough. During the war the Sydney suburbs had been ringed by internment camps for German nationals and even, in time, naturalized British subjects of German nationality, including, in some camps, women and children. The last of these, twenty miles from Sydney, had closed only in 1920. Arriving in the city, Lawrence sensed the animosity of this lingering xenophobia at once, and, as he and Frieda took their first walk, thought some of the working class around them suspected them on sight as "Fritzies, most likely," even if Frieda and Lawrence "were talking English." Despite her "pure Teutonic consciousness," Frieda seemed unaware of these associations, or would not admit to any fear, which may have enraged Lawrence all the more. She wrote to Mrs. Jenkins in Perth, "I feel I have packed all old dull Europe in the old kit bag and thrown [it] into the sea." She enjoyed "the domestic part after all our wanderings—I seem to *cook* with a zest that is worthy of higher things."

Frieda "housewifes," Lawrence wrote Earl Brewster, though he, too, took pleasure in the quotidian tasks of homemaking, and in addition to his own tasks—lighting a fire in the morning, for instance—he joined Frieda in the baking of cakes and tarts that they ate, he added, "*all* ourselves," the gluttony intertwined with loneliness (itself intermingled with relief) that they had no guests with whom to share them. But this was not the whole, or at least not the only, truth. Many years later, an old man who had been a delivery boy in Thirroul in 1922 told a different, perhaps apocryphal, story of the Lawrences' time in the town. He remembered approaching the gate of Wyewurk and then quickly going away again, "frightened by the voices within."

But whatever contentment Lawrence and Frieda shared in Wyewurk, he was still not writing anything more than letters. He had banished his muse but had become impatient now that she had continued to stay away. By the end of May, with no other ideas in mind, he thought that the voices within the bungalow, his and Frieda's, might make a novel of their own.

* * *

What a twelve months for writing it had now been for Lawrence. It had been almost exactly a year since he had written a single word of a new novel. After *The Lost Girl* was published, in 1920, he worked on a novel, *Mr. Noon*, but put it aside in January 1921 to resume the novel he had put aside before that, *Aaron's Rod*, itself a book he had begun and abandoned in autumn 1917, and which he had then picked up again without much hope in Taormina. He worked at it fitfully and, in the late spring of 1921, had arrived in Baden-Baden with the incomplete manuscript in his luggage. It was a novel of the Midlands, "the last of my serious English novels—the end of *The Rainbow, Women in Love* line," Lawrence thought. The title character, Aaron Sisson, is a union official and amateur flute player who abandons his wife and two children to pursue a musical career in Italy; it, too, was autobiographical, Lawrence and Frieda's departure from England, and Frieda's abandonment of her children, fractured into pieces reassigned and reassembled within various characters' lives. Aaron, like Lawrence himself, pursued his art, but it was actually another figure, a devoted friend of Aaron's, Rawdon Lilly, who is the Lawrence character, a writer who nurses Aaron when he becomes ill. Lawrence had written eleven chapters and then stopped.

In Baden-Baden, Lawrence went out into the woods every morning and was able to finish the novel in a rush amid the "strange stimulus" of the forest, where he found that the trees were like "living company, they seem to give off something dynamic and secret, and anti human—or non-human." But it was not just the forest itself. The inspiration was specific, he told a friend: "Especially fir-trees." (A different tree was to provide the inspiration for *Lady Chatterley's Lover*, which Lawrence wrote in the wood near the Villa Mirenda, near Florence, where he and Frieda were living in 1927. Then it was an umbrella pine. He sat under it, "almost motionless except for his swift writing," Frieda remembered, so still that lizards ran over him and birds came unusually close. Occasionally, a hunter would be startled by this silent figure in the forest.) He finished *Aaron's Rod* on the first day of June.

His difficulties with *Mr. Noon* and *Aaron's Rod* were an anomaly in one way, but crippling for that very reason. All through 1920, and 1921, and into 1922, Lawrence had been writing, and almost any writer might have looked back on the years as enviably prolific. He had written stories; he had written essays; he had written his "little travel book" *Sea and Sardinia*, which attracted Mabel Sterne's interest; he had written a number of poems; he had written articles; and he had worked on his translations. Seltzer and Secker had both been busy publishing his many books. Not the least reason behind his productivity was his need for money. The only income the Lawrences had was from the work he could sell.

The need for money was, of course, real, as was his ability to write almost at will. But for Lawrence, the novel was the crucial thing. Stories and essays, and then the books they were collected into, were what he called "my interim," written with a different effort. "The novels and poems come unwatched out of one's pen," he explained, flowing from "pure passionate experience." What he wrote in the interim were "inferences made afterwards, from the experience" of the others. Novels and poems arose unwatched, expressions of the present; his other work was more consciously derived from experience that had quickly and inevitably become the past. Lawrence had been writing during the year, as Virginia Woolf had, but he had not been successful at writing the fiction that mattered to him. It was progress in writing a novel that defined Lawrence to himself, just as Virginia's anxiety about her delay in finishing *Jacob's Room* defined Woolf to herself. They shared, as Eliot did, the frustrating conundrum Forster had described but had for too long been unable to escape: always working, never creating.

A new place to write a novel—that was what Lawrence had gone to Ceylon hoping to find, his exhaustion in Europe deepened by the fate of *Women in Love*. His friend John Middleton Murry not only wrote a scathing review of *Women in Love* when the Secker edition appeared in June 1921 but, four months later, in October, remarked in a review of another writer's work that Lawrence was among those novelists who "appear to have passed their prime long before reaching it." Lawrence would only have scoffed at Murry's criticism. But the fact that he had become stuck while writing his two most recent novels, had ultimately finished only one of them, and was not working on a new one unfortunately gave him, as it had given the similarly stymied Woolf and Forster, the same idea.

* * *

In Thirroul, Lawrence now set himself a task. Perhaps he could write a novel as he had written his "interim" books, quickly, often in a month or less. Could he leave for America with a finished manuscript in his trunk?

The book was not thought out, but in the experiment he might discover the new form he had envisioned at the start of the year. He had only its setting—it was "pitched" in Australia, as if it were a tent that could come down quickly if he needed to move on. He began work with one eye on the novel itself and another on the schedule of ships sailing to America from Sydney harbor. There were three ships departing at various points in July and August, one for any eventuality with the book, and he would stop, or keep on, writing, depending on what the schedule of boats imposed upon, or allowed, him.

He did not go outside to write this time—he needed no tree. He sat at a large table facing the windows that offered an expansive view of the Pacific. He wrote from memory, but of events that had taken place only days before. It was less a novel, at the start, than a diary of what he and Frieda had just been doing and saying. His novels had always been filled with characters based on the people he knew, sometimes without any (or at least enough) alteration, as the Heseltine libel action in 1921 had suggested. People closer to him than Heseltine, including Ottoline Morrell, whom he'd depicted parodically as Hermione Roddice in *Women in Love*, were hurt, while others were content, at least in retrospect, to have served a genius in his work. Frieda was one of these.

Lawrence started writing on June 3, almost precisely a year since he had finished *Aaron's Rod*. The novel begins as Lawrence and Frieda began the latest leg of their travels east, with the arrival of two characters in Sydney. A writer and his wife have come to Australia. There are workmen lying on the grass in a park. "It was winter, the end of May," as it had been for Frieda and Lawrence, and lying there in the sun the workmen had "that air of owning the city which belongs to a good Australian," as Lawrence, who at that point had met very few, was very happy to generalize. The writer and his wife cross the park, in search of a taxi, observed by the workmen.

"One was a mature, handsome, fresh-faced woman, who might have been Russian"—this was Harriet Somers, who might have been Russian if she had not been German, and a version of Frieda.

"Her companion was a smallish man, pale-faced, with a dark beard," in the novel Richard Lovat Somers, "a fanciful writer of poems and essays," and in life, David, poet, essayist, playwright, and novelist, who at five foot nine was small only in comparison to the larger Frieda, who in turn appeared especially buxom (and mature) next to her rail-thin husband, a "comical-looking bloke," only a "foreign-looking little stranger" who with his wife makes up a "pair of strangers." This is what the workmen saw. But Somers—Lawrence had used the same initials, R. L., for his doppelgänger in *Aaron's Rod*—looks back at a mechanic staring at him, and takes his own measure of himself, his bearing "so straight, so observant, and so indifferent."

This was Lawrence as he started to write his novel *Kangaroo*. He had abandoned *Mr. Noon*, a transparently autobiographical work, but despite that failure, he once again took his inspiration from his life with Frieda, and soon enough he was "suddenly writing again." He and Frieda quickly found a routine, he at work in the morning, Frieda at the same time doing her sewing and other chores at home. Then they swam, "when the sun is very warm and the beach quite, quite lonely, only the waves." Most afternoons, Lawrence wrote letters while Frieda slept, his prodigious correspondence, many letters written every day—to his friends, to his agents in the United States and England, to his publishers in New York and London—more evidence of the social nature of this man who professed to revel in isolation. Lawrence was rarely out of touch, and he often shared the same news and observations with many people, as if, by telephone, he had called a number of friends one after the other and told them each the same stories of what had happened to him in the days or weeks since they had last seen one another or spoken. On other afternoons, he would read to Frieda what he had written in the morning, as was their habit. Once Lawrence was at work on his novel, Frieda wrote, "the days slipped by like dreams, but real as dreams are when they come true."

If his writing of the novel "keeps on at the rate it is going," Lawrence expected it would be ready by August, he told his agent on the ninth of June, only days after he had begun it. "But it is a rum sort of novel, that'll probably bore you," he warned him. It was braided from two halves that joined uneasily. One part is a record of his and Frieda's daily life, their pleasures, and, more substantially and entertainingly, their disputes. The other is from the newspapers, a story of political unrest in Sydney fomented by a nascent fascist organization led by the apparently mythical (but ultimately quotidian) figure called "Kangaroo," the nickname his followers give "Benjamin Cooley," a Jewish lawyer of great charm. Somers, the Lawrence figure, becomes an unlikely admirer, wondering whether his destiny (that word again) is to put his literary art at the service of Kangaroo's revolution—as *Kangaroo* spends a dramatically unconvincing amount of time urging him to do—or whether he might join the union men who oppose Kangaroo from the left.

Kangaroo became the title almost as soon as he started work. Writing to Earl Brewster, he called it "a weird thing of a novel." The part that is a largely accurate domestic diary of Mr. and Mrs. Lawrence includes a fantasy of instant friendship with a younger couple who are neighbors of Somers and his wife, for which there was no counterpart intimacy in reality. In the novel, Lawrence's long-cherished and long-delayed Rananim was conveniently just across the garden, but just as conveniently without the demands made by the living people who usually got in the way of Lawrence's fulfillment of his utopian plans. But *Kangaroo* was also an experiment. The friendship with the couple, the Callcotts, is the hinge of a second fantasy. Callcott introduces Somers to Kangaroo, and from that meeting, the Rananim next door leads the writer, as Lawrence had also dreamed, to revolution. Will he be at its center—or will he balk from revolution as he had balked at going to America? *Kangaroo* was also to be a political novel set in an Australia that might be a kind of social laboratory, a "weird unawakened country . . . with huge unfolding breakers and an everlastingly folded secret," a place in which the "sustaining magic" of nature had given him the same impetus to write that the previous year he had found under the fir tree in Baden-Baden.

Only three weeks later, he had written more than half of what he thought the novel would in the end be. Frieda wrote to Mrs. Jenkins in Perth that Lawrence "has written his head off—nearly written a novel in a month." Lawrence told Thomas Seltzer, "the Lord alone knows what anybody will think of it: no love at all, and attempt at revolution." This was much the same promise he usually made to his agents and his publishers—that his *next* novel would have "no sex and no problems." This time it was largely true. Though there was love in it. R. L. Somers falls under the rapturous sway of Kangaroo just as in *Aaron's Rod* the "R. L." protagonist, Rawdon Lilly, fell under the sway of the title character of that novel. Lawrence describes the sexual energy of the surprising ideological attraction—"Richard's hand was almost drawn in spite of himself to touch the other man's body"—but *Kangaroo* was only about politics, Lawrence wrote to Seltzer, in part to reassure him and in part because he knew that politics were more alluring for Seltzer, a Socialist and the founder and former editor of the *Masses*.

Lawrence worked on the book steadily through the Australian autumn, at the rate of at least thirty-five hundred words a day, or higher if he took any days off. His notebooks were as neat and nearly free of substantive revision as ever. The story—the part that was not political—became entertainingly and revealingly about him and Frieda, particularly engaging when it is the wife's turn to pierce the arid (and frequent) theorizing of her husband. This is what Harriet does during one of Somers's disquisitions that particularly bores and enrages her. "Mr Dionysos and Mr Hermes and Mr Thinks-himself-grand," Harriet calls Somers, in a chapter Lawrence titled "Harriet and Lovat at Sea in Marriage." "I've got one thing to tell you," she says. "I've done enough containing and sustaining of you, my gentleman, in the years I've known you. It's almost time you left off wanting so much mothering. You can't live a moment without me."

Like Eliot, who recorded his wife's pleas for his attention in *The Waste Land* but did not attend to them in life, Lawrence, too, transcribed Frieda's justified tirades in *Kangaroo*, as in other books, without absorbing her meaning or changing his behavior. (Lawrence, also like Eliot, was unsparing enough to document his incriminating inattention and surpassed Eliot in also reporting the lengthy speechifying that provoked Frieda's outrage.) In *Kangaroo*, R. L. S. is unstoppable, "a determined little devil" who is self-aware enough to know "once he'd got an idea into his head not heaven nor hell nor Harriet would ever batter it out." When Somers—as the intransigent Lawrence tended also to do—resumed speaking in the tendentious metaphors his wife had tried with her outburst to clip, she looks at him, "speechless for some time. Then she merely said: 'You're mad,' and left him."

Then, after such quick progress, Lawrence faltered. On June 21, Lawrence wrote to Seltzer to say that he'd "done more than half" of *Kangaroo*. He was more forthcoming with Robert Mountsier, his American agent, on the same day—"now slightly stuck," he told him. He had hinted to Seltzer of his fears, though. "I do hope I shall be able to finish it," he told him, "not like *Aaron*, who stuck for two years, and *Mr Noon*, who has been now nearly two years at a full stop. But I think I see my way." His wording was circuitous, hedging. I do hope. I think I see my way. June 21 was the first day of the Australian winter. Lawrence had only just lived through a winter without writing fiction. Perhaps this second winter of the year would be as bad as the first.

Perhaps he did not want to disappoint Seltzer. His publisher needed a novel, considering the "depressing accounts of sales" for Lawrence's nonfiction, stories, and plays. As one of Lawrence's biographers noted of another period, "The trouble was that productivity was not the same as profitability."

The political parts of *Kangaroo* are largely invented, written by Lawrence in his role as "thought-adventurer, driven to earth." And it was that part of the novel that balked. It was not clear what he must do in order to press on toward the deadline he had set. "Seven weeks today till we sail," he reminded Seltzer, and himself.

Meanwhile, in America, Seltzer had published *Aaron's Rod*, which had not turned out to be as safe as he'd urged Lawrence to make it.

Seltzer had hoped to avoid any threat of suppression and wanted to publish a novel of Lawrence's free of controversy. This way Lawrence's talent would be the main thing on display. But whatever sensitivities Seltzer may have professed to Lawrence in urging him to be careful were ultimately less important to him than potential sales. He may have worried about the frank depiction of the protagonist's marriage in *Aaron's Rod*, but he highlighted rather than downplayed it when the time came for promoting the book. In advance of the novel's publication Seltzer prepared a pamphlet, "D. H. Lawrence: The Man and His Work," in which he so effusively described his author's genius that, as on other occasions, Lawrence himself was embarrassed by it and asked his agent to intercede with Seltzer to prevent any such rhetorical eruptions in the future.

> Have you ever stood on the shore watching a giant steamer come sailing in from the horizon? Out on the vague border line between sea and heaven it is a mere dot. Slowly, gradually, the speck expands, grows into a thing of dimensions, rises and broadens, and finally looms before you a Titian Leviathan. So with D. H. Lawrence . . .
>
> *Sons and Lovers* established D. H. Lawrence. Its bigness has never been questioned, and Lawrence has gone on producing works that show the man growing in stature, strengthening his power, adding to his material, and intensifying the beauty of his singular style. . . .
>
> D. H. Lawrence now has an ever-swelling host of admirers both here and in England. They look upon him as one of the greatest writers of to-day; some, as one of the greatest writers of all countries and all time.

The forthcoming *Aaron's Rod* Seltzer then described provocatively: "The book deals with the relation of man and wife, the passional struggles between the sexes that characterizes our day."

Seltzer touted Lawrence as a colossus but was smart enough to hint at more sensational elements that might inspire greater sales.

The headline above the very good review of *Aaron's Rod* in the *Brooklyn Daily Eagle* was not that different from what *John Bull* had decried in 1921: "D. H. Lawrence Completes His Love-Cycle." The critic knowingly addressed Lawrence's reputation before he praised the new novel. "We recognize, of course that Mr. Lawrence is sex-obsessed; we feel, also, that he hates sex. He would escape from it; and yet, whichever way he turns, he runs into it."

As summer in New York began, and the sales of *Aaron's Rod* peaked and trailed off sooner than expected, he was as much a prisoner of the reputation that demoralized—and bored—him as ever. And in Australia, Lawrence's progress on *Kangaroo* ended. He had become "stuck" with his third novel in a row.

Chapter 9

"DO NOT FORGET YOUR EVER FRIEND"

MORGAN HAD BEEN HOME IN ENGLAND for a month when, on April 8, he wrote in his diary, "Have this moment burnt my indecent writings or as many as the fire will take. Not a moral repentance, but the belief that they clogged me artistically." It is impossible to know what the stories were or what they contained. He did not burn *Maurice*, so it was not simply an erasure of the unpublishable, specifically homosexual, fiction he had written. He was not ashamed of them, and even though he burned his own stories, he kept "the indecent writings &ct of others." The pyre seemed to free him to follow Leonard's advice to give up journalism and to read his Indian fragment. They were a "wrong channel" for his pen, he thought now, and it was as if just having them in the house were an obstacle to future work.

On the last Friday of April, he listened to Beethoven's late quartets and was surprised to find that, despite the doleful music, he had, as he put it in his diary, "the happiest day I have passed for a long time." At the very same time he had been listening to Beethoven, it turned out, the young son of his friend Frank Vicary had been scalded accidentally while his mother was bathing him. "Frank's boy," was now "in hospital, probably dying," just as Mohammed—whom Morgan fondly called "My boy"—was in a similarly precarious state. Morgan heard in the melancholy of Beethoven's valedictory quartets the invigorating truth that there was life after unexpected tragedy. An old friend, visiting the next day, Saturday the twenty-ninth, asked him, "How can a great artist like you have stopped writing?" It was the question that Virginia and Sassoon had asked themselves after seeing Morgan, and though it was also the question Morgan had been asking himself for years, on that spring day he seemed to wonder it himself in a way he had not before, and to grasp that whatever had happened or would happen to the boy—or to Mohammed—he, Morgan, was alive. A farewell to Mohammed might mean a beginning for Morgan.

Two days later, on Monday, May 1, he noted a change in his diary. He had sat "gloomily before my Indian novel all the morning." Perhaps the great artist had not stopped writing. It was progress and was more than he had done in weeks or even years.

* * *

In retrospect, the "holocaust" he made of his "sexy stories" was a "curious episode," he thought, a "sacrificial burning . . . in order that a Passage to India might get finished." For the rest of his life the burning of his old stories remained an inexplicable, almost mystical breakthrough to the future: "I will try to connect it on to 'God,'" he was to write Christopher Isherwood decades later. But Proust and the pyre of his stories were not the only thing that spring that galvanized him.

Morgan read a poem called "Ghosts," by J. R. Ackerley, in the April issue of the *London Mercury*.

The title alone would have been enough to attract his attention, caught as he was in a mix of the morbid and romantic, thinking of the slowly dying Mohammed as a living ghost receding in distance and time—and of himself only as a living ghost of the writer he once had been. The poem, in twenty-four numbered stanzas, began with the question that had preoccupied him since he had left Egypt two months before.

Can they still live,
Beckon and cry
Over the years
After they die,
Bringing us tears
Meditative?

Those we once set
With us abreast,
Shielded and cherished,
Are they distressed
If we forget
After they've perished?

The poem seemed written from within his own mind. Would the link between Mohammed and him survive the grave, as his friend continually but unavailingly urged Morgan to believe? Reading the poem so soon after reading Proust, Morgan saw that both writers had found a way to conjure the dead. Forster saw it "all in the opening lines" of "Ghosts," as he had seen it immediately in his little sip of Proust.

At the heart of the poem Morgan found the narrator's recollection of a farewell almost exactly like his from Mohammed.

Then came his words
Back to my lips.

Softly they stole,
Wave upon wave,
Crushing my soul
Into his grave. . . .
"You will forget. . . .
You will forget. . . ."

The friend's remonstrance was an echo of Mohammed's own last words to Morgan, sent from his deathbed and written in the form of an accidental sonnet—fourteen short lines—that captured on paper the shortness of Mohammed's gasping, dying breaths.

> dear Morgan
> I am sending you the photogh
> I am very bad
> I got nothing more
> to say
> the family are good
> my compliment
> to mother
> my love to you
> my love to you
> my love to you
> do not forget your
> ever friend
> Moh el Adl.

Morgan had saved all of Mohammed's letters, collecting them together with some photographs and mementos of their friendship, including two of Mohammed's visiting cards, the tram ticket that was a totem of their first acquaintance, and, in a small loose-leaf notebook, four pages of aphoristic remarks Mohammed had made, "Words Spoken." Morgan kept the packet all his life, wondering decades later whether "my constant thinking of him an attempt to increase my own importance to show the universe that at all events *I* have had a great passion at all events."

* * *

The "middle age of buggers" might be as lonely as Virginia Woolf, or Morgan himself, feared; but even though Mohammed had failed him as a lover, Morgan understood more of what he himself desired now that he had been disappointed. He could now, in a sharper way, gauge the sympathy and understanding he wanted from people and what, in reality, they offered; he could not be satisfied with the shallow conviviality of most of his relations with friends in England. The burning of his erotic stories was not only a way to find a new channel for his pen. It might be a way of liberating himself from living out his sexual desires only on paper. Reading Ackerley's poem had an effect akin to the touch on the buttocks he'd received from Edward Carpenter's lover.

Finding camaraderie in the narrator's inability to forget, Forster wrote Ackerley a long letter of praise on April 26, taking advantage of Ackerley's facelessness beyond the poem itself to risk the revelation of his own sadness. "Yes, it is easier to write to strangers," Forster once told T. E. Lawrence, "and that is the objection to meeting: the illusion of social intimacy starts, and spoils the other thing."

* * *

Morgan's letter to Ackerley—J.R. stood for Joe Randolph—was equal parts modesty and need. He had been moved, he wrote, by the poet's sure-footed "combination of the reminiscent and the dramatic," and praised Ackerley in words that echoed his reaction to Proust. He was confessional but oblique. "What you have done is to drive home the strangeness of a creature who is apparently allowed neither to remember nor to forget," he wrote. He did not mention el Adl or his own artistic plight. And yet it was a letter demanding to be read between the lines, as if Forster trusted that if Ackerley were capable of writing with such sensitivity in "Ghosts," he would also do that. Invoking Proust, Morgan seemed to suggest a camaraderie of homosexuals. "I have been reading Proust who knows all about it too."

Citing Proust was a bit like quoting Oscar Wilde, a code already well understood in the literary world. Shortly after Forster's evening with Sassoon at the Reform Club, Sassoon had a long conversation with another group of members, all writers, including Arnold Bennett and H. G. Wells. The subject of Forster came up. He was maligned for his lack of productivity and for the fact that, as some of them thought, *Howards End* was "not really first-rate." His homosexuality was an open secret, and despite the paucity of his output, there were rumors of his unpublished novel: "everyone seems to suspect F. of that unpublished novel," Sassoon wrote, impressed, almost against his will, by the "astutely malicious" wit of one of the writers who joined in the talk, the now forgotten, but in his own time suitably productive, novelist Frank Swinnerton. "The usual subject?" Arnold Bennett asked. "That subject has been done once and for all by a man named PROUST."

Forster copied into his letter to Ackerley a passage of Proust that moved him in the way that Ackerley's poem had, a few paragraphs very near to the end of the first part of *Swann's Way*. If he usually transcribed to fill his emptiness, here he did it as a gesture toward friendship.

The passage he wrote out is memorably placed in Proust's novel, coming just before the famous incident of the *petits madeleines* from which the rest of the book flows, that day in winter when "as I returned home, my mother, seeing that I was cold, suggested that, contrary to habit, I have a little tea." When the narrator dips a madeleine into his tea, there is a seismic effect: "a delicious pleasure invaded me." Transformed instantaneously by the sensations induced by the madeleine and the tea, the narrator no longer feels "mediocre, contingent, mortal," and wonders, "Where could it have come from—this powerful joy?"

The passage that Forster shared with Ackerley was more melancholy. The narrator, speaking of the relation of the living to the dead, and as yet unaware of the key to the past that awaits him in the tea, sees a possibility of reclaiming the dead in the Celtic idea that the souls of those "we have lost are held captive in some inferior creature," an animal, or a tree. The souls of our beloved ones are trapped there, "effectively lost to us" until the day—which for many will never arrive—we pass close to the tree and perhaps recognize "the object that is their prison."

Morgan wanted to be among those to whom such a day would come, but he was not sure that he could share with Ackerley and Proust—or Mohammed—the belief that it might even be possible. " 'Out of death leads no ways' is more probably the fact," Morgan wrote to Ackerley, quoting the poet Thomas Beddoes.

In copying out the French for Ackerley, and taking up more than one sheet to do so, Morgan made a slip of the pen, a practically invisible error. Proust, looking forward to a meeting of the souls, to an eventual liberation and communion, wrote, "Delivrées par nous, elles ont vaincu la mort, et reviennent vivre avec nous." *Delivered by us, they have overcome death and return to live with us.*

But Forster wrote, "Delivrées pas nous." Delivered *not.*

In his version, there would never be deliverance, for the lost souls or for himself.

Forster could not have been unaware that linking Ackerley to Proust, and to Poe, which he also did in the letter, would be high praise from a

Virginia Stephen and Leonard Woolf,
July 23, 1912, three weeks before their wedding

Mohammed el Adl

"Mr. E. M. Forster in
his full official robes
at an Indian Court,"
October 31, 1921

[left] "Mrs. Eliot": Vivien Eliot at Garsington, 1921

T. S. Eliot and his mother, Charlotte, at the Eliots' Clarence Gate Gardens flat, summer 1921

T. S. Eliot and his brother, Henry, in Sussex, 1921

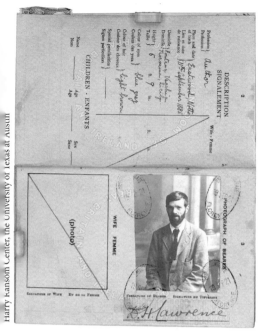
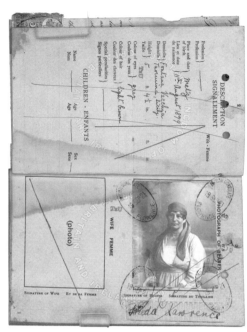

"Tired of Europe": D. H. Lawrence and Frieda Lawrence renewed their passports in Italy in September 1921.

D. H. Lawrence (center) with Frieda Lawrence (right) and Australian friends, on a trip to Lodden Falls, 1922

At Garsington, from Ottoline Morrell's Photograph Albums

Lytton Strachey and Virginia Woolf, 1923

Vanessa Bell (center) and Ottoline Morrell (right), with Morrell's daughter, Julian (left)

E. M. Forster

From Virginia and Leonard Woolf's Photograph Albums

Mary Hutchinson and Clive Bell

E. M. Forster (left) and T. S. Eliot, at Monk's House, September 1922

D. H. Lawrence, Santa Fe, 1922,
by Witter Bynner

Mabel Dodge Sterne, in Taos, circa 1920

Thomas and Adele Seltzer, early in their marriage

T. S. Eliot. On the reverse of the photograph, Vivien Eliot wrote, "Bosham/August 1922/Tom, looking like the Prince of Wales"

Scofield Thayer, 1921

Horace Liveright, 1922

From left: James Joyce, Ezra Pound, John Quinn, and Ford Madox Ford in Paris, 1923

"I was having a sitting for a drawing by Lewis and did not get home till nearly eight": T. S. Eliot, by Wyndham Lewis, June 23, 1922.

"I must sit for portrait to John o'London's on Monday": Virginia Woolf, "drawn from life," October 16, 1922, by H. L. Warren for John O'London's Weekly.

James Joyce, a portrait by Stuart Davis for the Dial, *June 1922*

"D. H. L. / dark mysterious within himself," by Knud Merrild, 1923

Marcel Proust, spring 1921

T. S. Eliot and Virginia Woolf, photographed by Ottoline Morrell, at Garsington, 1924

"Mrs Dalloway has branched into a book": Virginia Woolf in 1925, the year her novel Mrs. Dalloway *was published.*

welcome quarter. He wrote as an artist grateful to have encountered in a poem an effect that was perhaps beyond his own talent. Ackerley, who idolized Forster, accepted that as flattery enough, and the surprise and delight he felt upon receiving Forster's letter cannot be overstated. The letter was more important to him than the poem that had prompted it, and shortly before he died Ackerley would write that "Ghosts" was a "not very worthy midwife, I fear" to the lifetime of close friendship that ensued. Ackerley saved Forster's letter, the first of the more than one thousand, substantive or incidental, he was to receive from Forster over the next four decades. Morgan's salutation soon became—and remained—"D. M. J.," for Dear My Joe.

* * *

The next week brought to Morgan something of the same awakening that Virginia had exulted in in "Mrs. Dalloway in Bond Street," and the belated spring that had brought London itself to life. He recorded in his diary on Sunday, May 7, the "Sunshine and Happiness" that the *Times* would describe as arriving in London the next day. It was the first warm day since he had returned from Egypt, and Morgan spent much of it outdoors, in his aunt Laura's garden. He and Lily both fell asleep, he wrote in his diary, "with our mouths open to the sun."

But he noted a more momentous quickening than the change of weather: "Have made careful & uninspired additions to my Indian novel, influenced by Proust." The previous week he had steeled himself to spend one morning with pages of his novel. Now he had actually written something. He could not quite feel "happy" about it—that was "a silly word," he wrote—but even this measure of progress left him feeling "at all events more master of my surroundings and time." The first real days of spring also brought another letter from Mohammed, written, coincidentally, on the same day that Morgan had written Ackerley, April 26. Mohammed wrote that he was worse. But his letters had lost their power to move or to surprise Forster, who had read in Ackerley's poem the narrator's pained confession, "I had not cried when he was dead," and who now wrote a similar confession in his diary. "I want him to tell me he is dead, and so set me free to make an image of him. Latterly my great love prevents me feeling he is real."

Spring had not simply brought an end to winter. It was a new season of its own. Mohammed's death, he began to think, might not mark an end but a beginning, and a release. It was a reminder of what he had realized when he listened to the Beethoven quartets: there was life—and art—after tragedy. He might use his "memories and expressions to illustrate his state of mind," as he had been impressed, onboard the SS *Delta*, that Proust had done. Then he had not thought it would be possible for him. But Ackerley, in "Ghosts," had done it, too.

At the end of the week, he wrote in his diary, "Determined my life should contain one success I have concealed from myself and others M's frequent coldness towards me." Mohammed's "occasional" warmth might only have been politeness, gratitude, or pity, he wrote.

"Moh. worse again: the end? The prospect of his death gives me no pain."

* * *

Leonard had not only advised Morgan to go back to his unfinished pages and to give up journalism. He also advised him to be "out & about again." Morgan's reliance on Leonard was, Virginia thought, one of his most endearing characteristics. Because Leonard had been proved right about the Indian fragment, Morgan once again did as Leonard urged, accepting invitations widely and realizing he could not afford to let others continue to wonder, as the Cambridge man or T. E. Lawrence had, whether he was dead.

Virginia wrote in April to Ottoline Morrell to arrange a long-delayed visit for herself and Leonard to Garsington. She proposed they come on May 27. Ottoline, in turn, invited Forster to join them. T. S. Eliot was also to be a guest that weekend, she told Morgan. If he were not free, would he come the following weekend, when Wyndham Lewis was then to be her guest?

"The month of May was gorgeous & hot—& we had crowds of people here—Every Sunday they flocked over from Oxford," Ottoline wrote in her diary of a month of weekend parties that included the young men from the university whom she invited to meet the visiting writers and artists.

Morgan replied that he would be visiting Lytton Strachey, Ottoline's cousin, on her Eliot and Woolf weekend. "My future is as an uncharted sea, except where it is crossed by Lytton's system of soundings," he wrote in a letter full of chivalrous humor.

Morgan knew he was out of practice among the smart set—he had not been to Garsington since 1920—and, as if to prove his bonhomie, wrote Ottoline in the manner of "one who, despite considerable delay . . . is reading Proust," his letter full of long sentences and proliferating subordinate clauses in playful homage to the author he had begun to read so recently.

"Why do we do such things? Just to catch a glimpse of life—it don't matter much what," Virginia wrote to her sister Vanessa in April, explaining why, after a winter of influenza, she and Leonard had accepted H. G. Wells's invitation to spend five days at Easter with him "playing Badminton and discussing fiction." This was just like Morgan at Garsington, willing himself, at Leonard's urging, into a glimpse of life.

But the settled fabric of the two weekends quickly became frayed, to Morgan's delight. His weekend with Lytton included the Woolves, surprise guests who were to have been his companions at Garsington with Eliot, a visit Virginia had canceled by claiming, with some truth, the recurrence of her influenza. Virginia suggested a late June or early July visit to Garsington instead and, begging Ottoline's indulgence—"But please don't say you will have nothing more to do with me—annoying as these habits are"—she and Leonard went to Strachey's.

Forster wrote his mother of the near unraveling of the charade: a wire from Ottoline summoned Lytton and Morgan to the all-day garden party then, as always, in progress. They did not dare refuse, so they went, but without the Woolves, "whom we had to leave behind and conceal."

They arrived to find a scene as exotic as anything Morgan had described in his long letters about the doings of the court of Dewas: the whole company had been bathing in the pond, and at the center was "Lady O in bright yellow satin and a picture hat" alternating her "cries of joy and farewell" amid the bustle.

Ottoline, "once seen, could not be forgotten." She was best appreciated as an abstract painting, Quentin Bell, Virginia's nephew and biographer, remembered, "one admired the colours, the *matière*, the disposition of forms, one was amazed by the brilliance and the audacity of the composition, it was all stupendous, gorgeous, a little overwhelming and highly dramatic." Lytton spent a "not very stimulating" weekend with her in 1922 and was less awestruck, indulging himself to Virginia with a picture of a grotesque. "Ott. was dreadfully dégringolée"—"tumbled," an apt word for how far she had fallen in his estimation: "her bladder has now gone the way of her wits—a melancholy dribble; and then, as she sits after dinner in the lamplight, her cheek-pouches drooping with peppermints, a cigarette between her false teeth, and vast spectacles on her painted nose, the effect produced is extremely agitating. I found I want to howl like an Irish wolf—but perhaps the result produced in you was different." Virginia, almost equally harsh in private, could also be sycophantic, or at least fawning when required, as she was when she had written to Ottoline that spring, "It's such an age since I was at Garsington, and it never seems to me a house on the ground like other houses, but a caravan, a floating palace."

When Morgan and Ottoline talked about his own impending weekend, it turned out that she would have preferred him to visit with Tom Eliot. She was surer than ever that Wyndham Lewis "isn't nice," she told Morgan. "Why ask such?" Morgan wondered to Lily. (Lewis, and for that matter Lytton and Virginia, was no less "nice" than Ottoline herself could be, often unprovoked. At one of her garden parties Morgan met a poet. "I liked him but thought him a bit crazy and a bit of an ass, also conceited," he wrote in his diary. But Lady Ottoline did not like him, he added, and, in the course of her remarks, "managed to inform" Forster and the others that the poet had syphilis. Delighted as Forster was with the gossip, he was anxious that he would be the subject of it when out of earshot.)

The next weekend, Morgan arrived at Garsington in time for dinner on Saturday. "Suspicious and hostile glares" exchanged between Morgan and the other guests quickly gave way to fun, and, in particular, to a surprising ease with Lewis, who Morgan discovered was "a curious mixture of insolence and nervousness." Lewis even drew him away for a private walk, which disappointed Ottoline, who had counted on them "to be figuring separately," as ornaments among different groups of the guests.

Morgan thought the visit "a succès fou." He had weathered his first weekend back in England playing "Morgan Forster" and not as a guest among close friends like Lytton or the Woolves. But Lewis, however confidential and ingratiating he appeared, was in the end as unkind as Ottoline had feared he would be. He recalled in his autobiography that at Garsington he had once met Forster, "the 'Bloomsbury novelist,'" attaching the

moniker as if it were a known insult, which in Lewis's lexicon it was. Forster was a "quiet little chap," so anodyne and minor that no one could be
jealous of him, which was the key to why, Lewis wrote, Forster "hit it off
with the 'Bloomsburies,' and was appointed male number opposite to
Virginia Woolfe [sic]," whose name Lewis willfully misspelled more than
once in his book. Forster and "Woolfe" were both equally sexless and sterile, merely "roosters of the 'post-war'" who quickly "crowed themselves
hoarse or to a standstill," with Forster's long silence particularly advanta-
geous in a paradoxical way because "the less you write, in a ticklish position of that sort, the better."

* * *

A few days after Morgan returned from Garsington, everything changed.

It all began unexpectedly enough—with a mildly unfavorable review
in the *Times* of *Da Silva's Widow, and Other Stories*, the latest collection
of vaguely supernatural stories by Lucas Malet, an elderly writer whose
popularity had peaked many years before. The review itself, published on
Tuesday, June 6, promised little. It was fairly short, not prominently featured, and the headline, "Pale Souls," not calculated to draw readers,
seemed rather to be apologizing to them. Which perhaps it was. The first
sentence of the review—"Hardly one of these short stories does not carry a
reminder, by its subject, of some other author"—urged people away not
only from Malet's book but seemingly from the review itself. The second
sentence, however, invoking Henry James as the superior author most
often echoed, ended with a different comparison, that Malet "once or
twice" was instead more like "the Mr. E. M. Forster of *The Celestial Omnibus*." The similarity was "peculiarly unfortunate" because, in provoking
comparison with Forster, Malet's work would only leave the reader "wondering what Mr. Forster would have made" of the material.

The Celestial Omnibus had collected six stories of Forster's written in
a fantastical vein very different from his novels. Forster struggled, even
after the success of *Howards End*, to find a publisher willing to issue them;
his own regular publisher, Edward Arnold, declined. Eventually Sidgwick
and Jackson published the book in 1911, hoping that by doing so it might
have a chance at Forster's next novel. But there had been no next novel or
next book. Despite some good reviews, *The Celestial Omnibus* had not
been a commercial success, stories, then as now, generally less lucrative

than novels. But the reviewer's mention of it in the *Times* brought an unexpected second life that played out in the letters columns of the newspaper over the next ten days.

Lucas Malet was the pseudonym of Mary St. Leger Kingsley, born in 1852, the author of many novels and stories, the first published in 1882, the last in 1930, a year before her death. Malet, the daughter of Charles Kingsley, author most famously of *Westward Ho!*, and a writer who in her heyday had become a friend of James's and earned favorable comparisons to George Eliot and to Rudyard Kipling, was insulted by the review and by what she took to be the suggestion that her own stories were plagiarized.

Indignant at that charge—which had not been made or implied—Malet wrote to the newspaper that she was unaware of *The Celestial Omnibus* and of Forster's work; in fact she had never even heard of Mr. E. M. Forster. Her letter was published on Thursday. Frank Sidgwick, of Sidgwick and Jackson, was in his turn equally indignant at Malet's profession of ignorance of Forster. Sidgwick wrote to the *Times* as a publisher whose literary sensitivity had been offended, but in reality he was seizing a promotional opportunity. *The Celestial Omnibus* was eleven years old, and Sidgwick had not had confidence in it even as he went ahead with it, agreeing to use only six of the ten stories Forster wanted in the book and adding illustrations and decorated endpapers that were silly and trivialized the work, Forster thought. Sidgwick had reprinted the stories in a cheap edition in 1920 that was still available, and now he ran to the publicity barricades.

His letter was published on Saturday. "Having seen 'Lucas Malet's' letter in *The Times* of to-day, we have at once sent her a copy of *The Celestial Omnibus*, and we should be glad if you will announce that we will readily send a free copy of that book to any British novelist who, in our judgment, is as distinguished a writer as 'Lucas Malet,' if that novelist will make a similar public confession in your columns that he or she has never heard of Mr. E. M. Forster or read any of his books."

Confessions of admiration came quickly from readers, some of them novelists, who, almost every day for the next week, offered encomiums to Forster, praising one or the other of his books. (One of the letters was signed "C. K. S. M.," the initials of the man soon to publish his translation of Proust's *Du côté de chez Swann*.) The correspondence appeared under the recurring headline "Mr. E. M. Forster's Books." Many wrote that they wondered what Mr. Forster had been doing for the last decade. He had been silent but was not forgotten.

Lucas Malet's injudicious comment on Forster was another proof that it is never a good idea for an author to respond to an unfavorable review. The aggrieved victim never gets the last word and only draws more attention to the review that caused unhappiness in the first place. In this case, the ill-informed Malet also drew renewed attention to Forster. A newly, if warily, confident Morgan shared the exciting news with Masood, who was in Japan.

"I am well and suddenly famous. A most mysterious transition. Letters every day about me in the Times, ¾ column article upon me, imploring letters from publishers, missives from unknown admirers—all for no reason. I have done nothing. A trivial accident started in the Times. I am pleased and for one of my temperament the experience is good. You can't know—or perhaps you alone do know—the torture my diffidence often caused me, and a boom like this helps me forward."

The correspondence in the *Times* made him "so frisky and pleased," he wrote to Siegfried Sassoon. He was "more composed and able to face people" than he had been for a long time, and this affected the mood with which he wrote his Indian novel. He had been working diligently in the last month, neither satisfied nor dissatisfied with his writing but simply pushing ahead. His additions were not bad, he thought, but he was still not convinced that the novel would ever be finished. His track record was not one to give him faith, and he saw a "fundamental defect" in the novel that he worried he might not solve. The characters, he thought, were "not sufficiently interesting," and he found himself tempted to emphasize atmosphere at the expense of drama.

But even this doubt represented a significantly new perspective: the defect was in the novel rather than in himself as the novelist, as he had thought for a decade. He was working "terribly slowly," but if he continued to work, he might make a novel of what he had, just as Leonard had advised would happen.

Three months before, he had confessed to Sassoon that he thought his powers of observation were failing him. Now he was not so certain. He must get the conviction he could finish the book, he wrote Sassoon more optimistically at the end of June. He was not quite sure what he had to do. "By looking blandly ahead? By screaming? How? By Living?"

Living, and living as he wished to, might, after all, be the answer. Even when Morgan had been away on his weekend visits, he wrote long letters to Lily in order to reassure her, as he had written from Garsington in May, that he "longs to see her again and has often thought of her." But now a change between them was necessary, he told Lily. He could no longer bear her criticisms "and still more the prohibitions." He was roused against her at last, vibrant, even reckless, as he cataloged his complaints. But he could shed his submissiveness only so much, and he charged at her but retreated, too, using an awkward third person: "He wants to ask Mummy to try not to interfere with him so much. If he wants to take his clock to London, let him take it . . . if he wants to give away his great coat, let him—if he loses his glove, accept the fact." Each thing was so trivial in itself, it seemed absurd to mention them, "but they all add up into a loss of independence," he wrote. And he must gain his independence from her, as he had from Mohammed, if he were to finish the novel.

He closed with conciliatory chatter about how busy he was. He was to see Roger Fry, he had had his watch repaired, he had bought a volume of Hardy's poems. Morgan signed the letter, "Ever love as ever," as if signaling that in the end he was resigned that things would go on as before.

Morgan saved the letter, even as he burned successive rounds of his old correspondence in the decades after Lily's death. He may or may not have shocked Lily. But he had shocked himself. He wrote on it in the shakier hand of his later years, "Poppy kicks."

Chapter 10

"ELIOT DINED LAST SUNDAY & READ HIS POEM"

HEARING OF VIRGINIA'S LATEST RELAPSE in May, Tom wrote in sympathy to Leonard and added, "We know what constant illness is, and I think very few people do." This was as close to a personal confession as Eliot came in any of his letters to the Woolves at this time, a small shedding of the armor Aldous Huxley had described to Ottoline Morrell. Dealing with constant illness was a bond, usually left unspoken, that he and Leonard as husbands understood, and that he and Virginia, and indeed the two couples, also shared. Tom left unsaid, as he had in the autumn, that he, like Virginia, had relapsed, too, the return of his anxiety and depression more insidious in one way than influenza because it was without a foreseeable course. It was as if it were the autumn of 1921 all over again, as if his trip to Margate, and his treatment with Vittoz, had not happened at all; as if even his contentment at having finished his poem had dissipated now that, because of his own recalcitrance and procrastination, he was making the business of getting it published so difficult. To this were added the strains and delays involved in planning the *Criterion*, another way in which his ambitions for 1922—publishing his long poem, inaugurating his literary magazine, solidifying his position—seemed to slip farther from reach.

"I do not know whether it will work," he had written from Lausanne, before he and Pound had edited the nearly thousand-line poem into its final form of half that length. Now, the doubt was whether it would be published, a surprising turn of events. He had seemed so confident when he visited the Woolves at Hogarth House during the first week of March, when Virginia had written in her diary that he seemed to take heart having it safe in his desk. The difficulties with Thayer had already begun. But he had been able to hide any worry he might have begun to have behind his composed shell, and his cadaverous cosmetics. Now, after his high-handed, high-dudgeon demand for more money, the prospects for his poem seemed vastly different.

The uncertainty of the poem's future, his multiplying overdue assignments, including as yet unwritten work still owed the *Dial*, Vivien's worsening illnesses, even more physically debilitating than his own increasing depression through the spring—it all became too much to manage, the kink in his brain apparently no match for the techniques Vittoz had trained him in for attaining calm and mental control. There is nothing in any of Tom's or Vivien's voluminous and often very frank correspondence that spring to explain why the exercises that had so effectively calmed him in the winter were of no use or had been forgotten.

By mid-May, his mind, he confided to a friend, had "run down, so that at present I have to flog it for hours to produce the feeblest result," the latest of which was his next letter for the *Dial*, as much Vivien's work as his own, however. ("He was in a state of collapse," Vivien wrote a friend, "so *ill—he asked me what he should say* . . . and he just wrote it down, *anything*, not caring . . . in despair.") He and Vivien tried to live out of town, in Royal Tunbridge Wells, "for a needed change of air," though even the relatively easy commute to London, the hotel "only one step from the station," meant he had to get up every morning at six thirty, which, along with his constant anxiety about missing trains, meant, he wrote a friend, that "I get no benefit out of the country." Richard Aldington, a writer and former assistant editor of the *Egoist*, whom Eliot had asked to help with planning the *Criterion*, thought the situation catastrophic. "T. S. Eliot is very ill, will die if he doesn't get proper and complete rest for a long time," he wrote to the American poet Amy Lowell in the first week of May. The "sunshine and happiness" that returned to London that week, and that had such a revivifying effect on Forster and Woolf, brought no relief to Tom Eliot.

To get away for a long time was not possible, but his father-in-law offered a respite, what amounted to a second rest cure in Switzerland, a "4tnight's holiday," as quickly arranged with his indulgent superiors at Lloyds as his leave in the autumn had been, from May 20 to June 4, at the Hotel Bristol in Lugano, paid for completely by Mr. Haigh-Wood.

It turned out to be the tonic he needed to rescue him from collapse. He had "never felt quite so lazy and languid," he wrote, and spent his time "boating, bathing, eating, sleeping and making little trips about the lake," which was very beautifully "smothered in roses and wisteria," even if the town itself was overcrowded with hotels and "American trippers." He met Hermann Hesse for the first time, having already successfully solicited an article on "Recent German Poetry" from him for the first issue of the *Criterion*. The trip also allowed him to spend two days with Ezra Pound in Verona. Despite his difficulties with the London Letter for the *Dial*, the only thing he had attempted writing in the previous two months, the trip freed him to put *The Waste Land* through the sieve with Pound, in person, one more time.

Eliot had not seen Pound since January. The public announcement of the Bel Esprit plan had embarrassed Eliot, but as doubtful as Eliot was of how such a subsidy would work, or whether it would be generous enough, he did not ask Pound to stop his efforts. Nor did he actually express any willingness to leave the bank were a sufficient sum raised. Now the poet and his midwife were meeting on neutral ground, far away from the urban life that was overwhelming both of them for different reasons.

Pound and his wife, Dorothy, were in Italy to be away from Paris, where Pound had begun to find it impossible to work, not incidentally because of his efforts on Eliot's behalf. Through the early spring, Pound wrote privately to many potential supporters, including the poet William Carlos Williams and others, in what it became clear had been a rehearsal for the plan he soon announced publicly in the *New Age*. "I have been on the job, am dead tired with hammering this machine," he wrote. One reason it might have been convenient for Pound to publish the Bel Esprit plan in the *New Age*—whatever the cost to Eliot's pride and reputation—was simply that Pound would no longer have to write so many letters in search of individual subsidies. His personal pleas were reworded into the *New Age* manifesto, but then he left town, dramatically undercutting the likelihood that Bel Esprit would get off to a quick or lucrative start, his departure also suggesting he knew it was not feasible, a dream of a patronage that could not exist, even if it ought to.

Pound had warned friends that he was about to disappear, writing to John Quinn, "I shall be dead to the world," and to another friend, more definitively, "I am dead." He was writing from the World of Spirits, he added, and "had it put about" that he had died on Good Friday, telling his father of his temporary suicide, "I shall rise again at a suitable time," a resurrection—and return to Paris—that would come in three months rather than Christ's three days.

Just as Eliot had written geographical markers—King William Street, Margate Sands, Lac Leman—into his poem, Pound recounted his meeting with Eliot in the poem he was drafting during his trip, the "Malatesta Cantos," named for Sigismondo Pandolfo Malatesta, who was a fifteenth-century counterpart to Pound himself, both poet and patron of the arts and artists. In the draft, Pound described himself and Eliot in conversation with other friends at a café near the Roman arena in Verona. Pound styled Tom as "Thomas amics," a Provençal version of the French *ami*, friend or lover, and the scene outside the arena is more vital than the tired trappings of the show inside the arena—"the footlights, the clowns, dancers / performing dogs." Tom and Pound and their friends are drinking, but Eliot drinking with him in Verona was not the only thing on Pound's mind as he wrote. His several lines about Eliot were in effect the story of a quarrel over the fate of Eliot's poem, the progeny he had been the midwife to, and what milestone it might have been—and perhaps would yet be—in the future of poetry. Pound began his canto where Eliot's poem ended, his first line a "combative allusion" to one of Eliot's penultimate lines, written in Lausanne, "These fragments I have shored against my ruin," the very part of the poem that remained as Tom had written it and in which Pound had had the least hand. "These fragments you have shelved (shored)," Pound wrote, pointedly inserting "T. S. E." after "you" on one draft, a reference not only to Eliot's poem but also to the fact that Eliot had so far botched its publication. "Thomas amics" had shored his fragments at Lausanne, put them through the sieve with Pound, and then effectively shelved them—and their greatness—despite Pound's efforts.

Pound submitted the "Malatesta Cantos" to Eliot for the *Criterion* in 1923. Eliot requested one change. "I object strongly on tactical grounds to yr first line," he wrote. "People are inclined to think that we write our verses in collaboration as it is, or else that you write mine [and] I write yours. With your permission we will begin with line 2." Pound cut the line, which, once *The Waste Land* had been published, was no longer a private joke, but restored it when he published the poem in book form in 1925.

* * *

Leonard and Virginia returned to Richmond on Saturday, June 10, having spent ten days at Monk's House. The weather had been so good, "perfection is such that it becomes like a normal state," Virginia wrote in her diary. But it was not only the weather. The isolation of Rodmell had meant she could "slip easily from writing to reading with spaces between of walking," the seamless simplicity with which she lived "in the brain" there leaving her with the feeling that happiness, too, was normal. Back in Richmond, they were busy entertaining, but she was not distracted from her work, was in fact "working too hard; talking too much," and preparing *Jacob's Room* for the typist, Miss Green. Her temperature still fluctuated, despite the extraction of her three teeth. She was regretful at their loss, but on the other hand, here was more evidence that her doctors' prescriptions could profitably be ignored in the future. Even her "premonitory shivers" about the reception of *Jacob's Room*, which Leonard had yet to read, did not seem to weigh heavily on her.

Virginia had resolved to guard herself against what she called "my season of doubts & ups & downs" about *Jacob's Room*, convinced after her success with "Mrs. Dalloway in Bond Street" that the best answer to self-doubt was not to choose between her work on the story she wanted to write for Eliot, or continuing with her essay on reading, or accepting a review assignment that might be attractive. Doing one would not compromise the other or her vision. She saw herself, instead, moving easily among them, and had a "clever experiment" in mind. She would "vary the side of the pillow" as her mood suggested.

* * *

Morgan, in the wake of his "boom" in the *Times*, stayed at Hogarth on Thursday, June 15, after meeting Leonard for a dinner in London with Cambridge friends. The change over the past three months had been remarkable. In part he was buoyed by fame, in part by the work he had done, however careful and uninspired he sometimes thought it. In part it was also the social life he had resumed. It was revivifying to be talked about so favorably and so publicly, after so many months and years during which the main question among his friends, and even in his own mind, had been what was wrong with him. Far from the inanition of March, he was now "very calm, serene, like a kettle boiling by some private fire, a fire at Weybridge," Virginia wrote in her diary, her expansive mood fortified by the pleasure she was taking in her own work at the time. Morgan's old, fussy, exacting mother was still at Weybridge, of course, but Poppy was kicking, and he was feeling less subject to Lily's whims and prohibitions. He sat up late with Virginia and Leonard, talking about his book. It had been a long time since he had had a book to talk about, and now there was to be another one, as if he, too, saw some virtue in guarding himself against a season of doubts and ups and downs, as Virginia had decided to do. He agreed to collect some articles on Egypt for a book that the Hogarth Press would publish in 1923.

On Friday the sixteenth, he replied to Edward Arnold, who after reading about his long-silent author in the *Times* had written him inquiring whether Forster might be writing another novel. Forster was vague, only promising, "If I ever finish a novel, you shall certainly hear of it. Financial considerations alone, are tempting, for it ought to have a good sale thanks to Lucas Malet's timely tap. Public interest in me this morning has attained ¾ columns. It is all very queer."

A few days later, on Monday, June 19, he was back in London for a meeting of the Memoir Club. Both he and Lytton read contributions, another piece of work completed.

* * *

The night before the Memoir Club meeting, Eliot came to see Leonard and Virginia for the first time since his return from Switzerland and his visit in Verona with Pound. He came for dinner and, more significantly, had with him the poem that he had told them about in March. Then, too, he had come at almost the same time as Morgan. In March the contrast between the two of them had been very great, Tom confident of his best work, safe in his desk, and Morgan depressed to the point of inanition. Now, the two of them—and Virginia, too—were equally content and voluble.

Tom's time in Lugano had revived him even more than his visit to Lausanne had done, and by the time he saw the Woolves, on the evening of Sunday, June 18, he felt, he wrote a friend, "in very much better health than before I left, in fact in better physical health than I was when I came back from Switzerland in January." It showed in his demeanor during dinner with the Woolves, and it showed in the performance he gave afterward.

"Eliot dined last Sunday & read his poem," Virginia wrote in her diary.

"He sang it & chanted it rhythmed it. It has great beauty & force of phrase; symmetry; & tensity. What connects it together, I'm not so sure. But he read till he had to rush—letters to write about the London Magazine—& discussion was thus curtailed. One was left, however, with some strong emotion. The Waste Land, it is called."

It was fitting enough that Eliot had no time to discuss the poem. Distractions and obligations had shaped the writing of it, too, over many years. But his hasty departure may also simply have been a convenient excuse for him to avoid answering questions about his work, as he preferred to do whenever possible. After he had become a successful dramatist he remarked in an essay that in writing "other verse," nondramatic verse, "one is writing, so to speak, in terms of one's own voice: the way it sounds when you read it to yourself is the test. For it is yourself speaking." For Eliot, this did not mean that he was speaking of himself but rather that the rhythm, the chant, was the poet speaking. What the poet expressed was sound; what the reader wanted, usually, was sense. But this was not the poet's concern. "The question of communication, of what the reader will get from it, is not paramount." If the poem "is right to you, you can only hope that the readers will eventually come to accept it. The poem can wait a little while." Leaving the Woolves on Sunday, with or without letters to write, was a way of stating his case, and, conveniently, avoiding communication.

Eliot was better that June, but Vivien's condition was increasingly worse, her suffering as much the result of her doctors' ministrations as from the symptoms and pains of her colitis and other illnesses that had driven her to undertake more and more extreme and desperate regimens. At the recommendation of Ottoline Morrell, she had seen a new specialist, whose fashionable diagnosis was "glands." The "perfectly new and violent" experimental treatment the doctor proposed—doses of animal glands, together with a "very strong internal disinfection" requiring her to fast for two days a week—left her too weak, almost literally at wit's end, to see the Woolves or anyone else. Vivien's "constant illness" was once again left unspoken, the snippets of her pleas to her silent husband in the poem Tom sang and rhythmed and chanted a vivid enough reminder of her condition, and a revelation of his.

The next night, after the meeting of the Memoir Club, Clive Bell hosted a dinner at his home in Gordon Square. Tom's poem came up in conversation. It—and Eliot's friends—had not waited a little while at all. And it seemed that, in fact, it was the poet speaking, but not in the way Eliot's theory would have it. Mary Hutchinson had heard the poem, too, she said, and told the others she interpreted it to be "Tom's autobiography—a melancholy one."

"Mary Hutch," Virginia knew, was a confidante of the Eliots in a way she never truly had been. Occasionally jealous of Mary's intimacy with Eliot, more frequently dismissive of her charms (and intelligence) despite Clive's romantic attachment to her (she may have been occasionally jealous of that, too), Virginia on this evening was softened by Mary's solicitous warmth to her. "Yes, Mary kissed me on the stairs," she wrote in her diary. Mary had "crossed the room & purred in my ear." Perhaps in consequence of this show of affection, Virginia let Mary's interpretation of *The Waste Land* stand as her own at least tentative conclusion, and added nothing more.

* * *

Virginia's description of Tom's rhythming and chanting of *The Waste Land* caught an essential thing about Eliot, and his idea of the poet speaking. Tom's sister Ada, thirteen years his senior, wrote in her last letter to him before her death, in 1943, at seventy-four, "When you were a tiny boy, learning to talk, you used to sound the rhythm of the sentences without shaping words—the ups and downs of the thing you were trying to say. I used to answer you in kind, saying nothing yet conversing with you as we sat side by side on the stairs at 2635 Locust Street. And now you think the rhythm before the words in a new poem! . . . Such a dear little boy!"

His practice, in writing, was similar, sounding out the rhythm "to the accompaniment of a small drum," which was actually advice he passed along to at least one younger poet, and a style he followed in his readings, not only as Virginia described it, but in his two recordings of *The Waste Land*, made much later. Virginia had written that after hearing the poem she was left with "some strong emotion," but it was part of Eliot's design of the poem, and of his performance, that whatever emotions of Eliot's lay behind the poem were obscured. Eliot chanted, and did not emote, his voice absolutely flat, without inflection, what Leonard recalled, describing another of Tom's recitations, as "that curious monotonous sing-song in which all poets from Homer downwards have recited their poetry," all hints of implied meaning drained, the poet no more an authority on the meaning of the poem than the reader or listener: April | is | the | cruellest | month. Not *April* is the cruellest month, as if emphasizing there are other months more or less cruel, and that others, to whom the poet is responding, have said so. Not April *is* the cruellest month, as if to suggest there might be an argument, or any doubt, whether April is in fact the cruellest. Not April is *the* cruellest month, with any singularity to its cruelty. Nor that April is the *cruellest* month, as if to contradict the proposition that it is the kindest month, or that April is the cruellest *month*, emphasizing the interminable duration of what might sometimes seem a quickly moving thirty-day span in spring. One reader might hear the line any one of these ways, at one time or another. But the poet did not favor one, or suggest that there might be a particular meaning in the line at all.

When John Quinn once questioned Eliot about a passage in *The Waste Land*, Eliot replied not with the expected explanation but rather by laying out the method of his prosody. Perhaps Quinn didn't hear the poem the way Eliot did, the poet wrote. Eliot told Quinn that "the line itself punctuates" and was a self-contained entity of sound. He himself always paused at the end of a line, whether the punctuation, or perhaps even what appeared to be the sense, suggested otherwise. The pause between lines was another of the drumbeats that, as Virginia had heard, imposed a symmetry of sound and rhythmed the poem into a chant.

The sound of Tom's poetry and the sound of his conversation were not very different from one another, his general manner of speaking the same when he was a boy on Locust Street in Saint Louis or a grown man in a London drawing room. Ottoline Morrell recalled the frustration that, during one conversation with Eliot at Garsington, had led her to a "desperate attempt to break through his veil of reserve" by speaking in French. She hoped to disarm him but found that in French, as in English, he spoke with the same controlled forethought, "slowly, precisely and flatly." Another friend was to recall after Eliot's death that she was beguiled by the way he spoke in a "slightly booming monotone, without emphasis." His voice "lacked vanity," she thought, and was akin to a "bow drawn gently over a 'cello string & because of this one missed the exact sense. He didn't galvanize you with his words."

* * *

In the week following his dinner and performance at Hogarth House, Tom focused with renewed vigor on doing what he could to get his poem published in America in the autumn if there were still any chance it could happen. He had finally written to Knopf in mid-April, inquiring about Knopf's interest in his new poem for the autumn and adding rather mildly that he had met Liveright in Paris and he had made an offer. Knopf had replied on May 1 that though he wanted to publish more of Eliot's poetry, it was already too late for him to add a book to his list this year; his catalog of autumn books was ready to print. He advised him to accept Liveright's offer and said he would look forward to publishing Eliot's next work of prose instead. But now it was nearly July, and Eliot had not yet accepted Liveright's offer.

Liveright had, in the meantime, sent Eliot a contract—a very bad one, Eliot thought, and far more disadvantageous to the author than the contract John Quinn had negotiated for him with Knopf in 1919. It had been a long time since Eliot had been in touch with Quinn, who, when the Knopf negotiation had been finished, had advised Eliot that he should find a literary agent, which would be easier to do now than when he was unpublished, and unknown, in America. But Eliot had not sought a literary agent, and now he had no other alternative than to contact Quinn, by cable, despite the expense, on Wednesday, June 21.

DISSATISFIED LIVERIGHTS CONTRACT POEM MAY I ASK
YOUR ASSISTANCE APOLOGIES WRITING ELIOT.

Quinn cabled his reply immediately.

GLAD TO ASSIST EVERYWAY POSSIBLE YOUR CONTRACT.

He would be willing to see Liveright in person, if necessary, and awaited further instructions from Eliot by the letter his cable had promised.

Quinn's reverence for artists and writers and his generous financial support of many were at odds with his general misanthropy and the anti-Semitic tirades prompted by the slightest imagined offense of Liveright's or Knopf's. When in the course of dealing with Eliot's contract he had difficulty getting either on the phone in the summer of 1922, he complained to Eliot about their congenitally inconstant work habits and told him he had ultimately "treed" both of them: "You may observe this use of the Simian-verb 'to tree' with reference to these two publishers." And if either did not respond with alacrity to some request of his, he took it, as he called one of Liveright's delays, "a dirty piece of Jew impertinence, calculated imperti-nence at that, for that is the way that type of Jew bastard thinks that he can impress his personality. . . . I never forget things like that and I always repay with justice and exactitude."

But he was loyal to those for whom he had affection and regard, includ-ing Eliot, whose work he thought important. His avuncular embrace of Eliot was strengthened by the fact that Eliot had never asked him for finan-cial assistance, as Joyce had (though Quinn had promised Pound a gener-ous subscription to the Bel Esprit plan). Eliot and Quinn never met in person, but despite their many differences, of age, and income, and tem-perament, they had in common exhausting lives lived, as Eliot once wrote to Quinn, "with the leisure that you want always a mirage ahead of you, your holidays always disturbed by unforeseen (or foreseen) calamities." Responding in kind, Quinn was likely to offer advice far afield from the literary or legal. "Now, take off the time and go to your dentist," he wrote Eliot on one occasion. "That is rather important, much more important than having your hair cut. I know just what it is to be so busy that one cannot go to the dentist or have one's hair cut. But it is a mistake to allow yourself to be that driven," advice that was easier for Quinn to offer than to follow.

In response to Quinn's reassuring cable, Eliot wrote a letter similar to the other letters of apology and excuse he had become practiced at writing to Thayer and to others that year, begging pardon for his unavoidable inattention to serious matters, regretful as he was that he must ask for extra time or another indulgence because of his wife's or his own health.

The Liveright contract was unnecessarily vague, Eliot thought, "and gives all the advantage to the publisher," with Eliot seeming to sign away to Liveright world rights, translation rights, control of periodical and anthology publication, all of which made it "tantamount to selling him the book outright" for $150 and a 15 percent royalty. It was not a matter of money—this was the arrangement Liveright had proposed in Paris—but Eliot hoped Quinn could negotiate one closer to the terms of the Knopf contract for his previous book, encompassing only American and Canadian book rights and a copyright in Eliot's own name. Quinn agreed and, in turn, told Eliot that if Liveright would not accept the terms Quinn demanded, it was just as well for Eliot. There were other publishers, and Quinn, in any case, was always eager to slip out of business with a Jew, preferring that writers simply dealt with publishers named Harper or Scribner. Liveright had been interested in publishing the Eliot poems that Knopf had ultimately done in 1920 but had backed off at the last moment. Now Knopf was not to publish Eliot's new book, and here they were dealing with Liveright again. Must Quinn's own work always be "to tree" a Jewish publisher on Eliot's behalf?

Quinn's dissatisfaction with Liveright was particularly intense at the moment, since fresh in his mind was Pound's account of Liveright's other offer over dinner in Paris, to publish *Ulysses*. Quinn knew Liveright had not had the courage to do so the previous year, and knew, too, that he would not do it in 1922, despite the offer. Liveright was making good on his Paris offer to Eliot, but with a contractual perfidy that made him no more trustworthy on this than on the *Ulysses* question. Quinn assured Eliot it would be easy for him to arrange for another publisher to do the book, which might have calmed Eliot if he were not so anxious that *The Waste Land* be published this year. Quinn's letter would not have arrived in London until the first week of July at the earliest. Quinn was sure about eventual publication, by another publisher, ideally of non-Semitic origin. Eliot was concerned with publication as soon as possible.

Still hopeful that the poem would be published in the autumn, Eliot nevertheless gave Quinn power of attorney to do as he liked with the Liveright contract, including to refuse it. In a letter he wrote on Sunday the twenty-fifth, a week after his visit to the Woolves, he told Quinn he would send him a copy of the poem "as quickly as possible . . . merely for your own interest." He now planned to add notes, partly a stratagem to bulk up the book, addressing Liveright's concern in January that the poem might be too short on its own. He also promised Quinn he would send the complete typescript "in the form to be handed to the publisher." Liveright still had not read the poem.

Eliot had read the poem aloud to the Woolves. Presumably he did not read it from memory and there was some typed version available. But it now took him three more weeks to do what he'd promised Quinn to do quickly, once again undermining, and perhaps fatally, his hope that his poem would be published soon.

It had been in nearly finished form since January. It is impossible to explain why Eliot could not find, and did not make, any time in all those months to type a new draft of the poem, possibly even to take advantage of yet another time through Pound's sieve, or his own, in the realistic anticipation that a publisher would eventually need a clean typescript from which to set the poem, whether for book publication or in a periodical. (In April, Pound had written to a friend in New York inquiring whether *Vanity Fair* might be interested in the poem, and how much it might pay Eliot, but nothing came of it.) It is even harder to conceive why he did not have a professional typist type one or perhaps more copies, at a likely minimal expense, if he did not have time to do it himself.

Since he had not typed it, and did not type it, he had more apologies to make, even as he left it to Quinn to negotiate with Liveright. On July 19, Eliot sent Quinn a provisional version for Liveright, regretful that he had not yet been able to "type it out fair, but I did not wish to delay it any longer." The version Eliot was sending would be enough for Liveright "to get on with," if the contract was signed, "and I shall rush forward the notes to go at the end."

The entire publication of *The Waste Land* was a litany of apologies. Knowing it was his best work, Eliot urged the publisher's special care with the typescript—"I only hope the printers are not allowed to bitch the punctuation and the spacing, as that is very important for the sense," he wrote to Quinn about Liveright—and yet he had not taken the time to retype a fresh copy for Liveright to work from, as he had promised to do a month before. The delays he had created compounded his worry about the text, because with so little time before publication, it was impossible for the typesetting and correcting of proofs to proceed at a normal pace. Time was too tight, and it would take too long for Eliot to receive and return more than one set of corrections across the Atlantic. Nor had he yet written the promised notes, a new endeavor at just the moment he was also becoming most worried about the *Criterion*.

Chapter 11

WOMEN IN LOVE IN COURT

AN ATTRACTIVELY PRINTED BROCHURE announced that a 1,250-copy limited edition of D. H. Lawrence's *Women in Love* would be published by a new firm, Thomas Seltzer, Inc., in November 1920. The brochure, alluding to the scandal of Lawrence's *The Rainbow* and promising the same kind of reading experience with its sequel, did as much as possible to entice readers while doing what it could to avoid provoking the censors.

> With Lawrence passion looms large, but great passion is always near to great spirit, and "Women in Love" will eventually baffle the sensation hunters, because Lawrence, although unhesitatingly accepting, even celebrating the flesh, is quick to discover and proclaim the divinest essences.

The title page of the book listed no publisher ("Privately Printed for Subscribers Only"), and the edition sold steadily but modestly over the next eighteen months. Lawrence's reputation continued to grow, particularly with the successful publication of *The Lost Girl* in the United States, by Seltzer, and in Britain, but at $15 the subscription edition of *Women in Love* was an item for rarefied wallets in any case. And when, on a hot Friday afternoon in early July 1922, John Sumner, of the New York Society for the Suppression of Vice, paid an unwelcome call at Seltzer's offices across the street from St. Patrick's Cathedral, there were plenty of unsold copies of Lawrence's novel available to be seized.

Lawrence was in Australia, Eliot in London—but at the beginning of July, New York was the place that mattered most to their futures.

* * *

The New York Society for the Suppression of Vice, founded in 1873, was approaching its fiftieth anniversary. It had been a pioneering organization, the first of its kind in the United States, a private group that, upon its founding, was given law-enforcement responsibilities. Its founder and guiding spirit, Anthony Comstock, had led the organization, funded by the crusading Comstock's wealthy patrons, for more than four of those decades. When he died, in 1915, he was succeeded by Sumner, a figure who loomed smaller in the public imagination. Comstock's legend—his belly and whiskers as grandiose as his "lush" prose fulminating against "Base Villains"—proved enduring enough that Margaret Anderson, whose *Little Review* excerpts of *Ulysses* were first suppressed in 1917, recalled in her memoirs that the magazine had been "suppressed by Anthony Comstock," even though he had been dead for two years by then.

The continuing prosecution of the *Little Review* for its *Ulysses* excerpts and now of Seltzer for *Women in Love* was the handiwork of Comstock's successor, a Long Island stockbroker whose hobbies were golf and driving. Sumner, as nettlesome and indefatigable as Comstock, never escaped his shadow, though he was relentless and successful at policing the "many subdivisions of commercialized vice," including motion pictures, plays, and photographs and artwork for sale. He was also more inventive than Comstock. Sumner proudly recalled in an unpublished memoir that it had been his own innovation to prosecute a fiction magazine—the *Little Review*—which was something his predecessor had never thought to do.

Vice societies had proliferated across America in the late nineteenth century, to counteract the supposed loosening of moral codes brought on by the evils of urbanization and immigration. Their crusade against immoral literature as an incitement to crime and as a perversion of youth was part of a campaign dedicated to progressive causes, including anti–child labor laws and the elimination of poverty. Even Comstock himself, who had "conspicuously made an ass of himself" on many occasions, was respected by many, including some of his enemies, for having done much good if literature were left out of the accounting. It was a big if.

For it was true of Comstock, and true of Sumner, that fulminating about the dangers of a book didn't warn readers away: the attacks made it easier for them to pay attention, giving publicity to novels and nonfiction books that in almost every case would have had a lower public profile, and smaller sales, had they been published without prosecutorial fanfare. A *New York Times* editorial criticizing Sumner's efforts ran under the headline "Advertising Bad Books."

The society's targets were publishers and booksellers: Margaret Anderson and her partner in the *Little Review*, Jane Heap, not Joyce; Thomas Seltzer, not D. H. Lawrence. The author was both victim and innocent bystander, an interested party left out of the equation, except for the cost to his reputation. When *The Rainbow* had been suppressed in England, in 1915, and Methuen, the publisher, agreed to withdraw all copies, Lawrence wrote to his friend Cynthia Asquith, "This is most irritating. Some interfering person goes to a police magistrate and says, 'This book is indecent, listen here.' Then the police magistrate says, 'By Jove, we'll stop that.' Then the thing is suppressed." An appeal against the damning verdict was available only to the publisher, Lawrence complained—it was "an entitlement useless to the author," who, no matter how offensive his work was deemed to be, was not the offending party.

Sumner, "Decency's local representative," took the name of his society seriously and lived up to it, though he rejected the word "censorship" as a misrepresentation of his work because "the word was offensive to people in general." Instead, he thought of himself as a kind of curator, who culled the unsuitable in service of a higher and purer ideal of what literature or art or entertainment—and people—ought to be.

Of the sensational in books, Sumner wrote, "We are told that this literature merely reflects the life of the time and that this is what the people want. Neither statement is true. Such literature may and probably does reflect the life of a certain minor element of the population and there is a certain type of reader who no doubt demands it. Well, there is a certain part of the public that wants narcotic drugs, but very strict laws prohibit their sale.

"Does not the demand for salacious literature also come from a newly created class of addicts?"

Hapless readers were as much victims of predatory miscreants as those lured into gambling dens or lives of iniquity as prostitutes, and in his 1922 annual report, Sumner complained of new dangers then spreading like an infection: an "ebbtide of moral laxity, as a result of the great war, has revealed itself ominously," and led to a market for, and tolerance of, objectionable material of every kind, from postcards to motion pictures. Sumner's detailed monthly reports to his board of managers suggest he and his small staff were almost submerged beneath the weight of the moral infirmity around him. Books were only one part of a vast, creeping danger. Calls and letters came in from an army of concerned citizens, or busybodies. Every variety of moral affront was their daily business; the society's most public acts, and its most publicized, were against books and theater, but more time was spent, on a daily and monthly basis, with "vice" of a private nature. The society reported—to its managers and to the police— on "degenerates" lurking on street corners, in high schools, in subway stations, and even in fine neighborhoods. In the weeks before his July call on Thomas Seltzer, Sumner received a letter signed "McK. Hotchkiss" informing the society of "activities of [a] negro woman, Fanny Woods, using premises 230 Riverside Drive for immoral purposes." The report was referred to a police inspector for "investigation and action." Nothing was too small to escape the notice of a nosy neighbor, or Sumner's enumeration of it to those paying his salary: "Anonymous woman called stating that indecent pictures and writings on the walls appeared in premises 163 West 21st Street and 22 West 21st Street." The society "investigated and at both places the janitor promised to remove the objectionable matter." Sumner also wrote to the lessee of 163—a "Mr. Rappaport"—to suggest "that walls be painted a dark color which would discourage those inclined to deface them in this manner." Quite conveniently for the offended woman and for Sumner, these addresses were around the corner from the society's own offices on West Twenty-Second Street.

Even older than the society was the precedent that still for the most part controlled legal decisions regarding obscenity. *Regina v. Hicklin*, decided in 1868, in England, but followed in American courts into the twentieth century, had deemed a publication obscene if "the tendency of the matter . . . is to deprave and corrupt those whose minds are open to such immoral influence and into whose hands publication of this sort may fall." This definition, which in effect meant isolated passages of supposedly questionable purity could condemn an entire work, was used effectively in 1921, when Margaret Anderson and Jane Heap were once again on trial for publishing an excerpt of *Ulysses* (in the July–August 1920 issue). Anderson thought the essential question was "the relation of the artist—the great writer to the public. . . . *I state clearly that the (quite unnecessary!) defense of beauty is the only issue involved.*" But the law did not agree with her. Though not required to, the judges in that case allowed the defense attorney, John Quinn, the lawyer who was also Eliot's patron, to call three experts to the stand to testify to the literary quality of Joyce's work. This was a defense of beauty; but though their testimony was allowed, it did not affect the result, which was conviction, in February 1921, setting in train the wriggling of Huebsch and Liveright that was to so enrage Quinn, and once again infuriated him a year later when Pound told him of Liveright's professed interest in publishing *Ulysses*.

Between the publication of the *Little Review* in summer 1920 and its trial the following winter had come Seltzer's edition of *Women in Love* with its title page pointedly without a publisher. At the same time that Sumner seized it and two other Seltzer books, *Casanova's Homecoming*, by Arthur Schnitzler, and the anonymous *A Young Girl's Diary*, another case was decided. It set a new precedent of which Seltzer might take advantage.

* * *

The limited edition of *Women in Love* had been among the first books published by the new company created by Thomas Seltzer after the dissolution of a brief partnership, Scott & Seltzer, which he had formed with an editor named Temple Scott. Seltzer had published his first Lawrence book, *Touch and Go: A Play in Three Acts*, in June 1920. *Women in Love* followed in November, and by the spring of 1921 there would be three more, *The Lost Girl*; *The Widowing of Mrs. Holroyd*, a play; and *Psychoanalysis and the Unconscious*, an essay. This would have been a glut of the marketplace—Lawrence's essay sold only seven hundred copies—even if 1921 had not been a disastrous year for publishing. Seltzer had started his firm at a time of "business panic," as his wife, Adele, explained to her family about her husband's new venture. "The salesman in the West says if things keep on the same way, he'll starve, and he represents some of the largest houses besides Thomas Seltzer, Inc."

The Lost Girl had, however, sold four thousand copies within a few months of publication in 1921, persuading Seltzer to postpone *Aaron's Rod*, the novel Lawrence had completed that June, until the spring of 1922 so that he could continue to promote *The Lost Girl*. "Business is extremely dull, practically dead," Seltzer wrote to Lawrence's agent, Robert Mountsier. Despite the business doldrums, they were nevertheless in the midst of what Seltzer rather grandly—and self-aggrandizingly—called a "Lawrence boom," which really meant that *The Lost Girl* was selling. Sales of the several other Lawrence books he'd published were weak, but there was "hardly a literary page we pick up that has not some mention or other" about one of them. Seltzer assured Mountsier he was still "spending money freely on publicity for Lawrence." (Perhaps this was why Seltzer and his wife, however much they were "benefactors of writers," were also "never very far from insolvency.") Seltzer had faith in Lawrence's nonfiction and thought that even *Psychoanalysis and the Unconscious* might sell, given a chance. He also hoped *Sea and Sardinia*, excerpts of which Mabel Dodge would see in the *Dial*, would be a lucrative spring 1922 title. *Aaron's Rod* should come after that, Seltzer proposed.

Lawrence had initially been wary of tying himself up with Seltzer's new firm at all and had specifically not wanted a "semi-private publication" of *Women in Love*. But he agreed to go ahead, prophesying that the book would be either a *succès d'estime* or a *succès de scandale*. He had not thought, it seems, that it might be one at first and the other later.

Women in Love sold steadily enough, "considering the times," that after six months Seltzer thought a second subscriber edition, including signed copies, would soon be necessary. A sold-out edition would be lucrative, but the key to the publisher's hope for Lawrence's future, he wrote to Mountsier in June 1921, was whether *Aaron's Rod* is "really unobjectionable," as Lawrence had told him it was. Lawrence had only just finished writing the book, and Seltzer had not yet read it. But he was confident that to follow the popular *Lost Girl* with another novel "against which there is no definite objection . . . would give Lawrence a very strong position here. After that we need fear no antagonism." Seltzer predicted (wrongly, as it turned out) that by January 1922 the limited edition of *Women in Love* would be exhausted. But he also believed that following large sales of an unobjectionable *Aaron's Rod*, even *Women in Love* could at last be published for general circulation later in the year.

But Seltzer was too sanguine. The success of *The Lost Girl* did not change Lawrence's reputation. Secker had found this out, too: his English edition of *Women in Love* in the summer of 1921 ran into the familiar trouble with *John Bull*. The critic for the *Brooklyn Daily Eagle* might praise *Aaron's Rod*, but he also knew its author was still "the sex-obsessed Mr Lawrence." However much Seltzer claimed to worry about Lawrence's reputation or his own, he continued to capitalize on it. His June 1922 advertisement for *Aaron's Rod* in the *New-York Tribune* echoed his circular for the 1920 *Women in Love* and his spring promotional pamphlet "D. H. Lawrence: The Man and His Work," and declared, "The work of a great genius and a bestseller. Love and Marriage in our day as Lawrence sees it." The same month Lawrence's name could be invoked as comic shorthand for the risqué at the "offish little" Neighborhood Playhouse in lower Manhattan, where a revue, *The Grand Street Follies*, was drawing crowds. The show, riding the coattails of the *Ziegfeld Follies* of 1922, was a "delightfully carefree" hit, the *Tribune* reported, a "low-brow show for high-grade morons," using quotation marks that suggest this may have been the production's own tag line.

In one skit, a young man was trying to get the attention of his sweetheart, who was content to read a book instead. "Don't interrupt me," she told him. "I am in the midst of one of the most passionate passages of D. H. Lawrence."

Seltzer included the anecdote in one of his long business letters to Mountsier, who was out of town in rural Pennsylvania for the summer. "This, they say, always brings the house down." That Lawrence had entered into common parlance brought credit to him as his publisher, and reporting it might serve as yet another defense against Mountsier's complaints about Lawrence's generally weak sales and Seltzer's unfavorable contractual terms that the agent suggested other publishers would be willing to better.

But here was a joke about the very thing that most worried John Sumner and the Society for the Suppression of Vice: the poisoning of a young girl's mind by reading a book.

Knowing nothing of the *Follies*, Lawrence wrote Seltzer from Australia on June 9 to report on his progress on *Kangaroo*, and the fact that there was "no love interest at all so far—don't intend any—no sex either." And he made his own joke. "Amy Lowell says you are getting a reputation as an erotic publisher: she warns me. I shall have thought my reputation as an erotic writer (poor dears) was secure. So now I'll go back on it."

The erotic writer soon enough got stuck again. But that was not to be Lawrence's—or his erotic publisher's—only problem that summer. The *Follies* joke, and his own, soon shared a different punch line.

* * *

Late in the afternoon of Friday, July 7, Sumner raided the Seltzer offices, at 5 West Fiftieth Street. Nearly eight hundred copies of the three books, Lawrence's, Schnitzler's, and the anonymous *Diary*, notable for its foreword by Sigmund Freud, were "pinched by the PO-lice."

Seltzer was charged with violating Section 1141 of the New York State Penal Code, the statute dealing with "the publication and sale of obscene literature," as the *Times* decorously put it. The sweep of Seltzer's office was so complete that copies of books from other publishers were "taken by Mr. Sumner's command," after they were discovered in Seltzer's locked desk, which he agreed to open "under threat of having it forced."

Sumner's target was *A Young Girl's Diary*, about which he had received a complaint in June from an informer. Sumner immediately deputized a colleague who "called on Thomas Seltzer," as Sumner collegially reported to his board, and purchased a copy of the book from him. Sumner read *A Young Girl's Diary*, believed it to be actionable, and, beginning official action, "marked [it] for presentation" to the Seventh District Court. The complaint was filed, and on July 7, Sumner was given a summons and search warrant. He went to the Seltzer offices with a warrant officer of the West Side Police Court, who with Sumner oversaw the packing up of the hundreds of books. Seltzer was given a receipt for the copies; they had left it up to him whether he would hire—at his own expense—a trucker to take the books away, or whether Sumner would send a police patrol wagon for them. Seltzer decided to pay for it himself, a way of symbolically affirming at the outset his refusal, all along, to concede any criminality in the publication or distribution of the books. The receipt was in the name of the district attorney, a reminder that Sumner was a private citizen still working under a city license granted nearly fifty years ago to Comstock. Copies of A Young Girl's Diary were also seized from Brentano's, on Fifth Avenue and Twenty-Seventh Street. It was the only one of the three Seltzer books available there, the Times reported. (The society ignored Aaron's Rod during its visit to Brentano's, despite the novel's popularity at the moment. It was listed that week in the Tribune as Brentano's best-selling novel. F. Scott Fitzgerald's The Beautiful and Damned was number five.) Mary Marks, a clerk at Womrath's, a circulating library, was also arrested, and charged with lending A Young Girl's Diary to "divers persons."

There had been no mention of Women in Love in Sumner's monthly board reports before the seizure, and it seems he read the book only after it was taken, blandly noting among his activities for the month of July, "Also read books: 'Women in Love.'" Sumner had received complaints about Casanova's Homecoming in 1921 but, unusually, had taken no action.

The title of Women in Love was obviously suggestive enough, even without any knowledge of its contents or its author's reputation. It might almost be a sequel to A Young Girl's Diary, chronicling that anonymous author's continuing sexual development. The title of the third book, Casanova's Homecoming, was as damning as Schnitzler's foreign name. And though the "young girl" who had written the diary was anonymous, the penumbra of the alien (and sexual) hung over it, too. Freud's name and endorsement of the book's importance were featured on the cover.

That Sumner and the society seized books from so many Jewish publishers—Liveright, Knopf, and Ben Huebsch were perennial targets—was not a coincidence. He was ecumenical enough that he prosecuted publishers with names like Harper, Scribner, and Lippincott whenever possible, too, but Sumner did not think of them in league with one another against good taste and American purity as he did of the Jewish publishers whose offerings he deplored. Sumner's crusade against obscene plays was even more aggressive than his attacks on publishers in 1921 to

1923, and he fulminated against the Jewish producers who were responsible for polluting the city's stages, urging Americans "to rescue its theatre from 'foreigners.'"

Seltzer, born in Russia in 1875, had immigrated to the United States with his family in 1887. He graduated from the University of Pennsylvania, a scholarship student, in 1897, and did postgraduate work in modern languages, so that in addition to English, Russian, and Yiddish, the languages of his childhood, he was conversant in Polish, German, French, and Italian. He translated Maxim Gorky, and before starting his imprint he was a journalist and a founding editor of *Masses*, one of the intellectual "giants of the Village." (Seltzer had more "spark" than Martin Secker, Lawrence's English publisher, Frieda once wrote.) Seltzer was also the uncle of Liveright's partners Albert and Charles Boni, with whom he had formed the imprint Boni & Liveright in 1917.

The seizure was a catastrophe for Seltzer's firm and for him personally. His wife, Adele, had only just left for a summer vacation in Ontario, where he was to join her at the end of the month. He waited a week to write her, holding off until he thought news of the "dramatic occurrence" could not be withheld from her any longer. The invasion of his office, the seizure of the books, the publicity, his outrage: "Of course the burden upon me was terrific. . . . At first I thought I'd break under it—all alone and with so much other work," he told Adele, an even greater champion of Lawrence than her husband. Lawrence "enslaves me," Adele wrote a friend in the summer of 1922. "But he is lots more to me than that. Lawrence is the throbbing vital life of today with the genius of a sort of a combination of Shakespeare and Dostoevsky."

Seltzer had also waited until he could tell Adele what he had decided to do. On the twelfth, Seltzer's lawyer, Jonah Goldstein, announced that he would not seek to have the charges dismissed. Seltzer had been buoyed by supportive letters praising him for having published the books, he told Adele, and convinced, as she was, that Lawrence was the greatest writer of his time, he wanted to protect his investment but also his principles. Goldstein told the *Times* that he had read the books carefully and was confident that they were "in my judgment, classics of the day." The three books that had been seized had just the opposite effect than Sumner charged, Goldstein claimed, and in fact they tended "to elevate the tone and the morals of the community."

The case "is being conducted properly, I think, and it looks hopeful," Seltzer assured his wife. "We are up against a gang of toughs, but Goldstein seems to know how to fight them. . . . The papers are all with us and we are putting up a big fight."

* * *

Nothing about the seizure of *Women in Love* could have surprised "the sex-obsessed" Mr. Lawrence, except perhaps the society's long delay in discovering the novel, particularly after the *John Bull* attacks on Secker's edition the previous year in England. But he did not hear about it from either Seltzer or Robert Mountsier in the five weeks between Sumner's visit to Seltzer's office and his departure from Sydney, on August 11.

Why neither Seltzer nor Mountsier felt news of "the big fight" was urgent enough to cable to Lawrence is unclear. Seltzer wrote a letter that did not reach Lawrence before he left Australia. Lawrence read it only after he arrived in the United States, by which time it was no longer news. Lawrence's June 21 letter, reporting that he'd finished more than half of *Kangaroo*, would have likely reached Seltzer not long after the publisher's first appearance in court.

The prospects for Lawrence's *next* novel, even one without any love at all in it, were likely to be an afterthought, given Seltzer's preoccupation with his defense against Sumner. But it turned out that the hiatus in productivity Lawrence feared had been only days, not years, as it had been for his two previous "stuck" novels. It had been a fortuitous pause. He had found his way forward.

Kangaroo is set entirely in Australia—except for the one chapter Lawrence wrote after he resumed work. But in order to account for why Richard Lovat Somers—or David Herbert Lawrence—was there, he began to write about the one episode in his life that he had not yet touched on in his fiction: his and Frieda's experiences during the war. Frieda had told Mrs. Jenkins that Lawrence had written "his head off" until chapter eleven. The twelfth chapter is set in England during the first years of the war. The fear Lawrence had felt at the vastness of the Australian bush during his short stay in Perth was a fear he carried within him, and which he gave to his protagonist. Lawrence broke off writing after an unnerving conversation between Somers and Kangaroo. Will Somers stay loyal to him? Is his future with the movement Kangaroo leads? Somers doesn't know. And apparently neither did Lawrence. Somers is walking through Sydney on a Saturday night. The shops are closed, and the streets were, Lawrence wrote, "dark and dreary, though thronging with people. Dark streets, dark, streaming people. And fear. One could feel such fear, in Australia." The chapter ended. The inspiration that had carried him two-thirds of the way through the novel had unexpectedly failed. It was if Lawrence had written at full tilt until he could simply not see where Somers might go next.

In the next chapter, Lawrence explored where the fear had set in. Forster had told the Memoir Club in his recent contribution that he had looked into the "lumber-room of my past" and had found things that "were mine and useful." Lawrence, at the same moment, did it, too. He wrote as if his protagonist (and he himself) had taken to a psychoanalyst's couch, with Somers "lying perfectly still and tense" as he thought out "detail for detail . . . his experience with the authorities, during the war. . . . Till now, he had always kept the memory at bay, afraid of it. Now it all came back, in a rush. It was like a volcanic eruption in his consciousness."

In a novel of eighteen chapters, all of them roughly ten to twenty pages, the twelfth chapter, which Lawrence called "The Nightmare," is the longest and, at almost fifty pages, more than twice as long as any of the others.

Lawrence went through all that had happened to Frieda and him between the start of the war and their departure from England in 1917. "It was in 1915 the old world ended. . . . The integrity of London collapsed, the city, in some way, perished, perished from being a heart of the world, and became a vortex of broken passions, lusts, hopes, fears, and horrors . . . the genuine debasement began, the unspeakable baseness of the press and the public voice, the reign of that bloated ignominy, John Bull." He described the shock of the "very strict watch" on Frieda and himself, and the humiliation of being "called up"—the judgment of his "thin nakedness," the "ignominious" rejection as "unfit" that was a relief to him. "Let them label me unfit. . . . I know my own body is fragile, in its way, but also it is very strong, and it's the only body that would carry my particular self."

The exhortation of the doctor who decided he was unfit was to "find some way for himself of serving his country." Somers, as Lawrence did, "thought about that many times. But always . . . he knew that he simply could not commit himself to any service whatsoever. In no shape or form could he serve the war, neither indirectly or directly." He would be "forced into nothing" not of his own volition. He would "act from his soul alone."

Finally the military authorities order the couple to leave the county of Cornwall "within the space of three days." Then, wherever it was they would go in England, they must "report themselves at the police station of the place," and give their address, within twenty-four hours. As they left Cornwall Somers experienced "one of his serious deaths in belief." And so began the "long adventure" that led Richard and Harriet Somers out of England and to "this free Australia," where they came to feel the "same terror and pressure" of being "suspect again, two strangers."

When Lawrence finished the chapter, he, and the novel, returned to the present and to the story of Frieda and himself in Australia, and to the story of Kangaroo, who is killed in a street fight between his vigilante forces and the union men. Lawrence, less a visionary than he sometimes fancied himself, could not prophesy the future of fascism, and it seems he did not know how the novel should end. Halfway through it he called it a "funny sort of novel where nothing happens and such a lot of things should happen." He understood that figures like Mussolini, who had risen to political prominence as Lawrence was preparing to leave Italy, would gain, or seize, power; he made the danger of their seductive rhetoric clear in the clarity with which he depicted Somers's overwhelming but seemingly unwilled physical attraction to Kangaroo that leads to at least a temporary political acquiescence, too. But Lawrence stopped short of imagining, at least in *Kangaroo*, what the ramifications of such an attraction would be, for Somers, or for the masses. Kangaroo's death was a convenient plot twist, and convenient for Lawrence's projected schedule. Lawrence wanted to send off the manuscript of his novel so that it might reach the United States before he did. It, like he and Frieda, had a boat to catch. He wrote the rest of the book in little more than two weeks after he resumed work and was able to mail it to the United States at the end of the week that had begun with Seltzer's promise to put up a big fight.

Kangaroo, the novel, has as unceremonious an end as Kangaroo himself. Lawrence came to the end of a notebook, and he has Somers and his wife leave Australia, just as he and Frieda were about to do. Their boat sets sail. And the novel is over. Lawrence's experiment in form had been a complete success. He had written a novel in six weeks. Its first sentences described Richard and Harriet's arrival, and its last sentences their departure. In America he revised the ending of the novel, or rather added to it by adding an account of his and Frieda's last three weeks in Australia. This made it neater. Mountsier advised that "The Nightmare" should be cut. It was a digression. It had nothing to do with the story.

Lawrence considered it. But when he had revised the novel and sent it off, he was adamant. "The Nightmare" must remain. The key to the whole book, and to what he had hoped to achieve in writing it, had been to recall Frieda's and his experience as it had really been. "Have kept in the *War* piece," he wrote Mountsier, "it must be so. The book is now as I want it."

It had not seemed to him when he went to Ceylon, or to Perth, or to Sydney or Thirroul, that he was coming closer to unlocking a past that he had so completely—but so uneasily—kept at bay. Lawrence, like Proust and like Forster, had discovered during his months at Wyewurk how to make use of his memories and impressions. Somers's fears were Lawrence's, and waking from his nightmare by writing about it, Lawrence decided, along with his counterpart, "The judgments of society were not valid to him. . . . In his soul he was cut off, and from his own isolated soul he would judge."

Virginia was at work on "Mrs. Dalloway in Bond Street" at the time Lawrence wrote his "Nightmare" chapter. Their approaches reflected their different styles and aims, and also their different experiences of the war itself, but they both wrote from the same awareness of it as a present thing, and even with the same fictional provocation for their characters. Somers, walking in Sydney on a Saturday night, thinks the city streets will be an escape, except that "by bad luck," the crowds of people terrify him as in a way he hasn't felt in years, and the past returns to him as he walks. Mrs. Dalloway, setting out on her errand, is walking in London and thinks, "The war is over," but her thought was, of course, proof that the war wasn't over. It is still in Clarissa's mind, as it was in the shopgirl's, still a way of measuring everyday experience, including the quality of gloves. The sound of Big Ben with its eleven chimes was a reminder of the war; the noise from the street an unnerving sound that could no longer simply be an automobile backfiring. Any kind of explosive report might never be just a noise in the street again.

The war had affected not only the men who died. Neither Somers nor Clarissa could be distracted from what Eliot's narrator, amid the crowds flowing over London Bridge, also knew: that "death had undone so many." Memories that had been buried persisted. This was the "modern twist" of the Proustian "adventure" that Forster identified: art could render the internal in ways that had never been tried before. "Mrs. Dalloway in Bond Street," *Kangaroo*, and *The Waste Land* all depicted the glaring contradiction of 1922: the war was over but had not ended.

* * *

Thomas Seltzer's "big fight" against John Sumner and the New York Society for the Suppression of Vice was made easier by a decision of the New York State Court of Appeals in another obscenity case, coincidentally announced on the very day that Seltzer's lawyer was interviewed about his plans by the *Times*. This case had its roots in the society's November 1917 arrest of a bookseller, Raymond D. Halsey, for selling a copy of the nineteenth-century French novel *Mademoiselle de Maupin* by Théophile Gautier. Halsey had been arrested, as Seltzer and Mary Marks were, for violating Section 1141 of the penal code, for having sold a book that was, according to the statute, "obscene, lewd, lascivious, filthy, indecent and disgusting." Halsey was tried and acquitted in the Court of Special Sessions, and in turn sued the society for malicious prosecution. He won, in a jury trial. The society appealed, and the jury's decision was affirmed. The society appealed again to the court of appeals, and on July 12, 1922, after almost five years of litigation, the court found in Halsey's favor. He was also awarded $2,500 plus accrued interest. Most important, the court's 5–2 decision established for the first time in New York that in determining "whether a book is obscene or indecent within Penal Law, § 1141, it must be considered broadly as a whole, and not judged from paragraphs alone which are vulgar and indecent."

* * *

Gautier's *Mademoiselle de Maupin* had been published in 1835 and was immediately acclaimed in France and abroad. It was also equally notorious and had long been the object of censors' ire in the United States and elsewhere. The court of appeals cited the book's many admirers and noted that even though it had its critics, "No review of French literature of the last 100 years fails to comment upon it." The court pointed to the author's "felicitous style" and cited the book's many "passages of purity and beauty." It also quoted Henry James's remark that "in certain lights the book is almost ludicrously innocent." The court acknowledged that the book contained many paragraphs, "however, which, taken by themselves, are undoubtedly vulgar and indecent."

The "however" was key, for the essential point of the majority opinion was it did not matter that, printed separately, the apparently objectionable paragraphs might, "as a matter of law, come within the prohibition of the statute." That might also be true, the court added, of a similar selection of excerpts from "Aristophanes, Chaucer or Boccaccio, or even from the Bible."

Opponents of censorship, including Quinn in his defense of the *Little Review*, had made this argument about selective and misleading passages many times. But no court had agreed. The judgment established as a legal precedent what Ezra Pound had told Joyce in October 1920, when the *Little Review* issue with the "Nausikaa" episode of his novel was seized by Sumner: "The excuse for parts of *Ulysses* is the WHOLE of *Ulysses*."

* * *

The timing was fortuitous, uncanny. On the previous day, Sumner had testified in the West Side Police Court about Seltzer's three books. The headline in the *New-York Tribune* bordered on the satiric. "Blushed Through 254 Pages of 'Young Girl's Diary,' He Says," ran over the subhead, "'Women in Love' and 'Casanova's Homecoming' Also Shocking Vice Crusader Sumner Tells Court While Bookseller Asserts They Are Educational." The *Tribune* reporter took particular enjoyment in recording details that undermined the censorial assiduousness of the so-called crusader, highlighting the fact that Schnitzler's *Casanova* and the anonymous *Diary* had been available for eight months, and the limited edition of *Women in Love* for nearly two years. Surely they could not be so damaging if they'd been poisoning minds for that long without any discernible impact.

"Salacious matter," Sumner said "crisply," as he closed the copy of *A Young Girl's Diary* that he had been holding in court. He had been "profoundly shocked when he got to reading" it, the *Tribune* reported of Sumner's testimony. (The newspaper's headline came from its reporter's account of Sumner's testimony: "He began to blush at page 17 and his cheeks reddened with increasing fervor all the way from there to page 254.") Goldstein's defense of *A Young Girl's Diary* was limited that day. It was, as its cover proclaimed, "intended only" for parents, educators, those in the legal and medical professions, and "students of psychology." "Anybody, of course, may be a student of psychology," the *Tribune* noted. The warning on the cover was as much a way to advertise a "bad book" as Sumner's own activities often were and did not forestall a trial, which was set for the end of July.

The voluminous and favorable press coverage "more than pleads the case for us," Seltzer wrote his wife, but the Halsey case had come as a greater relief, "as precedents are so much, perhaps everything, in lawsuits, this is splendid." The July heat, which he'd hoped to escape in Canada, was another pressure. "Today is the worst day we have had yet," he wrote Adele one evening a week before the trial. "Last night I could not sleep." But rain, beginning at about five p.m., seemed to portend, as the Halsey decision had, that the "hot spell is broken."

* * *

Because it would test the new parameters of the Halsey case, and because Jonah Goldstein would call witnesses, the Seltzer trial quickly became, as *Publishers Weekly* noted, "one of the most widely discussed cases in book censorship that has ever been before the courts." Magistrate George Simpson heard testimony on Monday, July 31. The next day, the *Tribune* ran a summary of the day's proceedings under a sequence of cheeky headlines, "Fizz Taken Out of Seltzer's Books at Hearings on Vice Charges / Doctors, Professors, Editors, Mothers and Even 'Sunday School Review' Cited to Convince Judge That 'A Young Girl's Diary' Hasn't Any 'Kick.'" Sumner testified that he had read both the *Diary* and *Casanova's Homecoming* in their entirety but that, even in the month since he seized *Women in Love*, he had "perused only passages" of the novel, inadvertently underscoring the weakness of his case in the wake of the Halsey decision, before which that might have been enough to sway a sympathetic judge. The main focus of the experts' testimony was the *Diary*, but they were also asked their opinions of *Women in Love* and *Casanova's Homecoming*. An attorney, Miles M. Dawson, of West Ninety-Fifth Street, was called as "an authority on realistic literature of all classes" and had worked as a translator, though his true authority may have been political, as a well-known colleague of Charles Evans Hughes, the Republican former governor of New York and Supreme Court justice then serving as President Harding's secretary of state. The *Diary* was "harmless," Dawson testified, also praising "David Lawrence" as a "great English stylist."

Gilbert Seldes, the *Dial* managing editor, testified that the *Dial* had published pieces by Lawrence and Schnitzler, giving weight to Goldstein's contention that both were literary writers who must be judged by a different standard. Speaking also to the issue of whether it was necessary, as Sumner and his allies had long claimed, to ban a book because of "its putative effect on immature readers," Seldes gave it as his expert opinion that *Women in Love* "would not interest a child and be no more exciting to an adult than a railroad timetable."

* * *

The "hot spell" Seltzer had complained of in July had been broken. On September 12, Magistrate Simpson found against Sumner and dismissed the complaints against Seltzer and Miss Marks of Womrath's. Simpson had read the three books with "sedulous care," he announced and, praising each of them as a "distinct contribution to the literature of the present day," found that in *Women in Love*, "the author attempts to discover the motivating power of life." Quite apart from the quality of the three books, however, "Mere extracts separated from their context do not constitute criteria by which books might be judged obscene," Simpson wrote in his opinion, the recent court of appeals ruling in Halsey obviously the controlling precedent.

Seltzer said of the decision, "Technically it was a case of the people *vs.* Thomas Seltzer. In reality it was a case of the people *vs.* Mr. Sumner." Simpson had, at least in part, framed his decision that way, offering a more general defense of literature itself—"Books will not be banned by law merely because they do not serve a useful purpose or teach any moral lesson"—and adding to his finding for Seltzer a warning to Sumner. "It has been said with some justice that the policy of pouncing upon books too frank for contemporary taste, without regard to the motive or purpose for which they were written or to the use to which they are to be put is objectionable and should be curbed."

For his part, Sumner was philosophical, saying, "You can't win every case."

The evening papers ran lengthy stories on Sumner's second defeat in quick succession, and the next morning the *New York Times* announced, "Book Censorship Beaten in Court." Seltzer wrote Adele, "Everybody is happy about it. It was really a popular cause in the true sense."

Simpson also instructed Sumner to return the hundreds of books he'd confiscated. Soon orders were "rushing in for the three 'obscene' books," Adele wrote a friend. "Can you understand that we've been busy?"

The last signed copies of the $15 edition of *Women in Love* sold out before the end of September. "We haven't a copy left," Seltzer wrote to Mountsier the next week, outlining his plans for a three-thousand-copy trade edition at $2.50 to be published quickly. Seltzer also announced he would sue Sumner for $30,000 in damages, $10,000 for each book seized, for false arrest and injury to his business, while Miss Marks, who had also been exonerated when Simpson dismissed Sumner's charges, sued for $10,000. This might serve Seltzer's sense of justice, but it also brought a new round of stories that served as ideal publicity for the forthcoming trade edition, which was published on October 18 and quickly sold out. A second printing was available the first week of November, and a third printing quickly followed. Sales reached upwards of fifteen thousand copies by the end of the year.

The next June, Lawrence received an accounting from Seltzer of his sales for 1922. *Aaron's Rod* had done well enough at Brentano's, perhaps, but it was a brief, local success at best, and sales of it, *Sea and Sardinia*, *Fantasia of the Unconscious*, and volumes of his stories, including *England, My England*, seemingly well timed in November, and his poems and plays had been far more modest. "I should still be poor *sans* Women in Love, shouldn't I?" Lawrence wrote in reply, more sorry for Seltzer, whom he tried to cheer up, than he was for himself. "Pazienza!" he counseled, worried, despite the commercial breakthrough, that his publisher would be "getting a bit tired of me if the sales are so small."

At the end of 1921, as he had argued with Mabel Dodge about the necessity of paying her rent, he had written her, "I hope I needn't all my life be so scrubby poor as we have been: those damned books may sell better." At least one had. *Women in Love* had found a belated success, and so would others of his books, he was sure. As for his "rather depressing sales," he wrote his agent, "All we can do is grin and bear it, for the present. I shall still have my day."

* * *

Mabel Dodge sent Lawrence a newspaper cutting about the case, and it was awaiting him when he and Frieda arrived in San Francisco on September 4.

"Pfui!" he wrote Seltzer in New York the next day. "I thought I should have had a word from you—but there is nothing. . . . I shall be glad to hear from you & to know what is happening. Apparently I have arrived in the land of the free at a crucial moment."

Lawrence would finally see Seltzer's correspondence about the events of July when he arrived in "New Mexico, U. S. A." on September 11. The next day, Simpson dismissed the charges against Seltzer and, in doing so, exonerated Lawrence, too. He and his books were welcome in America. What quickly became clear, in Taos, was that Lawrence did not particularly welcome being in America.

Chapter 12

THE WASTE LAND IN NEW YORK

WYNDHAM LEWIS HAD BEEN WRONG. ELIOT had not lied to him when he said Lady Rothermere's review was going forward, though it is likely that Lewis hadn't shared his suspicion only with Mrs. Schiff—and equally likely that he was not the only one wondering why the "Hypothetical Review" seemed to become more and more so as time went on. By the end of June, "the current rumours of its having been abandoned" were so widely discussed that Eliot wrote to Richard Cobden-Sanderson, the printer he and Lady Rothermere selected as their partner, to say it was imperative a notice announcing otherwise must be distributed as soon as possible. The unwelcome expense of it would be worth the effect it would have "upon certain groups in London."

In fact, the magazine had a name now, the *Criterion*, which was Vivien's idea ("simply because I liked the sound of the word"; Lady Rothermere and Tom also liked it, if only because it was "apparently harmless" and so many other possibilities had been discarded). The rocks ahead that

Vivien had feared the previous year, when Lady Rothermere agreed in principle to finance the quarterly, had materialized in their lives, but not because of the magazine. In fact, though progress had been delayed by Eliot's poor health and two absences from London, its development had otherwise been relatively smooth.

More surprising was the great degree to which Tom had staked his future position on the *Criterion* rather than *The Waste Land*.

* * *

Eliot envisioned a journal that would balance longer essays of up to five thousand words on contemporary subjects—in the first issue, an essay by the French critic Valery Larbaud on the importance of Joyce's *Ulysses*—against "more historical work," for example, an article on the Tristan and Isolde myth by an English writer T. Sturge Moore.

The *Dial*, despite the international range of its contents and the distinguished roster of its contributors, was an American magazine, its headquarters in a brownstone on West Thirteenth Street, in Greenwich Village, in Manhattan, and with only a modest English circulation. The *Criterion*, by contrast, was to be a successor to earlier now defunct English journals—*Arts & Letters*, the *Egoist*, where Eliot himself had worked as an assistant editor—and focused narrowly, Eliot explained to a potential contributor to his magazine, on introducing "an elite readership of English letters to the most important representatives of foreign thought . . . to channel towards London the deepest foreign currents."

Eliot might see in the *Dial* an apt (and possibly lucrative) place for his long poem, but he also saw weaknesses and room for competition in the very variety of its contents, designed to appeal to an intelligent but not necessarily elite set of American readers. Thayer's plan had been that the *Dial* would expand English circulation after the magazine was firmly established, and he hoped, until late 1921, to come to an agreement with Lady Rothermere to make efficient distribution possible. When it became clear that instead of collaborating, Lady Rothermere would fund her own magazine, and that Eliot would edit it, Thayer offered congratulations to Tom but was doubtful that "the multiplication of magazines" would help either of them. "It was to avoid just such a thing that I had been to so much bother in re the Rothermere bunch," Thayer wrote to Vivien, who was at that point writing Tom's correspondence for him. "The more artistic journals you publish the more money is wasted upon printers and paper dealers and the less is left for the artists themselves."

A magazine to compete with his own, and a decisive bit of business quite contradicting Eliot's seeming incapacitation—it is no wonder that Thayer, who'd contended with Eliot's missed deadlines and claims of illness, was distrustful of Eliot when he was offered *The Waste Land* but not allowed to read it. And it was not surprising that when the negotiations became protracted, he was less interested in making allowances for a troubled poet than he might have been a year before. It was now clear that by publishing *The Waste Land*, the *Dial* would be showcasing the work, and boosting the reputation, of an unrepentantly demanding poet at its own expense: Eliot would have to capitalize on his own name to draw in some from the roster of international contributors that the *Dial* was already publishing or pursuing in order to make the *Criterion* work. There were only so many international writers of commanding-enough stature to go around, and quite apart from the duplication of production costs that Thayer suggested left less for the artists themselves, in fact the opposite might be true: more places to publish meant that the artists themselves might demand, and get, higher prices. In other words, transatlantic competition might mean a greater need to accede to the kind of demands Eliot had just made.

The *Dial* was hardly a paying concern, running a deficit for 1922 of $65,000, which required a monthly subsidy from Thayer and Watson of $2,700 each, as Pound made clear in outlining the math for his father in 1921. "Dial costs 46 cents to print," he wrote, "why the hell shdnt. Thayer charge 50 for it. He makes the public a present of several $1000 each month."

Eliot planned to print five hundred copies of the first issue and had asked Cobden-Sanderson for estimates, including circulars for potential subscribers as well as other related material, before he left for Margate. Eliot promised they would begin "the business afresh" upon his return, and he and Cobden-Sanderson had dinner with Lady Rothermere on February 2 at her home. "Lady Rothermere dines at 8," Eliot informed him the day before, reminding him of her address. "I shall wear a dinner jacket myself." Cobden-Sanderson submitted revised estimates, as well as paper and type samples, "a good small format and paper, neat but no extravagance and not arty," Eliot told Pound. There would be no illustrations, which "do more harm than good," Eliot added, perhaps not just because of their cost but as a reproval of Thayer's pretensions in the *Dial*, full as it was of Chagall and Brancusi. Lady Rothermere and Eliot agreed to pay contributors the rate of £10 for five thousand words—a not particularly generous amount given Eliot's demands of Thayer—with the guarantee, as Eliot wrote to Pound, "that the selection of contributions is entirely in my hands."

As it became clear that a first issue would not appear until autumn, Eliot solicited work and suggestions from editors and writers across Europe, in order to be "certain of the right contributors for the first four numbers," among whom he wanted the Woolves, as he had proposed to them in March. Before Tom left for Lugano, and despite his having been "handicapped by a good deal of illness and worry," he had copied out, by hand, a list of six hundred names and addresses the Hogarth Press had provided—time he might better have spent preparing a typescript of *The Waste Land* for a prospective publisher. He promised Cobden-Sanderson that in due course he would have this typed "so that your staff can read it."

Back in London, he resumed work on the review, prepared to devote the next three months "of entire concentration on this one object," he told Ottoline Morrell, apparently forgetting *The Waste Land* for the moment. "I shall not go out anywhere and must not contemplate any weekends," he wrote her, begging off from an invitation with less than sterling honesty. The next week he spent a "perfect" evening with Mary Hutchinson, who introduced him to Léonide Massine, the Russian dancer and choreographer; sat for a portrait by Wyndham Lewis; and went to another dinner and a dance, at which "Vivien starved," he told Mary, while he "enjoyed myself, and got off with the Aga Khan." Busy with correspondence for the *Criterion*, as he claimed when he departed from the Woolves after reading his poem, and still unable to "drop my attempts to make money by writing" whatever assignments he was offered, he had to hire a shorthand typist to come in two evenings a week. He began dictating letters to her, further confounding any explanation of why, by the end of July, he had still been unable to have one or several copies of *The Waste Land* prepared for Liveright or for the editors of the *Dial*.

* * *

Eliot and Thayer had not written to each other since before Eliot saw Pound in Verona. Eliot had, in April, refused "to dispose of the poem to The Dial" at the price Thayer had offered. There things stood into the late summer, the unfortunate aftermath of Eliot's "endocrine boil over," as Pound had called it, and a matter of pride more than business or literary differences, as Pound knew. "My present impression of the case is 'Oh, you two bostonians [sic],'" he wrote Thayer from Italy in May, expressing friendship—Amicitia—from his hideaway in the World of Spirits, and seeming to throw up his hands for the moment in favor of pursuing his own work. He closed his note to Thayer, "Ora Pro Nobis"—pray for us.

Eliot sent his London Letter for the July issue to Gilbert Seldes, the Dial managing editor, before leaving for Lugano, and then had no further communication with either Seldes or Thayer until July 24, when he sent another London Letter to Seldes in time for the September issue. He did not mention his poem, and because Quinn had been negotiating in earnest with Liveright about the book, it is possible he had decided that publishing it in a periodical was not necessary, or at this point would not be lucrative enough to jeopardize whatever sales might materialize from Liveright's edition. Thayer, who knew Seldes admired Eliot's work and would himself be eager to publish a poem of Eliot's at last, had in the meantime warned his managing editor—whose judgment he distrusted and whom he had been trying, without luck, to replace—"to correspond with Eliot only in the meagerest and barest form observing courtesy," presumably to forestall any discussion of the poem, but also, conveniently, preventing any second-guessing of Thayer's behavior in the matter.

With Thayer in Vienna and Watson, his partner, having left for Europe himself, "Young Seldes," as John Quinn called him, was concerned that the editorial reserves of the Dial were running very low. Even as managing editor, he had no authority to accept material on his own, a situation Thayer would not alter because of his dissatisfaction (from a literary point of view, unjustified) with Seldes. In fact, Seldes wrote widely, and perceptively, for the Dial as well as other publications and was a responsible enough literary expert to be asked by Thomas Seltzer's lawyer to testify on behalf of his client and to attest to the artistic merits of D. H. Lawrence.

The September issue had to be done—and the article well was running even more dangerously dry than it had in August. "When are you coming home? The milk is getting sour on the doorstep," Seldes wrote to Watson. He had, he added, "enough material, I think," for September, but the October issue was looking thin, apart from a serial by Sherwood Anderson already scheduled to begin that month. But the Anderson serial was only so long, and Seldes warned Watson, "there is not a poem nor a filler nor a loose line cut in hand." Given that "nothing of astounding brilliance" had arrived, it was now a question of finding "a few things acceptable" in order to get the October issue out at all. "Seriously, we will be in rather a mess . . . very soon," he added. Seldes wanted to publish a play by Yeats, *The Player Queen*. It was good, worth publishing, and long enough to fill forty to fifty pages.

Watson saw Pound in Paris at the end of July, and though his enthusiasm to publish Eliot was genuine—and untainted by the long history and personal strain that marked Eliot's relationship with Thayer—he was also realistic about the magazine's desperate need for copy. Pound wrote a "coy veiled hint" to Eliot about Watson's interest, and on July 28 Eliot promised to send a copy of *The Waste Land* "for confidential use" as soon as he could make one; he'd had only two copies and had sent one to Quinn "to present to Liveright on the completion of the contract," which Liveright was, at that moment, about to sign. Perhaps because Liveright's publication of the poem was now certain and because he was no longer dependent on the *Dial*, Eliot told Pound that he had no objection to letting Watson and Thayer see it.

"Cher S. T.," Watson wrote on August 12. "Eliot seems in a conciliatory mood."

* * *

Eliot sent the copy to Pound in Paris, rather than to Thayer in Vienna, which meant that Watson, unusually, read it first. "The poem is not so bad," he wrote his partner, though he amended the sentence to "better than not so bad" before sending the letter. Not a passionate endorsement, but then, Eliot had been a mainstay of the magazine, and his first poem for the magazine deserved a benefit of the doubt. This would have been the case had the editorial well not run dry. But now, the magazine could not stand on ceremony or afford to remain affronted by Eliot's earlier demands. A few days later, Watson wrote to Thayer again and forwarded a copy of the poem. It had taken some getting used to, he realized. "I found the poem disappointing on first reading, but after a third shot I think it up to his usual—all the styles are there, somewhat toned down in language (adjectives!) and theatricalized in sentiment." Watson also told Thayer that

Liveright was to publish the poem in book form. He thought, though, that "Gilbert could get around Liveright" and that they could publish the poem in the *Dial* first, if they acted quickly.

And, after all these months in which they had not seen the poem, act quickly they must. Seldes's worries about the upcoming issues had deepened. But the lack of copy was not the only problem the *Dial* now faced. The question of the lucrative Dial Prize was also on Watson's mind. The *Dial* had inaugurated the award in December 1921 and given it to Sherwood Anderson. The announcement of the award, and its munificence— $2,000—had garnered a great deal of publicity at a time when literary awards were rare. (The Pulitzer Prize for Poetry was given for the first time only in 1922, to Edwin Arlington Robinson, for his *Collected Poems*; three earlier prizes awarded by the organization had been sponsored by the Poetry Society of America.) Almost as soon as the *Dial*'s first award was made, Thayer and Watson looked ahead to the next one and settled on E. E. Cummings as the likely recipient.

But Watson had come to think that Cummings was "less and less supportable" as the recipient. To Thayer he proposed this idea about Eliot: "Shall I try to persuade him to sell us the poem at our regular rate with the award in view?" The announcement of the second Dial Prize would not be made for months yet, but here was a sleight of hand that would allow them to raise the effective price that Eliot would be paid for his poem. Watson said he favored giving Eliot the prize even without *The Waste Land* factored in. But because of Bel Esprit, Eliot was widely known to have financial problems and to have had a nervous breakdown. "I don't see why we shouldn't be doing something moderately popular in giving him the award." Watson and Thayer could open their pocketbooks to show that the *Dial* was above the petty politics of transatlantic literary wars. Thayer relented, though a record of his initial thoughts on Eliot's poem do not survive. Whether Eliot was in a conciliatory enough mood to accept the offer Watson had persuaded Thayer they must make was another question.

* * *

To Eliot, the success of his own magazine had become a question of personal pride—and "at least from the point of view of its contents, if not from that of circulation," also a matter of survival. The *Criterion* must not fail, because he must not fail. The open canvassing for Bel Esprit had exposed him to pity and perhaps even ridicule. If the first issue of the magazine were not dazzling, the personal cost would be great. "I am quite aware," Eliot wrote Aldington, who had become Eliot's de facto assistant as plans for the magazine proceeded, "how obnoxious I am to perhaps the larger part of the literary world of London and that there will be a great many jackals swarming about waiting for my bones." The failure of the *Criterion* would mean not only that he had "gained nothing" but that, more significantly, he would have lost "immensely in prestige and usefulness and shall have to retire to obscurity or Paris like Ezra."

Eliot confided that alternative only partly in jest. It was not "persecution mania" that led him to believe that his own public fate was intertwined with the success or failure of the *Criterion*, he wrote Aldington. He knew—and could not escape hearing the chatter of others confirming—that many in London's various literary sets, including friends like Virginia Woolf and Wyndham Lewis, viewed him with disdain or suspicion or pity (or envy), and that there were those on all sides who saw his vaunted hopes for his magazine as only another way in which he assumed an air of personal "superiority." This word was used in anger by Aldington, when Eliot reacted unfavorably to an essay he'd sent for his approval. In a further burst of unkindness, Aldington had also passed along to Eliot that people were saying he was "getting bitter and hypercritical," a report surely meant to hurt rather than to have a cautionary effect, and which Tom, who shared the remark with Pound, felt was a betrayal by a man in whom he'd confided so much and whose work he usually praised.

* * *

Through the summer Eliot flattered, cultivated, and ingratiated himself with as many eminent writers and editors as he could, for he knew that the table of contents for the first issue and the roster of promised contributors were battle lines drawn against competitors and rivals. Later in the 1920s, Leonard Woolf was involved with the creation of a magazine called *Political Quarterly*. One of his associates, the journalist Kingsley Martin, wrote Woolf with the disappointing news that John Maynard Keynes was working on a book and would therefore be unable to contribute to the first issue. Keynes's name, whatever he could have been persuaded to contribute, would have been, Martin wrote Woolf, "uniquely valuable intrinsically and 'publicitically'—(a good word that)."

Eliot, like Martin, knew the intrinsic and also the publicitical value of those whom he sought for the *Criterion*. But if it was clear why the *Criterion* needed celebrated names, it was certainly not clear why those with celebrated names would need the *Criterion*. This conundrum was much on Eliot's mind, particularly as he pursued the imprimatur of one whose prestige was greater than almost anyone's—Marcel Proust. Eliot's anxiety to publish him in the *Criterion* was a precise measure of Proust's exalted reputation in England by the summer of 1922.

"I am *not* anxious to get many French people for the *first* two numbers, more anxious to get other (foreign) nationalities," Eliot wrote Pound, "the French business is so usual (in London) that it doesn't raise a quiver; the only name worth getting is Proust, whom I am fishing for."

The importance of Proust was publicitical above all. Eliot, though otherwise deeply immersed in French poetry and criticism, had not read Proust, and there is not even a passing mention of Proust in Eliot's correspondence until he began to plan the first issues of the *Criterion* in 1922. His friend Sydney Schiff did know Proust and, a novelist himself who wrote under the name Stephen Hudson, had hoped to translate *À la recherche* into English. In this, he had been foiled by C. K. Scott Moncrieff, whose translation of the first volume, *Swann's Way*, was soon to appear. In June, Eliot asked Schiff to intercede on his behalf for a contribution, or at least the promise of one for a following issue. Eliot was hoping for a double coup, an English translation of an as-yet-unpublished section of Proust's novel. (In October 1920, the *Dial* had published an excerpt in translation from *Le côté de Guermantes*, which had appeared in France, together with an enthusiastic appreciation by Richard Aldington.) Schiff agreed to do so and suggested that Eliot also write to Proust directly.

On July 4 Eliot told Schiff he had written Proust at his "private address," as instructed. "I await consequences eagerly." The pressure was to secure Proust's name for the first promotional circular, the copy for which was due in mid-July. A week later there had been no response. "I have been waiting every day to hear from Proust, but have heard nothing," Eliot wrote Schiff. "I am very disappointed." Still, he hoped that Proust would, he added flatteringly, "yield to your persuasion if to anybody's."

Schiff's fishing expedition produced little, but Eliot did not know that Schiff was fishing on his own behalf as well as Eliot's and was hoping to arrange for the serialization of his novel *Elinor Culhouse* in France. Schiff had asked Proust to intervene with his own publishers, Jacques Rivière, the editor of *La Nouvelle Revue française*, and Gaston Gallimard, the head of NRF Éditions, the magazine's book publishing operation. Schiff praised Eliot to Proust as "possibly our best critic and certainly our best poet," but Proust did not reply to Eliot, writing instead to his publisher Gallimard, on July 7, proposing that he try to arrange with Eliot a more practical solution for publication in the *Criterion*, an excerpt published in French but not yet translated. But, he cautioned Gallimard, "cette question Eliot" was "all mixed up with" the more delicate issue of Schiff, in whose work Gallimard was not interested.

Proust, as aware as Eliot of the international importance of his imprimatur, was generally unswayed by the blandishments of editors, journalists, writers, and other favor seekers, eager as they were to flatter him. Eventually, at the end of a long letter to Schiff on July 18, Proust wrote, "I'm too tired to go on. I still haven't written to M. Eliot."

He never would. Proust died on November 18, 1922, and had been certain, all summer, that he was close to death. But Proust's talk of his imminent death was such a fixture of his conversation that no one took him seriously. In 1919, his friend Paul Morand had written in "Ode to Marcel Proust":

> *I say:*
> *You're looking very well.*
> *You reply:*
> *Dear friend, I nearly died three times today.*

Proust would not be published in the *Criterion* until July 1924, when an excerpt, "The Death of Albertine," appeared. It is unlikely that Eliot ever read much more of Proust than the excerpt he published. The writer William Empson later recalled Eliot's telling a group of students at Cambridge, "I have not read Proust," only to hear him, the following week, offer a "very weighty, and rather long, tribute" to Scott Moncrieff's translation, which he said was "at no point inferior to the original."

Eliot's lack of interest in reading Proust was perhaps conditioned by

Pound's opinion. He had early on been impressed but by 1921 had become bored, referring in the *Dial* to the French publication of *Le côté de Guermantes* and *Sodome et Gomorrhe* as the "new lump of Proust," with "nearly two hundred pages of close type" Proust devoted to describing a dinner party given by the Duchesse de Guermantes. "The pages of Proust's beautiful boredom roll on, readable, very readable," Pound wrote, "and for once at least the precise nuance of the idiocy of top-crusts is recorded." This was his public comment. Privately, he was appalled by the opening scene of *Sodome*, an extended sex scene between two older men. "The little lick-spittle wasn't satirising, he really thought his pimps, buggers and opulent idiots were *important*, instead of the last mould on the dying cheese."

* * *

Quinn finally received Eliot's typescript on Friday, July 28. He telephoned Liveright that day to tell him that the typescript had arrived and that he would send it to him on Monday, July 31, after one of the stenographers in his office was able to make a "careful copy" of it. Eliot would send the notes to Liveright directly at some point after the contract was signed. Liveright asked his opinion of the poem. Quinn told him he had not read it—that his plan was to "read it over Sunday."

Early on Saturday morning, John Quinn called his secretary Jeanne Robert Foster and asked her to come to his apartment at 58 Central Park West. She went up immediately, she was to recall. Here, in an eleven-room apartment on the building's top floor that he'd leased in 1919 for $3,200 a year, Quinn kept his massive collections of books and manuscripts, about eighteen thousand items, including multiple copies of many books—he had bought thirty-five copies of Eliot's first book of poems, many as gifts, but also as an investment—as well as the complete manuscript of *Ulysses* and almost all the manuscripts of Joseph Conrad's major works. And that didn't include his collection of paintings and sculpture. Despite how large the apartment was, on the building's top floor, it was not large enough "to show adequately, or even to store adequately, his immense accumulation" of books and art, which, insured for $350,000, nevertheless stood in piles in several rooms that "resembled not a gallery but storerooms of a museum."

When Foster, who was also Quinn's lover, arrived at the ninth-floor apartment, Quinn asked her to "read something to him that he had received from Elliot" (Foster misspells Eliot's name in virtually all of her surviving papers). He handed her the copy of *The Waste Land* he had just received from London.

One of Mrs. Foster's "unromantic duties" in Quinn's office was to "read over his law briefs to him before he appeared in court," Quinn's biographer wrote. Quinn had what might be called a phonographic memory. Foster would read the brief twice, after which Quinn was able to remember it almost verbatim. Now Foster did with the poem what she did at the office. "I read it twice that morning," she recalled, a task that would have taken about an hour. Foster was a poet herself; she, too, had a contract with Liveright for a book of poems, and her reading is likely to have been extremely good.

Meanwhile, on Thursday, Quinn had dictated a new Liveright contract based on Eliot's contract with Knopf. Liveright accepted the more limited terms without comment and signed the contract on Saturday, July 29, the same day Foster read the poem to Quinn. Liveright sent it back to Quinn's office on Monday, following which Quinn sent the typescript to Liveright. (This was the same day that Gilbert Seldes testified in the Seltzer case.) It had been almost seven months since Liveright had first offered to publish the poem. He had still not read it, but at least the contract had been signed. Liveright asked Quinn the title of the book. He didn't know either, Quinn said, though he soon remembered that it was "tucked away" in the postscript of a seven-page letter that Pound had recently written him. He inserted the name of the poem into the contract: *The Waste Land*.

By Monday Quinn had read "the poems," apparently thinking the five parts were five poems, "last night between 11:50 and 12:30," he told Eliot, which would mean Sunday evening, July 30, into the early morning of July 31. (Quinn's remark to Eliot that he had "read" the poems may also suggest the level of his intimacy with Foster and of his reliance on her; Foster's reading it to him was his reading it, just as he might have told a client he had read whatever legal briefs were germane to his case.)

The first two people outside Eliot's immediate circle of intimates to read the poem were unusually attuned to its discontent. Jeanne Foster had been seriously ill in early summer, and Quinn thought that she, like Eliot the previous autumn, was "close to a nervous breakdown as well." Quinn himself had been "working too hard to quit, and too hard to continue."

They were Tom and Vivien on the other side of the Atlantic, and the poem made a deep impression on Quinn. "*Waste Land* is one of the best things you have done," he wrote to Eliot, worried that, for all its excellence, "Liveright may be a little disappointed in it." It was, after all, a poem "for the elect or the remnant or the select few or the superior guys, or any word you choose, for the small number of readers it is certain to have."

Quinn was also worried about the length of the poem: "the book is a little thin," he thought, perhaps one of the reasons he had given Eliot such a precise accounting of the hour he had spent with it. He thought it might make for unflattering comparisons with the range of Eliot's first book of poems. Even though he foresaw only a small audience for it, Quinn thought it would be worth adding four or five more poems, even if by doing so the book were to be delayed another month.

"I give you my impression. . . . You won't mind my suggestion."

* * *

On June 3, Liveright had cabled Eliot, "Cable deferred rate our expense title of fall book and very brief description for catalogue." On the same day he sent Eliot the contract, by mail, that precipitated Eliot's cable to Quinn asking him to intercede. Eliot provided neither the title nor the copy as requested. Two months later, Quinn retrieved the title from Pound's letter. But Boni & Liveright's catalog of "Good Books" for autumn 1922, printed even with autumn nearly under way, did not reflect Quinn's instruction. Eliot's poem was announced to booksellers and the press as *The Wasteland*. Perhaps when Eliot sent the notes for the poem to Liveright, he also sent him a description. Eliot was good at this kind of work. He wrote the prospectus for the *Criterion* that summer, and later in his career as an editor at Faber and Faber, he made an art of the copy he wrote for the books he published. Whether Eliot wrote the copy, or Liveright did, the "Good Books" catalog read:

> Many poets who became prominent during the contemporary American poetic renascence have sunk quietly into forgetfulness. T. S. Eliot is a name which has acquired a leading significance in the same period. The qualities of Mr. Eliot's verse are enduring. They represent in many ways the keenest inquiry into our lives which American poetry can boast since Ezra Pound entered the lyric lists. Subtle, ironic, and molded to the peculiar form of Mr. Eliot's mind, this poet's work, highly individualistic, has run to caricature of

genuine realities, set off by flashes of rhythm and color. He knows how to draw people—not always within the knowledge of a poet—and he deals largely with the people he sees around him.

The Wasteland is the longest poem T. S. Eliot has written and the first poetry that he has written in the last three years. Mr. Eliot writes from London that this volume represents a new phase in his development, being the ripe fruit of his experimentation in all of his previous work.

T. S. Eliot is a man to be reckoned with, now, and hereafter, among the few unique talents of the times.

The Wasteland will be one of the most beautifully printed and bound books that has ever borne our imprint.

To be published October 1st . . . $2.00

* * *

Everything seemed to be settled. Quinn prepared to go on an upstate vacation for the month of August. In Liveright's office a ledger for the book was created. The contract was for The Waste Land, but in the Boni & Liveright accounting department the title was entered as "Wasteland." The first end-of-month entry, on July 31, is an overhead cost for inclusion in the fall catalog, $37.

But the poem would not be published by Liveright on October 1, as his catalog announced. There were to be more delays. It would not appear until December.

Chapter 13

"I LIKE BEING WITH MY DEAD"

MORGAN HAD HEARD NOTHING FROM Egypt for quite some time, but in mid-June he was still writing letters to Mohammed once a week—"on the chance," he told Florence Barger, happier to confide in her by letter than to spend too much time in her presence. He also wrote to Masood, with whom he could similarly share the continuing intensity of his feelings, and whose disapproval he did not fear. *On the chance.* The letters helped him to believe Mohammed was still alive, he wrote to Florence. "It will be painful stopping, for then I shall realise for ever that he is not there."

The boom had helped him forward—but he was still caught in the vise of his grief.

* * *

On the same day in late June that Morgan wrote to Masood about the "boom" of the Malet review in the *Times*, he received two letters from

Egypt, one from Mohammed's wife and the other from his brother-in-law, reporting what he had anticipated all spring: Mohammed was dead. The news, now that it had come, was unsurprising, an anticlimax, and Morgan realized that the "nearest approach to a shock" he'd had in the final months of their relationship had been when his boat had docked at Port Said and Mohammed was not there to greet him. The rest had been inevitable. The letters gave a confusing account of Mohammed's estate—he had owned three houses and had left £60—and this apparent financial security again raised the question of whether Mohammed had taken advantage of him, though Morgan's worry on this point was at least in part dispelled by a vision he had of Mohammed's ghost "as one needing forgiveness" appearing from behind a curtain, "conceived of as taller than normal." This relieved Morgan enough that he concluded, "The affair has treated me very gently." Mohammed's lingering death, which had tried Morgan's patience was now, retrospectively, more clearly a time in which the letters they exchanged had been full of expressions of love. Morgan noted the date of Mohammed's last letter—May 8—in his diary and realized that Mohammed must have died "almost directly" afterward.

Poppy kicked that summer by traveling—not quite running away from home as he had done in going to India, but it was neater and simpler to be away from Lily than to confront her too boldly about his need for freedom. Forster spent a month on the Isle of Wight, visiting his aunts the Miss Prestons at Brighstone, where he walked the downs. From Brighstone, he went to Dorchester, where in mid-July he visited Thomas Hardy and his wife for what he was disappointed to find was a rather dull afternoon tea, "nice food and straggling talk," he wrote to Lily. Hardy took him to see the graves of his pets, their names on headstones overgrown with ivy. The elderly author was pleasant and friendly, but as the visit wore on, Forster decided it was too much of a "dolorous muddle," with Hardy enumerating the death of each one, many of whom had been run over by trains. Snowbell, Pella, Kitkin, "she was cut clean in two, clean in two," Hardy told Forster, his sentence trailing off into silence. When Forster finally asked, "How is it that so many of your cats have been run over, Mr Hardy? Is the railway near?" Hardy replied, no, it was not near. And then, he added, there were the many who had simply gone missing. "I could scarcely keep grave," Morgan told Lily, the caricature of Hardy's own novels and poems too great.

Even away from home, he was thinking about his novel. Before he left on his trip, he had been worried about the "fundamental defect" his resumption of work had revealed: that he was emphasizing atmosphere too much, rather than characterization. One advantage of his visits through the summer, then, was that, in recording conversations, he was reminded of how people talked. He returned home in midsummer, and in August, after a brief stay, resumed his travels—to Belfast to visit Forrest Reid, and then to Edinburgh.

* * *

He made progress on the novel, but as he wrote to Siegfried Sassoon, the fact that he was not "dissatisfied with what I do" was not the same as having "the faintest conviction that it will be finished." He was still not sure that he could simply *become* a novelist again, and in the piece he wrote for the Memoir Club not long after his return from India, he tried to work the problem out. If he could find the conviction, he had told one friend, then everything would be all right—he could continue with the novel. But he did not have that faith, and for the Memoir Club he wrote of a moment in his past when that faith had been given to him from outside himself. He recalled the inspiration it had been for him, when still an undergraduate, he went to say good-bye to his tutor and to talk about his prospects. The man, Nathaniel Wedd—well known to those in the club, many of whom had met Forster at Cambridge— had "brought not only help but happiness" by telling Morgan, "Of course I could write—not that anyone would read me, but that didn't signify."

Wedd had praised Forster highly and had told him, he remembered, that "I had a special and unusual apparatus, something which philosophy and scholarship and athletics all despised, still I had it and they hadn't." Morgan's problem then, in 1901, was Morgan's problem now, though he did not make (and did not need to make) the connection explicit as he read the essay aloud to his friends. He recalled that as an undergraduate he had begun a novel, but that once under way, "the manuscript broke off. . . . The apparatus was working, not inaccurately, but feebly, and dreamily because I wasn't sure it was there." The tutor's benediction had given him some measure of confidence, he explained, enough that, in due course, while traveling abroad—a long trip of ten months—he wrote "The Story of a Panic," which became his first published story. Speaking before the Memoir Club two decades later, he was, as the members knew, back from another long trip abroad he had taken in search, at least in part, of himself as a writer.

Describing the long-ago scene in the tutor's rooms at King's, Morgan obliquely elided his post-undergraduate past and the present. Recalling his farewell to the tutor, he said of the encounter, "And now he helps me again, for he tells me that I might write, could write, might be a writer." From the memory he might draw faith for today. But it would not be easy to do. He had changed from the early days of his career, Morgan told his friends as he went on. He spoke of his second novel, *The Longest Journey*, published in 1907, which had been the last book of his that had "come upon me without my knowledge." The others had come with greater effort of mind and will, he said. He did not speak that night about the novel he was at present writing, but in calling the talk "My Books and I" he did not shy away from the question it would raise in the others' minds: Would there be another book? The doubt for Morgan was the doubt Eliot had shared from Lausanne. Morgan did not know whether the novel he was writing would work, and sometimes he had to give himself over to nothing more or less than "the motion of my pen," he told the Memoir Club, for the simple reason that all of a writer's faculties, "including that very valuable faculty, faking—do conspire together thus." In India, he had not been able to assimilate or arrange. Perhaps now that he was back in England—his preoccupation with Mohammed, tiresome even to himself—he could continue to fake it with his careful and uninspired additions.

Virginia and Leonard were at least two members of the Memoir Club who knew that he was making his perhaps uninspired additions and hoping for the best. Not long after the meeting, Morgan wrote to Ludolf about his progress and asked him to say nothing of the novel to any of their mutual acquaintances in Egypt: "secresy [sic] conveniences me."

* * *

Home in early August, Morgan was overwhelmed by ghosts, or by one ghost—Mohammed's. The liberation he expected Mohammed's death to bring had come to him only fitfully. After his travels he settled in at Weybridge to find that he was more akin to the narrator of Ackerley's poem in the *Mercury* than he had been when he first read it in the spring. It had now been six weeks since he received confirmation of Mohammed's death. But this had not put Mohammed behind him at all, and "most nights" were alive with visions and dreams of Mohammed, just as the poem had foretold. He himself had indeed been *delivrées pas.* Delivered not.

He wrote in his diary on August 4 of a "Confused dream about Mohammed, then someone else who produced w.d."—a wet dream, "the first time this year." But the erotic dream was a reminder of the thwarted desire that had defined their relationship, and Morgan was unsentimental—"always know that he has died." The next day, after another dream of Mohammed, Morgan wrote in his diary, "My boy I am oppressed with you—you are dead and cannot know. I only speak to my memories when I speak your name. I don't want you alive but to know exactly what you were like—this I can't do—nothing extra will turn up to help me. . . . I tried to come near you last night—no use."

He now did as Ackerley's narrator had done:

> *. . . I reeled*
> *Free from sleep's fetters*
> *Out of my chair*
> *Over to where*
> *I had concealed*
> *Certain old letters.*
>
> *Holding a taper*
> *Over my head,*
> *Thrust I aside*
> *Bundles of paper,*
> *Labelled and tied,*
> *Seeking my dead.*

His own bundle of papers included all the mementos and photographs he had saved. But looking at them was as dispiriting as the dreams were disappointing—"always this sober trying," he wrote.

He thought of a new way to seek his dead and, in order "to know exactly what you were like," sat down to write one more letter to Mohammed, "with my mind on you and with the illusion that your mind still exists and attends." He wrote it formally and dated the letter on the evening he began it, August 5, 1922, as if it were really to be sent.

But, like Mabel's papyrus to Lawrence the year before, this was a letter that was not a letter. Morgan did not write it on stationery but on the first page of a fresh notebook. He began with the usual salutation, "Dear Mohammed," greeting a recipient who would never read it, but confided to his lost friend that he was writing a book "for you and me."

There was the other book he was trying to write, the Indian novel, and now this one, too, written pretending Mohammed was still alive, "although I know that a putrid scrap in the Mansourah burial ground is all that was you." Morgan had not published a book while Mohammed was alive, but now that Mohammed was dead, and because "I am professionally a writer and want to pay you this last honour," he was writing a book for him, though one he was not sure that anyone other than himself would see. "I write for my own comfort and to recall the past," he told Mohammed, an echo of what he had told the Memoir Club, and what he had learned from Proust, about the uses of the past. To honor Mohammed, as his subject and as the recipient of this last gift, he gave the letter the elements of a book and did what he could to make it look like a real book, even if he were faking it.

He wrote out a dedication in short lines that mimicked both a printed book and the poetical form of Mohammed's last letters to him.

> To Mohammed el Adl,
> who died at Mansourah shortly
> after the 8th of May, 1922,
> aged about twenty three: of consumption;
> his mother, father, brother, and son
> died before him; his daughter has
> died since, his widow is said to
> have married again:
> and to my love for him.

Morgan also added an epigram from A. E. Housman's most recent book, *Last Poems*, published in 1922, that had touched him as Ackerley's "Ghosts" had:

> Good-night, my lad, for nought's eternal
> No league of ours for sure,

Tomorrow I shall miss you less,
And ache of heart and heaviness
Are things that time should cure.

Morgan wrote the letter in an extraordinarily neat hand, a clarity to each word that was very different from his often difficult to decipher "mediaeval" handwriting (Morgan himself called it "cacography"), as if this astonishingly intimate letter, part memento, part billet-doux, must be read.

Like the novel Morgan was writing, his book for Mohammed was, for now, to remain unfinished. He wrote a number of pages, and then broke off and resumed it in November ("dead six months . . . you are decayed to terrible things by this time. . . . I do not want to prate of perfect love, only to write of you as if you are real . . . pretend that you are still alive"). He wrote additional parts of the letter at longer intervals, often several years, and finished it only after another trip to Egypt, more than seven years after he had begun, signing it, "Mohammed el Adl—my love, Morgan, December 27th, 1929," a farewell also to the decade just ending. The letter was by then eighteen pages, but over time continued to grow. Morgan added a further seven pages of Mohammed's "Words Spoken," tran-scribed in 1960 from an earlier memento, and then copied out sixty-two pages of Mohammed's letters to him from their meeting until Moham-med's death, Mohammed's autobiography in letters "written" in Morgan's hand and preserving all of Mohammed's errors of grammar and spelling. After Mohammed's last letter, Morgan drew the kind of decoration often used in printed books to indicate a break. He added as a postscript to the letter—or as an epilogue to this "book"—the two further letters that arrived for him from Egypt after Mohammed's death, an end to the story that Mohammed's own letters could not tell. And then he pasted a book plate in the flyleaf: "This book belongs to E. M. FORSTER."

Morgan had begun when he was not certain he would ever write another book. By the time he put his finishing touches on it four decades later, "this book" was ninety-two handwritten pages, and his last.

* * *

The hope of his epigraph from Housman did not prove true. Morgan did not miss Mohammed less and less after beginning his letter. Writing to Masood from Edinburgh, he told him he had been going through Mohammed's letters and that doing so had been more disturbing than he had expected. "I get so miserable yet gain no clearer vision of the past," which had been the point of his writing to "Dear Mohammed" in the first place.

But disheartened as he was, he continued to write his Indian novel. He soon gave his dilemma to one of his protagonists, Dr. Aziz, a young widower who looks repeatedly at a photograph of his dead wife, only to find that the more he looks, the less he sees: "She had eluded him thus, ever since he had carried her to her tomb . . . the very fact that we have loved the dead increases their unreality, and the more passionately we invoke them the further they recede."

All through the summer he had been "absolutely battered at by people"—because of the "boom in the Times" he had gone from as good as dead to alive and in demand. But, he wrote to Masood, his new fame was for the wrong reasons: "they think I am amusing without being alarming." Declining another invitation to Garsington, he apologized to Ottoline for the "accumulation of muddle" that he must see to after his long summer absences. "I am in several other universes," he wrote, meaning he had been to so many places recently, the "queerest" of which had been Ireland. He said nothing to her of the other universe he was inhabiting at the moment, the realm of Mohammed's letters to which he was writing a posthumous reply.

He shared with Florence the news that while he was still working on the novel—"terribly slowly," he told her, as he had told everyone—he now worried that what he was writing would lack a continuity of emotion. He did not brood upon it, though, even when, one evening, he was "quite alone in the house." His solitude was not lonely, and it seemed to inspire him. "I like being with my dead—they are so far very different from most people's and any how they have eternal youth."

When Morgan added to the letter, he wrote in an odd mix of the present and the past, of "the occasional nights we have slept in one bed" and the details of the "last instants we sat together in the train at Cairo," in particular that moment when, Morgan recalled, "you nudged me twice with your right elbow out of love." Mohammed had been "the greatest thing in my life," and if he were to fade into nothingness, then so might Morgan.

To the bundle of Mohammed's papers, he had been able to add another memento. "This day I received my friend's ring, sent me by his sister," he wrote in his diary on October 10. This was the only thing of

Mohammed's he had asked for from Mohammed's family, a ring with a dark yellow stone that Mohammed used to wear. In June, he had asked Florence to write to Egypt to request it on his behalf and, perhaps to prevent its being opened by Lily during his summer travels, he had also asked her to have it sent to her. He had not really expected to receive the ring, but when he opened the envelope from Florence he discovered the ring cocooned inside "a silk bag inside cotton wool inside a cigarette box inside a coat of pyjama-skin inside a coat of sacking." He could hardly believe the "absurd care" with which it had been packed, each layer he unfolded bringing him no closer to the secret of Mohammed's intentions or affections. He showed it to a local merchant and asked what kind of stone it might be. Mr. Hill hesitated, Morgan reported to Florence, and only "after due pretending not to hurt my feelings" told him it was "the kind of stone used to decorate the tops of umbrellas, and of no value! But we agreed that didn't matter."

He wrote this to Florence while wearing the ring, which "just goes on to my little finger," and even though he did not like to wear rings, he wore it once a day, "generally at night." He also put it on occasionally when he added to his letter to Mohammed. He guarded it but was not overly sentimental about the totem or about his attachment to it. He wrote to Masood, "I know that if I lost it it would be nearer to him, because he is lost."

* * *

While in Brighstone, in June, Forster thought of D. H. Lawrence, whom he had not seen since 1915 but whose works he continued to read. He asked Siegfried Sassoon whether he had a copy of *Women in Love* or another book by "D. H. L." that he had missed while he was in India. Soon after, Forster wrote to D. H. L. for the first time in years. The letter missed him in Australia and, along with Seltzer's letters about Sumner, was waiting for him when he arrived in Taos. Lawrence's reply is dated September 20. Forster preserved it even when late in life he destroyed other correspondence. On the reverse, he wrote "1922" in his elderly hand.

Evidently Forster had asked him a question of great importance, to which Lawrence replied, "Yes I think of you—of your saying to me, on top of the downs in Sussex—'How do you know I'm not dead?'—Well, you can't be dead, since here's your script. But I think you *did* make a nearly deadly mistake glorifying those *business* people in Howards End. Business is no good." Here was his script, but of course there had been no books to remind Lawrence of Forster, as Lawrence's books had reminded Forster of the younger novelist. It seems Forster mentioned he was writing again.

"Do send me anything you publish, & I'll order Seltzer to send you two of my books which are only published here—one appearing just now.

"Taos is a tiny place 30 miles from the railway high up—6000 ft—in the desert. I feel a great stranger, but have got used to that feeling, & prefer it to feeling 'homely.' After all, one is a stranger, nowhere so hopelessly as at home."

It was an idea with which Forster could sympathize, which is why he, like Lawrence, had spent so much of the recent months away. He might, as he had written, "like being with my dead," but there was less to enjoy being with Lily, and so he continued to travel in the autumn too. Morgan visited the Woolves in September and was not the only guest. Joining them was T. S. Eliot.

Chapter 14

A SEPTEMBER WEEKEND WITH THE WOOLVES

FROM LONDON TO LEWES WAS AN EASY TRIP by train, about an hour south from Victoria Station, and it was only a mile's further ride by pony trap from the station to the tiny village of Rodmell, where Leonard and Virginia Woolf lived in a small house mostly hidden behind high hedges. They had bought Monk's House after the war, in July 1919, three summers ago, and though the name of the house was redolent of a history, beginning in the fifteenth century, as a retreat for the monks of the nearby Lewes Priory, it was, despite this heritage, an "unpretending house," Virginia wrote, "long & low, a house of many doors," the ideal retreat from the "incessant nibble nibble" of London for two twentieth-century writers in search of a quiet to be broken only by the scratching of a nib pen or the striking of typewriter keys.

The house, on the town's single main street, was two stories, built of brick and flint, "very humble and unromantic," Virginia warned a friend, in comparison to the country house, Asheham, for which they would be exchanging it. Before moving in, Virginia had wondered in her diary, "but why do I let myself imagine spaces of leisure at Monks [*sic*] House? I know I shall have books that must be read there too . . . this dressing up of the future is one of the chief sources of our happiness, I believe."

Monk's House had few rooms, no electricity, and no heat or indoor plumbing. Its countervailing charms, though, included an "old chimney piece & the niches for holy water" the monks had required on either side of the fireplace, as well as expansive views across the downs to and beyond the river Ouse.

Despite a "distinctly bad" kitchen that had only an oil stove for cooking and that did double duty for heating the bath water, the pedigree conjured a Sussex home built for isolation amid natural profusion. Virginia had felt upon first sight "profound pleasure at the size & shape & fertility & wildness of the garden"—"an infinity of fruitbearing trees," "unexpected flowers sprouted among cabbages" and "well kept rows of peas, artichokes, potatoes"—and she was filled with rapture in the direction of the river, "the garden gate admits to the water meadows, where all nature is to be had in five minutes." Leonard had seen it the next day and agreed. "He was pleased beyond his expectation. The truth is he has the making of a fanatical lover of that garden," Virginia wrote. Elsewhere in England there might be "very good" country with "mystic mounds & tombs of prehistoric kings," Leonard thought. But everywhere else lacked the distinctive character and atmosphere of the Sussex countryside, he wrote to Virginia not long after their wedding, when they first thought of buying a house.

When, a few years later, Lytton Strachey was buying a country house, he became frustrated that the seller was fighting him penny by penny into a price he feared was too high. "Still I advised the leap, as I always advise leaps," Virginia wrote in her diary. In 1919, they had leapt at Monk's House.

How "ironical" it was to find the "so savagely anti-clerical" Leonard in a house for monks. And, to some, how appalling: Leonard, "a born writer and a born gardener," was also Jewish. "As soon as a Jew has enough money to buy a place in the country he always chooses one that is called the Priory, Abbey, Minster, Chantry," the Baron de Charlus says in Proust's *Sodom and Gomorrah*.

But the name "Monk's House," it turned out, was entirely a snare. It was a realtor's invention, "quite fraudulent," used for the first time when the house was advertised for sale the summer the Woolves bought it, as Leonard, usually the most careful of businessmen and the most meticulous of record keepers, discovered almost five decades later. He was then in his eighties, still very much in residence, and writing the fourth volume of his autobiography. The house had been expanded and modernized in stages, as Virginia's income from writing had increased book by book, and then again many times during the almost three decades he lived there alone after her death. In the more than two hundred years of its history before he and Virginia bought it for £700, no monks, but rather a carpenter and a miller and their relations, had ever retreated to its plain rooms. The house had been known as "The Cleers," for one of the three families that lived there.

* * *

On the side away from the meadows, Monk's House abutted the local church, its school, and its graveyard. The church bell's chiming of the hour so close by brought its own punctual frustration—as did the noisy interruption of children on their way to and from the church school or singing. These sounds found their way into *Jacob's Room*. One character is a painter, who, "loving children," is nevertheless "exasperated by the noise" of one child calling to another outside his studio as he "picked nervously at the dark little coils on his palette." Noise had been a worry, too, when she and Leonard had been thinking of moving to Hogarth House, in Richmond. "We walked to Hogarth this afternoon, to see if the noise of schoolchildren is really a drawback," Virginia had written of their inspection, relieved to find it would really "only affect Suffield," the other half of the early-eighteenth-century residence from which the two adjoined houses had been divided.

In such "rather shabby, but very easy surroundings, the members of Bloomsbury gathered to eat and talk," Quentin Bell, Virginia's nephew and her biographer, remembered decades later of homes like Monk's and Hogarth House. "I don't think they needed much else to amuse them." In 1922, Virginia and Leonard were hosts at Monk's House to many more guests than usual—the "most sociable summer we've ever had," Virginia wrote in her diary, the contrast with the summer of 1921 stark and refreshing.

They ended their London "season," at the end of July, with Rodmell "summers" running from August into autumn and the first week of October. "What is the sense of coming to London in September?" Virginia wrote to a friend trying to arrange a visit. "You must know that the Woolves aren't there then. How could we be? Why should we be? And then you pretend to expect to see us." Why should they be, when every year, as Leonard put it, "Sept. is so magnificent here," and he could spend nearly every afternoon in the garden.

So there could be no reason to return to Hogarth House before October, one annual rite being that the servants would "have to go on their holidays." But then the last week of September would arrive and Leonard would awaken one morning and feel "the summer dying out of the year, and the chill of autumn in fact immediately descended . . . a regular grey, damp Rodmell autumn with the clouds right at the foot of the downs and the smell of dead leaves burning." Then they could go back to London.

After the war, what Leonard called "civilization" had begun to penetrate into Sussex. There was even a bus that made it easier to travel between Rodmell and Charleston, the grander, if even more unorthodox, house nearby, where Vanessa and Clive Bell lived with their children.

"Nothing could exceed the monotony of life at Charleston except the pleasantness of that monotony," Clive wrote to Mary Hutchinson. "One comes down to breakfast as much before ten as possible, hopes for letters, kills a wasp, smokes a pipe, contemplates nature, writes till lunch, reads The Times, goes for a walk, drinks tea, reads Proust, shaves, writes to Polly"—Clive's nickname for Mary herself—". . . dines, lights a fire, smokes a cheroot, reads the Grenville memoirs, smokes a pipe, reads Proust, goes to bed. Sometimes it rains."

At Monk's the monotony, by contrast, consisted of days parceled up into routine activities of work, just as it was in Richmond.

* * *

On Sunday, July 23, Leonard read through *Jacob's Room*. The novel had had to be postponed, but Leonard's reaction went very far to redeem the loss of a season and to alleviate Virginia's fear that delaying it would render it only "sterile acrobatics": "He thinks it my best work. But his first remark was that it was amazingly well written." He told Virginia it was a work of genius, "unlike any other novel." They disagreed about whether her people "were puppets," as he thought, and she did not. But he found it "very interesting, & beautiful" and almost completely "without lapse. . . . I am on the whole pleased." He thought she ought to consider using her "method"—

her focus on the internal—more narrowly next time, burrowing in "on one or two characters" rather than on the larger chorus of *Jacob's Room*. She had already been doing this, in "Mrs. Dalloway in Bond Street," and Leonard's advice, so attuned to the experiment she had under way in the story she was continuing to revise, gave her encouragement to go on thinking about the ways in which that story might be developed further. His identification of her "method" in *Jacob's Room* was a ratification of her own burgeoning conviction that what she had begun to do with Clarissa Dalloway was a further advance on the novel that preceded it. She had made a kind of formal breakthrough that she must now recognize, and lay possession to, as hers.

* * *

She could savor the last days of July in London. They had dinner with Vanessa, Duncan, Tom, and Hope Mirlees, another poet they published, and *Jacob's Room* was at last on its way to Donald Brace, her publisher in New York. She noticed, too, "On the whole, L. & I are becoming celebrities," she wrote in her diary, knowing that Leonard would deny it, but convinced that she was right, her observation "drawn from other sources." Clive had likely been one, or perhaps even the only one, of these, because it was from him that she presumably heard the opinion of an acquaintance of his who was longing to be introduced to Virginia: "Mrs Nicolson thinks me the best woman writer—& I have almost got used to Mrs Nicolson's having heard of me. But it gives me some pleasure." Mrs. Harold Nicolson was Vita Sackville-West.

Then, on Monday, July 31, the day of the Seltzer trial and Seldes's testimony in New York, they had a farewell dinner at Commercio, their regular spot on Frith Street, celebrating with Roger Fry and Clive, who, just back from Paris, was a last-minute addition, having run into Virginia in the street unexpectedly. Taking advantage of the prewar liberties that the recently extended licensing hours allowed, they savored "our usual talk," as Virginia put it in her diary, Clive's "bits of gossip" about adulterous entanglements among Rodmell villagers and, via his mistress Mary, the "literary and fashionable intelligence." Tom had been invited, but was too busy, and spent his evening "dictating to his typist," Clive reported to Mary. Tom did join them afterward, at Clive's flat in Gordon Square, arriving "very neat from the type-writers," Clive told her. Tom solicited a contribution for the *Criterion* from Fry, who had been showing his paintings to the group, and though Tom had heard from John Quinn by cable on Saturday that his contract with Liveright had been signed, he was apparently completely silent on the subject of his poem. Neither Clive, writing to Mary, nor Virginia, in a colorful account of their evening in her diary, mentions what both would likely have recorded as the major news it was.

There was something Cheshire Cat about Tom that night, though. He was "sardonic, guarded, precise, & slightly malevolent, as usual," Virginia wrote.

* * *

The next morning, Clive and the Woolves took the train to Lewes together, the journey, with servants and voluminous luggage and packages, "organized with uncommon skill: we chattered all the way down—I hardly know about what," Clive told Mary, surprised to learn that his cook, Mrs. Harland, was a "most engaging companion" who seemed to know "all the theatrical profession and to have seen all the plays—they send her tickets . . . and rather respects me because she thinks I am in with the theatrical world and lead a loose life."

Packed to go to Sussex was a deceptively simple way of putting it, Virginia once joked, given that it meant also packing up the Hogarth Press. "We travel with a selection of our books placed in hampers," and the cumbersome array was in addition to their dog. (Their summer convoy one year also included "a tortoise, bought for 2/-yesterday in the High Street.") Virginia left Leonard to preside over the decampment and the wrangling of humans, beasts, and luggage, "with considerable mastery—poor devil," she wrote. "I make him pay for his unfortunate mistake in being born a Jew by discharging the whole business of life. This induces in me a sense of the transitoriness of existence, and the unreality of matter, which is highly congenial and comfortable."

* * *

As if to test her after her winter illnesses, this summer the Sussex weather upset her daily routines. August was full of "rain, wind, & dark London looking skies," only a scattering of good days, and the paths often too muddy to walk along. This meant an "almost constant stream across the floor" of the Monk's House kitchen so extreme it might have been "one of the main tributaries" of the nearby Ouse.

But the disruption did not prove fatal for Virginia, as variations so often had been and were to be. Now it seemed Virginia had almost effortlessly persevered. The "gift of summer," which had for too long been "promised & then withheld," had now, she saw, brought a garden blooming as never before—apples and pears, and green peas that arrived in time to eat before they returned to Richmond.

And the summer's gift to her was a new freedom of mind she was unused to experiencing: "There's no doubt in my mind that I have found out how to begin (at 40) to say something in my own voice; & that interests me so that I feel I can go ahead without praise." With *Jacob's Room* finished, she thought again about her reading essay and also made expansive plans about the fiction she might be able to write in autumn. And even though she dreaded the reviews of *Jacob's Room* and admitted, "I can't write while I'm being read," what others were to say then seemed less essential than her own confidence at Monk's House now. "At last, I like reading my own writing. It seems to me to fit closer than it did before."

* * *

Their most sociable summer might, like the weather, have had its own cost.

"Visitors leave one in tatters," she wrote on the sixth of September, but they kept inviting them, because, she added on the other side of a semicolon, they also left her "with a relish for words." Lytton Strachey was coming for several days in mid-September, for the second part of a visit that began at Charleston with Vanessa and Clive Bell. When Clive asked whether the order of the visits might be reversed, he discovered it couldn't be done: "Woolf & Virginia had arranged everything as neatly as a Chinese puzzle." Yet it had all come together despite the fact that, Virginia wrote a friend, "neither of us wishes for visitors. Of course they threaten us from all sides—Partridges, M[olly], Hamilton, Americans, Lytton, Morgan, Tom, Sangers—no: leave me, leave me, is all I say: to work my brain."

Morgan and Tom had missed their weekend together at Garsington in the spring and would be visiting together the third weekend of September. They would be the final guests of the season.

* * *

Tom arrived on Saturday, after his morning's work at Lloyds. A letter from John Quinn, written on September 7 and received just before he was to visit Monk's, outlined the final arrangements for publication of *The Waste Land*, first in the November issue of the *Dial* and then afterward as a book, by Liveright.

The poem would be published within weeks, running in the *Dial* issue scheduled to appear about October 20. Eliot would be paid the $10 a page that Thayer had offered in January, but as Watson had proposed, Eliot would also get the Dial Prize, and its $2,000 cash award, for his "services to the cause of literature." Liveright would publish the book in December, paying Eliot $150 upon publication, and the *Dial* would buy 350 copies of his $2 edition, at a 40 percent discount, to "push mightily" as promotional copies for subscribers. The arrangement basically ensured that Liveright would not lose money on the book and that the *Dial* would not, either, since, as Seldes noted, even it were to be a total loss they would have paid only about $350. The notes that Eliot had written were to appear only in Liveright's edition, which Seldes regretted because, as he reported to *Dial* co-owner Watson, they were "exceedingly interesting and add much to the poem . . . but don't become interested in them because we simply cannot have them."

Once Quinn and Liveright had signed the book contract at the end of July, Eliot no longer cared very much whether the *Dial* would publish *The Waste Land*, still angry at Thayer despite what he thought had been Watson's charming manner, even though "it's my loss, I suppose," he wrote to Pound on August 30.

But it would also be the *Dial*'s loss—of prestige but also of copy to fill the magazine—and Seldes, worried about it, as he had been all summer, took matters into his own hands at the end of August and proposed privately to Liveright the arrangement that Quinn formalized. "It was a close shave," Quinn wrote Eliot, reporting on a meeting with Liveright and Seldes in his office. "There was a good deal of chinning" about terms, and "Seldes made Liveright promise in nine different forms that he would keep The Dial's intention to award you the $2,000 prize confidential." But Liveright, with his penchant for publicity, knew the importance of the award and the value to him of keeping it secret. By the terms of the agree-

ment, he would not be able to publish it on October 1, as his autumn catalog had indicated—but with 350 sold before he even needed to print the
book, the delay was a lucrative one.

When Liveright published the book in December, to take advantage
of the *Dial*'s publicity, he put the news of the Dial Prize on the front cover,
so that it was nearly as prominent as the title and author. He also followed
Seldes's suggestion to number copies of the first edition to give the book
"bibliographical value." He printed one thousand copies. And he lowered
the price to $1.50.

* * *

Just before leaving for Sussex, Eliot wrote to Quinn in gratitude, "quite
overwhelmed by your letter, by all that you have done for me, by the results
that have been effected, and by your endless kindness. In fact, the greatest
pleasure of all that it has given me is the thought that there should be
anybody in the world who would take such an immense amount of pains
on my behalf."

But he was as silent in September as he had been sardonic and guarded
at Gordon Square on the evening of July 31. Whether out of discretion or
modesty, Tom seems to have said nothing about the imminent publication
of his poem during his weekend at the Woolves', even though they discussed the fellowship fund in detail. Virginia wrote two long diary entries
about the weekend. She analyzed Tom as she usually did and described
their conversation about the fund, but made no mention of *The Waste Land*.

* * *

Morgan arrived on Friday, allowing an evening's visit before Tom arrived for
the weekend, too. Forster, by contrast with the formal Eliot, dressed shab-
bily, traveling lightly with a frayed rucksack for luggage. (He had been teased
about his clothes for years, and during the war el Adl had "gently" complained to him, "You know, Forster, though I am poorer than you I would
never be seen in such a coat" as the tattered one Forster wore. "I am not
blaming you—no, I praise—but I would never *be* seen, and your hat has a
hole and your boot has a hole and your socks have a hole.")

As overnight guests Forster and Eliot were an unlikely pairing—
never to be repeated—particularly in a house of such close quarters and
with so little privacy. Morgan did all he could to keep to himself, writing

an article in his room upstairs, busy, largely out of sight, until Tom had left after tea on Sunday. Then the three old friends "snuggled in & Morgan became very familiar; anecdotic; simple, gossiping about friends & humming his little tunes," Virginia wrote in her diary.

Morgan did not always mix well with other guests, she had found, and, after one uneasy weekend, thought that "Forster would come out better alone," which, in the end, was true of this weekend, too. On the earlier occasion Morgan had been "easily drowned" by the vivacity of the others, struggling himself with an awkwardness he had described in *Howards End*: "I don't believe in suiting my conversation to my company," one of Forster's protagonists says. "One can doubtless hit upon some medium of exchange that seems to do well enough, but it's no more like real conversation than money is like food. There's no nourishment in it."

Morgan was "often melancholy and low-temperature," particularly when faced with those, like Eliot, with whom he was cordial, but about whom he was decisive and judgmental. "He never effused," Virginia wrote in her diary, and he could not easily hide it if "he didn't like you." The cozy ebullience Virginia was often able to spark in Morgan, Tom's presence almost instantly stifled. Eliot could not encounter the playful Morgan, and perhaps like Wyndham Lewis at Garsington, he didn't witness that when enjoying a bit of gossip Morgan's blue eyes would "sparkle" with pleasure and amusement. This was often the amused prelude to a "sort of suppressed sneeze, which became a surreptitious laugh . . . a little sneeze of joy."

Tom's mind, Virginia noted that weekend, "is all breadth & bone compared with Morgan's," as if seeing them at such close quarters for the first time revealed each anew. Morgan had "something too simple about him—for a writer perhaps, mystic, silly, but with a childs [sic] insight." Tom, she felt, retained little of the directness that was the foundation of Morgan's observant, insightful nature. Tom, too guarded at least in her presence, was earnest and pedagogical, playacting at the convivial guest and tending even in casual conversation to the oracular pronouncement, the whole weekend another stage set for him to play a role.

Alone with Leonard and Virginia, Morgan told them that Tom had asked him to contribute to the *Criterion*, flattery of the eminent novelist, so recently boosted by the *Times*, by the younger editor seeking recognizable names for the table of contents of his new magazine.

But flattery and compliments could "scarcely touch" Morgan, and Morgan, Virginia noted approvingly, was very different from herself, caring "very little I should think what people say. . . . I dont think he wishes to shine in intellectual society; certainly not in fashionable. . . . To dominate the talk"—as Eliot did—"would be odious to him."

* * *

Much of the talk was about *Ulysses*.

It had now been two years since the September 1920 weekend when Eliot's praise of Joyce had left Virginia feeling that what she was doing, in her stories, was "probably being better done by Mr Joyce." And it had been nearly six months since she had cut the pages of *Ulysses*, left the book for Leonard actually to read, and then begun to read Proust instead. In the summer it had been the other way around: she had been in the second of her two-volume edition of *Swann*, when she put it aside to read *Ulysses* again, resenting that Joyce was one of "these undelivered geniuses" whom one couldn't neglect, "or silence their groans, but must help them out, at considerable pains to oneself," she wrote to a friend in June. That certainly proved truc. By August she had read two hundred pages—"not a third." She had decided she was "amused, stimulated, charmed[,] interested by the first 2 or 3 chapters—to the end of the Cemetery scene; & then puzzled, bored, irritated, & disillusioned as by a queasy undergraduate scratching his pimples," she wrote in her diary, eliding the distinction between the writer and his work. "An illiterate, underbred book it seems to me: the book of a self-taught working man, & we all know how distressing they are, how egotistic, insistent, raw, striking, & ultimately nauseating." But was the novel or the working man distressing, egotistic, raw, striking, and ultimately nauseating?

She had written to Clive in frustration and disbelief—she was going to give Tom a piece of her mind about Joyce and *Ulysses* when he visited. And in seeing no difference between the man and his work, Virginia had a particularly fitting interlocutor in Clive, to whom she had, in 1917, confessed her boredom with *A Portrait of the Artist as a Young Man*.

Clive had met Joyce for the first time in Paris on May 6, 1921, and wrote Mary the next morning about the encounter, memorable for all the wrong reasons.

Bell and some friends had started the evening at the Deux Magots, and then went to dinner at Michaud. One of Clive's companions saw a man he knew sitting in an adjoining room with a friend of his own. Bell did not recognize either of the men but was told one of them was "un critique anglais qui devait être americain . . . un sale type—qui parle tout le temps dans un français de l'anglais de l'opéra-bouffe de ses livres et de leur valeur"—an English critic who must be American—a bad sort—who speaks only about his own books and their value in a French out of an opera bouffe.

"And who do think the critique anglais qui devait être americain was?" Clive wrote Mary.

> The creature immediately thrust an immense card under my nose and on it was the name of your favorite author—James Joyce. His companion, who happily spoke not one word of French, was called McAlmon . . . and gives himself out as the most intimate friend of the well-known American poet—T. S. Eliot. God, what a couple. Joyce did not seem stupid, but pretentious, underbred and provincial beyond words: and what an accent. McAlmon is an American. They both think nobly of themselves, well of Ezra Pound and poorly of Wyndham Lewis.

Clive spoke in English to "Mr. Mac"—Robert McAlmon, a poet and editor who was an acquaintance of Eliot's but not an intimate friend by any means—while the "little nuisance" who had brought the two over, "broke in drunkenly on Joyce's incessant monologue of self-appreciation." It was not a compliment when Clive described Joyce to Mary as "exactly what a modern genius ought to be"; he looked like "something between an American traveller in flash jewellery and a teacher in a Glasgow socialist Sunday-school."

It is unlikely that in the more than a year since that evening, Clive had not repeated to Virginia at least some of what he told Mary, given that Joyce had been a recurring topic between them for years. More likely is that he repeated a version of the Joyce story in a letter that does not survive or that he told her about the meeting upon his return to London. In October 1921, in fact, Virginia had written to Roger Fry about an evening's talk, "Eliot says that Joyce's novel is the greatest work of the age—Lytton says he doesn't mean to read it. Clive says—well, Clive says that Mary Hutchinson has a dressmaker who would make me look like other people." Not long after that, Clive was in Paris again. He had a drink on his way home one night and reported to Mary that the evening had been a success on at least one count: he had avoided Joyce, "who grinned at me from les deux maggots [*sic*]."

Now that she was reading *Ulysses* in earnest, Virginia, as if channeling Clive, judged the book by the man and his manners, using an array of adjectives she spewed in her diary that repeated Clive's to Mary. The book was "underbred," as Joyce in Paris, in person, had been. Even the appalling provincial accent that had horrified Clive she heard, too, in this book by the pretentious and egotistic "self-taught working man" who had immediately and inelegantly thrust his card upon the refined Clive Bell.

Ulysses had also come up when Clive visited Virginia one afternoon in mid-August. Virginia was "utterly contemptuous" of the book, Clive told Mary, and had asked him, with the same surprise she had had at Tom's reaction, "Did Mary really admire it?" Clive replied by hedging. Mary "had only read a bit here and there," he said, or at least was protesting to Mary that he had tried to keep her safe from Virginia's scorn. But Virginia that afternoon sounded much like Virginia writing in her diary: *Ulysses* was "feeble, wordy, uneducated stuff, cheap as a preparatory school," she told Clive. Clive took playful satisfaction in passing on Virginia's excoriation of the book; but knowing that Mary and Virginia were not always on good terms, he also took pleasure in having a little fun at his opinionated sister-in-law's expense. Clive suggested Virginia might simply have been reading the book at the wrong time, and reported to Mary that he had "found Virginia down with the monthlies, but brisk and gay enough in the head for all that."

But neither her monthlies nor her echoing of Clive's disdain could hide the fact that Joyce and his book were as worrisome a specter as they had been in 1920. She rephrased the question in a new way almost two years later: "When one can have the cooked flesh, why have the raw?" she wrote in her diary. It was a rhetorical question and a statement of purpose. She saw her own method reflected in *Ulysses*, saw her own work reflected in it as if in a fun house mirror, the method unrecognizable, the "raw" work distorted from what it ought to become, and left unfinished.

"I may revise this later. I do not compromise my critical sagacity. I plant a stick in the ground to mark page 200," she wrote in her diary in

August. The next sentence was about her own work, as if she paused in *Ulysses* not only from boredom and exhaustion but also so that she could think more deeply about her own aims before continuing work on the short story she had begun writing in the spring. "For my own part, I am laboriously dredging my mind for Mrs Dalloway & bringing up light buckets. I don't like the feeling I'm writing too quickly. I must press it together."

As always, the question of what the men were doing sharpened her sense first of inadequacy, and then of her own ambition. She might judge herself superior to the underbred working man she had called Joyce, but then perhaps she wasn't: if it were a difference not only of class but of education, Joyce had a university degree and it was she herself who was self-taught. At the heart of her anxiety and her anger were questions of literary apprenticeship and approbation, and what it meant to be a woman writing.

The burr, examined, became, as usual, a spur. As was her other fear, that perhaps in too easily finding critical common ground with Clive, she was falling in with the facile way of thinking he made attractive and entertaining but that she at other times recognized was superficial and incomplete. One sentence in her diary about *Ulysses* and the next about *Mrs. Dalloway*. In the reading of the one she saw something of the writing of the other.

* * *

By September, as if preparing for Tom's visit, Virginia had finished *Ulysses*— read "the last immortal chapter"—"think it is a mis-fire," she wrote in her diary. Once again, she thought of Joyce's work and her own in uneasy tandem. *Ulysses* might be a misfire, but she feared the same was true of *Jacob's Room*. Only two months before, she had noted her satisfaction in reading her own writing. Now, correcting the proofs had left her feeling the novel "reads thin & pointless; the words scarcely dint the paper," even as her fears about it encouraged her to think, or to delude herself, that whatever she would write next would be "something rich, & deep, & fluent, & hard as nails, while bright as diamonds."

From her hopes about what she would write eventually, she turned to analyzing the particulars of Joyce's failure. "Genius it has I think; but of the inferior water." She called it "brackish"—it was *not* rich and deep, like the work she would next write, but murky, and she phrased it as if to suggest what she had discovered of it was a relief to her and her future hopes. And then she repeated Clive's words once more, calling it pretentious and also underbred, "not only in the obvious sense, but in the literary sense," as if on further reading and reflection, making a distinction between man and book was not only impossible but unnecessary. The novel was simply a writer "doing stunts," and a first-rate writer, which Joyce obviously was not, "respects writing too much to be tricky," she thought. Joyce was exactly her own age, younger by only a week, and as she had judged herself as a writer at forty all year, now she judged him on the maturity he ought to have. "I'm reminded of some callow board school boy . . . so self-conscious & egotistical that he loses his head, becomes extravagant, mannered, uproarious, ill at ease, makes kindly people feel sorry for him, & stern ones merely annoyed; & one hopes he'll grow out of it." But at Joyce's age, "this scarcely seems likely."

Though she thought she might have "scamped the virtue of it more than is fair," she was confident enough to conclude that the effect of *Ulysses* was "myriads of tiny bullets" that spattered but were too weak to give that "one deadly wound straight in the face." That was what reading Tolstoy was like—but she stopped herself, saying "it is entirely absurd to compare him with Tolstoy," as she was shocked that Tom had done: "And Tom, great Tom, thinks this on a par with War & Peace!" She had, in this last rush, read it as much through his eyes as her own, trying, and failing, to make sense of his ecstatic praise, which had "over stimulated" her and perhaps left her with "my back up on purpose."

Myriads of tiny bullets. Virginia framed her response to *Ulysses* differently, but she had had a similar reaction to *The Waste Land* when she had heard it in June. Her question then had been, What connected it together? She had not been sure and was not sure now of what held the tiny bullets of *Ulysses* together, either. She was sure only that in *Mrs. Dalloway* her goal, as she had put it in her diary, must be to press it together.

* * *

On September 7, the day after she had written out her thoughts in her diary, Leonard gave her a review of the novel that had appeared in an American magazine the previous week. It was by Gilbert Seldes, who had been simultaneously rescuing *The Waste Land* from Scofield Thayer's purgatory and doing what he could to champion *Ulysses* to an American readership who could not yet purchase it for themselves. (Seldes's review appeared in the *Nation*, its editors, like Seltzer's lawyer, having more faith in his good judgment than his boss at the *Dial* did.) Seldes's review was very intelligent, Virginia thought, and had cleared away some of the obscurity that had defeated her, making the book "much more impressive than I had judged." But there was "some lasting truth in first impressions" that would not cancel hers, she decided, even though she thought she must read some of the chapters again. (If she ever did so, she does not mention it.) Still, even after reading Seldes's review she realized that she ought to have been "bowled over" by *Ulysses* and was not. Her first impression did hold.

When Tom came the last weekend of September, he was as definitive as she had been in her diary, but in the other direction: "The book would be a landmark, because it destroyed the whole of the 19th century." Perhaps to qualify this a bit for Virginia's benefit, or his own, he pointed out that this left Joyce himself "with nothing to write another book on. It showed up the futility of all English styles." Tom said that there was no "great conception" behind *Ulysses*. Joyce was more interested, Tom argued, in the individual character of Leopold Bloom, what the workings of his mind could reveal of character rather than of human nature. Joyce had done what he had meant to do—"completely." Joyce's "new method of giving psychology" had destroyed the nineteenth century, or at least its literary conventions.

But Woolf could not agree. William Thackeray's *Pendennis*, she thought, was more illuminating of an individual than Joyce's approach to Leopold Bloom in *Ulysses*. Here, again, was the question of how to create character in fiction. Had Joyce really found a new way? It did not seem so to her. "We know so little about the people," she complained.

The question raised by Thackeray's *Pendennis* and by Tom's contention that Joyce's *Ulysses* had destroyed the nineteenth century was a signal to Woolf "how far we now accept the old tradition without thinking." As she put it in a note to herself, "Its [*sic*] a very queer convention that makes us believe that people talked or felt or lived as J. A. & Thackeray & Dickens make them—the only thing is that we're used to it."

In *Jacob's Room* and in "Mrs. Dalloway in Bond Street," she, too, had begun a new method of giving psychology. But this was not enough if it missed out at a representation of life. Austen and Thackeray and Dickens made readers—made her—believe that people talked and felt and lived as they described them. Joyce had not. And Leonard, at least, did not think she had done enough to represent life in *Jacob's Room*. But, she wondered, "What is life? Thats [*sic*] the question. Something not necessarily leading to a plot." She must master her intention, as Joyce had. She thought she "could have screwed Jacob up tighter," as she put it in her diary.

* * *

Morgan was, apparently, of two minds about Joyce, though he was so far from dominating the conversation, or perhaps even joining it, that his comments, if any, go unrecorded by Virginia. He had discovered Joyce's *Portrait of the Artist as a Young Man* not long after it first appeared, in 1917, and had been impressed, at least, by Mohammed's request for a copy of it and his friend's description of it as "a very remarkable product." Evidently Forster shared that opinion, and continued to think so, or at least treasured the memory that Mohammed had been so charming when he said it. Years later, in 1930, when he met Bob Buckingham, the police constable who would be his emotional mainstay for the rest of his life, the two men talked about books. Buckingham had been reading Dostoyevsky, he told Forster. Forster, in turn, offered when they met again, as they did a few days later at Forster's London apartment, to lend him two books: his own *A Passage to India* and Joyce's *Portrait of the Artist*.

Nonetheless, in 1959, on the occasion of his eightieth birthday, Forster was interviewed for television and, as part of the program, was shown writing at his desk. Shortly after the broadcast, V. S. Pritchett asked him what he had been writing when the camera was rolling. One sentence "over and over again until they had got their picture," Forster replied. " 'James Joyce is a very bad writer.' I kept on writing it."

* * *

Virginia was done with Joyce and was ready to sell him for whatever small profit she could—£4 10s, even, she joked to David "Bunny" Garnett, the bookseller from whom she had bought it. She was also going to get back to Proust. She had been bound to *Ulysses* "like a martyr to a stake." But it was "far otherwise" with Proust, she wrote to Roger Fry, in her last letter from Monk's House in October, marking not only her return to Richmond but also to Proust's happier pages and the "great adventure" he had become for her.

Fry had urged her to read Proust long before. Now he was the confessor to whom she could speak rhapsodically, ecstatically, of "devoting myself" to Proust. She managed a rare combination of religious fanaticism and reason in her response, admitting that there might be faults to be found in Proust—"I suppose"—but that she did not see them and was "in a state of amazement; as if a miracle were being done before my eyes."

> How, at last, has someone solidified what has always escaped—and made it too into this beautiful and perfectly enduring substance? One has to put the book down and gasp. The pleasure becomes physical—like sun and wine and grapes and perfect serenity and intense vitality combined.

"Well, what remains to be written after that?" Virginia asked.

She returned to Richmond and, within a few days, she knew. She wrote in her diary: "Mrs Dalloway in Bond Street has branched into a book; & I adumbrate here a study of insanity & suicide: the world seen by the sane & the insane side by side—something like that."

She had gleaned from Joyce and Proust different answers to the question hearing Tom read *The Waste Land* had raised: What connects it together? And in autumn, as in the spring, she would begin the further development.

Chapter 15

DAVID AND FRIEDA ARRIVE IN TAOS

HALFWAY AROUND THE WORLD, FIVE thousand miles from Rodmell, and six thousand feet above sea level, D. H. Lawrence was thinking about *Ulysses*, too. The same Friday in September that Morgan came to Monk's House, Lawrence, in Taos for about ten days, wrote to Thomas Seltzer, "Can you send me also a copy of James Joyce's *Ulysses*. I read it is the last thing in novels: I'd best look at it."

It had taken more than three weeks to sail from Australia, on the *Tahiti*, like "a big boarding-house staggering over the sea," the passage £60 in first class, meaning that they "shall have blewed [*sic*] all our money on steamships." On board, Frieda won at whist, and a man could be overheard practicing the saxophone in the music room. The stop at Tahiti itself was disappointing—"dead, dull, modern, French and Chinese"—and practically the only excitement of the trip was on the last leg, when "a Crowd of cinema people" came aboard. They had been in Tahiti to film a melodrama called *Lost and Found on a South Sea Island*, about a white woman nearly forced to marry a native chieftain before she is rescued, and Law-rence was appalled that the cast and crew of the film, produced by Samuel Goldwyn and directed by Raoul Walsh, who had played John Wilkes Booth in *Birth of a Nation* (and later discovered John Wayne), were utterly undistinguished, the women only "successful shop-girls" and the men "like any sort . . . at the sea-side." All of them were "so common" and "hat-ing one another like poison, several of them drunk all the trip." They rep-resented the worst of a louche sexuality that Lawrence saw as the enemy of the higher sensual and spiritual communion men and women might attain (the sex-obsessed Mr. Lawrence's strictures on who constituted the worthy as rigid as those of any sectarian). Encountering them did not give him any more faith in the America that awaited him. Frieda was as usual more relaxed and also as usual took pleasure in noting her husband's petty condemnations and the difference between his reputation and the more conflicted reality.

* * *

David and Frieda arrived in San Francisco, "a fine town but a bit dazing," on September 4. They had been twenty-five days at sea and were, the next day, "still landsick—the floor should go up and down, the room should tremble from the engines . . . the solid ground almost hurts."

They were to spend five days there. "San Francisco very pleasant, and not at all overwhelming," Lawrence wrote after a sunny day's automobile tour of the city. But within a dozen words of this happy beginning, he had descended into a description of the "terrible" noise of "*iron* all the while," the trolleys and cable cars crisscrossing the city into a fearsome metropolis of black and glossy streets marked by steel rails that were "ribbons like the path of death itself." It was a "sort of never-stop Hades," the relentless noise and activity day and night of which "breaks my head."

They stayed four cocooned nights at the Palace Hotel. "Everybody is very nice, everything very *comfortable*," he wrote in German to his mother-in-law, the Baroness von Richthofen. "I really hate this mechani-cal *comfort*," he concluded, as wear and tear as ever.

The letter, on the hotel's elaborate notepaper, spoke of the luxury he described to Frieda's mother, Anna, and the hotel, at $7 a night, was extremely expensive for a man who had arrived with less than $20 in his pocket. The first words Lawrence wrote in America were a telegram to his agent,

ARRIVED PENNILESS TELEGRAPH DRAFT CARE PALACE HOTEL SAN FRANCISCO, and his first order of business to wait for American money from Mountsier.

Then, it was a two-day journey to New Mexico by rail—"the time-table, that magic carpet of today"—and with tickets provided by Mabel, he and Frieda boarded the Grand Canyon Limited, arriving in Lamy, twenty miles from Santa Fe, on Sunday, September 10. It was another seventy miles to Taos, and after a night just outside Santa Fe, with the poet Witter Bynner and his lover Spud Johnson, they drove to Taos, across the flat desert, that Monday, the eleventh, his thirty-seventh birthday.

Ten days later, he wrote to Seltzer about *Ulysses*. Lawrence had in common with Joyce that they were both victims of John Sumner, and little else. Lawrence, of course, was triumphant over his suppression, even if, by law, the victory was Seltzer's. He now set about getting his hands on a copy of Joyce's elusive blue-covered book.

The status of the complete *Ulysses* had not been tested in court, and though neither Liveright, Huebsch, nor Knopf had been willing to risk publishing it, it was not explicitly banned. Quinn ordered fourteen copies of *Ulysses* from Sylvia Beach and wrote her early in 1922 that he did not want to take a chance that they might be confiscated by customs. He had seen her advertisement for the book in the most recent issue of the *Little Review*, and, he warned her, "I know that Sumner is watching the Little Review, particularly because of the 'Ulysses' mess. He is therefore sure to have instructed the customs authorities to confiscate all copies of 'Ulysses' that come by mail or any other way." Quinn agreed to pay for his copies in advance so that, he told her, "they will become my property and then I must be consulted as to how they are to be sent here." He did not know, or care, what she planned to do about mailing anyone else's copies to the United States, but once paid for, his must be set aside, "carefully wrapped up, and *held subject to my order*." He proposed that a friend who was visiting Paris might bring them back for him, or he might ask her to send the books to Canada, where a dealer would receive them on his behalf and either mail them or bring them to New York himself. In fact, many copies of Beach's first thousand-copy limited edition were sent to buyers in the United States or brought into the country by returning travelers, without incident.

In his letter to Seltzer, Lawrence had also asked for some other books, a Spanish-language primer, Spanish-English dictionary, and a recently published book about Melville. When these arrived, but without a copy of Joyce's novel, he wondered, "Couldn't you find *Ulysses*? If you could just *lend* it to me, to read."

Ulysses had been on his mind even in Australia, where there was press coverage of the publication of the Shakespeare and Company edition. "I shall be able to read this famous *Ulysses* when I get to America. I doubt he is a trickster," he had written to a friend in London in July—using the same formulation Virginia Woolf had—though reserving judgment. Like Virginia, he could not help but see his own work in tandem or in opposition to it, and added about *Kangaroo*, "I have nearly finished my novel here—but such a novel! Even the Ulysseans will spit at it." His argument was less with Joyce than with the acolytes and critics, among them Pound, who valorized Joyce's genius as if the (by comparison) more conventional novels Lawrence wrote—less visibly experimental in form, without the same obscuring emphasis on the internal, everything perceived by the characters rather than anything observed by an omniscient narrator—were not making a formal break with tradition, too.

Lawrence's novel *Aaron's Rod* had, meanwhile, appeared in England that summer. It was, inevitably, compared to *Ulysses*, as no novel published after it, particularly so soon after it, could avoid. Lawrence was less self-conscious of this comparison than Virginia Woolf, but he was as aware as she was that any fiction published in the wake of even its excerpts was being read at least by critics in Joyce's shadow.

John Middleton Murry in the *Nation and Athenaeum* proclaimed, in August, that *Aaron's Rod* was "much more important" than Joyce's novel, his worry that with *Women in Love* Lawrence had passed his peak now completely allayed. Spit the Ulysseans might at Lawrence, and he might welcome their dismissal, but Murry embraced the difference: the intellectual armature of *Ulysses*, the foundation of it in the ancient Homeric myths, rendered it "sterile"; by contrast, *Aaron's Rod* was "full of the sap of life." The "whole of Mr Joyce is in *Ulysses*," Murry wrote, as if the novel had exhausted Joyce as much as it exhausted Murry. Murry did not damn Joyce completely. He recognized *Ulysses* as a literary milestone, but thought that even if *Aaron's Rod* were undoubtedly a smaller work in one way, it was not the whole of Mr. Lawrence, but rather a "fruit on the tree of Mr. Lawrence's creativeness. . . .

No other living writer could drive us to a frenzy of hostility as he has done; no other fill us with such delight."

Eliot, who had told Virginia Woolf at Monk's House that Joyce had left himself nothing to build on after *Ulysses*, might have been surprised to find himself in relative agreement with Murry's conclusion that it represented the "whole of Mr Joyce," particularly given the personal and literary animosity he and Murry often felt for each other, and even more so because he thought *Ulysses* an unadulterated triumph. But he and Virginia spoke of Lawrence, too, at Monk's House, and there remained some ground of opposition to Murry. Eliot had read *Aaron's Rod*, he told Virginia, and thought that in it Lawrence "came off occasionally." He "had great moments," even if overall he was "a most incompetent writer."

* * *

Mabel had spent the better part of a year willing Lawrence to come to Taos, but all along she had accurately understood Lawrence's delays as a result of his fear of her. "They wanted to see me, take a look, even a bite, and be able to spit me out if they didn't like it" she was to write in her memoirs. But whatever Lawrence's considerable misgivings about America itself and about his hostess, he had anticipated his arrival in Taos as at least another fresh beginning for him as a writer. He had written his Australian novel as planned and left. Now, in a new place, he would revise it, and he planned to write another. "I build quite a lot on Taos—and the pueblo," he had written Mabel from Australia. He would write "an American novel from that centre. It's what I want to do."

Lawrence immediately fell in love with the landscape, and his first impression of it affirmed the foretaste of the primordial and fantastical that Mabel had wafted his way the year before. He was immediately curious, too, about the Indians, a people whose ancient ways persisted, he imagined, unsullied by the modern world, their pueblo a living symbol of the wellsprings of humanity he sought in the Far West. But Mabel was the center of things in Taos, as far as she was concerned, her domination of what was more of an outpost than a village complete enough that it was really "Mabel-town." He had not come so far to be a citizen, or acolyte, of that little world, an ancient land populated by modern fools, the "subarty" here no different from the Mad Hatter's Tea Party he had fled in

Taormina. But he had understood in Taormina that it would not be any different in Taos—had heard the similarity even in the sound—and yet here he was.

For Lawrence, the erasure of the ancient was perhaps most disappointingly epitomized by Mabel's lover Tony Lujan. He drove them all in Mabel's Cadillac from the train station, a too willing victim, it seemed to Lawrence, of the automobile, and money, and, ultimately, of Mabel's "terrible will to power—woman power." In Lawrence's eyes, Tony was more a symbol of Indian man rather than an Indian man.

They moved into "Tony's house," which Mabel had completed in anticipation of the Lawrences' arrival. It was as spacious and comfortable as promised, and lived up to expectations, too, in being a little too near to Mabel's larger house, only about two hundred yards away.

A few days after settling in, Lawrence came over to her house early in order to begin what Mabel was to describe as "our work together." But that they would do any kind of work together was more likely Mabel's fantasy than anything Lawrence would have promised her. Mabel retold the story of Lawrence's arrival that morning in her memoirs. He was there early enough that she had not yet dressed and was sunbathing on the roof terrace outside her bedroom. She called to him to come up and, walking through her bedroom on the way out to her, he was, she either saw or imagined, shocked by the sight of her unmade bed, "a repulsive sight" to him. By his glance around the room, she wrote, he had "turned it into a brothel . . . that's how powerful he was."

The Lawrence of the SS *Tahiti* had arrived in Taos. Mabel was disappointed by the small-mindedness of this man who had come to loom so large in her imagination. For Lawrence, the "brothel" of Mabel's unmade bed was the grave of whatever ancient aristocracy Lawrence had envisioned persisting.

Mabel would go on to perfect the art of paying tribute to Lawrence while denigrating him. (T. S. Eliot was to write of Lawrence that he was a Johnson "surrounded by a shoal" of Boswells, "some of them less tender towards the great man than was Johnson's biographer.") And if Lawrence had been shocked that morning, it might have been less at the implicit display of any wanton sexuality than at the untidiness of the room, fastidious as he was; or perhaps it was surprise at her outfit, a voluminous white cashmere burnous designed, as all her clothing was, in "so-called flowing lines" to mask that "longing to be like a willow, I have always resembled a pine tree . . . the Christmas-tree variety," Mabel would write.

Lawrence wrote to his sister-in-law that Mabel "very much wants me to write about here. I don't know that I ever shall." The distinction between "here" and her—Mabel herself—was unclear and meant more to him in any case than to Mabel. In her recollection, it was not only her desire but his choice to write a book about *her*. "Of course it was for this I had called him from across the world," and she waited for him to announce it as his intention to write this very book. "He said he wanted to write an American novel that would express the life, the spirit, of America and he wanted to write it around me."

"You have done her," Mabel remembered she told him, referring to Frieda, who had appeared, in one way or another, as the female protagonist in all of his novels written after he met her, most explicitly in *Kangaroo*, which she had not yet read. "She has mothered your books long enough. You need a new mother!" But Frieda would not let him, Mabel reported as Lawrence's reply to her. "She won't let any other woman into my books."

Mabel also wanted Lawrence to join her crusade against legislation proposed in Congress that would make it more difficult for Indians to seek redress. She asked him to write an article on the subject, which he did, willingly, the request a collaboration easier to accept, and one that might postpone the other thing entirely.

Mabel and Frieda now went to war over Lawrence, or at least Mabel saw it that way. In her eyes, the "tall and full-fleshed" Frieda overwhelmed Lawrence in sheer pulchritude, his head too heavy for his too slim body, over which it hung forward, the "whole expression" of his figure, slightly built and so stooped, one of "extreme fragility." This was no match for Frieda's imposition of weight and will. Nor might it be for Mabel's own weight and will, which is where, briefly, she thought she saw her opening. And yet for all her disappointment in the sight and sound of Lawrence, or because of it, Mabel felt at the very first instant that she understood Lawrence's "plight." He was a husband in thrall, she thought, to a "limited" wife—Frieda, from whom he must be saved. She herself was the person who could do it, the impulse one she described, elementally, as "the womb in me roused to reach out to take him," an act of psychic rescue selfless, as she saw it. Lawrence and Frieda, naturally, saw things differently.

Lawrence dubbed Mabel the *padrona* and acknowledged her kindness

to him and her generosity even if he was constitutionally unable to recon-
cile himself to patronage, in general, or to the ravenous brand of physical
absorption that Mabel demanded. Not long after arriving in Taos, Lawrence wrote his agent that he thought he could be happy there—if they had
more time to themselves. Tony's house was, as he knew it would be, too
much Mabel Sterne's "ground," and whether she was ravenous or generous made little difference in the end. He wouldn't be bullied, "even by
kindness," which created a debt more costly than money and more insidious than "if one had been left to make one's way alone."

Lawrence was of two minds (as he was about most things) about
Mabel and Tony. He was at ease with them—Tony "a big fellow—nice—
they have been together several years"—but judged more harshly the
pretension of Mabel's performance of the grande dame liberated from
convention. "Mabel Sterne has an Indian lover [who] lives with her," he
wrote a friend. "She has had two white husbands and one Jew: now this.
She is pretty rich."

Mabel fancied herself Lawrence's muse, and she was sure that if it
weren't for Frieda's opposition, she would have been, for misperceiving
Lawrence she thought he "had no will of his own . . . Frieda tried to stand
with a flaming sword between him and all others." But settling in at Taos,
and with access to his American money, including $1,000 from Hearst for
the rights to "The Captain's Doll," he was intent on paying off old debts,
not incurring new ones. (This was the most he ever had received for a
story, or ever would. Hearst never actually published it, a bit of American
profligacy of which he could perhaps approve.) Very soon after he arrived,
he sent £15 to Ottoline, thanking her for the money she had kindly lent
"during the hard days" of the war, exorcising the aftermath of the suppression of *The Rainbow* and the rough times in Cornwall as he had done
in the chapter "The Nightmare" of *Kangaroo*. Now free of that debt and
other small obligations to other friends, he did not want to mortgage
whatever he would write in Taos to Mabel. That was at least one promise
the New World had kept—he had his money.

* * *

Nevertheless Lawrence tried to play his part, and after his first morning's
visit Lawrence began to write something that grew out of his conversation
with Mabel and from his own first impressions of Taos. Whether it would

be the novel Mabel dreamed of is doubtful, a͏ ͏ ͏ ͏ ͏ ͏
his agent, Mountsier, that he was working on a͏ ͏
here," pointedly emphasizing "here" rather than "͏
placate her or because he would take inspiration whe͏
and would as happily use her as a foundation as he ha͏
Jessie Chambers in *Sons and Lovers* or Heseltine in *W*
Lawrence obligingly asked Mabel to write out some notes ab͏ ͏ ͏ ͏ ͏ ͏ ͏ ͏ ͏ ͏ ͏ ͏ar
crossroads in her life, listing eleven to begin with, includin͏ her marriage to Sterne, her feelings about Tony, and her arrival in New Mexico.
"You've got to remember also things you don't want to remember," he
warned her, perhaps aware that the more difficult he made her task, the
less likely she would undertake it. Perhaps to flatter her that it really
was their work "together," he told her he might eventually incorporate
her own writing—a story she'd written about her marriage to Maurice
Sterne, some poems she had written about Tony—so that "your own
indubitable voice [be] heard sometimes." He would not show her what he
wrote until the end, he told her.

Frieda supposedly put a conditional stop to Mabel and Lawrence's
collaboration. He and Frieda "had had it out," Lawrence told Mabel. Their
work on the novel, if it were to proceed, would have to take place not at
Mabel's house, where they would have the privacy Mabel required, but at
the Lawrences', where Frieda could, he said, keep a watchful eye. In the
event, Frieda did all she could to distract them, stamping around the
house, "sweeping noisily, and singing with a loud defiance." But this stratagem seems more of Lawrence's design than Frieda's own.

It is impossible to believe that if Lawrence had wanted to write a story
or a novel with Mabel in it, he would have compromised his vision for
Frieda's sake, for he rarely if ever did anything on her behalf solely, which
was why, despite her desire to stay put anywhere, they were actually in
Taos in the first place. She had chosen him over her children, long ago,
and, as Mabel was to put it, with great sympathy, suffered "loneliness that
was like a terrible hunger." Lawrence was contemptuous of that loneliness. "He couldn't admit any rivals," Mabel wrote. Lawrence had long
bristled at practically any mention of Frieda's children; this may have
been guilt as much as egotism. But, as Frieda knew, Lawrence's true
egotism was that he would not admit any rivals to the work he must do.
His writing came first, before his wife, and certainly before any other

as that children, or affection, might be. And about this he felt guilt. Nor did Frieda ever want him to, believing in his work as fiercely as he did, and perhaps all the more so for the sacrifices she had made to be his wife.

For Mabel it was more satisfying to find grand psychological forces at work in why Lawrence could not proceed with the novel, easier to resent Frieda than to blame herself or Lawrence for the dead end his little sketch met. "I never even saw the chapter he did; I presume she tore it up," Mabel was to remember, referring to Frieda. But it was not a chapter so much as notes for a chapter. And Frieda had not torn it up. She actually was quite pleased with Lawrence's work. "It's *very* clever at the beginning, it will be rather sardonic!" she wrote to Mountsier.

* * *

And it was. In the letter Lawrence wrote Forster after he arrived in Taos, he had complained of Forster's "nearly deadly mistake glorifying those *business* people"—Henry Wilcox and his son—in *Howards End*. Perhaps because that continued to bother him, or perhaps because after venting his spleen Lawrence recalled a little of what he had first felt about the book—that it was "exceedingly good and very discussable"—Forster's novel was on his mind when he began to work on whatever it was he was going to write about Mabel.

The character based on Mabel is called Sybil Mund. On her father's side she is descended from the Hamnetts, from whom she has inherited her "force." But all her "push" comes from her mother's family—the Wilcoxes. This family heritage has "culminated" in Sybil, "this one highly-explosive daughter." The "push" of the business people in *Howards End* was what still angered Lawrence, after all these years—or perhaps after thinking about the novel again, he realized that Forster, too, had derided the "push" and that he and Forster were more on the same side than in opposition. In the novel, Forster had written that the Wilcoxes "avoided the personal note in life" and, as one of the Schlegel sisters realized, "All Wilcoxes did. It did not seem to them of supreme importance. Or it may be as Helen supposed: they realized its importance, but were afraid of it." Mabel was afraid of the personal, Lawrence saw. She lived too much from theory and was too insulated by her money to interest him very much, or for him to tolerate her even as a specimen he might observe in fascination or disgust. He had most certainly not come to America to merge with the highly explosive daughter of the Wilcox tradition.

Frieda may have been pleased with Lawrence's sardonic start, but it was not a vein in which Lawrence could write for very long. He was not a satirist, and Mabel—so ripe for satire, as he had known she would be—enraged him too much once they'd met. She "hates the white world, and loves the Indians out of hate," Lawrence wrote his mother-in-law. Instead of pursuing the "M. Sterne novel of *here*," he revised *Kangaroo* so that Seltzer could publish it in 1923, and he left in "The Nightmare" as he told Mountsier he must.

* * *

Two months of Mabel-town turned out to be all Lawrence could stand. This was longer than he had survived the heat and mosquitoes of Ceylon, and the haven he now found, a nearby ranch, higher in the mountains, promised the isolation they had found alongside the Pacific in Australia. As usual with Lawrence, the move he contemplated could not be made simply. He must make the move a manifesto, and just as at the start of 1922 he had heralded the new year to Earl Brewster as a "new incarnation," he wrote to Mabel at the end of the first week of November to tell her of his decision. It was as intolerable in mind as in body to live on Mabel Sterne's ground, and he would not do it, he announced in a letter, including ten itemized points, he wrote in response to a lost letter of hers that perhaps made new demands he could not countenance.

He, too, he told her, would "put it in black and white" and began with the item, "I don't believe in the 'Knowing' woman you are." Mabel may have provoked him, but his response was a condemnation of the modern world, more revealing of Lawrence than of Mabel.

She was "bullying and Sadish"—for sadistic—against Tony as well as himself and Frieda, not to mention the others in her orbit, and despite (or because of) her three marriages and her affair with Tony, she was "*antagonistic* to the *living* relation of man and wife." In what might be the most poignant thing he ever wrote or said about Frieda, Lawrence told Mabel, "I believe that, at its best, the central relation between Frieda and me is the best thing in my life, and, as far as I go, the best thing in life." And the letter went on.

It gives one a sense of Lawrence to know that after having written this letter—however correct he was in his bill of particulars against her—he could still believe, as he wrote to Seltzer, "Of course there is no breach with Mabel Sterne."

At first it seemed he and Frieda might be able to move to a ranch owned by Mabel's son. But it needed too many repairs, which could not be done before winter set in, and in any case was still too much on "Mabel Sterne's territory."

The new ranch, Del Monte, was set in a triangle with the house of the rancher from whom they rented it. There was also another house on the property, a smaller house in which, once again reaching for Rananim, he put up two young Danish artists he had met, his own generosity as *padrone* very different in spirit from Mabel's and a plain rebuke to her. Their little Lawrence-town made him glad to be "on free territory once more."

In the mountains, the snow was deep and coyotes could be heard howling by the gate to the property. As if to revel in their freedom, he and Frieda went riding, both of them fully American at least on the outside, in cowboy hats and boots.

But Lawrence would not have been himself if, however happy he was, he were not also equally unhappy. Just as he had loved swimming in the Pacific but then complained about how crashingly noisy it was, at Del Monte he exulted in the landscape but qualified it, loving the land "in bits." The pureness of the air and the clearness of the sky, the beauty of the clouds and the stunning sunsets, these were glorious. But then the expanses became shadowed for him, albeit in white: the snow-covered mountains above the ranch, and the flat table of the deserts below, combined to weigh on his mind and spirit and felt to him "so heavy and empty. . . . It is very depressing."

One of the Danes, the painter Knud Merrild, was to recall that Lawrence conjured Del Monte as an endangered Eden delicately poised so near to Mabel-town, but his own territory free of the "cobra." Merrild recollected Lawrence's conversation as perhaps more lyrical and apocalyptic than it was, but he captured what was then, and always, at stake for Lawrence. The world must be remade, and it had gone wrong at the start, at the very birth of man—and woman. Mabel was the Queen Cobra in a coterie filled with snakes, their fangs "full and surcharged with insult," and ready to bite him at the slightest bending toward them. This was more of the "beshitten" world he had wanted to flee when he first proposed leaving Taormina in the autumn of 1921, a year before.

"God in Heaven, no, they shall not bite me," he cried, "I must make my own world," he told Merrild, away from "beastly humans," in search, as he had been a year before, of that place, "somewhere away by myself," that he had not yet found.

The mountains themselves and the desert were tainted by the simple fact that they were American. For beyond Del Monte was the rapacious United States that with its country of materialism and hypocritical egalitarianism had killed the Indian magic he had dreamed of finding in the ancient West. His experience of America confirmed in him the idea with which he had arrived, that it was a country with, as he put it now, "no inside to life: all outside."

He recalled a conversation in Taormina with a Mrs. Ashley, an American. "In *my* country," he had heard her say to the sister of an Italian duke, "we're *all* Kings and Queens." This was the problem. "And by Jove they are—of their own muck-heaps, of money if nothing else."

* * *

Eventually Seltzer had been able to find a copy of *Ulysses* for Lawrence. It arrived in Taos on November 6, together in a package with copies of three of his own books, *Fantasia of the Unconscious*; *England, My England*; and the trade edition of *Women in Love*, "all very nice, but a terrible wrapper on *Women in Love*," Lawrence thought, put off by the head of a woman with streaming hair it depicted.

Seltzer had procured the copy of *Ulysses* from an acquaintance, "F. Wubbenhorst," a New Yorker, otherwise unidentified. Believing that Seltzer had only borrowed it from Mr. Wubbenhorst, Lawrence promised to read it within about a week and return it. Seltzer, though, had actually bought it, at his own expense, as a gift. When Lawrence later learned this, and that the price might have been $25 or more, he was grateful but adamant, perhaps even more on his guard living as he still was on Mabel's "ground." "I do *not* want you to pay for books for me. Please charge them to me, or I feel uneasy."

Lawrence was no more impressed by *Ulysses* than he had thought he would be. No Ulyssean he. When Lawrence sent the book back to Wubbenhorst on November 14, he was thankful for the loan but glad to be rid of it. "I am sorry, but I am one of the people who can't read *Ulysses*. Only bits," which was not far from Virginia's reaction, though he did not persevere as she had done, having only barely cut the pages before he'd had enough to plant his own stick in the ground. Perhaps with Murry's review of *Aaron's Rod* in mind, he wrote to Wubbenhorst, "I am glad I have seen the book, since in Europe they usually mention us together—James Joyce and D. H. Lawrence—and I feel I ought to know in what company I creep to immortality."

He expected that Joyce "would look as much askance on me as I on him" (Joyce, in fact, had less regard for Lawrence and felt less need to know in what company *he* was creeping to immortality). But Lawrence was good-natured about the true kinship he had with Joyce, as a victim of Sumner, and of the fury of *John Bull*. "We make a choice of Paolo and Francesca floating down the winds of hell," he wrote Wubbenhorst, invoking characters of Dante's *Inferno* who inhabit the second circle with other sinners condemned for illicit sexual activity, the buffeting of the winds an external counterpart to the internal passions Paolo and Francesca had succumbed to and that Lawrence and Joyce had gone their separate ways to depict.

Lawrence had read his Dante, but he would read no more of *Ulysses*, though he continued, as Virginia Woolf had done in August, to fabricate his own case "for & against." It was more against, and he resisted when Seltzer suggested that his offhand commentary to Wubbenhorst be published. "Do you really want to publish my James Joyce remarks," he wrote as they were planning a trip the Seltzers were to make to Taos for Christmas. "No, I don't think it's quite fair to him."

Both Lawrence and Woolf might have been pleased to have read John Quinn's October 1922 letter to Harriet Weaver, Joyce's publisher at the Egoist Press. Thanking her for some clippings she had sent him, he told her Joyce's novel was a "great thing, a unique thing, and will probably remain unique." But the intensity of people's reactions, on either side, was overwrought, and the jousting of critics one against the other in personal terms was ridiculous, Quinn thought. "It is no proof that a man is a fool because he does not admire *Ulysses*," he told Weaver, and no proof, either, that someone was a genius for admiring it. "If everyone admired it or if it was generally admired, I should doubt the soundness of my feeling that it was a great work of art," he wrote.

"It is absurd for people to get angry *at Ulysses* or *at* Joyce. But it is equally absurd for people who like and admire *Ulysses* to get angry *at those who get angry at* Ulysses."

* * *

In America, as elsewhere, Lawrence felt like a foreigner in exile. But the one bright side to America was that the trial of *Women in Love* had led to tremendous sales. "Why do they read me?" he wondered to Catherine Carswell about his American audience. "But anyhow, they *do* read me—which is more than England does."

Seltzer's trade edition of *Women in Love* appeared nearly simultaneously with an originally scheduled collection of stories published as *England, My England*. Lawrence sent copies of both books to friends around the world as Christmas presents. The title that had seemed an elegy for a lost land, the England he had left five years before, had become a greeting, a herald of homecoming, a wish for this Englishman in the teeth of all the world, even in the teeth of England, to make it his own again, somehow.

* * *

Earlier in the year Seltzer had thought he might travel west to meet Lawrence's boat when it docked in San Francisco. The seizure and the subsequent trial, as well as the press of other business, had made that impossible. Now, to celebrate "Victory" and flush, at last, and for the only time, with unanticipated revenue from *Women in Love*, he and his wife would come to Taos for Christmas. Writing to Adele Seltzer about the visit, Frieda warned, "You will find it a different sort of life after New York—Bring warm clothes and *old* clothes and riding things if you like riding—It's primitive to say the least of it—but plenty of wood and cream and chickens."

Last year, in Taormina, Lawrence had had the flu and been glad of it. He hated Christmas. This year, he was more happily settled and ready to celebrate the holiday with the Seltzers and the Danes. Together they decorated an outdoor Christmas tree, under which, in warmer weather, he might have been writing.

Chapter 16

"MRS DALLOWAY HAS BRANCHED INTO A BOOK"

"WELL—WHAT REMAINS TO BE WRITTEN after that?" Virginia had wondered to Roger Fry, returning to the sublime world of Proust she had sacrificed for *Ulysses*. At Hogarth House she began to see that what remained to be written was her own new book.

Leonard and Virginia returned to Paradise Road on Thursday, October 5. She was ready for autumn to begin and for the publication of *Jacob's Room*. Just before they left Rodmell, Virginia heard from Donald Brace, "my first testimony from an impartial person," who thought *Jacob's Room* "an extraordinarily distinguished & beautiful book . . . or words to that effect" and praised her "own method," as Leonard had done. Brace's letter left her feeling "a little uppish . . . & self assertive," ready to follow the plan she had laid out in the spring, "two books running side by side," fiction and once again her book on reading. "Mrs. Dalloway in Bond Street" and her chapter on Chaucer, for the other book, were done. She had read five books of the *Odyssey* and *Ulysses*, was returning to Proust, and after that would undertake an ambitious course of "reading with a purpose": Homer, Aeschylus, Sophocles, Euripides, a Plato dialogue, and more.

In January she had started her diary in the "odd leaves at the end of poor dear Jacob," at least in part because of parsimony. Now she did something similar, taking up the third notebook she had used to write *Jacob's Room* to make some detailed notes. "Thoughts upon beginning a book to be called, perhaps, At Home: or The Party," she wrote. She saw the book whole, and almost all at once, her idea for it growing out of challenges of form and characterization she felt she'd left unresolved in *Jacob's Room*.

"Mrs. Dalloway in Bond Street," she decided, was to be the first in a series of perhaps eight stories she would write at roughly the rate of one a month, each "complete separately" but with "some sort of fusion," which was, of course, the element missing in *Ulysses* and *The Waste Land*. Seeing the new book *whole* was the key. Her relief when she read Donald Brace's letter had been a certainty that what she had seen as the disconnected rhapsodies of *Jacob's Room* would at least "make *some* impression, as a whole," upon readers; that it "cannot be wholly frigid fireworks." Now she made a list of chapters: "Mrs. Dalloway in Bond Street," then "The Prime Minister," which she had thought about at Rodmell and began to write on the same day she wrote out her notes, October 6. Then there were to be six more, she projected. Important details were to change—the title of the book, for one; the names of the chapters she planned and then whether there would even be chapters—but in the more than two years' work that were to follow from these notes, Virginia honed, but did not veer from, her initial conception.

The sequence, she outlined for herself, "must converge upon the party at the end," as if in laying out this challenge she aimed to correct the only lapse Leonard had identified in *Jacob*: the party in that book. She had been thinking since the spring about how a party might draw together a disparate group of people and as a scene-setting device make them, and the story in which they appear, a coherent whole. She had written the dinner party scene in "Byron and Mr. Briggs" that had ended when Clarissa Dalloway told her friends it was time to go to Clara Durrant's party. That had led to "Mrs. Dalloway in Bond Street," and in writing this party she must get it right this time. She acknowledged how the threads of one had led her to the others in the label she pasted on her notebook: "Book of scraps of J's R. & first version of The Hours," one of the several titles she would give the book while working on it.

In the six weeks between October 6 and November 19, Woolf made four substantive sets of notes, two in October and two in November, in each month setting them down ten days apart, as if the intervals were pauses designed to spare mental reserves between sprints. But she was not resting. The intervals of time were like her afternoon walks: she was working through what she was to write, foreseeing it all while seeming to be engaged in another task entirely. She periodically urged herself on in her diary—"I must get on with my reading . . ."; "I want to think out Mrs Dalloway"— while she also ruminated on the reviews of *Jacob's Room* and reluctantly attended to problems at the Hogarth Press and other quotidian details. But all the while she was thinking out *Mrs. Dalloway*, the building of her structural and thematic plan work she was then able to commit to paper quickly and virtually without a single crossing out, in short lines that run down the pages of her notebooks like poetry.

Mrs. Dalloway "ushers in a host of others, I begin to perceive," and though she was not sure who these other characters would be, her notes were a tool, like binoculars, to bring these characters far off on the horizon into better focus. These as-yet-unknown figures must be depicted "much in relief," she wrote, the challenge for her to present them from the outside in a way that would join those sections seamlessly with the depiction of Clarissa from within that had been her breakthrough in "Mrs. Dalloway in Bond Street." Perhaps there could be "interludes of thought, or reflection, or short digressions." But then how would these sections "be related, logically, to the rest"? How could she keep it "all compact, yet not jerked"? She didn't know yet. The stories must be drawn together into a story. The characters must converge on the party. She must fuse the sculpture of the external view with Clarissa's internal view that was like an X-ray. She would later call this technique of revealing the character's mind and past, "tunneling."

In the end, Woolf drafted most of the stories, which were published posthumously. "The Prime Minister" did indeed become the next chapter of "Mrs. D.," and Virginia began it exactly where "Mrs. Dalloway in Bond Street" left off. The sound from the street heard in the glove shop was heard again, by others, at the start of the second story, which solved one mystery: "the violent explosion" from the street was the backfiring of a car. The scene drafted in the story was eventually "fused" to its predecessor in a new way when Virginia jettisoned the idea of chapters as too great a break in the texture of the book.

* * *

Jacob's Room was published on October 27, in an edition of one thousand copies. It turned out that Virginia could write, and contentedly enough, while being read, the mixed reviews—the *Times*'s "long, a little tepid"; "Pall Mall [Gazette] passes me over as negligible"; the *Daily Mail* called her "an elderly sensualist"—a contrast to the letters that satisfied her, from Morgan ("the letter I've liked best of all"), and Ottoline, and from Lytton, who "prophecies immortality for it as poetry," though his letter praised the book "too highly for it to give me exquisite pleasure." She was either "a great writer or a nincompoop," but the lack of the public "splash" didn't bother her when weighed against private enthusiasm that was the "most whole hearted" she had ever had.

"It's odd how little I mind," she noticed, reflecting on the negative reviews, surprised at the equanimity that seemed to have come along with her conviction in the summer that at forty she had found out how to say something in her own voice, now affirming in her diary, "At last, I like reading my own writing. . . . At forty I am beginning to learn the mechanism of my own brain—how to get the greatest amount of pleasure & work out of it." She was certain she could "go on unconcernedly whatever people say," as distrustful of Clive's telling her *Jacob's Room* was a masterpiece as she was unmoved by being "sneered at" by some reviewers. At least *Jacob's Room* was selling—six hundred fifty of its one thousand copies gone, enough to order a second edition of another thousand.

One friend, the writer and bookseller Bunny Garnett (from whose shop, Birrell and Garnett, she had bought *Ulysses*), telephoned her to tell her "it is superb, far my best, has great vitality & importance." Two days later he wrote to expand upon what he had only been able to begin to share on the phone. The novel gave him more pleasure than anything of hers he'd read, and then he went further—it gave him more pleasure than anything written by anyone of their generation. Garnett concluded with the observation, "You are perfectly free of a heritage that didn't suit you—the legacy of the realist."

Replying to Bunny's praise—and to his assurance that he was going to fill a window of his shop with it and sell as many copies as he could—she framed the question she had been pursuing in *Jacob's Room* and was preparing to explore further in "At Home, or a Party." "But how far can one convey character without realism? That is my problem—one of them at least," she wrote. There were no scenes in *Jacob's Room* as there were in *The Voyage Out* or in *Night and Day*, no conversations or traditional dialogue that gave voices to the characters. She instead sketched them in through their impressions; working to leave no sense of a narrator, or the novelist herself, in whose hands and through whose eyes the reader saw things. Garnett appreciated the rhapsodies, and whether they were disconnected or not, as she had feared, his letter at least assured her there was beauty in what she had achieved. She could not "do" the realism, she told him, and had exhausted her interest in it with *Night and Day*. Even though she admired writers who could—she was soon to praise Sinclair Lewis's *Babbitt*—her own aim was to "try to get on a step further in the next one, now that I've got rid of some of my old clothes." She wrote to Bunny on the twentieth, having taken the "step further" a week before, now that "Mrs. Dalloway" had branched into a book. She had thought to move from "Mrs. Dalloway in Bond Street" to "The Prime Minister." Now she saw that there must also be another character. "Septimus Smith?—is that a good name?" she wondered.

On October 16 she wrote in her notebook under the heading "*a possible revision of this book*":

> Suppose it to be connected in this way:
> Sanity and insanity.
> Mrs. D. seeing the truth. S. S. seeing the insane truth . . .
> The contrast must be arranged . . .
> The pace is to be given by the gradual increase of S's
> insanity. on the one side; by the approach of the party on the other.
> The design is extremely complicated . . .
> All to take place in one day?

If, as she told Bunny, she could not "do" the realism, she knew, too, that she could not do modernism as Joyce or Eliot or anyone else were doing it. That had become clear enough to her after finishing *Ulysses* and talking about it with Tom at Monk's House. But Bunny made another comparison in his letter. It was not only that her novel was more full of beauty than any piece of modern prose he could remember. He had been looking through the *Criterion* and had read *The Waste Land* just the day before.

> I compared him with you—simply because he represents some-
> thing I suppose. But the difference between you is that you have a
> sense of beauty; you see beauty in the world about you, you are alive
> to it all the time. Mr Eliot seems to me entirely to lack it. And lack-
> ing a sense of beauty he is profoundly bored. Boredom seems to me
> the mainspring of his work and of a good many other frightfully
> clever people's work. He is a schoolboy at the top of his class, first in
> every subject and bored by each—and to tickle his palate can only
> try new combinations of subjects.

Virginia was flattered but told Bunny, "I expect you're rather hard on Tom Eliot's poem." (She might also have cautioned him he was rather hard on Eliot himself. Like Clive, Bunny had completely elided the distinction between the writer and his work. Of course he had done the same thing with Virginia, to a happier purpose.) Virginia told him she had not read *The Waste Land* herself. "I only have the sound of it in my ears, when he read it aloud; and have not yet tackled the sense. But I liked the sound."

But the sense of her new book, and what connected it together—she had not resolved that yet. She desired to "foresee this book better" than her first three novels in order to "get the utmost out of it" in a way that Joyce and Eliot had not with their latest works. One of the most interesting comments on *Jacob's Room*, in fact, was one she was unlikely to have seen but might have agreed with. Her friend Desmond MacCarthy, the literary editor of the *New Statesman*, told Vanessa that it was the best thing Virginia had ever written but added a caveat: "he said it is like a series of vignettes," Vanessa relayed to Clive in Paris. "I don't know that that matters but I gathered he thought it lacked coherence though very brilliant. Each chapter is like the beginning of a very good novel. That is his description. As I have only read the first chapter I can't say."

She could have indeed "screwed Jacob up tighter," Virginia decided, but she had had to "make my path as I went." Her path, like her method, was to be her own.

* * *

Virginia began writing "The Prime Minister" on October 6, the same day that she wrote out her first notes for "At Home: or The Party" (or "the 10th of June, or whatever I call it"). It was writing the first ten pages that had given her the idea for her possible revision of the scope and structure. Septimus Smith was mentioned only once in the story until then, one of a group of half a dozen friends who gather for lunch every Wednesday at half past one at a restaurant in Leicester Square. Something about him provoked her attention even at this earliest stage: "Septimus Smith was utterly different," she wrote in her first sentence about him. "He was goat-toothed and laughed very violently." Virginia shifted her focus to Septimus Smith in the next seven pages of the story, but his background remained mysterious, his link to the other people at lunch not stated. He is twenty-seven, and therefore likely a veteran. He leaves lunch and the thought occurs to him that he will kill the prime minister and then himself. But his mind seems to drift in other directions: "All the enmities and motives of life came across him in a flash." He lights his cigarette but forgets to smoke it. He drops it to the pavement. He thinks of his wife. His mind wanders. Other characters drift in again. The story ends with what Virginia intended to be the next link in the chain of stories, an airplane flying overhead that, like the sound in the street, fused the two chapters and their characters together. The airplane is writing letters in the sky.

"Mrs Dalloway saw people looking up," she wrote. The story ended.

On November 9 she decided that "The Prime Minister" and "Mrs. Dalloway in Bond Street" were "too jerky & minute" for her purposes, not joined by a "general style." Now she saw more clearly what her novel would be.

Suppose the idea of the book is
the contrast between life and death.
All inner feelings to be lit up.
The two minds. Mrs. D. and Septimus.

She thought through upon whom "S.S." would be "founded," and did the same with the other characters. Septimus's wife would be called "Rezia," and she thought to draw on Leonard. "She to be founded on L?" she wrote, though there were to be significant differences between her own husband and her fictional wife, who was to be "simple, instinctive, childless." About Septimus she had a decision to make: "Had been in the war? or founded on me?" She thought she might base his character, and his look, on Ralph Partridge, a young man who was their (largely unsatisfactory) assistant in the Hogarth Press. But if she attained the right "generalised" sense of him that she wanted to achieve—"left vague—as a mad person is"—then he "can be partly R.; partly me." She had thought of Septimus's name before she wondered whether he was to be "founded" on herself, but to make him "partly me" may have been her unconscious intention to begin with. His name is Latin for "seventh," and Virginia was the seventh of her parents' eight children. Her father, Sir Leslie, had one child from his previous marriage to Harriet Thackeray, and her mother, Julia, had three children by her first husband, Herbert Duckworth. Sir Leslie and Julia were married in 1878 and had four children: Vanessa, Thoby, Virginia, and Adrian Stephen, who was younger than Virginia by one year.

* * *

But "S.S." would not, in 1922, have been shorthand only for Septimus Smith. It had meant something else almost since the beginning of the war, a meaning that received renewed attention only recently. Ten days after Leonard and Virginia arrived at Monk's, the *Times* published news of a War Office report on shell shock. The study had been the work of more than two years, undertaken in April 1920, almost eighteen months after the end of the war. The inquiry was under the leadership of Lord Southborough, a response to public outrage at the ill treatment of veterans, and also to resolve whether those who claimed shell shock had in fact been ill. The committee met forty-one times beginning in September 1920, and examined fifty-nine witnesses before ending on June 22, 1922. The *Times* article, under the headline "The Anatomy of Fear," urged a wide readership of the two-hundred-page report, calling it "a document of so great interest as to merit the attentive study of every one interested in human nature. . . . It probes far into the dim processes of the mind which determine character and conduct." It was as much a challenge to a novelist as it was an invitation to the public.

The report, and the extensive coverage of it in newspapers over the course of the next month, was another reminder that the war had not ended with the Armistice. The plight of wounded veterans, mentally and physically scarred, was visible all around. The care of wounded veterans was an exorbitant cost to the public. But if these veterans' mental infirmities had never been established as true wounds of war, then was it worth the public's money to support them? Or was it indulgence of continued malingering? And why were so few who were treated recovering?

The committee concluded that the array of mental illness among sol-diers in the war was a large one, not usefully termed "shell shock" because the problems were found among soldiers who did not hear, literally hear, shell explosions. The web of mental diseases were, Lord Southborough summarized in a separate article for the *Times* published the first week of September, also a result of the "wear and tear of a prolonged campaign of trench warfare, with its terrible hardships and anxieties, and of attack and perhaps repulse." Shell shock itself was a "wholly misleading" term, he wrote. "Shell-shock" was so firmly "established" that it was impossible to erase it from the vernacular, however. "The alliteration and dramatic sig-nificance of the term had caught the public imagination, and thencefor-ward there was no escape from its use."

The "condition of mind and body" produced under the battle condi-tions Southborough enumerated were more properly termed "war neuro-sis." And the manifestations of war neurosis would be "practically indistinguishable from the forms of neurosis familiar to every doctor under ordinary conditions of civil life."

It was not, then, a choice for Virginia whether she must found "S's character" on his experience on the battlefield or on her own history. To use the alliteration would suggest one obvious "reason" for Septimus's insanity—he was another shell-shocked veteran of the war. But his having been in the war was irrelevant. It could not be news to her that there was a continuity of neuroses in peace and in war. This was the deeper psycho-logical truth—sanity vs. insanity—she was pursuing in fusing the stories of Clarissa and Septimus.

* * *

Morgan was a frequent overnight guest at Hogarth House in the autumn and winter, visiting at monthly intervals that, incidentally, charted the course of his own progress on his Indian novel.

Just after Morgan had left Monk's House in September, Virginia wrote in her diary, "I was impressed by his complete modesty (founded perhaps on considerable self-assurance)." He had rediscovered some of this confidence because of his continuing work. "He is happy in his novel, but does not want to discuss it," she wrote.

A few days later he wrote to Masood, his grief over Mohammed abat-ing, at least for the moment, after the letter he had begun in August. He shared no more with his friend than he had with Virginia. "I am in excellent form and have hopes of finishing my Indian novel," he wrote, urging Masood, too, to keep his secret, because "if people know the news and get talking, I become worried & cannot write." He was far enough along to ask Masood whether he would accept the dedication. "I always intended this, but warn you that you will find yourself initialling much you will consider inaccurate, pernicious, and banal."

He had a new conception of it, far different from what Masood might have imagined after urging Morgan to look to India for a subject in the early years of their friendship. He warned Masood, "When I began the book, I thought of it as a little bridge of sympathy between East and West," recalling it at this distance almost as a romance intended to strengthen the bridge of sympathy between the two of them into something deeper than friendship. Returning to the book now, Forster had realized "this conception has had to go, my sense of truth forbids me anything so comfortable." Perhaps there had been value in having visited India again, even though being there had not helped him forward in the writing. But he had gained a perspective he now thought essential to the new spirit of what he was writing. "I think that most Indians, like most English people, are shits and I'm not interested whether they sympathise with one another or not. Not interested as an artist: of course the journalistic side of me still gets roused over these questions." Morgan had, in fact, written another article for the *Nation* to pour out "that part of my soul," the part that hoped, given new trouble in India and the Middle East, "the whole bloody Empire was over." Journalism and fiction might not be so mutually exclusive after all; he might not be expending energy on the one at the expense of the other but, like Virginia, he might vary the side of the pillow as his mood, or as necessity, required. He had given the important news incidentally: he was an artist again.

A month later, at Hogarth House, where he stayed from Friday to Sunday, October 20 to 22, Morgan was once again "very charming," Virginia wrote to Roger Fry, her letter a long and warmly confidential one even though she was sorry she had no gossip to share. But she did have news about Morgan. She and Morgan had gone for a walk in Richmond Park on Saturday. It was now almost exactly three years since that evening in November 1919 when they had walked together along the Thames after dinner at Hogarth House and Morgan had confided to her that he was "in trouble with a novel of his own . . . fingering the keys but only producing discords so far." Now he was finishing the novel, he told her, though Morgan, as in September at Monk's House, said little or nothing about it before he "snuggled in" again, and they became engrossed in "very very minute domestic details: the cat, the maid, the cousin, and Miss Partridge of Ashstead." Virginia gave him a copy of *Jacob's Room*, and he left.

Two days later, on the twenty-fourth, once more at home with his mother, the cat, and the maids, Morgan wrote to her about the book, which he had read immediately and had only just finished. It was "an amazing success," he told her, and his mind was occupied with "wondering what developments, both of style and form, might come out of it." He had read it, in other words, as a novelist thinking about the use it might be to him. He was confused on that point, so "of course am reading the book again" to see how she had made the "tremendous achievement" of it work, and what he might learn from it. She had kept readers'—and his—interest in Jacob as a character even though he was absent from the book, present in the thoughts others had of him.

His praise seemed connected to his work on his own novel and some of the problems with which he been struggling. She had been able to "clean cut away" the difficulties that seemed insuperable to him: "all those Blue Books of the interior and exterior life of the various characters— their spiritual development, income, social positions, etc., etc.," that he had worried in reading *Night and Day* "were gaining on you," the sheer amount of information that added detail to the pages of a novel but did not bring life to them. He had worried earlier in the year that this tendency might be gaining on him, too, that he might be stressing atmosphere at the expense of character, adding color without depth. She, in *Jacob's Room*, had found a "general liberation" from convention, and also, it seemed, from compromise: "I don't yet understand how, with your method, you managed it," but that was why he was already reading the book again.

For Virginia had found an answer to at least one issue that had frustrated him as he worked, his impatience with the "tiresomeness and conventionalities of fiction-form." In *Jacob's Room* she had made a leap beyond the conventions, and though sparked by Proust, Morgan had not yet been able really to do so. He was working, but it was in the old vein. It was frustrating, he had written to Goldie in the spring, to be limited to viewing "the action through the mind of one of the characters; and say of the others 'perhaps they thought', or at all events adopt their view-point for a moment only." Proust had done it: his first-person narrator became an omniscient third-person narrator to tell the story of Swann and Odette, after which long sequence the "I" returned. This had not broken the texture of Proust's embroidered ribbon. But Morgan was concerned that in his lesser hands, the "illusion of life may vanish." It had happened to others, the creator degenerating into the showman, he told Goldie. Reading *Jacob's Room* five months later, he saw that Virginia had managed, in her way, to do what Proust had done and what he might want to do: "pretend" to get inside "all the characters." That she had done this was the greatest achievement of the book, and "the making of the book . . . it's full of beauty, indeed is beautiful."

In working on the Indian novel before the war, Forster had written himself into a cul-de-sac with the central "incident" in the book. His early draft of the book included largely the same cast of characters as appear in the published novel, and the first scenes are also largely alike, focusing on a small group of characters, some English, including administrators of the Civil Station at Chandrapore, and some Indians. These include Ronny Heaslop; the woman, Adela (at various times called Edith or Janet), who comes from England to decide whether she should marry him; Ronny's mother, Mrs. Moore; Cyril Fielding, an English teacher; and the Indian doctor Aziz. Adela wants to see "the real India," and Aziz impulsively suggests they visit the Marabar Caves. The question of the novel is the question of what happens there. Adela claims that Aziz has assaulted her. He is arrested. There is a trial. And at its climax Adela withdraws her charge. She decides that he has not assaulted her, she perhaps imagined it. But then what did happen in the caves? Forster himself did not know, he claimed, even to Goldie, who wrote him immediately after reading the book, in June 1924, to ask why Forster did not say. He was sure Forster must have a good reason and was, for himself, more curious about the reason than about the incident.

"In the cave it is *either* a man, or the supernatural, *or* an illusion," Forster replied. "And even if I know! My writing mind therefore is a blur here—i.e., I will it to remain a blur, and to be uncertain, as I am of many facts in daily life." If it were to remain a blur for him, he must ignore his own drafts, where before the war he had made the sexual attraction between Aziz and Adela much more explicit than he made it in the published novel. And here had been his problem, and where he had stopped writing. He could get inside the cave, but he could not get himself out again.

In Forster's 1913–14 draft, Adela (still Janet) "looked up in his face" and thought, "How handsome he was, and no doubt his wife was beautiful, for people usually get what they already possess." In the caves, they "drift into one another's arms—then apart." (Here Forster wrote some notes to himself: "Discovers she loves him . . . Marriage impossible. She— theoretically—immoral: he practically, but believes it is impossible with an Englishwoman.") In the draft, Aziz "got hold of her other hand and forced her against the wall, he got both of her hands in one of his, and then felt at her breasts." In the novel, Adela swings wildly—perhaps at air. In the draft, she "wrenched a hand free" and pushes at Aziz's mouth: "She could not push hard, but it was enough to hurt him." She runs out of the cave in both the draft and the novel. But only in the draft is it clear what she is running from. In both the draft and the novel, Forster ends the chapter when Adela finds help.

That is also where he stopped writing, and where he resumed in 1922.

Forster's way forward from Proust and from *Jacob's Room* might not be to "pretend" to be in any character's head as easily as he would be in any other. For him the development was to be less inside a character's head than as the novelist he had the right to be. Virginia had cut away the Blue Books of the interior and exterior life of the various characters. He, too, would cut away and perhaps in the blur find the "general liberation" he had seen Virginia make for herself. He had begun his letter to Moham- med in search of this, and now, as autumn turned to winter, he continued writing in search of a general liberation as the artist he was once again beginning to feel himself to be.

Chapter 17

"WHAT MORE IS NECESSARY TO A GREAT POEM?"

ON OCTOBER 13, 1921, VIVIEN HAD WRITTEN to Scofield Thayer of Tom's serious breakdown, that he must stop all work and would be going away for three months. One year later, the earliest copies of the first issue of the *Criterion* began to appear in London, and with them *The Waste Land*. Tom received his own six copies on Monday, October 16, and wrote to Cobden-Sanderson, his printer, that the magazine lived up to his expectations: "all that I could have desired; it is a model." The first words of praise of *The Waste Land* arrived that same day, from Sydney Schiff. The letter is lost, but Tom replied that afternoon, "You could not have used words which would have given me more pleasure or so have persuaded me that the poem may possibly communicate something of what it intends." Tom shared Schiff's letter with Vivien, who wrote her own much longer reply to Schiff's "real and true appreciation" of the poem. "Perhaps not even you can imagine with what emotions I saw The Waste

Land go out into the world," she wrote. "It was a terrible thing, somehow, when the time came at last for it to be published."

Vivien's faith in Tom had been vindicated but she was also perhaps anxious at the poem's revelation of herself and their marriage. The poem might, as Mary Hutchinson had said, be Tom's melancholy autobiography, but it was, in that case, Vivien's history, too. Schiff had "exactly described" her own response to the poem, Vivien wrote, adding, as if to acknowledge by confession what he already knew, "it has become a part of me (or I of it) this last year." Schiff's additional compliments about the *Criterion* she took, along with the poem, as a testament to Tom's triumph over circumstances she had in part imposed, his work fitted into evenings compromised not only by exhaustion after days at the bank, but by his being forced, she wrote self-deprecatingly, to fill hot water bottles and prepare invalid food for "his wretchedly unhealthy wife."

A week later, Tom again left London for the seaside, exhausted as he had been a year before, but in happier circumstances—and with different prospects awaiting him upon his return from what was to be about ten days away, the remainder of his annual leave from Lloyds. Everything about this year's trip was as markedly different as he could make it. He went to Worthing, this time, on the southern coast, hours in the other direction from Margate, and he went alone, the regimen and limited diet imposed upon Vivien too strict for her to "visit, travel, or stop at hotels," as he wrote to one friend, offering an excuse for refusing a weekend invitation but, perhaps unintentionally, also an indication of what he was relieved to be escaping from. He gave his address only to their partner Cobden-Sanderson, in case of emergency. He was back in London on November 1.

Reviews of the *Criterion* were favorable, including an auspicious notice in the *Times Literary Supplement*, which was the most important. Worrying about the review of *Jacob's Room* that would appear in "the Supt.," Virginia wrote in her diary that it was the only one she was anxious about—"not that it will be the most intelligent, but it will be the most read & I can't bear people to see me downed in public." Eliot was not downed. The *Criterion* was "that rare thing among English periodicals, a purely literary review . . . of a quality not inferior to that of any review published here or abroad," and the *Times* said of *The Waste Land* that it seemed to be "a complete expression of this poet's vision of modern life. We have here range, depth and beautiful expression. What more is necessary to a great poem? . . . Life is neither hellish nor heavenly; it has a purgatorial quality. And since it is purgatory, deliverance is possible."

The downing of Eliot came from an unlikely source, the Books and Bookmen column of the *Liverpool Daily Post and Mercury*, which on November 16, 1922, reported that *The Waste Land*, "a long poem by Mr. T. S. Eliot" published in the first issue of a quarterly review called the *Criterion*, was "attracting considerable attention." The article did not say anything more of the poem but described the Bel Esprit fund in detail, mixing sensation and error and noting that though friends of Mr. Eliot "endeavoured strenuously to keep the affair a secret . . . it has come to light (by way of America)." This was strange, given that Pound had published his manifesto in an English periodical eight months before. According to the newspaper report, "Until quite recently Mr. Eliot was earning his livelihood in a London bank," which was of course false; he was very much still employed there. The newspaper then recounted an "amusing tale" presumably from its American source: that well before Bel Esprit, a sum of £800 was presented to Mr. Eliot by "admirers to persuade him to give himself up for literature." On that occasion, he had "accepted the gift calmly and replied, 'Thank you all very much; I shall make good use of the money, but I like the bank!'" This fabricated event had supposedly occurred two years before, but the poet had "held out" in the bank until the past spring, according to the newspaper, "when he suffered a severe nervous breakdown which necessitated a three months' leave of absence." It was then that Bel Esprit "was hatched in secret and carried through, the poet's wishes not being consulted." This last phrase was a direct quote from Pound's article in the *New Age*.

But the part about Eliot's nervous breakdown was correct, even if the newspaper was wrong about when it had occurred. Eliot was outraged, feared "how calamitous these statements may be for me," and wrote to Richard Aldington and to Pound that it had not come as a surprise that such a story would be published "as I have suspected for some time that something of the sort might happen." Here, months later, was the fruition of what he had feared when putting the prospectus for the *Criterion* together: the "great many jackals swarming about waiting for my bones" if it were to fail. Then he had worried about the immense loss of prestige he might suffer. He had been blind, in his worry, to the fact that the jackals might swarm more venomously with the gain in prestige he made when the *Criterion*—and his own poem—proved successful. He did not say to Pound what was also true: if Pound's Bel Esprit plan had not been published, he might not be in this situation, ready to pursue a libel action against the newspaper.

He spent the next two weeks meeting with solicitors and getting legal advice. Eventually he wrote a letter to the *Post and Mercury* that was published on November 30 and settled the matter without a recourse to the "protracted and immense strain" it would have been to take the matter to court. "The circulation of untrue stories of this kind causes me profound astonishment and annoyance and may also do me considerable harm," he wrote. There had been no collection or presentation; he had not received any money; he had not left the bank. It was slightly less true that the Bel Esprit plan "referred to by your correspondent is not in existence with my consent or approval," given that Eliot knew about it and had allowed Pound—and Ottoline Morrell and Virginia Woolf, continuing to pursue the separate Eliot Fellowship Fund they had started in the spring—to proceed with fund-raising while also stating conditions for accepting the money to be raised. These included whether the initial guarantees the plans promised would be renewed, "for my life *or for Vivien's life*," he had written to Pound only the day before the Liverpool article appeared. "If the contributors cannot give such guarantees, then they are people who ought not to be in such an enterprise at all."

* * *

The appearance of *The Waste Land* in New York was a brilliantly orchestrated occasion. A few weeks before the November *Dial* was to appear, Seldes wrote to Beatrice Kaufman, the wife of the playwright George S. Kaufman, who worked as a publicist for Liveright, to arrange a meeting. "I want to talk about publicity for T. S. Eliot with you very shortly, and I think that these lofty business matters are always settled at lunch, paid for by the office. Let us go to Child's some morning or afternoon."

The first reader of the poem beyond Eliot's immediate circle seems to have been Edmund Wilson, then an editor at *Vanity Fair* and a friend of Seldes's whom he asked to write a review of the poem to appear in the December *Dial* along with the announcement of the prize.

Seldes knew that Wilson would be sympathetic to Eliot, and knew, too, that Wilson had a great deal in common with the poet. In the winter of 1922, Wilson had written in his notebook, "I sometimes feel as if all the tires of my mind were deflated and my intellectual wheels were running rackingly and joltingly on their rims," an echo of Tom's poem much like Ottoline Morrell's private vision recorded in her diary. Seven years Eliot's junior, Wilson was, like him, an impecunious journalist who needed every assignment, and he recognized himself in the poem, just as he had seen his plight in Pound's Bel Esprit manifesto: he was working at a magazine as an editor rather than writing full-time and living with a roommate in a cheap railroad apartment on Lexington Avenue, above a furrier's loft, that smelled like wet cats. His enthusiasm for Eliot's earlier work—and the announcement of Bel Esprit—had prepared him for what he would discover in *The Waste Land*, and after getting it from Seldes, he began to read it immediately, sitting on the upper deck of a Fifth Avenue bus, so engrossed in it he felt "bowled over," his own "Unreal City," its crowds and its noise, all around him as he read.

Wilson wrote immediately to the poet John Peale Bishop that he was "much excited" about the poem. "It will give you a thrill, I think." Though he had read the poem two or three times in quick succession, and too cursorily, he told Bishop, he saw that it was Eliot's masterpiece, and something more—"nothing more or less than a most distressingly moving account of Eliot's own agonized state of mind during the years which preceded his nervous breakdown." Wilson knew Eliot's previous poems, and they had corresponded only in Wilson's capacity as an editor at *Vanity Fair*. But he saw in *The Waste Land* just what Mary Hutchinson had, and just what Eliot had been anxious others would see in it: Tom's melancholy autobiography, and a little bit of his own.

"Never have the sufferings of a sensitive man in the modern city chained to some work he hates and crucified on the vulgarity of his surroundings been so vividly set forth," Wilson wrote to Bishop. "It is certainly a cry *de profundis* if ever there was one—almost the cry of a man on the verge of insanity." In fact Eliot's breakdown prefigured Wilson's own stay in a sanitarium later in the 1920s. The review Wilson published in the December *Dial* was laudatory but contained no reference to Eliot's own agonized state.

The book columnist for the *New-York Tribune*, Burton Rascoe, reviewed

THE WORLD BROKE IN TWO   283

the poem on November 5, after it appeared in the *Dial*. Rascoe was a friend of Wilson's and also of Gilbert Seldes. Wilson often complained that Rascoe relied too much on his opinions for his columns (he also complained that Rascoe frequently misquoted him). Rascoe called *The Waste Land* "perhaps the finest poem of this generation," and echoed Wilson's private comments for public consumption: "it gives voice to the universal despair or resignation arising from the spiritual and economic consequences of the war, the cross purposes of modern civilization . . . and the breakdown of all great directive purposes which give joy and zest to the business of living." Four of the most influential of the reviews that appeared—Wilson's in the *Dial* and Rascoe's in the *Tribune*; and two more, by Seldes himself, in the *Nation*, and Conrad Aiken's in the *New Republic*—were all by men who knew of Eliot's private drama. None mentioned it, and Eliot's despair became, in the reviews, a universal one.

* * *

Eliot, in January, could hardly have anticipated the success that November and December would bring. Liveright's fear that *The Waste Land* was too short to make a book on its own would soon prove unfounded, and Quinn, too, had been wrong in cautioning Eliot in July that *The Waste Land* might have only a very small, select audience. One of the few people who was not pleased was Scofield Thayer. When the November issue of the *Dial* appeared, a week or so after the *Criterion*, *The Waste Land* had been given the "place of honor," appearing first, a decision Seldes and Watson made without telling Thayer, who when he saw the issue in Vienna was very angry. In fact, the worst review of *The Waste Land* was Thayer's.

Thayer wrote to Seldes from Vienna with his detailed postmortem and, as usual, included some praise as well as criticism that "drew blood." The November issue was a disappointment to him, and nothing was more disappointing than *The Waste Land*. He thought it "quite beyond words" that Yeats's *The Player Queen* had been placed "anywhere other than at the beginning of the number," and he complained about Yeats's loss of eminence and that the play had been set in type that was far too small. Thayer's letters went on for pages, noting every typographical error, and he sent so many in succession about each issue, repeating points made earlier, that Seldes could defend himself adequately only by responding "paragraph by paragraph," apologizing on one occasion "if in answering two, i.e., letters, I seem to retrace my steps."

Seldes justified the placement of *The Waste Land* by saying that the *Dial* frequently published Yeats and had never published a poem by Eliot before. He had also given Eliot pride of place to set the tone for the following issue, in which the Dial Prize would be announced. Almost incidentally he added of the poem, "in our opinion it was a very fine piece of work," leaving it diplomatically unclear to whom his royal we referred.

Thayer had not warmed to the poem as Watson had on rereading it. He did not see himself reflected in the "cry *de profundis*," as Wilson had or, if he did, he disliked the poem even more. Publicly he wrote in extravagant praise of it in the required editor's note announcing the $2,000 prize in the December issue. But writing privately to Alyse Gregory, another *Dial* editor whom he hoped to persuade to take Seldes's place as managing editor, he described his vision of what they should be doing, and what he hoped she would agree with him they must do: "as to the literary contents too I feel forced to refrain in the future from publishing such matter as the silly cantos of Ezra Pound and as the very disappointing 'Waste Land' and I should like to secure for The Dial the work of such recognised American authors as Edith Wharton."

But whatever offense Thayer took in Seldes's insubordination about giving Eliot's poem the "place of honor" ought to have been subsumed by his pleasure in the success of the publicity campaign Seldes engineered. What Thayer had lost of face he was making up in circulation. The November and December issues of the *Dial*, the former with the poem and the latter with the announcement of the prize, sold better than any in the magazine's history, almost 50 percent more at newsstands than an average issue, reaching over 4,500 in November, and even more for December, over 6,200 copies. Subscriptions also rose at the end of 1922, to more than 6,300 at year's end, and by another thousand, to 7,440, by February 1923, much of it, if not all, directly accountable to the expectations created by publishing *The Waste Land* rather than Edith Wharton.

As the *Dial* soon touted to potential advertisers, it had a "rapidly increasing circulation" among "wealthy, cultured, intelligent people," and its "typographical perfection" would be an ideal showcase for prestigious brands. By February 1923, Colgate and Company, Steinway and Sons, American Express, and the Underwood Typewriter Company had all come aboard.

* * *

Liveright's edition sold as well as the *Dial*, and his first edition of one thousand copies sold quickly enough that he ordered another printing. On Christmas Eve, a Sunday, a large photograph of Eliot appeared on the front page of the *New-York Tribune*'s Book News and Reviews section, alongside Burton Rascoe's In Retrospect on the literary year. The caption mentioned the Dial Prize of $2,000 and said of *The Waste Land*, it is "generally considered the outstanding poem of the year."

Liveright advertised *The Waste Land* in the *Tribune* as "probably the most discussed poem that has been written since Byron's Don Juan." He quoted Clive Bell, "the distinguished English writer," who had published an article in the *New Republic* calling Eliot "the most considerable poet writing in English," though Liveright, of course, did not know that Bell's private proclamations, particularly to Mary Hutchinson, were often more unkind.

Liveright also took a Christmas advertisement in the *New York Times Book Review* that ran under the headline "Between Ourselves" and included chatty squibs about a dozen of his autumn books. About *The Waste Land* he wrote: "The Dial's annual award of $2000.00 has been given this year to T. S. Eliot, the American poet now living in England. The contract for The Waste Land, Mr Eliot's longest and most significant poem, which we have just published, was signed in Paris on New Year's Eve and was witnessed by Ezra Pound and James Joyce. A good time was had by one and all—even by the publisher."

The story read well, but there was not a word of truth in it.

* * *

The end of 1922 arrived for Eliot in January 1923, when copies of Liveright's edition reached him in London. He sent one to Vivien, away in Eastbourne, and she wrote her "Dearest darling Wing," on January 11, "I think Waste Land book *very nice*." The same day Tom wrote to Edmund Wilson, thanking him for his "more than generous appreciation" of the poem in the *Dial*. "I think you have understood it remarkably well, perhaps a little over-understood it! I mean read more into it than it contains here and there. I am very sensible of its fundamental weaknesses, and whatever I do next will be, at least, very different; I feel that it [is] merely a kind of consummation of my past work, not the initiation of something new, and it will take me all my courage and persistence, and perhaps a long time, to do something better. But 'something' must be better. *The Waste Land* does not leave me well satisfied."

Wilson had been generous in his appreciation of *The Waste Land*, but he wrote harshly of Ezra Pound, whom he called an "imitator" of Eliot and whose "extremely ill-focused" recent Cantos presented, in contrast to *The Waste Land*, "a bewildering mosaic with no central emotion to provide a key." In his letter, Tom reminded Wilson of his "vast indebtedness" to Pound. He told Wilson without false modesty that it was plain to him that "there are unquestionably respects in which he is far more a master than I am." For Tom was not always the schoolmaster that he seemed to play when he was with Virginia Woolf. As he wrote later to Pound, "I always envied James Joyce his apparent conviction of the importance of his own work. I have never felt so convinced as he appeared to be. Often very doubtful."

Perhaps it was in writing to Wilson he got the idea for the inscription in the copy he gave to Pound in January 1923: "For E. P./Miglior Fabbro," the better craftsman.

EPILOGUE

FORSTER CONTINUED THROUGH 1923 TO work on his novel. Late in the year, he gave it the title *A Passage to India*, taken from a poem by Walt Whitman. On the last day of 1923, on the eve of his forty-fifth birthday, he wrote again in his diary about Mohammed. "Good bye Mohammed. I meant to review the year, but my eyes have gone fut. I can only say 'Good bye—I saw you and kissed you last year.'" Three weeks later, on January 21, 1924, he recorded a different farewell: he had finished *A Passage to India* that day. Forster dedicated the novel to Masood, "and to the seventeen years of our friendship," but writing in his diary, he paid private tribute to another friend by using Mohammed's pencil to "mark the fact" that the novel was done. All of the entries in the hundreds of pages of his diary, from 1909 to 1967, are written in various inks. Except that one.

Morgan also wrote to Leonard Woolf, at whose urging, almost two years before, he had looked at his Indian fragment "with a view to continuing it." He paid tribute, now, to the Woolves, and was as touchingly dependent on Leonard's advice as ever.

"I have this moment written the last words of my novel and who but Virginia and yourself should be told about it first?" There would be revisions, and "of course there's the typing. . . . Do you know a typist—cheap? . . . It would save time if I could give out say 20,000 words."

Virginia wrote in her diary after reading Morgan's letter, "He is moved, as I am always on these occasions."

* * *

A Passage to India was published by Edward Arnold on June 4, 1924, and in the United States by Harcourt Brace in August. By then it had been fourteen years since the publication of *Howards End*. One reviewer admitted to his worry that *Howards End* "was to be Forster's end." Another, praising the "admirable self-restraint" by which Forster "limited his output," regretted the gap meant that the public was now not familiar enough with his style to appreciate that "no modern writer is so distinctive in all his work." The book received nearly unanimous praise, including a not completely unbiased review by Leonard Woolf in the *Nation and Athenaeum*: "A little while ago I wrote in these columns that the book of this publishing season to which I looked forward most eagerly was Mr. E. M. Forster's new novel, *A Passage to India*. And now it has appeared and I have read it and—Well, there are few things more exciting than to look forward to the publication of a new book, by a living writer, to read it, and to find one's hopes realized." The book quickly became the biggest success of Forster's career, and by the end of 1924 had sold seventeen thousand copies in England and more than fifty-four thousand in the United States. Forster had an idea about why *A Passage to India* was his first novel to sell at all well in America. "A few years ago I wrote a book which dealt in part with the difficulties of the English in India," he wrote in a 1926 essay. "Feeling that they would have had no difficulties in India themselves, the Americans read the book freely. The more they read it the better it made them feel, and a cheque to the author was the result."

A Passage to India was Forster's last novel, though he published many works of nonfiction before his death in 1970 at ninety-one.

* * *

By the end of 1922, Lawrence was no longer so "scrubby poor" as he had been. His income for the year was $5,439.67, and he owed the U. S. government $70 in taxes. But his Christmas idyll at Del Monte Ranch did not last long, and he was not able to "pitch" a novel in Taos as he had done in Australia. He went to Mexico in 1923 and traveled across America that year, to Texas, New Orleans, Washington, DC, and then on to New York City, Buffalo, and Los Angeles. He and Frieda spent part of July and August 1923 at a cottage in New Jersey that Thomas and Adele Seltzer rented for the two couples, and which the publisher renamed "Birkendele," in honor of the character Rupert Birkin in *Women in Love*. It was here, in the hills above Morris Plains, that Lawrence corrected the proofs of *Kangaroo* and other books, a collection of poems, and the translations of Giovanni Verga he had begun on his ocean voyage to Ceylon, which Seltzer planned to publish in the autumn. The house was as inaccessible and isolated as Del Monte Ranch, and as Wyewurk, in Thirroul, and Fontana Vecchia, in Taormina, had also been: "very quiet, pretty, peaceful, quite alone. . . . A horse and buggy: 4 miles from station." Seltzer and his wife commuted to New York and returned in the evenings, an arrangement that worked well enough, perhaps because it was not intended to last. Frieda returned to England without Lawrence in early August 1923, and he sailed shortly afterward. He planned to visit his sisters in the Midlands just after Christmas. But it was "hateful here" in England, he wrote to Mabel, who had married Tony that year. "It's all the dead hand of the past, over here, infinitely heavy." He postponed his visit and stayed in Nottinghamshire only a few days to mark the new year. The rest of the winter he and Frieda spent traveling in Europe, before returning to Taos in the spring.

While in Baden-Baden, he read Forster's *Pharos and Pharillon*, the book of essays on ancient and modern Egypt that the Hogarth Press published in 1923. Forster had sent it to him, and when Lawrence wrote to thank Forster for the book, he told him it seemed as "sad as ever," the call of a lost soul to a departed world of glory. After his years of wandering, Lawrence saw a camaraderie with Forster that he had not felt before, though he thought of himself as more eager to turn toward the future than Forster. "To me you are the last Englishman," Lawrence wrote him. "And I am the one after that."

Kangaroo received respectful reviews and some very high praise, in both the United States and England, but as a novel apparently "about"

Australia, it had perhaps less appeal than it might have if it had had "so much of the letter S of sex" in it, particularly because Judge Simpson's exoneration of Seltzer was not a New York court's final word on *Women in Love*. In February 1923, Judge John Ford, of the New York State Supreme Court—outraged that Lawrence's "loathsome" novel had been recommended to his daughter by a clerk at a lending library—began an attack that, coordinated with John Sumner, was as widely covered in the newspapers as the 1922 seizure and trial had been. Seltzer was arrested again, in July 1923, and indicted by a grand jury for publishing "unclean" books, though the grand jury did not find *Women in Love* objectionable, and Lawrence was once again exonerated. The publication of *Kangaroo* shortly afterward had Lawrence's good reputation to capitalize on, but this, unsurprisingly, led to less sensational sales than *Women in Love* had achieved. Few reviewers appreciated the autobiographical experiment that the novel marked for Lawrence, who wrote in *Kangaroo* as honestly of himself and his wife as he had written of his family life and youth in *Sons and Lovers*.

Lawrence died in March 1930, in France, of tuberculosis. He was forty-four. A few weeks later, Forster gave a talk about Lawrence on the BBC. He ranged widely and generously over the work of a writer he called "one of the glories of our twentieth-century literature." But at the time of his death, Lawrence had two publics, Forster said, "neither of them quite satisfactory." The general public thought him "improper and scarcely read him at all." This was the Lawrence who, book after book, had been in trouble with the law—*The Rainbow*, *Women in Love*, and, finally, *Lady Chatterley's Lover*, so sensational that Lawrence published it privately, which did not prevent its becoming, long before it could be published legally in the United States and in England, his most famous, and lucrative, book. By contrast, Lawrence's "special public" read him in too narrow and fanatical a way, Forster thought. But the Lawrence with whom Forster himself felt kinship had been forgotten, and however flawed his work, the "pages and chapters of splendour" that he had written when "the whole fabric of his mind catches fire" ought to be remembered. The "Nightmare" chapter of *Kangaroo* was one of the splendors and was, Forster said, "the most heart-rending account of non-fighting that has ever been written." This was Forster's way of affirming what he, too, had always known. Lawrence was wear and tear, and had always been fighting, in his life and in his art.

* * *

"Mrs. Dalloway in Bond Street" was published in the July 1923 issue of the *Dial*, in the same issue as a review of *Jacob's Room* by David Garnett that largely repeated the praise he had offered to Woolf in his October letter, though without any of the doubts about *The Waste Land* that he shared with her. The story was also published without any of the difficulties that Eliot and Thayer had experienced in their negotiations. Raymond Mortimer, a young graduate of Balliol College, Oxford, whom Woolf met through Ottoline Morrell, was working unofficially as a London agent for Thayer after Eliot became editor of the *Criterion*. He wrote Thayer in February 1923 that he had "the promise of a story from Virginia Woolf," a story, she had suggested to him, "which she does not want to print here (probably because she has done a portrait of some one in it, at least that is my guess)." This may have been a playful insinuation by Woolf that her protagonist was based on Morrell, to whom Woolf had written in the summer of 1922 that she had finished "2 chapters of my Garsington novel, you'll be glad to hear." This perhaps had been more flattery than truth, but Mortimer's interest was piqued by Woolf's hint, and he was gratified by the story he received from her a few weeks later. Mortimer sent it to Thayer in Vienna with a note, "I enclose Mrs. Woolf's story (very badly typed, as she said). . . . I think it is most exquisite, & hope you will like it. I am coming to think her the best writer we have."

Thayer agreed "as to the exquisiteness of Mrs. Woolf's story" and forwarded it to the New York office to calculate her payment. This came to $60. Woolf's handwritten note, dated May 21, 1923, acknowledging "The Dials [sic] cheque received today," is among the Dial Papers at Yale's Beinecke Library.

Woolf worked on *Mrs. Dalloway* for more than two years. She varied the side of her pillow so successfully that, just before Christmas 1924, she was "putting on a spurt" so that the novel could be copied in time for Leonard to read at Monk's House, and so that she could then "deliver the final blows" to her book on reading. The Hogarth Press published *The Common Reader* at the end of April 1925, and *Mrs. Dalloway* three weeks later, on May 14, 1925. At first her reading book was little read—a few days after publication she wrote in her diary, "so far I have not heard a word about it, private or public: it is as if one tossed a stone into a pond, & the waters closed without a ripple." Though she saw her disappointment about it "floating like an old bottle in my wake," she was on to "fresh adventures." She hoped the same thing would not happen to *Mrs. Dalloway*. It didn't.

Woolf was gratified by the nearly universally ecstatic reviews the novel received but wrote in her diary, "The only judgment on Mrs. D. I await with trepidation (but thats [*sic*] too strong a word) is Morgan's." A few days later, he visited. "Well, Morgan admires," she wrote. "This is a weight off my mind." Though "sparing of words," he told her it was better than *Jacob's Room* and kissed her hand. As he left he told her he was "awfully pleased, very happy (or words to that effect) about it."

Mrs. Dalloway soon began to sell, and, more surprisingly to her, so did *The Common Reader*, in both England and the United States, where both books were published by Harcourt Brace. If sales kept up, "We are going to build a W. C. and a bathroom at Rodmell," she wrote a friend.

Woolf read Proust again as she was finishing *Mrs. Dalloway*. "I wonder if this time I have achieved something?" she wrote in her diary shortly before her novel was published. "Well, nothing anyhow compared with Proust, in whom I am embedded now." Proust was unlike any other writer in his combination of "the utmost sensibility with the utmost tenacity. He searches out these butterfly shades to the last grain. He is as tough as catgut & and as evanescent as a butterfly's bloom," the last words she had once used to try to encompass Morgan's unique characteristics, too. She had already begun to think of her next novel, *To the Lighthouse*, and, she wrote, "he will I suppose both influence me & make me out of temper with every sentence of my own." Once again, the question was what remained to be written after Proust. *Mrs. Dalloway* had been one answer. *To the Lighthouse*, "to have father's character done complete in it; & mothers [*sic*]; & St Ives; & childhood" was perhaps another. The title she gave to the brief but central section of the novel, published in 1927, has an echo of Proust. Woolf called it "Time Passes."

* * *

Virginia Woolf committed suicide on March 28, 1941. She was fifty-nine. She left instructions that Leonard should choose one of her manuscripts as a gift for Vita Sackville-West, whom she had met just before Christmas

1922, at a dinner party Clive arranged. Vita was a "lovely gifted aristocrat," Virginia wrote in her diary the next day, but "Not much to my severer taste . . . florid, moustached, parakeet colored, with all the supple ease of the aristocracy, but not the wit of the artist." A decade younger than Virginia, she was also too prolific, wrote too quickly, published too much—five books of poetry and three novels between 1909 and 1922. She "knows everyone— But could I ever know her?" Vita invited Virginia to dinner soon afterward, and it turned out she could. Their deep romantic attachment became a lifelong friendship, the singular significance of which Virginia underscored with the legacy she gave uniquely to Vita.

Vita asked Leonard for the manuscript of Virginia's 1931 novel *The Waves*. Leonard wanted to keep that for himself and instead sent her the manuscript of *Mrs. Dalloway*, coincidentally the novel Woolf had begun just before meeting her.

* * *

Tom Eliot was, as Wyndham Lewis saw, an indecisive Prufrock "to the life," particularly as it related to Bel Esprit and to the Eliot fund that Ottoline Morrell and Virginia Woolf had also started. Woolf coordinated their separate efforts through Richard Aldington and sent "poor Tom" £50 at the end of 1922. She worried that Eliot would refuse it. Instead, he deposited it and the $2,000 he received from the *Dial* in a special account he set up "as a Trust," for himself and for Vivien. Solicitations for the fund continued for more than another two years. Tom left Lloyds Bank in the summer of 1925, when Geoffrey Faber, setting up a new publishing house, took over the publishing of the *Criterion* and appointed Eliot to the board of his new company. Faber and Gwyer, named for his partners Maurice Gwyer and his wife, Lady Alsina Gwyer, was renamed Faber and Faber in 1929. Eliot worked at the company until his death in 1965, at the age of seventy-six.

Eliot had been grateful to Edmund Wilson for his generous praise of *The Waste Land*. He would, perhaps, have not been surprised by what Wilson had written privately to his friend John Peale Bishop about the poem, in September 1922, or by Mary Hutchinson's confidence to Virginia and Leonard Woolf that summer that the poem was "Tom's autobiography—a melancholy one." He thought so, too, and wrote to his mother before the poem was published that "he had put so much of his own life into it."

His letter to her does not survive, but a May 1923 letter that Charlotte Eliot wrote to her brother-in-law, also named Tom, does. He had written Charlotte that he did not understand the poem, and in reply, she confessed that she, too, had been puzzled when she first read it. But Tom had written her to explain that it described, at least in part, the loss of "an ideal world" in which he had lived: "Certainly up to the time of his marriage and residence in England," Charlotte wrote her brother-in-law. "Since then he has had pretty hard times." She told him about Tom's financial difficulties and of his three months' leave from Lloyds Bank and his treatment in Lausanne. Vivien's continuing illnesses, and his own, were once again, that spring, almost more than he could bear. "Under these circumstances you can easily imagine some of his ideals are shattered."

* * *

Ezra Pound wrote to H. L. Mencken in March 1922 that the "Christian Era" had ended at midnight on October 29, 1921, the night that James Joyce finished *Ulysses*. The magnitude of Joyce's achievement was incalculable, but it was as important to Pound that the year "1 p.s.U"—post scriptum *Ulysses*—had then begun. Seeing *The Waste Land* in print confirmed for Eliot a similar truth. The poem was "a thing of the past so far as I am concerned and I am now feeling toward a new form and style," he wrote in November 1922. The decisive end to one thing must be the start to something else. He was convinced of this all his life, and in *Little Gidding*, published in 1941, he put it another way:

> For last year's words belong to last year's language
> And next year's words await another voice.

It was the question Virginia Woolf had asked Roger Fry—and herself—while reading Proust in 1922: "Well—what remains to be written after that?"

NOTES

Introduction

3   "How these writers live in their works": Virginia Woolf, *The Diary of Virginia Woolf*, ed. Anne Olivier Bell, vol. 2, *1920–1924* (London: The Hogarth Press, 1978), 163. Future references will be to *VW Diary 2*.

3   "It is after all": T. S. Eliot, *The Letters of T. S. Eliot*, ed. Valerie Eliot and Hugh Haughton, rev. ed., vol. 1, *1898–1922* (London: Faber and Faber, 2009), 628. Future references will be to *TSE Letters 1 2009*.

3   "apparently the favourite breeding ground": Virginia Woolf, *The Letters of Virginia Woolf*, ed. Nigel Nicolson and Joanne Trautman, vol. 2, *1912–1922* (New York: Harcourt Brace Jovanovich, 1976), 504. Future references will be to *VW Letters 2*.

5   "frosty morning": D. H. Lawrence, *Lady Chatterley's Lover*, ed. Michael Squires (New York: Penguin Classics, 2006), 41.

5   "'One *must* preserve . . .": Ibid., 43.

7   "Poppy Day": "Lord Haig's New Scheme for Ex-Service Men," *Times*, October 6, 1921, 7.

7   "November 11 shall be a real Remembrance Day," Ibid.

7   Eight million sold: "The Poppies of Flanders," *Times*, November 12, 1921, 6.

7   "licensing hours": "London Licensing Hours," *Times*, October 3, 1921, 7; and "Licensing Meeting To-Day," *Times*, October, 1921, 7.

8   prewar "liberties": "New Drink Hours To-Day," *Times*, September 1, 1921, 10.

1: Virginia Woolf Nears Forty

11   "Oh but the cold was too great at Rodmell": Virginia Woolf, *The Diary of Virginia Woolf*, ed. Anne Olivier Bell, vol. 4, *1931–1935* (London: The Hogarth Press, 1982), 4. Future references will be to *VW Diary 4*.

11   Even "a few staggering sentences": Ibid.

11   "Oh its [*sic*] so lovely on the downs now": Virginia Woolf, *The Sickle Side of the Moon: The Letters of Virginia Woolf*, ed. Nigel Nicolson and Joanne Trautmann, vol. 5, *1932–1935* (London: The Hogarth Press, 1982), 141. Future references will be to *VW Letters 5*.

12   "parsimony . . . odd leaves at the end of Poor Jacob": *VW Diary 2*, 155.

12   "quite truthfully, the Hogarth Press": Ibid., 144.

12   Paradise Road basement for a print shop: *VW Letters 2*, 487.

12   "I shall think of another novel, I daresay": *VW Diary 2*, 142.

12   "Will my fingers stand so much scribbling?": Ibid.

12   "I was shivering over the fire": Ibid., 156.

12   "Winter is upon us; fog, frost, every horror": *VW Letters 2*, 492.

12   "We go to bed under": *VW Diary 2*, 143.

12   "a north east wind sweeping": Leonard Woolf, *The Letters of Leonard Woolf*, ed. Frederic Spotts (New York: Harcourt Brace Jovanovich, 1989), 537. Future references will be to *LW Letters*.

12   "one creeps about the house": *VW Letters 2*, 492.

13   loping her own "delicate" way "a little unevenly": Diana Gardner, *Rodmell Papers: Reminiscences . . . by a Sussex Neighbor*, Bloomsbury Heritage Series #52 (London: Cecil Woolf, 2008), 18.

13   "I keep thinking of different ways to manage my scenes": Virginia Woolf, *The Diary of Virginia Woolf*, ed. Anne Olivier Bell, vol. 1, *1915–1919* (New York: Harcourt Brace Jovanovich, 1977), 214. Future references will be to *VW Diary 1*.

13   "Tomorrow my reading begins!": *VW Diary 2*, 156.

13   "Work morn Walk w V aftn": Leonard Woolf's pocket diaries are arranged chronologically in Leonard Woolf Papers, SxMs-13/2/R/A, University of Sussex Monk's House Papers, including SxMs-13/2/R/A/5 (1913); SxMs-13/2/R/A/7 (1915); SxMs-13/2/R/A/14 (1921); and SxMs-13/2/R/A/15 (1922).

13   "We should have felt it to be": Leonard Woolf, *Downhill All the Way: An Autobiography of the Years 1919 to 1939* (New York: Harcourt, Brace & World, 1967), 156.

14   "Its [*sic*] foul": VW to Elizabeth Bowen, May 20, 1934, Elizabeth Bowen Collection, HRC, Box 12, Folder 4.

14   "V came down for tea" and "Vanessa came dinner": Leonard Woolf pocket diary, 1922, SxMs-13/2/R/A/15 (1922).

14   "settled & unadventurous": *VW Diary 2*, 159.

14   "less normal": Ibid.

14   "binding": Ibid.

14   "I have seen all the cleverest people": *VW Diary 2*, 159.

14   "only sixpence a year": Ibid.

14   "Dearest Dolphin": *VW Letters 2*, 504.

15   "donkey that I am": *VW Diary 2*, 159.

15   "the sacred morning hours . . . Phrase tossing": Virginia Woolf, *The Diary of Virginia Woolf*, ed. Anne Olivier Bell, vol. 3, *1925–1930* (London: The Hogarth Press, 1980), 206. Future references will be to *VW Diary 3*.

15   "the habit of writing thus for my own eye": *VW Diary 1*, 266.

15   "consists of how many months?": *VW Diary 2*, 158.

15   "The machinery for seeing friends": Ibid., 157.

15   Talland House "untidy and overrun": Quentin Bell, *Virginia Woolf: A Biography* (New York: Harcourt Brace Jovanovich, 1972), 32.

16   "I feel time racing like a film at the Cinema.": *VW Diary 2*, 158.

16   the *Times* reported: *Times*, January 5, 1922.

16 "Winter sickness": *Times*, December 3, 1921, 7.

16 "V went concert[.] Could not sleep.": Leonard Woolf Papers, University of Sussex, SxMs-13/2/R/A/14.

16 "plagues": *VW Letters* 2, 478.

16 "days spent in wearisome headache": *VW Diary* 2, 125.

17 "What a gap!": *VW Diary* 2, 125.

17 "Oh what a damned bore!": *VW Letters* 2, 494.

17 "scribbling away": Ibid.

17 Among the particular symptoms: "New Influenza Outbreak," *Times*, January 9, 1922, 10.

17 Leonard monitored: Leonard Woolf's account books are at the University of Sussex, SxMs-13/2/R/A/65.

18 "the inexorable Jew": Clive Bell to Mary Hutchinson, September 15, 1924, Mary Hutchinson Papers, Harry Ransom Humanities Research Center, Box 6, File 6. Future references to the Harry Ransom Center will be abbreviated as HRC. Future references to Clive Bell will be abbreviated as CB, and future references to Mary Hutchinson as MH.

18 "an interval in which": Willa Cather, *Not Under Forty* (New York: Knopf, 1936), 139.

18 "continual nagging": Victoria Glendinning, *Leonard Woolf: A Biography* (New York: Free Press, 2006), 250.

18 "pronounced my eccentric pulse": *VW Diary* 2, 160.

18 "best advice": "The Influenza Epidemic," *Times*, January 12, 1922, 11.

19 "at a time when many": Virginia Woolf, *The Second Common Reader: Annotated Edition*, ed. Andrew McNeillie (Harcourt, 1986), 70.

19 "Nearing the end of the year": *VW Diary* 2, 78.

20 "K. M. bursts upon the world": Ibid., 161.

20 "in two days [*sic*] time": Ibid., 141.

20 "it will appear to me sterile acrobatics": Ibid., 161.

20 "We had thought that this world": Hermione Lee, *Virginia Woolf* (London: Chatto & Windus, 1996), 386. Future references will be to Lee.

20 the novel was "a lie in the soul": Ibid., 395.

21 "a kind of glittering village": J. H. Stape, ed., *Virginia Woof: Interviews and Recollections* (Iowa City: University of Iowa Press, 1995), 20. Future references will be to Stape.

21 "the cultured attitude": Fry to VW, September 4–5, 1921, in S. P. Rosenbaum, ed., *The Bloomsbury Group: A Collection of Memoirs and Commentary*, rev. ed. (Toronto: University of Toronto Press, 1995), 37.

21 "central heating": The remark was made by Clemence Dane, quoted in *LW Letters*, 543.

21 "Bloomsburial": TSE, "The Post-Georgians," *Athenaeum*, April 11, 1919, 171.

21 "La belle Virginia": CB to MH, September 11, 1924, Mary Hutchinson Papers, HRC, Box 6, File 6.

21 "suddenly felt the quintessence": Noel Carrington, *Carrington: Paintings, Drawings, and Decorations* (Oxford: Oxford Polytechnic Press, 1978), 32.

22 T. S. Eliot and his wife, Vivien: Eliot's wife was named Vivienne at birth. She adopted the spelling "Vivien" in her twenties, and during the period covered in this book she signed her letters this way. She later reverted to "Vivienne." See Carole Seymour-Jones, *Painted Shadow: The Life of Vivienne Eliot, First Wife of T. S. Eliot, and the Long-Suppressed Truth About Her Influence on His Genius* (New York: Nan A. Talese/Doubleday, 2002), 598.

22 "backwards and forwards to each other": Ibid.

22 Bloomsbury standards: TSE to John Hayward, July 7, 1941, The Papers of the Hayward Bequest of T. S. Eliot Material, King's College Archive Centre, Cambridge, HB/L/12/1/18. Future references to King's College Archive Centre, Cambridge, will be abbreviated as KCAC.

22 "We are at the tea table": Stephen Miller, *Conversation: A History of a Declining Art* (New Haven, CT: Yale University Press, 2007), 183.

22 "speech became the deadliest weapon": Vanessa Bell, in Stape, 3.

22 "her living presence": Gerald Brenan, in ibid., 45.

22 "I see she is very beautiful": Lady Ottoline Morrell Papers, British Library, Add. MS 88886/4/13, transcript, 51–52, entry for June 19, 1923. Future references to Lady Ottoline Morrell will be abbreviated as OM.

23   "O Philosophress of Garsington": Sassoon to OM, September 3, 1922, Ottoline Morrell Collection, HRC, Box 28, File 4.

23   "Yellow Cockatoo": *VW Letters* 2, 341.

23   "Yellow Bird of Bloomsbury": Ibid., 348.

23   "orchestral concerts": Gerald Brenan, in Stape, 89.

23   "From this distance": Sassoon to OM, April 6, 1920, OM Papers, HRC, Box 28, File 4.

23   "The London intellect": E. M. Forster, *The Longest Journey* (New York: Penguin Books, 2006), 246.

23   "Tenuousness and purity": *LW Letters*, 259n3.

24   "But the odd thing is": *VW Diary* 2, 116.

24   "I have made up my mind": Ibid., 168.

25   "I was stricken with the influenza": *VW Letters* 2, 498–500.

25   "evanescent, piping, elusive": *VW Diary* 4, 321.

25   "timid, touching, infinitely charming": *VW Diary* 3, 193.

25   "whimsical & vagulous": *VW Diary* 1, 291.

25   "vaguely rambling butterfly": Ibid., 295.

26   "the peculiar invalid's acuteness of emotion": Conrad to Ada Galsworthy, February 9, 1922, *Joseph Conrad: Life and Letters*, 2 vols. (New York: Doubleday, Page, 1927), 2:265.

26   "naturally abnormal": *VW Diary* 2, 161.

26   "I have taken it into my head": Ibid., 167–68.

26   lethargy of an alligator: *VW Letters* 2, 503.

26   "furious, speechless, beyond words indignant": Ibid., 504.

26   "going to make him let me out": Ibid., 504.

26   "a little air, seeing the buses": *VW Diary* 2, 169.

27   "The cat lets this mouse run": Ibid., 170.

27   "an occasional bite . . . like dead leaves . . . what a 12 months": Ibid., 161.

27   "exquisitely on a bed": CB to Vanessa Bell, March 1, 1922, The Charleston Papers, CHA/1/50/4/8, KCAC. Future references to Vanessa Bell abbreviated as VB.

27   "the fire dying out": *VW Diary* 2, 167.

28   "both very much liked your book": *LW Letters*, 262.

28   "Peace is rapidly dissolving . . . Instead of feeling": *VW Diary* 1, 217.

28   "There's practically no one": *VW Letters* 2, 293.

28   "interrupted somewhere on this page": *VW Diary* 1, 218.

28   "We literary people": *VW Letters* 2, 297.

28   "His sentences take": Ibid., 295–96.

29   "beneath the surface": 218.

29   "To go on with Eliot": *VW Diary* 2, 67.

29   "What happens with friendships": Ibid., 100.

29   "our damned self conscious susceptibility": Ibid., 104.

29   "on the strength of one visit": *VW Diary* 1, 235.

29   "I plunge more than he does": *VW Diary* 2, 104.

2: Eliot in January

30   "I suppose you wdn't come for the 24th?": *VW Letters* 2, 483.

30   "passed off successfully": *VW Diary* 2, 140.

31   "*why* it is cheaper to buy steel bars": *TSE Letters* 1 2009, 357.

32   "Have you ever been": Ibid., 546.

32   "hoard of fragments": Lyndall Gordon, *T. S. Eliot: An Imperfect Life* (New York: W. W. Norton, 1999), 539.

32   "the freedom of mind": *TSE Letters* 1 2009, 549.

32   "prey to habitual worry and dread of the future": Ibid., 617.

33   "lived through material for a score": Gordon, *T. S. Eliot: An Imperfect Life*, 540.

33   "engaged in some obscure & intricate task": Lewis to Violet Schiff, February 6, 1921, British Library, Schiff Papers, Add MS 52919.

33 "Eliot can not be depended on": Ezra Pound, *Pound/The Little Review: The Letters of Ezra Pound to Margaret Anderson: The Little Review Correspondence*, eds. Thomas L. Scott and Melvin J. Friedman (New York: New Directions, 1988), 64.

33 "chief drawback to my present mode of life": *TSE Letters 1 2009*, 557.

34 "invalid food for his wretchedly unhealthy wife": Ibid., 765.

34 Eliot published: See T. S. Eliot, *The Complete Prose of T. S. Eliot: The Critical Edition: The Perfect Critic, 1919–1926*, eds. Anthony Cuda and Ronald Schuchard (Baltimore: Johns Hopkins University Press and Faber and Faber, 2014), v-vii; https://muse.jhu.edu/book/32768.

34 "a moment's breathing space": *TSE Letters 1 2009*, 556.

34 "private worries": Ibid., 583.

34 "her migraines and malaises": *TSE Letters 1 2009*, 597.

34 "another anxiety as well as a joy": Ibid., 557.

34 "These new and yet old relationships": Ibid., 568.

35 "So I shall not rest": Ibid.

35 "emancipated Londoners . . . charmingly sophisticated": Ibid., 105.

35 "sleek, tall, attractive . . . sort of Gioconda smile": Ibid., 104n2.

36 "Vivien's smell peculiarly feline": Dial/Scofield Thayer Papers, Beinecke Rare Book and Manuscript Library, YCAL 34, Series VII, Box 80, Folder 2078.

36 "one sees it in the way": Peter Ackroyd, *T. S. Eliot: A Life* (New York: Simon and Schuster, 1984), 63.

36 "the author of Prufrock": *TSE Letters 1 2009*, 104n2.

36 "a handsome young United States President": Wyndham Lewis, *Blasting and Bombardiering* (Berkeley: University of California Press, 1967 [1937]), 270.

36 "be fully conscious of": TSE to Philip Mairet, October 31, 1956, T. S. Eliot Collection, HRC, Box 5, File 4.

36 "Our marriage was hastened": *TSE Letters 1 2009*, 117.

36 "The only really surprising thing": Ibid., 113.

37 "a maddening feeling": Craig R. Whitney, "2 More T. S. Eliot Poems Found amid Hundreds of His Letters," *New York Times*, November 2, 1991, 13.

37 "flirtation or mild affair": *TSE Letters 1 2009*, xix.

37 "too shy and unpractised": Ibid.

37 "very immature for my age": Ibid.

37 "because I wanted to burn my boats": Ibid.

38 "bolted up to the stage": Ackroyd, *T. S. Eliot: A Life*, 294.

38 "My nerves are bad" and Pound's and Vivien's notes: T. S. Eliot, *The Waste Land: A Facsimile and Transcript of the Original Drafts Including the Annotations of Ezra Pound*, ed. Valerie Eliot (London: Faber and Faber, 1971), 11. Future references will be to *TWL Facsimile*.

38 "To her the marriage brought": *TSE Letters 1 2009*, xix.

39 "has deteriorated": Ibid., 613.

39 "much less inspired": Ibid.

39 "to me he seemed": Ibid.

39 "always must be an American": Ibid., 613.

39 "keyed up, alert": *TSE Letters 1 2009*, xix.

39 "still-trailing Bostonian voice": Wyndham Lewis, *Blasting and Bombardiering* (London: Eyre and Spottiswoode, 1937), 275.

39 "recognizably English": Anthony Powell, *To Keep the Ball Rolling* (Chicago: University of Chicago Press, 1983), 309.

39 "the general run of Americans": Ibid.

39 "further exasperated": *TSE Letters 1 2009*, 592.

39 "some prominent person": Ibid., 593.

39 "He only really *expressed* himself": Ottoline Morrell journal, Lady Ottoline Morrell Papers, British Library, Add. MS 88886/6/13, transcript, p. 29.

40 "Good-bye Henry": *TSE Letters 1 2009*, 576.

40 Lady Rothermere, Mary Lilian Harmsworth, the wife of the publisher Harold Harmsworth, agreed: Ibid., 577.

40 "Hypothetical Review": Ibid., 580.

40 "Therefore I am immersed": Ibid., 579.

41 "It *is* going to be": Ibid., 576.

41 Even his typewriter: Ibid., 585.

41 "Look at *my* position": Ibid., 592.

41 "He had left New York": James Dempsey, *The Tortured Life of Scofield Thayer* (Gainesville: University Press of Florida, 2014), 97. Thayer was "[p]erpetually on the edge of sanity," Dempsey writes (120). Thayer's sessions with Freud ended in spring 1923, but he continued to edit the *Dial* from Europe. He resigned as editor in June 1926. He was frequently institutionalized and was legally certified as insane in 1937. He died in 1982.

41 His divorce from his wife: Ibid., 100.

41 "the Professor himself": Ibid., 102.

41 "the most celebrated specialist in London": *TSE Letters 1 2009*, 584.

41 "thoroughly . . . greatly overdrawn": Ibid.

41 "feel quite different after . . . As nobody": Ibid., 583.

42 "great name": TSE to Julian Huxley, October 26, 1921, Ibid., 593.

42 "without any difficulty at all": Ibid., 584.

42 "enforced rest and solitude": Ibid.

42 "strict rules": Ibid., 586.

42 "not exert [his] mind": Ibid.

42 Tom's release from the pressure and tension: Ibid., 585.

42 "to think of the future": Ibid., 586.

42 "fortunate opportunity": Ibid., 585.

42 "I have not described": Ibid.

42 "quite alone and away": Ibid., 586.

42 Standard treatment: T. J. Jackson Lears, *No Place of Grace: Anti-Modernism and the Transformation of American Culture* (New York: Pantheon, 1981), 52, quoted in Matthew K. Gold, "The Expert Hand and the Obedient Heart: Dr. Vittoz, T. S. Eliot, and the Therapeutic Possibilities of *The Waste Land*," *Journal of Modern Literature* 23, nos. 3–4 (Summer 2000): 522.

42 "getting on *amazingly*": *TSE Letters 1 2009*, 593.

43 "postcard to himself": David Seabrook, *All the Devils Are Here* (London: Granta Books, 2003), 8.

44 "quite the best man": *TSE Letters 1 2009*, 594.

44 "not solely due": T. S. Eliot, *The Letters of T. S. Eliot*, ed. Valerie Eliot and Hugh Haughton, vol. 2, *1923–1925* (New Haven, CT: Yale University Press, 2011), 5. Future references will be to *TSE Letters 2*.

44 "nerve man: *TSE Letters 1 2009*, 594.

44 "largely due to the kink in my brain": *TSE Letters 2*, 5.

44 "psychological troubles": *TSE Letters 1 2009*, 594.

44 "utterly dead & empty": OM journal, September 3, 1921, Lady Ottoline Morrell Papers, British Library, Add. MS 88886/4/12.

44 "nerves or insanity!": *TSE Letters 1 2009*, 598.

45 "more useful for my purpose": Ibid., 617.

45 "a dull place": Ibid.

45 "*carte postale colorée* country": Ibid.

45 "the food is *excellent*": Ibid., 608.

45 a 1921 French edition of which Eliot owned: Ibid., 594n1.

45 "system of mental control": Ibid., 835.

45 "steadying and developing": Ibid.

45 "extraordinary poise and goodness": Ibid.

45 "in short he is": Ibid., 608.

45 "every form of neurasthenia": Rogert Vittoz, *Treatment of Neurasthenia by Means of Brain Control*, trans. H. B. Brooke (London: Longmans, Green, 1921), vii.

45 "imperfections of that [brain] control": Ibid., viii.

46 "uncurbed brain": Ibid. 5.

46 "state of anarchy": Ibid.

46 "prey to every impulse": Ibid.

46 "painful confusion": Ibid., 7.

46 "I seem to have no time": *TSE Letters 1 2009*, 608.

46 "more calm than I have for many years": Ibid., 609.

47 "Apparently all of Western Europe": Ibid., 617.

47 "awful expense . . . little room . . . did not seem . . . *en pension* . . . too incredibly dear": Ibid., 618.

48 "most exquisite": Ibid.

48 "Now if I could secure . . . For Tom, I am *convinced*": Ibid.

48 "*What* a last impression": Ibid.

48 "about 800 or 1000 lines": Ibid., 617.

48 "in a trance—unconsciously": *VW Diary 4*, 288.

48 *The sea was calm*: These are the lines Eliot wrote in Lausanne. The phrases at the center of the stanza—"I left without you / Clasping empty hands"—which, perhaps not incidentally, also encapsulate Eliot's emotions as he left Vittoz's care, do not appear in the published poem. *TWL Facsimile*, 79.

49 "Everything is now postponed": *TSE Letters 1 2009*, 571.

49 "The Christian Era ended": Quoted in ibid., 625n1.

49 "furiously busy six days": Tom Dardis, *Firebrand: The Life of Horace Liveright* (New York: Random House, 1995), 86.

49 "sailed for YURUP": Ezra Pound, *Ezra Pound to His Parents: Letters 1895–1929*, ed. Mary de Rachewitz, A. David Moody, and Joanna Moody (New York: Oxford University Press, 2010), 492.

49 "guide and mentor": Dardis, *Firebrand*, 86.

49 "the last of the human cities": Richard Ellmann, *James Joyce*, rev. ed. (New York: Oxford University Press, 1982), 508.

49 "best of all": Dardis, *Firebrand*, 87.

49 Pound took advantage of serendipity and brought Liveright and Eliot and Joyce together for dinner: Ibid., 90.

49 "Joyce nearly killed": Pound, *Ezra Pound to His Parents*, 492.

50 "much more of a man": Richard Londraville and Janis Londraville, *Dear Yeats, Dear Pound, Dear Ford: Jeanne Robert Foster and Her Circle of Friends* (Syracuse: Syracuse University Press, 2001), 200.

50 "Glad Liveright is to see you": Homer Pound to Ezra Pound, January 13, 1922, Ezra Pound Papers, Beinecke Rare Book and Manuscript Library, YCAL MSS 43, Series II, Box 60, Folder 2684.

50 "a great 'fan' ": Lewis, *Blasting and Bombardiering* (1937), 285.

50 "Pound circus": Ibid., 269.

50 "Ezra's boyscoutery": Ibid., 254.

50 "Point I can never seem": Pound, *Pound/The Little Review*, 266.

50 "had an unforgettable look": Louis Kronenberger, "Gambler in Publishing," *Atlantic Monthly*, January 1965. Galley proofs in Manuel Komroff Papers, Rare Book and Manuscript Library, Columbia University, Box 2, item 10066F, galley 3.

50 "always dressed": Ibid.

50 "quite aware": Ibid.

50 "in a well-fitted Chesterfield": Manuel Komroff, "The Liveright Story," 48, unpublished manuscript, in Manuel Komroff Papers, Rare Book and Manuscript Library, Columbia University, Box 24.

50 "Horace's hangovers": Kronenberger, "Gambler in Publishing."

50 "discipline was about as out of place": Ibid.

50 "with a well-trained smile": Ibid.

50 "This is a hell of a time": Ibid.

51 "Authors in the waiting room": Paul S. Boyer, *Purity in Print: Book Censorship in America from the Gilded Age to the Computer Age*, rev. ed. (Madison: University of Wisconsin Press, 2002), 82.

51 "his unaffected love of alcohol": Komroff, "The Liveright Story," 48.

51 "A nice collection": Ellmann, *James Joyce*, 510.

51 "he was in the habit of frequenting": Ibid., 532.

51 "made no pretense": Ibid., 514.

52 "I had never realized": Ibid., 495.

52 "burdensome . . . Oh yes. He is polite": Ibid.

52 "But he is exceedingly arrogant": Ibid.

52 "pearl": Dardis, *Firebrand*, 86.

52 "U.S. publicators": Ezra Pound, *The Letters of Ezra Pound, 1907–1941*, ed. D. D. Paige (New York: Harcourt, Brace, 1950), 186.

52 Sherwood Anderson: Dardis, *Firebrand*, 180.

52 "offered to bring out Ulysses": Ibid., 90.

52 "Why the hell he didn't nail it": Ibid.

52 "slightly draped": B. L. Reid, *The Man from New York: John Quinn and His Friends* (New York: Oxford University Press, 1968), 484.

53 "the certainty of prosecution . . . He said he did not want": Ibid., 485.

53 "meat, cake, breads": Pound, *Ezra Pound to His Parents*, 490.

53 "so mountany gay": *TSE Letters 1 2009*, 631.

54 "As to Twentieth century poetry": Ezra Pound, "Prolegomena," in *Literary Essays of Ezra Pound*, ed. T. S. Eliot (New York: New Directions, 1968), 12.

54 "a portrait of failure": *TSE Letters 1 2009*, 63n2.

54 "false art": Ibid.

54 "last intelligent man": Ezra Pound to H. L. Mencken, October 3, 1914, quoted in T. S. Eliot, *The Poems of T. S. Eliot*, ed. Christopher Ricks and Jim McCue, vol. 1, *Collected and Uncollected Poems* (Baltimore: Johns Hopkins University Press, 2015), 400.

54 "I have yet had or seen": Ezra Pound to Harriet Monroe, September 30, 1914, Ibid., 365.

54 "move against poppy-cock": Pound, "Prolegomena."

54 "devil of it": *TSE Letters 1 2009*, 63.

54 "nothing good": Ibid.

54 "superfluities": Ibid., 625.

54 "caesarean operation": Ibid., 629.

55 and was why, very soon: In July 1924, Eliot sought the advice of Arnold Bennett, who wrote in his journal that Eliot was now ""centred on dramatic writing" and "wanted to write a drama of modern life . . . in a rhythmic prose." See *TSE Letters 2*, 465 and 465n3.

55 "period of tranquility": *TSE Letters 1 2009*, 502.

55 "He has written a particularly fine poem": Wyndham Lewis to OM, Ottoline Morrell Collection, HRC, Box 13, Folder 4.

55 "MUCH improved": *TSE Letters 1 2009*, 625.

55 the repetition of the word: Gold, "The Expert Hand and the Obedient Heart," 531.

55 "That is nineteen pages": *TSE Letters 1 2009*, 626.

55 "he had done enough": John Quinn to Homer L. Pound, November 29, 1921, John Quinn papers, Manuscripts and Archives Division, New York Public Library, Letterbook vol. 25, p. 117.

3: Edward Morgan Forster

56 "haze of elderly ladies": P. N. Furbank, *E. M. Forster: A Life*, 2 vols. (New York: Harcourt Brace Jovanovich, 1978), 1:28.

57 "The boy grew up": Forster, *Longest Journey*, 24.

57 "exciting game": Ibid.

57 "Will review the year": E. M. Forster, *The Journals and Diaries of E. M. Forster*, ed. Philip Gardner, 3 vols. (London: Pickering and Chatto, 2011), 2:3.

58 "I may shrink": Ibid., 62.

58 "India not yet a success": Ibid., 63.
58 "Am grinding out my novel": Ibid., 6.
58 "In your novels": Ibid., 5.
58 "There is no doubt": Philip Gardner, ed., *E. M. Forster: The Critical Heritage* (London: Routledge and Kegan Paul, 1973), 130.
58 "With this book, Mr. Forster": Ibid., 129.
58 7,662 copies: EMF to Edward Arnold, 27-2-23, The Papers of E. M. Forster, EMF/18/169, King's College Archive Centre, Cambridge. Future references will be to EMF Papers, KCAC.
58 "Let me not be distracted": Forster, *Journals and Diaries*, 2:17.
58 "I should satisfy myself": EMF to Edward Arnold, EMF Papers, KCAC, EMF/18/169.
59 "One 'oughtn't to leave one's mother'": E. M. Forster, *Selected Letters of E. M. Forster*, ed. Mary Lago and P. N. Furbank, vol. 1, *1879–1920* (Cambridge, MA: Harvard University Press, 1983), 228. Future references will be to *EMF Letters 1*.
59 "she unexpectedly read family prayers": "Memorandum on Mother," EMF Papers, KCAC, EMF/11/11/a.
59 "You see, I too have no news": EMF to Forrest Reid, 4-2-21, EMF Papers, KCAC, EMF/18/457.
59 "As you say, I shall go": EMF to Forrest Reid, 4-2-21, EMF Papers, KCAC, EMF/18/457.
59 "sububurban": Forster, *Longest Journey*, 32.
59 "a little builder's house": Forster, *Journals and Diaries*, 3:178.
59 "The house is littered with manuscripts": EMF to G. H. Ludolf, 6-3-20, EMF Papers, KCAC, EMF/18/333. Future references to G. H. Ludolf will be abbreviated as GHL.
60 "until its destructions": Ibid.
60 "How fatuous!": Forster, *Journals and Diaries*, 2:57. Forster crossed out the word "accomplishing" and replaced it with "creating."
60 "just the aimiable [*sic*]": Ibid.
60 "the proof being": *VW Diary 1*, 310–11.
60 "fingering the keys": Ibid.
60 "Indian M.S.": EMF to Goldsworthy Lowes Dickinson, 31-5-21, EMF Papers, KCAC, EMF/18/158. Future references to Goldsworthy Lowes Dickinson will be abbreviated as GLD.
60 "While trying to write": *EMF Letters 1*, 302.
61 "go for six months": Furbank, *E. M. Forster*, 2:67.
61 "get a passport and passage": EMF to Forrest Reid, 17-2-21, EMF Papers, KCAC, EMF/18/457.
61 "Morgan goes to India": *VW Diary 2*, 96.
61 "just the thing": Ibid.
62 "usual Bob style": Ibid.
62 "too submissive and deferential": Forster, *Journals and Diaries*, 3:143.
62 "was dignified and reticent": Forster, *Longest Journey*, 24.
62 "broke down at breakfast": Forster, *Journals and Diaries*, 2:57.
62 an early death: Forster, *Longest Journey*, 26.
62 "the sudden business of my life": Forster, *Journals and Diaries*, 2:18.
62 "naughtiness": EMF to Florence Barger, 5-20-21, EMF Papers, KCAC, EMF/18/38/1, vols. 34/1–2. Future references to Florence Barger will be abbreviated as FB.
62 "careless of this suburban life": Forster, *Journals and Diaries*, 2:45.
62 "treated with great kindness": E. M. Forster, *Selected Letters of E. M. Forster*, ed. Mary Lago and P. N. Furbank, vol. 2, *1921–1970* (Cambridge, MA: Harvard University Press, 1985), 8. Future references will be to *EMF Letters 2*.
62 One of his proposed tasks: Ibid.
63 "noble writings of the past": Ibid., 9n7.
63 "slight and the enthusiasm slighter": Ibid., 8.
63 "decently furnished": EMF to FB, undated fragment [October 1921], EMF Papers, KCAC, EMF/18/38/1, vols. 34/1-2.
63 "only distaste and despair": E. M. Forster, *The Hill of Devi: The Abinger Edition of E. M. Forster*, ed. Elizabeth Heine (London: Edward Arnold, 1983), 99.
63 "electric house": *EMF Letters 2*, 1.

63   "Perhaps it is the heat": EMF to Syed Ross Masood, 25-5-21, EMF Papers, KCAC, EMF/18/360/1. Future references to Syed Ross Masood will be abbreviated as SRM.

63   "does not use in me": EMF to GLD, 31-5-21, EMF Papers, KCAC, EMF/18/158.

63   "My Indian M.S. is with me": Ibid.

64   "silliness of Indian life": *EMF Letters 2*, 10.

64   "seemed to wilt and go dead": Forster, *Hill of Devi*, 99.

64   "dull piece . . . unattractive for the most part . . . mainly confined": EMF to FB, 13-10-21, EMF Papers, KCAC, EMF/18/38/1, vols. 34/1-2.

64   Morgan had a bad dream: Letter of August 24, 1921, quoted in Rama Kandu, *E. M. Forster's A Passage to India* (New Delhi: Atlantic Publishers and Distributors, 2007), 265–66.

64   "how unsuitable were my wanderings": Forster, *Journals and Diaries*, 2:64.

64   "felt caught in their meshes": E. M. Forster, *A Passage to India*, ed. Oliver Stallybrass (London: Penguin Books, 1983), 36.

64   "to escape from the net": Ibid., 37.

65   "Slowness and apathy increase": Forster, *Journals and Diaries*, 2:64.

65   "My mind is now obsessed": Ibid., 61.

65   "indecent" stories: Ibid., 66.

65   "something positively dangerous": Ibid.

66   "I could bear no more": Ibid., 19.

66   "Non respondit": Ibid.

66   "weariness of the only subject": Ibid., 27.

66   "Desire for a book": Ibid., 18.

66   "lustful thoughts . . . personal": Ibid., 46.

66   "a believer in the Love of Comrades": E. M. Forster, "Terminal Note," in *Maurice* (New York: W. W. Norton, 1971), 249.

67   "It seemed to go straight through": Ibid.

67   "for the first time in my life": *EMF Letters 1*, 243.

67   "do the motherly": Ibid., 237.

67   "all these young gods": Ibid.

67   "Nice": E. M. Forster, *Alexandria: A History and a Guide* and *Pharos and Pharillon: The Abinger Edition of E. M. Forster*, ed. Miriam Farris Allott (London: Andre Deutsch, 2004), 329.

67   "African-Negro blood": Ibid.

67   "in the prime of . . . physical glory": Ibid., 331.

67   "intervene or speak": Ibid.

67   "one great piece of good luck": *EMF Letters 1*, 253.

68   "age, race, rank": Ibid.

68   "hit on things of objective worth": Ibid.

68   "romantic curiosity . . . on both sides": Ibid.

68   "adventures": Ibid.

68   "a gracious generosity": *EMF Letters 1*, 258.

68   "my damned prick": Forster, *Alexandria*, 332.

68   "I am so happy": *EMF Letters 1*, 274.

68   "gruff demur . . . lean back": Forster, *Alexandria*, 333.

68   "frequent coldness": Forster, *Journals and Diaries*, 2:67.

69   "If the letters cease": *EMF Letters 1*, 300.

69   "snatch a meeting": Furbank, *E. M. Forster*, 2:67.

69   "four perfect hours together": *EMF Letters 2*, 2.

69   "great coat and blue knitted gloves": Wendy Moffatt, *A Great Unrecorded History: A New Life of E. M. Forster* (New York: Farrar, Straus and Giroux, 2010), 180.

69   "flowery day": EMF to Alice Clara Forster, 3-1-22, EMF Papers, KCAC, EMF/ACF I, 1922–24. Future references to Alice Clara Forster will be abbreviated as ACF.

70   "feeling rather like crumbs in the night": Ibid.

70   "Let us wish one another a Happy New Year": EMF to GLD, 1-1-22, EMF Papers, KCAC, EMF/18/158.

70   "True of M.": Virginia Woolf's notes are in vol. 15 of her holograph reading notes in the Berg
Collection, New York Public Library. See also Brenda R. Silver, *Virginia Woolf's Reading
Notebooks* (Princeton: Princeton University Press, 1983), 89–90.

71   "C/o Messrs T. Cook": EMF to ACF, 1-12-21, EMF Papers, KCAC, KCC EMF/ACF, August–
December 1921.

71   "for a splash in Upper Egypt": EMF to SRM, 8-2-22, EMF Papers, KCAC, EMF/18/360/1.

71   "inclined to a pot belly": Forster, *Journals and Diaries*, 2:61.

71   "make another great friend": EMF to GLD, 31-5-21, EMF Papers, KCAC, EMF/18/158.

71   "I shall be carried past . . . misery . . .": EMF to GLD, 1-1-22, EMF Papers, KCAC, EMF/18/158.

71   "not see him alive again": EMF to SRM, 25-1-22, EMF Papers, KCAC, EMF/18/360/1.

71   "haemorrage, night-sweats, exhaustion": EMF to SRM, 28-1-22, EMF Papers, KCAC,
EMF/18/360/1.

72   "a robber and probably a quack": EMF to SRM, 25-1-22, EMF Papers, KCAC, EMF/18/360/1.

72   "tubes of useless stuff": *EMF Letters 2*, 21.

72   "sit attempting to nurse": EMF to SRM, 25-1-22, EMF Papers, KCAC, EMF/18/360/1.

72   "irritable and hard": Ibid.

72   "sombre and beautiful": EMF to SRM, 28-1-22, EMF Papers, KCAC, EMF/18/360/1.

72   "I am very ill": Ibid.

72   would return to Mansourah for another week or two: EMF to SRM, 8-2-22, EMF Papers,
KCAC, EMF/18/360/1 and EMF to FB, 8-2-22, EMF Papers, KCAC, EMF/18/38/1, vols. 34/1-2.

72   Morgan was able to pay for a visit: EMF to SRM, 8-2-22, EMF Papers, KCAC, EMF/18/360/1.

72   "The leading doctor": Ibid.

73   "perked up by this good desert air": EMF to FB, 8-2-22, EMF Papers, KCAC, EMF/18/38/1,
vols. 34/1-2.

73   "oddly tranquil considering the circumstances": EMF to FB, 8-2-22, EMF Papers, KCAC,
EMF/18/38/1, vols. 34/1-2.

73   Only sixty-six copies: Forster asked Arnold for an accounting of the sales of his books in
February 1923. Arnold's reply is in EMF Papers, KCAC, EMF/18/169.

73   "How wonderful money is": *EMF Letters 2*, 22.

73   "I wish I knew how long": EMF to FB, 8-2-22, EMF Papers, KCAC, EMF/18/38/1, vols. 34/1-2.

73   "without difficulty": EMF to SRM, 8-2-22, EMF Papers, KCAC, EMF/18/360/1.

73   "very violent" sexual desire . . . "great loss of sexual power": Forster, *Journals and Diaries*, 2:76.

74   left Mohammed impotent: EMF to FB, 8-2-22, EMF Papers, KCAC, EMF/18/38/1, vols. 34/1-2.

74   "I had been looking forward": Ibid.

74   "half hour's stroll": EMF to SRM, 8-2-22, EMF Papers, KCAC, EMF/18/360/1.

74   "and we sit about at cafés": EMF to SRM, 18-2-22, EMF Papers, KCAC, EMF/18/360/1.

74   "little more than bones now": EMF to GLD, 25-2-22, EMF Papers, KCAC, EMF/18/158.

74   "He sat by me in the Railway carriage": EMF to FB, 25-2-22, EMF Papers, KCAC, EMF/18/38/1,
vols. 34/1-2.

74   "a very nice one": Ibid.

74   "out of love": Forster, *Alexandria*, 330.

74   "collapse may come any minute": EMF to SRM, 23-2-22, EMF Papers, KCAC, EMF/18/360/1.

75   Morgan had done all he could: Ibid.

75   "Ah me": *EMF Letters 2*, 22.

75   "the usual 25 years of his life": EMF to SRM, 23-2-22, EMF Papers, KCAC, EMF/18/360/1.

75   "for now he is silent": Ibid.

75   "We passengers": EMF to Laura Forster, 26-2-22, EMF Papers, KCAC, EMF/18/193/1, vol. 6/9.

75   "The public tragedy": EMF to SRM, 25-1-22, EMF Papers, KCAC, EMF/18/360/1.

75   "passed very pleasantly": EMF to Laura Forster, 26-2-22, EMF Papers, KCAC, EMF/18/193/1,
vol. 6/9.

75   "I must not forget": Ibid.

75   "The knack of a double life grows": *EMF Letters 2*, 59.

76   "that as soon as I leave": Ibid.

76   An uncle of Morgan's, Willie Forster: Furbank, *E. M. Forster*, 1:66.

76   "Depressing & enervating surroundings": Forster, *Journals and Diaries*, 2:27.

4: "Somewhere Away by Myself"

77 "our Bert's first book": Edward Nehls, ed., *D. H. Lawrence: A Composite Biography*, vol. 1, *1885–1919* (Madison: University of Wisconsin Press, 1957), 72. Future references will be to *Composite 1*.

77 "message after message": Edward Nehls, ed., *D. H. Lawrence: A Composite Biography*, vol. 3, *1925–1930* (Madison: University of Wisconsin Press, 1959), 505. Future references will be to *Composite 3*.

77 "no sign was given": *Composite 1*, 72.

77 "a genius for inventing games": Ibid., 13.

77 "the girls together to go blackberrying": Ibid., 17.

78 "hundreds of niggardly houses": Ada Lawrence and Stuart Gelder, *Young Lorenzo: Early Life of D. H. Lawrence* (London: Martin Secker, 1931), 13.

78 "was as white as lard": Mabel Dodge Luhan, *Lorenzo in Taos* (London: Martin Secker, 1933), 169–70.

78 "tousled head and red beard": Ibid., 170.

78 "indomitable, with a will to endure": Ibid.

78 "a fleshly Word": Ibid.

78 "Dicky Dicky Denches": *Composite 1*, 30.

78 "he had not much use": Ibid., 25.

78 "perpetually squeaked or squealed": Edward Nehls, ed., *D. H. Lawrence: A Composite Biography*, vol. 2, *1919–1925* (Madison: University of Wisconsin Press, 1958), 95. Future references will be to *Composite 2*.

78 "ill-bred and hysterical": Edmund Wilson, *Letters on Literature and Politics, 1912–1972*, ed. Elena Wilson (New York: Farrar, Straus and Giroux, 1977), 662.

78 "One saw . . . burst out": Edmund Wilson, *The Twenties* (New York: Farrar, Straus and Giroux, 1975), 149–50.

79 "It seemed inevitable": Lawrence and Gelder, *Young Lorenzo*, 40.

80 passport: D. H. Lawrence Collection, HRC, Series V, Miscellaneous.

80 "like flames": *Composite 1*, 59.

80 "funny little cackle": Robert Mountsier, in D. H. Lawrence Collection, HRC, Box 46, File 4.

80 "rising inflection . . . little scream": *Composite 2*, 106.

81 "I wish I could find a ship": D. H. Lawrence, *The Letters of D. H. Lawrence*, ed. Warren Roberts, James T. Boulton, and Elizabeth Mansfield, vol. 4, *1921–1924* (Cambridge: Cambridge University Press, 1987), 93. Future references will be to *DHL Letters 4*.

81 "so empty . . . life-empty": D. H. Lawrence, *Letters to Thomas and Adele Seltzer*, ed. Gerald M. Lacy (Santa Barbara, CA: Black Sparrow Press, 1976), 20.

81 "the great window": *DHL Letters 4*, 90.

81 "naked liberty": D. H. Lawrence, *The Letters of D. H. Lawrence*, ed. James T. Boulton and Andrew Robertson, vol. 3, *1916–1921* (Cambridge: Cambridge University Press, 1985), 417. Future references will be to *DHL Letters 3*.

81 "bog": *DHL Letters 4*, 420.

82 "You will hate it": D. H. Lawrence, *The Letters of D. H. Lawrence*, ed. George Zytaruk and James T. Boulton, vol. 2, *1913–1916* (Cambridge: Cambridge University Press, 1982), 669.

82 "a half imbecile fool": *DHL Letters 4*, 89.

82 *John Bull*: *DHL Letters 4*, 88n2. The text of the denunciation is in *Composite 2*, 89–91.

82 "to disapprove of me": *DHL Letters 4*, 115.

83 "at considerable pecuniary loss": Ibid., 94n1.

83 "the best of my books": Ibid., 40.

83 "come loose": Ibid., 97.

83 "continual Mad-Hatters tea-party": Ibid., 105.

83 "it feels so empty": Ibid., 165.

83 "What isn't empty": Ibid.

83 "a Columbus who can see": D. H. Lawrence, *Twilight in Italy and Other Essays*, ed. Paul Eggert (Cambridge: Cambridge University Press, 1994), 186.

83   "companion adventurers": *Composite 2*, 71.

83   "if only to leave behind": Ibid.

83   "America, being so much *worse*": *DHL Letters 3*, 25.

83   "dryrotted": Ibid.

83   "really away": *DHL Letters 4*, 96.

84   "forty-odd pounds": Ibid., 107.

84   "at the last crumbs": Ibid., 113.

84   because he had misplaced: Ibid., 103.

84   "without new possibilities": Ibid., 25.

84   "in a hell of a temper . . . dagger": Ibid., 108.

84   "beshitten": Ibid., 109.

84   "slippery ball": Ibid., 90.

84   "stolen": Ibid., 124.

85   Her letter was not a letter: Luhan, *Lorenzo in Taos*, 16–17.

85   "so long that it was rolled": Ibid., 17.

85   "*There* is glamour": *DHL Letters 4*, 125.

85   "just one long arcade": Ibid., 139.

85   "tell him every single thing": Luhan, *Lorenzo in Taos*, 16.

85   "full of time and ease": Ibid.

85   "carpentered right there in the house": Ibid., 20.

85   "I believe what you say": *DHL Letters 4*, 111.

86   "*very* practical": Ibid.

86   "very much cut up": Ibid., 107.

86   transforms Frieda and Lawrence into comic characters: Mark Kinkead-Weekes, *D. H. Lawrence: Triumph in Exile, 1912–1922* (Cambridge: Cambridge University Press, 1996), 622.

86   "annoying and uncomfortable . . . vivacity": Ibid., 623.

86   "mass of contradictions and shocks": Luhan, *Lorenzo in Taos*, 15.

86   "he made a fetish": Richard Aldington, *Portrait of a Genius, But . . . : The Life of D. H. Lawrence, 1885–1930* (London: Heinemann, 1950), 42.

87   "Still she thought": D. H. Lawrence, *The Rainbow*, ed. Mark Kinkead-Weekes (New York: Penguin Classics, 1995), 94.

87   "give a voice": Luhan, *Lorenzo in Taos*, 255.

87   "The white people like": Ibid., 23.

87   "severe homosexual fixation": Lois Palken Rudnick, *Mabel Dodge Luhan: New Woman, New Worlds* (Albuquerque: University of New Mexico Press, 1984), 195.

87   "Are there any trees?": *DHL Letters 4*, 111.

87   "I want to take the next step": Ibid.

88   "How far are you": Ibid., 112.

88   "I was so weary": "New Heaven and Earth," in D. H. Lawrence, *The Complete Poems*, eds. Vivian De Sola Pinto and F. Warren Roberts (London: Penguin Books, 1993), 256.

88   "I had a letter yesterday": *DHL Letters 4*, 112.

88   but her income: Brenda Maddox, *D. H. Lawrence: The Story of a Marriage* (New York: Simon and Schuster, 1994), 311.

88   "to earn our bread & meat . . . A round": *The Suppressed Memoirs of Mabel Dodge Luhan: Sex, Syphilis, and Psychoanalysis in the Making of Modern American Culture*, ed. Lois Palken Rudnick (Albuquerque: University of New Mexico Press, 2012), 102.

89   "I envy Mary Austin": Ibid., 104.

89   "he threw everyone over": Luhan, *Lorenzo in Taos*, 26.

90   "till I have crossed": *DHL Letters 4*, 111.

90   "it has got form": D. H. Lawrence, *The Letters of D. H. Lawrence*, ed. James T. Boulton, vol. 1, *1901–1913* (Cambridge: Cambridge University Press, 1979), 476.

90   "Why don't you write . . . copying and revising": *Composite 2*, 106.

91   "dull but nice": *DH Letters 4*, 187.

91   "Very well": *Composite 2*, 106.

91   "But I do want": Ibid.

91   "For where was life to be found?": D. H. Lawrence, *Women in Love*, ed. David Farmer, Lindeth Vasey, and John Worthen (New York: Penguin Books, 1995), 193.

91   "What do you think life is?": *Composite 3*, 593.

91   "all this intimacy . . . common emotion": Knud Merrild, *A Poet and Two Painters: A Memoir of D. H. Lawrence* (New York: Viking Press, 1939), 47.

92   "inner life . . . action and strenuousness": *DHL Letters 4*, 154.

92   "I hate Christmas": Ibid.

92   "through the blood": Ibid., 174.

93   "rest, peace, inside one": Ibid., 180.

93   "I feel it is my destiny": Ibid., 181.

93   "Lawrence *is* wear and tear": To Edward Garnett, January 1913?, in Frieda Lawrence, *The Memoirs and Correspondence*, ed. E. W. Tedlock, Jr. (New York: Knopf, 1964), 176.

5: "The Greatest Waste Now Going On in Letters"

94   "not very many others": *TSE Letters 1 2009*, 622.

94   *Unreal City*: The city was so persuasively unreal in this passage, beginning at line 60 of the published text, that when Virginia Woolf set the poem in type for the Hogarth Press in 1923, she made the mistake of having the crowd flow *under* the bridge. Tom did not catch the error in proofreading, though in presentation copies he crossed out the word and corrected it in the margin. In his typescript, on *TWL Facsimile*, 9, Eliot used the word "flow"—an urgent present tense. In the published poem it appears in the past tense, "flowed."

95   "crush hour": Eliot's friend John Hayward wrote in his notes to a 1947 French edition of Eliot's poetry—notes surprisingly biographical but presumably approved by Eliot, since they shared a flat at the time Hayward prepared them—that these lines about the Unreal City, with their echoes of Dante, described "a typical London scene during the morning 'crush-hours.' City workers are due at their offices by 9 a.m., hence the reference to St. Mary Woolnoth's bell." Hayward also noted that King William Street runs from the north side of London Bridge "into the heart of the City," adding, "T. S. Eliot worked for a time in the City in the Foreign Department of Lloyds Bank." These are found in the Papers of the Hayward Bequest of T. S. Eliot Material, KCAC, HB/V.4b, John Hayward's draft notes for his notes on *The Waste Land*, published in the French translation of Eliot's *Poèmes 1910–1930* (Paris: Seuil, 1947).

95   "London, the swarming life . . . B—ll—S": *TWL Facsimile*, 31.

95   Eliot's influenza: *TSE Letters 1 2009*, 624.

95   "excessively depressed": Ibid., 629.

96   "approximately what the *Dial* would offer": Ibid., 623.

96   "postpone all . . . but not more": Ibid.

96   "It will have been three times": Ibid.

97   "12pp. 120,": Ibid., 623n2.

97   "I only wish": Dial/Scofield Thayer Papers, Beinecke Rare Book and Manuscript Library, YCAL MSS 34, Series IV, Box 31, Folder 809. The Beinecke has penciled a date of 1921 for this letter, but it seems to be Thayer's response to a TSE letter of February 14, 1920.

97   "Why no verse?": *TSE Letters 1 2009*, 539n2.

97   "You must excuse": Ibid., 572.

97   "That at least is definite": Ibid.

98   "embarrassing situation": Ibid., 623.

98   "I was glad to hear": Ibid., 616.

98   "howsoever good your next": Ibid., 617.

98   a gap of seven months: For Eliot's excuse see *Letters 1 2009*, 623, and for Thayer's reply see *Letters 1 2009*, 632.

99   "await another case of influenza": Ibid., 631.

99   "that if she had realised": Ibid., 629.

99   "Three months off . . . undiplomatic": Ibid., 640.

99   "almost enough to make everyone": Walter Sutton, ed., *Pound, Thayer, Watson, and the* Dial (Gainesville: University Press of Florida, 1994), 227.

100   "incommodious delay": Ibid., 194.

100 "Some minds aberrant": *TWL Facsimile*, 37. For the dating of this passage, see Gordon, *T. S. Eliot: An Imperfect Life*, 541.

100 "life has been horrible generally": *TSE Letters 1 2009*, 652.

100 "two highly nervous people": Kate Zambreno, *Heroines* (Los Angeles, CA: Semiotext[e], 2012), 39.

100 "as good pay for a year's work . . . graciousness . . . more yielding": *TSE Letters 1 2009*, 641.

101 "I have no disposition": Ibid., 639.

101 "I have just got through to Eliot": Wyndham Lewis to Violet Schiff, 4-28-1922, British Library, Schiff Papers, BL Add MS 52919.

101 "glowed with a tawny light . . . it may not be . . . a real curiosity": *TSE Letters 1 2009*, 638n2.

102 "the other offers for it": Ibid., 638.

102 "CANNOT ACCEPT": Ibid., 639.

102 "I have had to notify . . . I trust your review": Ibid., 644.

103 "merely gone to pieces again": Ibid., 640.

103 "I dare say . . . so DAMN little genius . . . two offspring . . . tougher than Thomas . . . Three months off": Ibid.

104 "Let The Dial stew": February 7, 1922, John Quinn papers, Manuscripts and Archives Division, New York Public Library, Letterbook vol. 25.

104 "was much given . . . leaning sideways . . . in a bantering tone . . . flirtatious": Stape, 46.

104 "a little encouragement . . . throw off a cascade": Ibid., 47.

104 "was ever bookish": Ibid., 46.

104 "preen itself with self-confidence": Ibid., 47.

105 "yes, grown positively familiar": *VW Diary 2*, 170.

105 "irritable and exhausted . . . overwhelmed . . . having let my flat": *TSE Letters 1 2009*, 646.

105 "What, then, did we discuss?" . . . "He has written": *VW Diary 2*, 171.

105 "This is his best work": Ibid.

105 "V. went for short walk": LW pocket diary, Leonard Woolf Papers, University of Sussex, SxMs-13/2/R/A/15.

105 "I am back again": *VW Diary 2*, 170.

106 "Clive, via Mary": Ibid., 171.

106 "I sat next to Tom": James E. Miller, Jr., *T. S. Eliot: The Making of an American Poet, 1888–1922* (University Park: PA: Pennsylvania State University Press, 2005), 380–81.

106 "She asked me, rather pointedly": Ibid.

106 "invalid wife . . . work all day": *VW Letters 2*, 549.

106 "He still remains": *VW Diary 2*, 204.

106 "Knopf knows . . . dear publisher": John Quinn to TSE, October 3, 1919, John Quinn papers, Manuscripts and Archives Division, New York Public Library, Microfilm ZL-355, Reel 10.

107 "Israelite": John Quinn to Harriet Weaver, June 22, 1922, John Quinn papers, Manuscripts and Archives Division, New York Public Library, Letterbook vol. 25, 838.

107 "three New York Jewish publishers re: Ulysses": Ibid.

107 "apparently loved": Ibid., 839.

108 "You have asked me several times": *TSE Letters 1 2009*, 652.

108 "hammered all but incessantly": Allen Tate, ed., *T. S. Eliot: The Man and His Work* (New York: Delacorte Press, 1966), 264.

108 "hunted round like a ghost": OM journal, Lady Ottoline Morrell Papers, British Library, Add MS 88886/6/13, transcript, 158.

109 enjoyed herself "enormously . . . We are all lonely": Ibid., transcript, 25.

109 "sort of apologia": *TSE Letters 1 2009*, 107.

109 "the whole hog": Ibid., 110.

109 "As to the exact sum": Ibid., 112.

110 "No use blinking the fact": *TWL Facsimile*, xviii.

110 "Eliot is worth saving": John Quinn to Ezra Pound, July 12, 1922, John Quinn papers, Manuscripts and Archives Division, New York Public Library, Letterbook vol. 25, 965.

110 Bel Esprit: Ezra Pound, "Credit and the Fine Arts: A Practical Application," *New Age*, March 30, 1922, 284–85.

112 "I had not intended . . . *complete* liberty": *TSE Letters 1 2009*, 650.

112 "These things should be done privately . . . For Gawd's sake": John Quinn to Ezra Pound, April 28, 1922, John Quinn papers, Manuscripts and Archives Division, New York Public Library, Microfilm ZL-355, Reel 31.

6: "Without a Novel & With No Power to Write One"

113 "part of my trouble": EMF to FB, 15-10-19, EMF Papers, KCAC, EMF/18/38/1, vols. 34/1-2.

113 "A nice state of affairs": EMF to SRM, 10-3-22, EMF Papers, KCAC, EMF/18/360/1.

114 "I felt no enthusiasm": *VW Diary* 2, 172.

114 "That was obvious": Ibid.

114 "I suppose I value": *VW Diary* 1, 308.

114 "told us as much . . . inanition . . . To come back . . . having lost your Rajah": *VW Diary* 2, 171.

114 "devilish, shrewd, psychological pounces": Vita Sackville-West to Harold Nicolson, November 20, 1926, quoted in Nigel Nicolson, *Portrait of a Marriage* (Chicago: University of Chicago Press, 1998 [1973]), 212.

115 "sparrows that fly about": *VW Diary* 2, 171.

115 "Ransack the language": Virginia Woolf, *Orlando*, ed. Rachel Bowlby (Oxford: Oxford University Press, 1992), 45.

115 "The middle age of buggers": *VW Diary* 2, 171.

115 "Off he went": Ibid., 172.

115 "It was such a happiness": EMF to SRM, 10-3-22, EMF Papers, KCAC, EMF/18/360/1.

115 "so ridiculously inane": *DHL Letters* 2, 293.

115 Sassoon wrote in diary: *Siegfried Sassoon Diaries, 1920–1922*, ed. Rupert Hart-Davis (London: Faber and Faber, 1981), 126.

117 "I think we shall meet": Forster, *Alexandria*, 345.

117 The scrawl of el Adl's signature: The letter is in EMF Papers, KCAC, EMF/18/11.

117 commonplace book he had begun during the war: EMF Papers, KCAC, EMF 16/13/A.

117 "I have transcribed": Forster, *Journals and Diaries*, 2:75.

118 "I plunged into Proust": EMF to SRM, 10-3-22, EMF Papers, KCAC, EMF/18/360/1.

118 "it's great stuff": Sutton, *Pound, Thayer, Watson, and the Dial*, 74.

118 "how cleverly Proust": Forster, *Journals and Diaries*, 2:65.

118 "Everyone is reading Proust": *VW Letters* 2, 499. The editors transcribe Woolf on Proust, "I'm shivering on the brink, and waiting to be submerged with a horrid sort of notion that I shall go down and down and down and perhaps never come up again." I have used the more idiosyncratic punctuation of the letter, in the Berg Collection, New York Public Library, m.b. (Woolf).

118 "Plymouth Sound": Ibid.

119 "entering an enchanted forest": Marcel Proust, *Marcel Proust: Selected Letters*, ed. Philip Kolb, trans. Ralph Manheim, vol. 4, *1918–1922* (London: HarperCollins, 2000), 215n5.

119 "There have always been aunts": E. M. Forster, "Uncle Willie," written for the Memoir Club and provisionally dated to the period just after Forster's return from India in 1922. Published as Appendix B in Forster, *Longest Journey*, 354.

120 "I suppose that ours is a female house": E. M. Forster, *Howards End*, ed. David Lodge (New York: Penguin Books, 2000), 37.

120 Proust's "favorite formulas": Edmund Wilson, *The Shores of Light: A Literary Chronicle of the Twenties and Thirties* (New York: Vintage Books, 1961 [1952]), 385.

121 "introspective and morbid . . . a million words . . . adventure": E. M. Forster, *Abinger Harvest* (New York: Harcourt, Brace, 1936), 202–3.

121 "a sad person": EMF to GHL, 27-4-22, EMF Papers, KCAC, EMF/18/333.

122 "hardish line": EMF to SRM, 15-4-22, EMF Papers, KCAC, EMF/18/360/1.

122 Florence Barger . . . bored him, "feeble . . . inferior": Forster, *Journals and Diaries*, 2:66.

122 "had totally disappeared from every one's view": EMF to Alice Clara Foster, undated, EMF Papers, KCAC, EMF/ACF I, 1922–24.

122 "and it was the real thing": *T. E. Lawrence Correspondence with E. M. Forster and F. L. Lucas*, ed.

Jeremy and Nicole Wilson (Fordingbridge, UK: Castle Hill Press, 2010), 179. Forster recounted this incident in his contribution to *T. E. Lawrence by His Friends*, ed. A. W. Lawrence (London: Jonathan Cape, 1937), 282–86.

122   "I want to talk over": EMF to Leonard Woolf, March 25, 1922, Henry W. and Albert Berg Collection of English and American Literature, New York Public Library, Berg Collection, m.b. (Woolf).

122   Leonard offered Morgan two pieces of advice: Forster, *Journals and Diaries*, 2:66.

7: "The Usual Fabulous Zest"

123   "Summer time": *VW Diary* 2, 174.
123   "27 days of bitter wind": Ibid., 175.
123   "my Reading book": Ibid., 120.
124   "up to the fire . . . four hundred pages . . . between tea . . . perhaps with labour . . . career": Virginia Woolf, *The Essays of Virginia Woolf*, ed. Andrew McNeillie, vol. 3, *1919–1924* (San Diego: Harcourt Brace Jovanovich, 1988), 474. Future references will be to *VW Essays* 3.
124   "lewd": *VW Diary* 2, 151.
124   "Milton is alive": *VW Essays* 3, 477.
125   "new book by Mr Keats": Ibid., 479.
125   In the dozens of reviews: The Woolf articles to which I refer are collected in *VW Essays* 3.
125   "But if the sense": Ibid., 138.
125   "the usual fabulous zest": *VW Diary* 2, 172.
125   "In England at the present moment": *VW Essays* 3, 475.
126   "a little party": Ibid., 494.
126   "who will marry who": Ibid.
126   "Mrs Dalloway was so-and-so": Virginia Woolf, *The Voyage Out*, ed. Lorna Sage (Oxford: Oxford University Press, 1992), 38.
127   "for a season": Ibid., 37.
127   "a tall slight woman": Ibid., 39.
127   "Well, that's over": Ibid., 84.
127   "was quite nice": Ibid., 88.
127   "It's a pity to be intimate": Ibid., 89.
127   "And the Dalloways": Lytton Strachey, *The Letters of Lytton Strachey*, ed. Paul Levy (New York: Farrar, Straus and Giroux, 2005), 270.
127   "such a harlequinade": *VW Diary* 2, 17.
127   "the more alterations": *VW Letters* 2, 401.
127   "I have put it in": Ibid., 404.
128   "voluntarily . . . *extremely* good": *VW Diary* 2, 65.
128   "so few of the gifts": *VW Letters* 1, 383.
128   "my people are puppets": *VW Diary* 2, 186.
128   "on his mother's side . . . Mrs Dalloway confessed": *VW Essays* 3, 494.
128   "most sincere . . . she had an Englishwoman's . . . fetch her husband": Ibid., 495.
129   "very interesting, & beautiful": *VW Diary* 2, 186.
129   "Come" . . . It was time: *VW Essays* 3, 495.
129   "So what does it matter": *VW Diary* 2, 170.
129   "some queer individuality . . . I'm to write": Ibid., 168.
129   "almost impenetrably overgrown": McNeillie note, *VW Essays* 3, 473.
130   "solid, living, flesh-and-blood": *VW Essays* 3, 388.
130   "ticklish . . . When one wants . . . I can never tell . . . tearing me up . . . have a fling": *VW Letters* 2, 521.
130   "little creatures": *VW Diary* 2, 161.
131   "Mrs. Dalloway in Bond Street": A typescript of the story with Woolf's change of "silk" to "gloves" is in the Berg Collection, m.b. (Woolf) [Mrs. Dalloway Stories], "Mrs. Dalloway in Bond Street," New York Public Library. The story is printed in Virginia Woolf, *The Complete Shorter Fiction of Virginia Woolf*, ed. Susan Dick, 2nd ed. (San Diego, CA: Harcourt Brace Jovanovich, 1989), 152–59.

132   *Manchester Guardian*: "The Silence in Manchester," *Manchester Guardian*, November 12, 1919, https://www.theguardian.com/theguardian/2009/nov/12/remembrance-archive-manchester-1919.

132   "Gloves have never been quite so reliable": Woolf, *Complete Shorter Fiction*, 158–59.

132   "one has more pleasure": *VW Diary* 2, 45.

133   "walked with V" and other LW entries: LW pocket diaries, Leonard Woolf Papers, University of Sussex.

133   "Sunshine and Happiness": "Sunshine and Happiness," *Times*, May 9, 1922, 7.

133   deaths in England and Wales: "Influenza Epidemic Figures," *Times*, June 16, 1922, 7.

134   "my heart has gone rather queer": *VW Letters* 2, 525.

134   "3 I could ill spare": Ibid., 532.

134   "goes on like": Ibid.

134   "She must rejoice": *LW Letters*, 199.

135   "Somehow, one can't take Richmond": *VW Diary* 1, 29.

135   "Omnibuses joined motor cars": Virginia Woolf, *Complete Shorter Fiction*, 155.

135   "I love walking": Ibid., 153.

135   "a strip of pavement . . . some way further": *VW Diary* 2, 73.

136   "unused hour fresh": Virginia Woolf, *Complete Shorter Fiction*, 152.

136   "seemed a fine fellow . . . there is nothing": Ibid.

136   "sweating out streams . . . Proust's fat volume . . . to sink myself . . . Proust so titillates": *VW Letters* 2, 525.

137   "No 'method' is justified": Ezra Pound, Paris Letter, *Dial*, March 1922, 403.

137   "I see it is necessary": *VW Letters* 2, 519.

138   "if it goes on raining": Ibid., 521.

138   "Now Mr Joyce": Ibid., 522.

138   "unutterable boredom . . . I can't see what he's after": *VW Letters* 2, 167.

138   "The life of a man": *VW Diary* 2, 68.

138   "claims to be a writer . . . concealed vanity": Ibid., 67.

139   "I should have gone under": Ibid.

139   "is probably being better done by Mr Joyce": Ibid., 69.

139   "Then I began to wonder": Ibid.

139   "in the opinion of": Ibid., 115n22.

139   "women can't paint, women can't write": Virginia Woolf, *To the Lighthouse*, ed. Mark Hussey (Orlando, FL: Harcourt, 2005), 51.

140   "First there's a dog": *VW Letters* 2, 234.

140   "interesting as an experiment": Ibid.

140   "These five years": Virginia Woolf, *Mrs. Dalloway*, ed. David Bradshaw (Oxford: Oxford University Press, 1992), 61.

8: "English in the Teeth of All the World"

142   would never be able to work there: Keith Sagar, *D. H. Lawrence: A Calendar of His Works* (Austin: University of Texas Press, 1979), 121.

142   "for a bit, thank God": *DHL Letters* 4, 157.

142   "the people are so": Ibid., 103.

142   Their steward came at seven a.m.: Ibid., 205.

142   "yelling crowd . . . handsome Turks . . . hateful Christians . . . one can easily throw": Ibid., 211.

143   "lost Paradise": Ibid.

143   "on thorns, can't settle": Sagar, *D. H. Lawrence: A Calendar of His Works*, 120.

143   Ceylon: *Composite* 2, 117.

143   repulsed by the thought of America: *DHL Letters* 4, 207.

143   large bungalow: *Composite* 2, 118.

143   "curled up": Sagar, *D. H. Lawrence: A Calendar of His Works*, 121.

143   "affected consciousness": *Composite* 2, 118.

144   "good-looking": Ibid., 121.

144   "whose flow of blood": Ibid., 118.

144   "colourful" . . . monkeys . . . elephants: Ibid.

144   "need never tread . . . strange, pulsating": Ibid., 127.

144   "sad and forlorn . . . the *butt* . . . being a prince . . . periphery . . . most living clue . . . vital spark": Ibid., 121.

145   "English in the teeth of all the world": Ibid., 131.

145   "Heaven knows why . . . I think Frieda": Ibid.

145   "bush all around" . . . A land to lose oneself: *DHL Letters 4*, 266.

146   "raw hole": *Composite 2*, 131.

146   gave no hint: Ibid., 473–74n31.

146   "unhewn": Ibid., 136.

146   Lawrence of Arabia: Ibid.

146   "Why had he come?": D. H. Lawrence, *Kangaroo*, ed. Bruce Steele (Cambridge: Cambridge University Press, 2002 [1994]), 13.

146   "but—but—BUT": *Composite 2*, 135.

146   "an outsider . . . off the map": D. H. Lawrence, *The Lost Girl*, ed. John Worthen (Cambridge: Cambridge University Press, 1981), 117–18.

146   "to be one step removed": Lawrence, *Kangaroo*, 256.

147   "Sydney town": *DHL Letters 4*, 249.

147   Meat "is so cheap": Ibid., 256.

147   "you get huge joints": Ibid., 266.

147   the 1921 census: Joseph Davis, *D. H. Lawrence at Thirroul* (Sydney, Australia: W. Collins, 1989), 38.

147   "Thirroul's Gay Arena": Ibid., 250n74.

147   "under the brooding": Ibid., 24.

147   "the men here are mostly": Ibid., 44.

147   "I feel awfully foreign": *DHL Letters 4*, 253.

147   "very discontented": *Composite 2*, 142.

147   Australian gentry: Ibid.

148   "indescribably weary and dreary . . . so many forlorn": Lawrence, *Kangaroo*, 26.

148   The to-let advertisements: Davis, *Lawrence at Thirroul*, 27, 32.

148   The "holiday cottage": Ibid., 18.

148   "only we are on the brink": *DHL Letters 4*, 263.

148   "morose-looking fellow": Davis, *Lawrence at Thirroul*, 38.

148   "ignored the normal give-and-take": Robert Darroch, "The Town That Doesn't Want to Be Famous," *Australian Magazine*, Christmas 1976, 31–33.

148   preternaturally curious: Davis, *Lawrence at Thirroul*, 38.

148   "It doesn't pay": Ibid.

148   the estate agent: *Composite 2*, 144.

148   muse: *DHL Letters 4*, 243.

149   "Idle Here" . . . "Wyewurk" . . . "Wyewurrie": Davis, *Lawrence at Thirroul*, 18.

149   " 'Why work' ": Ibid., 19.

149   "very seaey water": *DHL Letters 4*, 271.

149   "You are so bad-tempered": Lawrence, *Kangaroo*, 26. I have drawn some details of the Lawrences' lives in Australia from this autobiographical novel. As Lawrence's biographer David Ellis notes, "In almost all respects that matter, Harriet and Richard Somers 'are' Frieda and Lawrence." See David Ellis, *D. H. Lawrence: Dying Game, 1922–1930* (Cambridge: Cambridge University Press, 1998), 43.

149   "boomingly crashingly noisy": *DHL Letters 4*, 271.

150   "Fritzies, most likely": Lawrence, *Kangaroo*, 8.

150   "pure Teutonic consciousness": Ibid., 238.

150   "I feel I have packed": Frieda Lawrence to Anna Jenkins, Papers associated with D. H. Lawrence collected by W. Forster, University of Nottingham Manuscripts and Special Collections, For L 1/3/4/1.

150   "housewifes": *DHL Letters 4*, 266.

150   "*all* ourselves": Ibid.

150   "frightened by the voices within": Margaret Barbalet, *Steel Beach* (Ringwood, Australia: Penguin Books Australia, 1988), 13. The part of Barbalet's novel about the Lawrences in Australia is based on her research.

151   "the last of my serious English novels": *DHL Letters 4*, 92.

151   "strange stimulus . . . living company . . . Especially fir-trees": Ibid., 25.

151   "almost motionless": Ellis, *D. H. Lawrence: Dying Game*, p. 324.

152   "little travel book": Sagar, *D. H. Lawrence: A Calendar of His Works*, 109.

152   "my interim": *DHL Letters 4*, 25.

152   "The novels and poems": D. H. Lawrence, *Fantasia of the Unconscious*, in *Psychoanalysis and the Unconscious and Fantasia of the Unconscious*, ed. Bruce Steele (Cambridge: Cambridge University Press, 2004), 65.

152   "appear to have passed their prime": John Middleton Murry, quoted in Kinkead-Weekes, *D. H. Lawrence: Triumph in Exile, 1912–1922*, 684.

152   quickly, often in a month or less: *DHL Letters 4*, 28.

153   "pitched": Ibid., 258.

153   "It was winter, the end of May . . . that air of owning": Lawrence, *Kangaroo*, 7.

153   "One was . . . Her companion": Ibid.

154   "suddenly writing again": *DHL Letters 4*, 255.

154   "when the sun is very warm": Ibid., 256.

154   "the days slipped by like dreams": Frieda Lawrence, *"Not I, But the Wind . . ."* (Santa Fe, NM: Rydal Press, 1934), 119.

154   "keeps on at the rate . . . rum sort": *DHL Letters 4*, 257.

155   "a weird thing": Ibid., 265.

155   "weird unawakened country": Ibid., 266.

155   "has written his head off": Frieda Lawrence to Anna Jenkins, Papers associated with D. H. Lawrence collected by W. Forster, University of Nottingham Manuscripts and Special Collections, For L 1/3/4/1.

155   "the Lord alone": *DHL Letters 4*, 267.

155   "Richard's hand was almost drawn": Lawrence, *Kangaroo*, 136.

156   At least thirty-five hundred words a day: Ellis, *D. H. Lawrence: Dying Game*, 39.

156   "Mr Dionysos and Mr Hermes": Lawrence, *Kangaroo*, 173.

156   "a determined little devil": Ibid.

156   "done more than half": *DHL Letters 4*, 267.

156   "now slightly stuck": Ibid., 268.

156   "I do hope": Ibid.

156   "depressing accounts of sales": Ibid., 276.

157   "The trouble was": Ellis, *D. H. Lawrence: Dying Game*, 345. About the period between October 1926 and March 1927, Ellis writes, "Lawrence was reconciled to being neither popular nor rich and prepared to regulate his expenses accordingly." Ellis quotes DHL's response to a November 1926 letter from the Seltzers "asking if he would consider publishing with them again. In his reply Lawrence said that he could promise nothing and added, 'Adele says I am to come back with a best seller under my arm. When I have written "Sheik II" or "Blondes Prefer Gentlemen", I'll come. Why does anybody look to me for a best seller? I'm the wrong bird.' "

157   "thought-adventurer, driven to earth": Lawrence, *Kangaroo*, 212. Robert Darroch, in his book *D. H. Lawrence in Australia* (Melbourne, Australia: Macmillan Australia, 1981), argued that the political parts of *Kangaroo* are not invented. Bruce Steele rebutted Darroch's claims in his introduction to the Cambridge University Press edition of *Kangaroo*, xiv–xviii. Darroch has continued his research into the issue, and it is presented, along with other information about Lawrence's time in Australia, on the website of the D. H. Lawrence Society of Australia:http://www.dhlawrencesocietyaustralia.com.au/.

157   "Seven weeks today": *DHL Letters 4*, 267.

157   "Have you ever stood": "D. H. Lawrence: The Man and His Work," Papers associated with D. H. Lawrence collected by W. Forster, University of Nottingham Manuscripts and Special Collections, For L 4/1/1/1.

158   "D. H. Lawrence Completes His Love-Cycle": *Brooklyn Daily Eagle*, May 6, 1922, 3.

9: "Do Not Forget Your Ever Friend"

159   "Have this moment burnt": Forster, *Journals and Diaries*, 2:66.

159   "the indecent writings . . . of others": Ibid.

159   "the happiest day I have passed": Ibid.

160   "How can a great artist like you": Ibid.

160   "gloomily before my Indian novel": Ibid.

160   "holocaust . . . sexy stories": E. M. Forster, *The Life to Come, and Other Stories* (New York: W. W. Norton, 1973 [1972]), xiv. Oliver Stallybrass wrote an introduction to this posthumous collection of Forster's short fiction. "Holocaust" is his word. He ascribes the second phrase to Forster, though without a citation.

160   "sacrificial burning . . . in order that": *EMF Letters* 2, 129.

160   "I will try to connect it": EMF to Christopher Isherwood, 10-2-44, EMF Papers, KCAC, EMF/18/271/2.

160   "Ghosts": *London Mercury* 5, no. 30 (April 1922): 568–73.

161   "all in the opening lines": *EMF Letters* 2, 24.

162   "dear Morgan / I am sending you": EMF Papers, KCAC, EMF/18/11.

162   "my constant thinking of him": Forster wrote this note to himself in the margin of his transcription of el Adl's "Words Spoken," in EMF Papers, KCAC, EMF/11/10/2/A. Because his second use of the words "at all events" fell directly underneath the same words on the line above, Forster used ditto marks to indicate them.

163   "Yes, it is easier to write to strangers": T. E. Lawrence, *Correspondence with E. M. Forster and F. L. Lucas*, ed. Jeremy and Nicole Wilson (Fordingbridge, UK: Castle Hill Press, 2010), 16. The letter is dated February 22, 1924.

163   confessional but oblique: Even two years on Forster was hesitant about too much confession. "Joe Ackerly [*sic*] has been my confidant," he wrote in his diary in October 1924, referring to an aborted sexual affair with a married man. "It may cause him to despise me" (Forster, *Journals and Diaries*, 2:75).

163   "I have been reading Proust": *EMF Letters* 2, 24.

163   "not really first-rate . . . everyone seems to suspect . . . astutely malicious. . . . The usual subject?": *Siegfried Sassoon Diaries, 1920–1922*, 129.

164   "as I returned home": Marcel Proust, *Swann's Way*, trans. Lydia Davis (New York: Viking, 2003), 45.

164   *"Delivered by us"*: Ibid., 44.

164   "Délivrées pas nous": E. M. Forster Collection, HRC, Box 3, Folder 3.

165   "with our mouths open to the sun": Forster, *Journals and Diaries*, 2:67.

165   "Have made careful & uninspired additions": Ibid.

165   "happy . . . a silly word . . . at all events": *EMF Letters* 2, 25–26.

165   "I want him to tell me": Forster, *Journal and Diaries*, 2:67.

166   "Determined my life should contain": Ibid.

166   "Moh. worse again": Ibid.

166   "out & about again": *VW Diary* 2, 178.

166   his most endearing characteristics: Ibid., 33.

166   Virginia wrote in April to Ottoline Morrell: *VW Letters* 2, 524.

166   "The month of May was gorgeous & hot": OM Journal, Lady Ottoline Morrell Papers, British Library, Add. MS 88886/04/012, transcript, 145.

166   "My future is as an uncharted sea": EMF to OM, 5-12-22, Ottoline Morrell Collection, HRC, Box 6, File 9.

167   "Why do we do such things?": *VW Letters* 2, 520.

167   "playing Badminton and discussing fiction": Ibid., 519.

167   "But please don't say": Ibid., 526.

167   "whom we had to leave behind and conceal": *EMF Letters* 2, 27.

167   "Lady O in bright yellow satin": Ibid.

167   "once seen, could not be forgotten": William Plomer, *At Home* (London: Jonathan Cape, 1958), 46.

167   "one admired the colours": Quentin Bell, "Ottoline Morrell," in *Bloomsbury Recalled* (New York: Columbia University Press, 1996), 161.

168   "not very stimulating" weekend . . . "Ott. was dreadfully dégringolée": Strachey, *The Letters of Lytton Strachey*, 521–22. The letter is dated September 19, 1922.

168   "It's such an age": *VW Letters* 2, 518.

168   Lewis "isn't nice . . . Why ask such?": *EMF Letters* 2, 27.

168   "I liked him but thought . . . managed to inform": Forster, *Journals and Diaries*, 2:59.

168   "Suspicious and hostile glares": *EMF Letters* 2, 29.

168   "a succès fou": EMF to Gerald Brenan, EMF Papers, KCAC, EMF/18/67.

168   Lewis, however confidential and ingratiating he appeared: Lewis, *Blasting and Bombardiering*, 239. The index to the book spells Virginia's surname correctly, but the misspelling in the text is preserved in the reset second edition, prepared by his widow Anne Wyndham Lewis and posthumously published in 1967 by the University of California Press, perhaps inadvertently, perhaps to preserve Lewis's original intention. On page 3 of the 1937 edition, Lewis writes that it is time to give the war a "fresh inspection" and that "the roosters of the 'post-war' have crowed themselves hoarse or to a standstill. . . . The 'frozen eagle,' Mrs. Woolfe, has not flooded the welkin for a moon or two. . . . It is many years since Mr. Forster opened his mouth" (3–4). He was presumably unaware of Forster's essay collection, *Abinger Harvest*, published in 1936; Woolf's *The Years* was published in 1937. The remark about "Mrs. Woolfe" is removed from the 1967 edition, perhaps in deference to her suicide, leaving the question of the misspelling even more confounding.

169   "Pale Souls": *Times*, June 6, 1922, 14.

170   she had never even heard: Ibid., June 8, 1922, 14.

170   "Having seen 'Lucas Malet's' letter": Ibid., June 10, 1922, 14.

171   "I am well and suddenly famous": EMF to SRM, 26-6-22, EMF Papers, KCAC, EMF/18/360/1.

171   "so frisky and pleased": EMF to Siegfried Sassoon, 12-6-22, EMF Papers, KCAC, EMF/18/489/3.

171   "fundamental defect . . . not sufficiently interesting": EMF to GHL, 6-13-22, EMF Papers, KCAC, EMF/18/333.

171   "terribly slowly": Ibid.

171   "By looking blandly ahead? By screaming? How? By Living?": EMF to Siegfried Sassoon, 12-6-22, EMF Papers, KCAC, EMF/18/489/3.

172   "longs to see her again and has often thought of her": *EMF Letters* 2, 29.

172   "and still more the prohibitions . . . He wants to ask Mummy . . . Ever love as ever": *EMF Letters* 2, 30.

172   "Poppy kicks": *EMF Letters* 2, 30n1.

10: "Eliot Dined Last Sunday & Read His Poem"

173   "We know what constant illness is": *TSE Letters 1 2009*, 667.

174   There is nothing in any of Tom's or Vivien's: Eliot seems never to have referred to Vittoz after leaving Lausanne; and even when his own mental state and Vivien's declined precipitously in 1924 and 1925, he seems never to have thought of returning to Vittoz for treatment. The only evidence of continued contact between them is in December 1923. Eliot sent Vittoz a copy of the Hogarth Press edition of *The Waste Land* as a Christmas present and inscribed it to the doctor with "eternal gratitude." Vittoz died in April 1925. "The Waste Land, T. S. Eliot, Presented by Senior Rare Book Specialist Adam Douglas," video, Peter Harrington Rare Books, http://www.peterharrington.co.uk/video/waste-land-t-s-eliot/; and Simon Reichley, "T.S. Eliot's *The Waste Land*, with Inscription to the Author's Therapist, Goes on Sale," Melville House, February 9, 2016, http://www.mhpbooks.com/t-s-eliots-the-waste-land-with-inscription-to-the-authors-therapist-goes-on-sale/.

174   "run down, so that at present": *TSE Letters 1 2009*, 669.

174   "He was in a state of collapse": Ibid., 701.

174   "for a needed change of air . . . only one step . . . I get no benefit": Ibid., 670.

174   "T. S. Eliot is very ill": Ibid., 669n1.

175   "4tnight's holiday": Ibid., 673.

175 "never felt quite so lazy and languid": Ibid., 675.
175 "boating, bathing, eating, sleeping": Ibid., 686.
175 "smothered in roses and wisteria": Ibid., 675.
175 two days with Ezra Pound in Verona: Ibid., 676, 687.
175 "I have been on the job": Pound, *The Letters of Ezra Pound, 1907–1941*, 172.
176 "I shall be dead to the world": Ezra Pound to John Quinn, April 12, 1922, in Ezra Pound, *The Selected Letters of Ezra Pound to John Quinn, 1915–1924*, ed. Timothy Materer (Durham, NC: Duke University Press, 1991), 208.
176 "I am dead": Ezra Pound to Jeanne Foster, April 12, 1922, in Londraville and Londraville, *Dear Yeats, Dear Pound, Dear Ford*, 200.
176 "had it put about": A. D. Moody, "*Bel Esprit* and the Malatesta Cantos: A Post–*Waste Land* Conjunction of Pound and Eliot," in *Ezra Pound and Europe*, ed. Richard Taylor and Claus Melchior (Amsterdam: Rodolpi, 1993), 80.
176 "I shall rise again at a suitable time": Pound, *Ezra Pound to His Parents*, 498.
176 "Malatesta Cantos" . . . "Thomas amics" . . . "the footlights": Moody, "*Bel Esprit* and the Malatesta Cantos," 81.
176 "combative allusion": Ibid., 79.
176 "T. S. E." after "you" on one draft: Ibid., 80n7.
177 "I object strongly . . . With your permission": *TSE Letters* 2, 141.
177 "perfection is such": *VW Diary* 2, 176.
177 "slip easily": Ibid.
177 "working too hard; talking too much": Ibid., 177.
177 "premonitory shivers": Ibid.
177 "my season of doubts & ups & downs": Ibid., 178.
177 "clever experiment . . . vary the side of the pillow": Ibid.
178 "very calm, serene": Ibid.
178 "If I ever finish a novel": EMF to Edward Arnold, 16-6-22, EMF Papers, KCAC, EMF/18/169/2.
179 "in very much better health": *TSE Letters* 1 2009, 686.
179 "Eliot dined last Sunday & read his poem": *VW Diary* 2, 178.
179 "He sang it & chanted it rhythmed it": Ibid.
179 "The Waste Land, it is called": Ibid. Virginia's reaction to the poem echoed Eliot's thoughts on Donne, whose gift, Eliot had written, was to make a poem from "the apparent irrelevance and unrelatedness of things" and to convey in a very personal way "his genuine whole of tangled feelings." Quoted in F. O. Matthiessen, *The Achievement of T. S. Eliot: An Essay on the Nature of Poetry* (Boston: Houghton Mifflin, 1935), 13.
179 "one is writing, so to speak": T. S. Eliot, "Poetry and Drama," in *Selected Prose of T. S. Eliot*, ed. Frank Kermode (New York: Harcourt Brace Jovanovich, 1975), 138.
179 "The question of communication": Ibid.
179 "is right to you": Ibid.
180 "glands . . . perfectly new and violent . . . very strong internal": *TSE Letters* 1 2009, 679.
180 "Tom's autobiography—a melancholy one": *VW Diary* 2, 178.
180 "Yes, Mary kissed me on the stairs": Ibid.
180 "When you were a tiny boy": Ada Eliot Sheffield to TSE, April 13, 1943, in *TSE Letters* 1 2009, xxxvii.
181 "to the accompaniment of a small drum": TSE to R. Ellsworth Larsson, May 22, 1928, in T. S. Eliot, *The Letters of T. S. Eliot*, ed. Valerie Eliot and John Haffenden, vol. 4, *1928–1929* (New Haven, CT: Yale University Press, 2013), 171. Future references will be to *TSE Letters* 4. Adam Mars-Jones cites this as an "outright mockery" of a younger poet and a conscious myth-making: "Of course, it's possible that he really did so, but wouldn't it have become part of the myth if he had? More likely that he gave in for once to irresistible impulse and took the piss out of a no-hoper." Adam Mars-Jones, review of *TSE Letters* 4, *Guardian*, January 10, 2013, http://www.theguardian.com/books/2013/jan/10/letters-ts-eliot-1928-1929-review.
181 "that curious monotonous sing-song": Leonard Woolf, *Downhill All the Way: An Autobiography of the Years 1919 to 1939* (New York: Harcourt Brace Jovanovich, 1975 [1967]), 109.
181 When John Quinn questioned Eliot: *TSE Letters* 1 2009, 557.

182   "desperate attempt to break through . . . slowly, precisely and flatly": Miranda Seymour, *Ottoline Morrell: Life on the Grand Scale* (New York: Farrar, Straus and Giroux, 1993), 257. The quotes are Seymour's summary of Morrell's journal entries.

182   "slightly booming monotone, without emphasis": Brigit Patmore, *My Friends When Young: The Memoirs of Brigit Patmore*, ed. Derek Patmore (London: Heinemann, 1968), 84.

182   bow drawn gently over a 'cello string": Draft of "T. S. Eliot: Some early memories," Brigit Patmore Collection, HRC, Box 3, File 6.

183   DISSATISFIED LIVERIGHTS CONTRACT POEM MAY I ASK YOUR ASSISTANCE APOLOGIES WRITING ELIOT: *TSE Letters 1 2009*, 680.

183   GLAD TO ASSIST EVERYWAY POSSIBLE: Ibid.

183   "You may observe this use of the Simian-verb 'to tree' with reference to these two publishers": John Quinn to TSE, July 28, 1922, John Quinn papers, Manuscripts and Archives Division, New York Public Library, Quinn Microfilm, ZL-355, Reel 10.

183   "a dirty piece of Jew impertinence": John Quinn to TSE, June 30, 1919, John Quinn papers, Manuscripts and Archives Division, New York Public Library, Quinn Microfilm, ZL-355, Reel 10.

183   "with the leisure that you want": John Quinn to TSE, May 9, 1921, John Quinn papers, Manuscripts and Archives Division, New York Public Library, Quinn Microfilm, ZL-355, Reel 10.

183   "Now, take off the time and go to your dentist": John Quinn to TSE, March 27, 1923, John Quinn papers, Manuscripts and Archives Division, New York Public Library, Letterbook vol. 26, 757.

184   The Liveright contract was unnecessarily vague: *TSE Letters 1 2009*, 681.

184   "and gives all the advantage . . . tantamount to selling": Ibid.

184   Quinn assured Eliot: Ibid., 680n1.

185   "as quickly as possible . . . merely for your own interest": Ibid., 682.

185   "in the form to be handed to the publisher": Ibid.

185   In April, Pound had written: Eliot, *The Poems of T. S. Eliot*, vol. 1, *Collected and Uncollected Poems*, 561.

185   "type it out fair, but I did not wish to delay": *TSE Letters 1 2009*, 707.

185   "and I shall rush forward the notes": Ibid.

185   "I only hope the printers": Ibid.

11: *Women in Love* in Court

187   "With Lawrence passion looms large": D. H. Lawrence Collection, HRC, Box 48, File 2.

188   New York Society for the Suppression of Vice: Boyer, *Purity in Print*, 3.

188   a private group: Andrea Friedman, *Prurient Interests: Gender, Democracy, and Obscenity in New York City, 1909–1945* (New York: Columbia University Press, 2000), 133.

188   "lush": Boyer, *Purity in Print*, 2.

188   "suppressed by Anthony Comstock": Ibid., 3.

188   "many subdivisions of commercialized vice": John S. Sumner, "The Truth About 'Literary Lynching,'" *Dial* 71 (July 1921): 65.

188   He was also more inventive: "Jurgen and the Censor," 4, in John Saxton Sumner Papers, Wisconsin Historical Society, Library-Archives Division, Box 1, File 8.

189   "conspicuously made an ass of himself": Boyer, *Purity in Print*, 29.

189   having done much good: Ibid.

189   "Advertising Bad Books": *New York Times*, March 15, 1923, 18.

189   "This is most irritating": *DHL Letters 2*, 431.

189   "an entitlement useless to the author": Edward de Grazia, *Girls Lean Back Everywhere: The Law of Obscenity and the Assault on Genius* (New York: Random House, 1992), 59.

189   "Decency's local representative": Newspaper clipping, April 1, 1951, publication name not included, John Saxton Sumner Papers, Wisconsin Historical Society, Library-Archives Division, Box 4.

189   "the word was offensive to people in general": "Forensics," p. 4, John Saxton Sumner Papers, Wisconsin Historical Society, Library-Archives Division, Box 1, Folder 7.

189   "We are told that this literature . . . Does not the demand": "Literature and the Law," p. 1, John

Saxton Sumner Papers, Wisconsin Historical Society, Library-Archives Division, Box 1, File 8, MS-44. The piece was written in 1931.

190 "ebbtide of moral laxity": The 1922 annual report is in John Saxton Sumner Papers, Wisconsin Historical Society, Library-Archives Division, Box 2, Folder 8.

190 The society reported: Sumner's monthly reports for 1922 are in ibid.

191 *Regina v. Hicklin*: de Grazia, *Girls Lean Back Everywhere*, 12.

191 "the tendency of the matter": Ibid., 193.

191 "the relation of the artist": Ibid., 11.

191 the result, which was conviction: Ibid., 10–11.

192 "business panic . . . The salesman in the West": Lawrence, *Letters to Thomas and Adele Seltzer*, 174.

192 *The Lost Girl* had, however, sold four thousand: Ibid., 207.

192 "Lawrence boom . . . hardly a literary page . . . spending money freely": Ibid., 211.

192 "benefactors of writers . . . never very far from insolvency": Alexandra Lee Levin and Lawrence L. Levin, "The Seltzers & D. H. Lawrence: A Biographical Narrative," in Lawrence, *Letters to Thomas and Adele Seltzer*, 175.

192 *Women in Love* sold steadily enough: Lawrence, *Letters to Thomas and Adele Seltzer*, 207.

192 "really unobjectionable": Ibid.

193 His June 1922 advertisement: *New-York Tribune*, June 11, 1922, D4.

193 "offish little": Alexander Woollcott, in a review of Eugene O'Neill's *The First Man*, *New York Times*, March 16, 1922, 15.

193 "Don't interrupt me . . . This, they say": Lawrence, *Letters to Thomas and Adele Seltzer*, 228.

193 Lawrence's generally weak sales: Neither Mountsier nor Seltzer seemed to think that Lawrence's sheer productivity—and the publication of so many books of his in so many genres in so short a time—diminished his overall prospects. Seltzer published twenty books of Lawrence's between 1920 and 1925, including an edition of *The Rainbow* in 1924. Seventeen appeared between 1920 and 1923 alone. Lawrence, working at the protean rate that was natural to him, appeared to calculate that small advances and perhaps limited royalties on many books would make for a better return than holding back in favor of the potentially lucrative novels that took him longer to complete (Lawrence, *Letters to Thomas and Adele Seltzer*, 279).

194 "no love interest at all so far—don't intend any—no sex either": *DHL Letters 4*, 258.

194 "Amy Lowell says you are getting a reputation": Ibid.

194 Late in the afternoon of Friday, July 7: "Seize 772 Books in Vice Crusade Raid," *New York Times*, July 12, 1922, 32.

194 "pinched by the PO-lice": The phrase is Ezra Pound's, from a letter he wrote in October 1920 to James Joyce about Sumner's seizure of the *Little Review* for July–August 1920, containing the "Nausikaa" episode of *Ulysses*, in *Pound/Joyce: The Letters of Ezra Pound to James Joyce, with Pound's Essays on Joyce*, ed. Forrest Reid (London: Faber and Faber, 1968), 184.

194 with "the publication and sale": "Seize 772 Books."

194 "taken by Mr. Sumner's command . . . under threat of having it forced": "Fizz Taken Out of Seltzer's Books at Hearing on Vice Charges," *New-York Tribune*, August 1, 1922, 5.

194 "called on Thomas Seltzer": Sumner's July 1922 report is in John Saxton Sumner Papers, Wisconsin Historical Society, Library-Archives Division, Box 2, Folder 8.

194 "marked [it] for presentation" to the Seventh District Court: Sumner monthly report, June 1922, ibid.

194 Sumner was given a summons and search warrant: "Blushed Through 254 Pages," *New-York Tribune*, July 12, 1922, 22.

195 "divers persons": "Censorship Beaten in New York Court: Magistrate Lets Thomas Seltzer Publish Three Criticized Books," September 16, 1922, *Publishers Weekly* 102 (July–December 1922): 802, https://books.google.com/books?id=rlo2AQAAMAAJ&pg=PA801&dq=censorship+beaten+thomas+seltzer+magistrate&hl=en&sa=X&ved=0ahUKEwjEmLuP9tzOAhXD7hoKHT9TBKUQ6AEIHjAA#v=onepage&q=censorship%20beaten%20thomas%20seltzer%20magistrate&f=false. See also "Important Censorship Case," August 5, 1922, *Publishers Weekly* 102 (July–December 1922): 463–64, https://books.google.com/books?id

=rlo2AQAAMAAJ&pg=PA463&dq=seldes+seltzer+1922&hl=en&sa=X&ved
=oahUKEwiZyYzB-tzOAhWqB8AKHUpSBOcQ6AEIVDAH#v=onepage&q=seldes%20selt
zer%201922&f=false.

195   "Also read books": Sumner's July 1922 report is in John Saxton Sumner Papers, Wisconsin
       Historical Society, Library-Archives Division, Box 2, Folder 8.

196   "to rescue its theatre": John H. Houchin, *Censorship of the American Theatre in the Twentieth
       Century* (Cambridge: Cambridge University Press, 2003), 86.

196   "giants of the Village": The phrase is Granville Hicks's, in his book *John Reed: The Making of a
       Revolutionary* (New York: Macmillan, 1936). The details of Seltzer's life are summarized in
       Levin and Levin, "The Seltzers & D. H. Lawrence," in Lawrence, *Letters to Thomas and Adele
       Seltzer*, 171–72.

196   Seltzer had more "*spark*": Lawrence, *Letters to Thomas and Adele Seltzer*, 108.

196   "dramatic occurrence . . . Of course the burden": Ibid., 233–34.

196   Lawrence "enslaves me . . . But he is lots more": Ibid., 237.

196   "in my judgment": "Seltzer to Fight Charges: Publisher's Lawyer Says Alleged Obscene
       Books Are Classics," *New York Times*, July 13, 1922, 29.

197   "is being conducted properly . . . We are up against a gang": Lawrence, *Letters to Thomas and
       Adele Seltzer*, 233–34.

197   Why neither Seltzer nor Mountsier felt: The letter would have taken about a month to arrive
       from the United States (see *DHL Letters 4*, 266, letter 2543 to Mabel Dodge Sterne). Like
       almost all correspondence to Lawrence, Seltzer's letter does not survive.

197   "his head off": Frieda Lawrence to Anna Jenkins, University of Nottingham Manuscripts and
       Special Collections, For L 1/3/4/1.

198   Somers is walking: Lawrence, *Kangaroo*, 211.

198   "the lumber-room of my past . . . mine and useful": Forster, *Longest Journey*, 366.

198   "lying perfectly still . . . Till now, he had always": Lawrence, *Kangaroo*, 259.

198   "It was in 1915 . . . John Bull": Ibid., 216.

198   "very strict watch": Ibid., 218.

198   "called up . . . thin nakedness . . . ignominious . . . Let them label me": Ibid., 221.

198   "find some way . . . thought about that many times . . . act from his soul alone": Ibid., 222.

199   "within the space of three days": Ibid., 241.

199   "report themselves": Ibid., 242.

199   "one of his serious deaths in belief": Ibid., 247.

199   "this free Australia . . . same terror . . . suspect again": Ibid., 259.

199   "funny sort of novel": *DHL Letters 4*, 271.

200   Mountsier advised: Ibid., 318.

200   "Have kept in the *War* piece": Ibid., 322.

200   "it must be so": Ibid., 323.

200   "The judgments of society": Lawrence, *Kangaroo*, 259.

200   "by bad luck": Ibid., 211.

201   "obscene, lewd, lascivious": Halsey v. N.Y. Society for Suppression of Vice, 191 App. Div. 245
       (N.Y. App. Div. 1920), https://casetext.com/case/halsey-v-ny-society-for-suppression-of-vice.

201   Halsey was tried and acquitted: Dawn B. Sova, *Literature Suppressed on Sexual Grounds*
       (New York: Facts on File, 2006), 156.

201   "whether a book is obscene": Halsey v. New York Soc. for Suppression of Vice, 136 N. E. 219
       (Court of Appeals of New York, July 12, 1922), reprinted in *National Reporter System: The New
       York Supplement*, vol. 195, September 11–October 2, 1922 (St. Paul, MN: West Publishing, 1922).
       Available online at https://books.google.com/books?id=guYKAAAAYAAJ&pg=PA964&dq
       =raymond+d.+halsey+maupin&hl=en&sa=X&ei=XhVbUa6eB4jD4AOxoIHACw&ved
       =oCD8Q6AEwAg#v=onepage&q=raymond%20d.%20halsey%20maupin&f=true, 964.

201   "No review of French literature . . . felicitous style . . . passages of purity": Ibid., 965.

201   Henry James's remark: Ibid.

201   The court acknowledged: Ibid.

202   "The excuse for parts of *Ulysses*": Ezra Pound to James Joyce, October 1920, in *Pound/Joyce*, 185.

202   "Blushed Through 254 Pages": *New-York Tribune*, July 12, 1922, 22.

202   "Salacious matter . . . profoundly shocked": Ibid.

203   "more than pleads the case": Lawrence, *Letters to Thomas and Adele Seltzer*, 235.

203   "Today is the worst day . . . hot spell is broken": Ibid.

203   "one of the most widely discussed cases": Boyer, *Purity in Print*, 384n31.

203   "Fizz Taken Out of Seltzer's Books": "Fizz Taken Out of Seltzer's Books."

203   "perused only passages": "Critics Find No Evil in 3 Impugned Books," *New York Times*, August 1, 1922.

203   The main focus of the experts' testimony: "Fizz Taken Out of Seltzer's Books."

204   "its putative effect on immature readers": Boyer, *Purity in Print*, 81.

204   "would not interest a child": "Fizz Taken Out of Seltzer's Books."

204   "sedulous care . . . distinct contribution . . . Mere extracts": "Book Censorship Beaten in Court," *New York Times*, September 13, 1922, 5. See also "His Books Held Lawful, Seltzer Says He'll Sue," *New-York Tribune*, September 13, 1922, 11.

204   "Technically it was a case": "Censorship Beaten in New York Court," *Publishers Weekly*, 801.

204   "Books will not be banned by law": Ibid.

204   "It has been said with some justice": "His Books Held Lawful, Seltzer Says He'll Sue."

204   "You can't win every case": Boyer, *Purity in Print*, 81.

204   The evening papers: Lawrence, *Letters to Thomas and Adele Seltzer*, 240.

204   "Everybody is happy about it": Ibid., 241.

204   "rushing in for the three 'obscene' books": Ibid.

205   "We haven't a copy left": Ibid., 243.

205   Sales reached upwards of fifteen thousand copies: Ibid., 244.

205   "I should still be poor *sans* Women in Love": *DHL Letters 4*, 457.

205   "getting a bit tired of me": Ibid., 277.

205   "I hope I needn't all my life": Ibid., 152.

205   "All we can do is grin and bear it": Ibid., 276.

206   "Pfui": Ibid., 292.

206   "New Mexico, U. S. A.": Ibid., 281.

12: *The Waste Land* in New York

207   "the current rumours of its having been abandoned": *TSE Letters 1 2009*, 685.

207   "upon certain groups": Ibid.

207   "simply because I liked the sound of the word . . . apparently harmless": Ibid., 701.

208   "more historical work": Ibid., 688.

208   "an elite readership of English letters": Ibid., 659n2.

208   "the multiplication of magazines . . . It was to avoid . . . The more artistic journals": Scofield Thayer to Vivien Eliot, October 20, 1921, Dial/Scofield Thayer Papers, Beinecke Rare Book and Manuscript Library, YCAL MSS 34, Series IV, Box 31, Folder 813.

209   running a deficit for 1922 of $65,000: Nicholas Joost, *Scofield Thayer and The Dial: An Illustrated History* (Carbondale: Southern Illinois University Press, 1964), 40.

209   "Dial costs 46 cents to print": Pound, *Ezra Pound to His Parents*, 481.

209   "the business afresh": *TSE Letters 1 2009*, 584.

209   "Lady Rothermere dines at 8 . . . I shall wear a dinner jacket myself": Ibid., 633.

209   "a good small format and paper": Ibid., 642.

210   "that the selection of contributions": Ibid.

210   "certain of the right contributors for the first four numbers": Ibid., 656.

210   "handicapped by a good deal of illness and worry": Ibid., 672.

210   "so that your staff can read it": Ibid.

210   "of entire concentration on this one object": Ibid., 678.

210   "perfect" evening . . . "Vivien starved": Ibid., 680.

210   "drop my attempts": Ibid., 690.

210   shorthand typist: Ibid., 688.

210   "to dispose of the poem": Sutton, *Pound, Thayer, Watson, and the* Dial, 239.

211   "endocrine boil over . . . My present impression of the case": Ezra Pound to Scofield Thayer,

May 1922, Dial/Scofield Thayer Papers, Beinecke Rare Book and Manuscript Library, YCAL MSS 34, Series IV, Box 38.

211 "to correspond with Eliot only in the meagerest": Scofield Thayer to Gilbert Seldes, April 30, 1922, Dial/Scofield Thayer Papers, Beinecke Rare Book and Manuscript Library, YCAL MSS 34, Series IV, Box 40.

211 "When are you coming home?": Sutton, *Pound, Thayer, Watson, and the* Dial, 243.

212 "there is not a poem nor a filler": Ibid.

212 "nothing of astounding brilliance . . . a few things . . . Seriously, we will be": Ibid., 244.

212 "coy veiled hint": Ibid., 245.

212 "for confidential use": *TSE Letters 1 2009*, 711.

212 "to present to Liveright": Ibid.

212 "Cher S. T. . . . Eliot seems": Sutton, *Pound, Thayer, Watson, and the* Dial, 247.

212 "The poem is not so bad": Ibid.

212 "I found the poem disappointing": Ibid., 248.

213 "Gilbert could get around Liveright": Ibid.

213 "less and less supportable": Ibid.

213 "Shall I try to persuade him": Ibid., 247.

213 "I don't see why": Ibid., 250.

213 "at least from the point of view": *TSE Letters 1 2009*, 699.

214 "I am quite aware . . . gained nothing . . . prestige and usefulness": Ibid.

214 "persecution mania": Ibid.

214 "superiority . . . getting bitter and hypercritical": Ibid., 708.

215 "uniquely valuable intrinsically and 'publicitically'—(a good word that)": Kingsley Martin to Leonard Woolf, September 7, 1929, Henry W. and Albert A. Berg Collection of English and American Literature, New York Public Library, Berg Collection, m.b. (Woolf).

215 "I am *not* anxious": *TSE Letters 1 2009*, 693.

215 Schiff . . . C. K. Scott Moncrieff: Schiff remained bitter about this, though after Moncrieff's death in 1930, he completed his rival's translation with the concluding volume, *Le temps retrouvé, Time Regained*, which he published under his usual pen name, Stephen Hudson.

215 "private address . . . I await consequences": *TSE Letters 1 2009*, 689.

215 "I have been waiting . . . I am very disappointed . . . yield to your persuasion": Ibid., 697.

216 "possibly our best critic": Richard Davenport-Hines, *Proust at the Majestic: The Last Days of the Author Whose Book Changed Paris* (New York: Bloomsbury, 2006), 268.

216 his publisher Gallimard, on July 7: Marcel Proust, *Correspondance*, ed. Philip Kolb, vol. 21, 1922 (Paris: Plon, 1993), 345.

216 "cette question Eliot" was "all mixed up with": Ibid.

216 "I'm too tired to go on. I still haven't written to M. Eliot": Ibid., 364.

216 "Ode to Marcel Proust": Proust, *Selected Letters*, vol. 4, 95n2.

216 "I have not read Proust . . . very weighty, and rather long . . . at no point inferior to the original": *TSE Letters 2*, 233n6.

217 "new lump of Proust": Davenport-Hines, *Proust at the Majestic*, 186.

217 "The little lickspittle wasn't satirising": Pound, *The Letters of Ezra Pound, 1907–1941*, 249.

217 Quinn finally received: *TSE Letters 1 2009*, 713–14n2.

217 Early on Saturday morning: Jeanne Foster's recollections are in her typescript "Notes on var. orig. 'Wasteland,'" Jeanne R. Foster–William M. Murphy Collection, b. 3, Manuscripts and Archives Division, New York Public Library.

217 eleven-room apartment: Reid, *The Man from New York*, 402.

217 thirty-five copies of Eliot's first book: Londraville and Londraville, *Dear Yeats, Dear Pound, Dear Ford*, 197.

217 complete manuscript of *Ulysses*: Reid, *The Man from New York*, 589.

217 "to show adequately": Ibid., 598.

217 insured: Ibid., 565.

217 "resembled not a gallery": Ibid., 598.

218 "unromantic duties . . . read over": Ibid., 402.

218 Foster would read the brief twice: Ibid., 403.

218   Quinn had dictated a new Liveright contract: *TSE Letters 1 2009*, 713–14n2.

218   "tucked away": Ibid.

218   Quinn had read "the poems": Ibid.

218   "close to a nervous breakdown": Reid, *The Man from New York*, 564.

218   "working too hard to quit": Ibid.

218   *"Waste Land* is one of the best things . . . Liveright may be . . . for the elect": *TSE Letters 1 2009*, 713–14n2.

219   "the book is a little thin . . . I give you my impression": Ibid.

219   "Cable deferred rate": Charles Egleston, ed., *The House of Boni & Liveright, 1917–1933: A Documentary Volume* (Detroit: Gale, 2004), 264. Egleston's transcription of Quinn's letter to Eliot records the time Quinn read the poem as between 11.30 p.m. and 12.30 a.m. (267). *TSE Letters 1 2009* records it as between 11.50 p.m. and 12.30 a.m. (713–14n2).

219   "Many poets who became prominent": In W. W. Norton and Company records, Columbia University Rare Book and Manuscript Library, Series III (Boni and Liveright, Inc./Horace Liveright, Inc. Records), Box 8.

220   a ledger for the book was created: Ibid., Box 7. "Wasteland" it remained. There are four pages of *Wasteland* entries, including the cost of additional printings and royalty payments to Eliot through December 31, 1929, long after Liveright had any right to print the book. All of them carry over *Wasteland* to the top of the next page. On the last days of October, November, and December 1922, further costs itemized include: proofs, $6.50; printing and binding 1,012 copies, $61.50 for the first 500 and $78.07 for the rest; paper, $31.50; dust jackets, $21.62.

13: "I Like Being with My Dead"

221   "on the chance . . . It will be painful stopping": EMF to FB, 17-6-22, EMF Papers, KCAC, EMF/18/38/1, vols. 34/1–2.

221   On the same day in late June: Forster, *Journals and Diaries*, 2:67. He refers to the news in his letter to Masood on June 26 EMF Papers, KCAC, EMF/18/360/1.

222   "nearest approach to a shock": Forster, *Journals and Diaries*, 2:67.

222   a vision he had: Ibid., 68.

222   "The affair has treated me": Ibid., 67.

222   "almost directly": Ibid.

222   "nice food and straggling talk": *EMF Letters 2*, 31.

223   "dissatisfied with what I do . . . the faintest conviction": EMF to Siegfried Sassoon, 12-6-22, EMF Papers, KCAC, EMF/18/489/3.

223   "Of course I could write": Forster, *Longest Journey*, 361.

223   "I had a special and unusual": Ibid.

223   "the manuscript broke off": Ibid.

224   "come upon me without": Ibid., 366.

224   "including that very valuable faculty": Ibid., 362.

224   "secresy [*sic*] conveniences me": EMF to GHL, 6-13-22, EMF Papers, KCAC, EMF/18/333.

225   "Confused dream": Forster, *Journals and Diaries*, 2:68.

225   "always know that he has died . . . My boy I am oppressed . . . always this sober trying": Ibid.

225   "to know exactly what you were like": Ibid.

225   "with my mind on you": Forster, *Alexandria*, 329.

225   dated the letter: Ibid.

226   "for you and me": Ibid.

226   "although I know": Ibid.

226   "I am professionally a writer": Ibid.

226   "I write for my own comfort": Ibid.

226   He wrote out a dedication: Ibid.

226   Morgan also added an epigram: Ibid.

227   "mediaeval" handwriting: K. Natwar-Singh, ed., *E. M. Forster: A Tribute, with Selections from His Writings on India* (New York: Harcourt, Brace & World, 1964), 24.

227 "cacography": John H. Stape, "Editing Forster," *Essays in Criticism* 26, no. 2 (April 1, 1976): 177–81; first draft ("superseded") in EMF Papers, KCAC, EMF/34/1, related to the Abinger edition of *Howards End*. The phrase "self-styled 'cacography'" is dropped from the published article.

227 "dead six months": Forster, *Alexandria*, 329.

227 "December 27th, 1929": Ibid., 334.

227 "This book belongs to ... ninety-two handwritten pages": The notebook is in EMF Papers, KCAC, EMF/11/10, vol. 3/1.

228 "I get so miserable": EMF to SRM, 30-8-22, EMF Papers, KCAC, EMF/18/360/1.

228 "She had eluded him thus ... the very fact": Forster, *Passage to India*, 68–69.

228 "absolutely battered at by people ... they think I am amusing": EMF to SRM, 30-8-22, EMF Papers, KCAC, EMF/18/360/1.

228 "I am in several other universes": EMF to OM, 28-8-22, Ottoline Morrell Collection, HRC, Box 6, Folder 9.

228 "terribly slowly ... quite alone in the house ... I like being with my dead": EMF to FB, 19-11-22, EMF Papers, KCAC, EMF/18/38/1, vols. 34/1-2.

228 "the occasional nights ... last instants we sat together ... you nudged me": Forster, *Alexandria*, 330.

228 "the greatest thing in my life": Ibid., 328.

228 "This day I received": Forster, *Journals and Diaries*, 2:68.

229 "a silk bag inside cotton wool": EMF to FB, 12-10-22, EMF Papers, KCAC, EMF/18/38/1, vols. 34/1-2.

229 "after due pretending": Ibid.

229 "just goes on to my little finger": Ibid.

229 "generally at night": EMF to SRM, 27-6-23, EMF Papers, KCAC, EMF/18/360/1.

229 He also put it on occasionally: Forster, *Alexandria*, 334.

229 "I know that if I lost it": EMF to SRM, 27-6-23, EMF Papers, KCAC, EMF/18/360/1.

229 a copy of *Women in Love*: EMF to Siegfried Sassoon, 27-6-22, EMF Papers, KCAC, EMF/18/489/3.

229 "Yes I think of you": *DHL Letters* 4, 301.

14: A September Weekend with the Woolves

231 "unpretending house": *VW Diary* 1, 286.

231 "long & low, a house of many doors": Ibid.

231 "incessant nibble nibble": *VW Letters* 5, 211.

231 "very humble and unromantic": *VW Letters* 2, 390.

232 "but why do I let myself": *VW Diary* 1, 291.

232 "old chimney piece": Ibid., 286.

232 "distinctly bad" kitchen: Ibid.

232 "profound pleasure ... an infinity ... unexpected flowers ... well kept rows ... the garden gate admits ... He was pleased": Ibid.

232 "very good" country ... "mystic mounds & tombs": *LW Letters*, 206.

232 "Still I advised the leap": *VW Diary* 2, 276.

232 "ironical ... so savagely anti-clerical": *LW Letters*, 552n2.

232 "a born writer and a born gardener": Ibid., 532n2.

232 "As soon as a Jew": Davenport-Hines, *Proust at the Majestic*, 70.

232 "Monk's House" ... a snare ... "quite fraudulent": *LW Letters*, 569.

233 "loving children ... exasperated": Virginia Woolf, *Jacob's Room*, ed. Kate Flint (Oxford: Oxford University Press, 1999.), 5.

233 "We walked to Hogarth": *VW Diary* 1, 19.

233 "rather shabby, but very easy surroundings": Quentin Bell, *Bloomsbury* (London: Futura, 1974 [1968]), 73.

233 "most sociable summer we've ever had": *VW Diary* 2, 202.

233 "What is the sense of coming": *VW Letters* 2, 549.

234 "Sept. is so magnificent here": *LW Letters*, 222.

234 "have to go on their holidays": Ibid.

234 "the summer dying out of the year": Ibid., 233.

234   "Nothing could exceed the monotony": CB to MH, August 7, 1921, Mary Hutchinson Collection, HRC, Box 6, File 2.

234   "He thinks it my best work": *VW Diary 2*, 186.

235   They had dinner with Vanessa: Leonard Woolf's appointment diary for Thursday, July 27,1922, Leonard Woolf Papers, University of Sussex, SxMs-13/2/R/A/15.

235   "On the whole": *VW Diary 2*, 187.

235   "Mrs Nicolson thinks me": Ibid.

235   farewell dinner at Commercio: Ibid.

235   "literary and fashionable intelligence . . . dictating to his typist . . . very neat": CB to MH, August 3 or 4, 1922, Mary Hutchinson Collection, HRC, Box 6, File 3.

236   "sardonic, guarded, precise": *VW Diary 2*, 187.

236   "organized with uncommon skill": CB to MH, August 3 or 4, 1922, Mary Hutchinson Collection, HRC, Box 6, File 3.

236   "We travel with a selection": Virginia Woolf, *A Change of Perspective: The Letters of Virginia Woolf*, ed. Nigel Nicolson and Joanne Trautmann, vol. 3, *1923–1928* (London: The Hogarth Press, 1977), 58. Future references will be to *VW Letters 3*.

236   "a tortoise": Ibid.

236   "with considerable mastery . . . I make him pay": Ibid.

236   "rain, wind, & dark London looking skies": *VW Diary 2*, 204.

236   "almost constant stream . . . one of the main tributaries": Bell, *Bloomsbury Recalled*, 121.

237   "promised & then withheld": *VW Diary 2*, 204.

237   "I can't write while I'm being read": *VW Diary 3*, 200.

237   "At last, I like reading my own writing": *VW Diary 2*, 205.

237   "Visitors leave one in tatters": Ibid., 198.

237   for the second part of a Sussex visit: CB to MH, August 25, 1922, Mary Hutchinson Collection, HRC, Box 6, File 3.

237   "Woolf & Virginia . . . Chinese puzzle": CB to MH, August 28, 1922, Mary Hutchinson Collection, HRC, Box 6, File 3.

237   "neither of us wishes for visitors": *VW Diary 2*, 192.

238   first in the November issue of the *Dial* and then afterward as a book, by Liveright: John Quinn to TSE, September 7, 1922, John Quinn papers, Manuscripts and Archives Division, New York Public Library, Letterbook vol. 26, 220–31. In the end, the *Dial* paid Eliot $130 for the poem, $20 less than Thayer had originally offered in the winter (Sutton, *Pound, Thayer, Watson, and the* Dial, 253).

238   "exceedingly interesting and add much": Sutton, *Pound, Thayer, Watson, and the* Dial, 254.

238   "it's my loss, I suppose": *TSE Letters 1 2009*, 736.

238   "It was a close shave": John Quinn to TSE, September 7, 1922, John Quinn papers, Manuscripts and Archives Division, New York Public Library, Letterbook vol. 26, 225.

238   "good deal of chinning": Ibid., 221.

239   "bibliographical value": Sutton, *Pound, Thayer, Watson, and the* Dial, 253.

239   "quite overwhelmed by your letter": *TSE Letters 1 2009*, 748.

239   "You know, Forster": *EMF Letters 1*, 268.

240   "snuggled in": *VW Diary 2*, 204.

240   "Forster would come out better alone": *VW Diary 1*, 294–95.

240   "I don't believe in suiting": Forster, *Howards End*, 132–33.

240   "often melancholy and low-temperature": *E. M. Forster: Interviews and Recollections*, ed. J. H. Stape (New York: St. Martin's Press, 1993), 230.

240   "He never effused . . . didn't like you": Ibid., 228.

240   "sparkle . . . suppressed sneeze . . . a little sneeze of joy": Ibid., 59.

240   "is all breadth & bone": *VW Diary 2*, 203.

240   "something too simple about him": Ibid., 204.

241   "scarcely touch . . . very little I should think": Ibid.

241   "probably being better done": Ibid., 69.

241   "these undelivered geniuses . . . or silence their groans": *VW Letters 2*, 533.

241   "not a third . . . amused, stimulated, charmed": *VW Diary 2*, 188–89.

241 "An illiterate, underbred book": Ibid.
241 confessed her boredom with *A Portrait*: *VW Letters* 2, 167.
241 Clive had met Joyce for the first time: Bell's encounter is described in a May 7, 1921, letter to MH, Mary Hutchinson Collection, HRC, Box 6, File 2. Clive also saw Joyce at a May 1922 party at the Majestic given by Sydney and Violet Schiff. Also invited were Proust and Stravinsky, among others. Joyce and Proust's meeting was brief and not illuminating. See Davenport-Hines, *Proust at the Majestic*, 38–46.
242 "Eliot says that Joyce's novel": *VW Letters* 2, 485.
243 "who grinned at me": CB to MH, October 26, 1921, Mary Hutchinson Collection, HRC, Box 6, File 3.
243 "utterly contemptuous . . . 'Did Mary really admire it?' . . . feeble, wordy, uneducated stuff . . . Virginia down with the monthlies": CB to MH, August 18, 1922, Mary Hutchinson Collection, HRC, Box 6, File 3.
243 "When one can have the cooked flesh, why have the raw?": *VW Diary* 2, 193.
243 "I may revise this . . . For my own part": Ibid., 189.
244 "the last immortal chapter": Ibid., 197.
244 "reads thin & pointless . . . something rich, & deep": Ibid., 199.
244 "Genius it has I think . . . not only in the obvious sense . . . doing stunts . . . respects writing too much . . . I'm reminded of some callow": Ibid.
245 "scamped the virtue": Ibid., 200.
245 "myriads of tiny bullets": Ibid.
245 "And Tom, great Tom": Ibid., 189.
245 "over stimulated . . . my back up on purpose": Ibid., 200.
245 It was by Gilbert Seldes: Ibid. This was published in the *Nation*.
246 "much more impressive . . . some lasting truth . . . bowled over": Ibid.
246 If she ever did so: Woolf did not read *Ulysses* again, and in her diary she wrote, "Thank God, I need not write about it" (*VW Diary* 2, 196). She had praised Joyce artfully in her article "Modern Novels," published in the *Times Literary Supplement* of April 10, 1919, and noted, "Any one who has read *The Portrait of the Artist as a Young Man* or what promises to be a far more interesting work, *Ulysses*, now appearing in the *Little Review*, will have hazarded some theory . . . as to Mr Joyce's intention" (*VW Essays* 3, 34). When she republished the article in *The Common Reader* in 1925, she left this line unchanged, though the complete *Ulysses* had been published three years before. In her July 1924 *Criterion* article, "Character in Fiction," Woolf wrote briefly of *Ulysses*, "Mr Joyce's indecency in *Ulysses* seems to me the conscious and calculated indecency of a desperate man who feels that in order to breathe he must break the windows. At moments, when the window is broken, he is magnificent. But what a waste of energy!" (*VW Essays* 3, 434).
246 "The book would be a landmark" . . . Tom said that there was no "great conception": *VW Diary* 2, 202–3.
246 Thackeray's *Pendennis*: Ibid., 203.
246 "We know so little . . . how far we now accept": Woolf's notes on Joyce are in Virginia Woolf, "Modern Novels (Joyce)," Berg Collection, New York Public Library, m.b. (Woolf), holograph notebook.
246 "a very queer convention": Ibid.
247 "What is life? Thats the question": Ibid.
247 "could have screwed Jacob up tighter": *VW Diary* 2, 210.
247 Mohammed's request: *EMF Letters* 1, 272.
247 to lend him two books: Furbank, *E. M. Forster*, 2:165–66.
247 "'James Joyce is a very bad writer'": V. S. Pritchett, "Three Cheers for E. M. Forster," *New Statesman*, June 12, 1970, 846, reprinted in *E. M. Forster: Interviews and Recollections*, 224.
247 Virginia was done with Joyce: *VW Letters* 2, 566.
247 "like a martyr to a stake": Ibid.
247 "far otherwise": Ibid.
248 "great adventure": Ibid., 565.
248 "devoting myself": Ibid., 533.

248   "I suppose . . . in a state of amazement": Ibid., 566.

248   "How, at last . . . Well—what remains": Ibid., 565–66.

248   "Mrs Dalloway in Bond Street has branched into a book": *VW Diary* 2, 207.

15: David and Frieda Arrive in Taos

249   "Can you send me also": *DLH Letters* 4, 306.

249   "a big boarding-house staggering over the sea": Ibid., 284.

249   "shall have blewed [*sic*]": Ibid., 260.

249   whist . . . practicing the saxophone: Ibid., 284.

249   "dead, dull, modern, French and Chinese": Ibid., 286.

249   "a Crowd of cinema people": Ibid., 287.

250   "like any sort": Ibid.

250   "hating one another": Ibid., 303.

250   "a fine town but a bit dazing": Ibid., 289.

250   "still landsick": Ibid.

250   "terrible . . . *iron* all the while . . . breaks my head": Ibid., 290.

250   "Everybody is very nice": Ibid., 289.

251   ARRIVED PENNILESS TELEGRAPH DRAFT: Ibid., 287.

251   "the time-table, that magic carpet of today": Lawrence, *The Lost Girl*, 285.

251   "I know that Sumner is watching . . . *held subject to my order*": John Quinn to Sylvia Beach, February 4, 1922, John Quinn papers, Manuscripts and Archives Division, New York Public Library, Letterbook vol. 25, 256.

252   "Couldn't you find *Ulysses*?": *DHL Letters* 4, 320.

252   "I shall be able to read this famous *Ulysses*": Ibid., 275.

252   "I have nearly finished . . . Even the Ulysseans": Ibid.

252   "much more important . . . whole of Mr Joyce": John Middleton Murry,*Reminiscences of D. H. Lawrence* (New York: Henry Holt, 1933), 228, reprinted from the *Nation and Athenaeum*, August 13, 1922.

253   "came off occasionally . . . had great moments": *VW Diary* 2, 203.

253   "They wanted to see me": Luhan, *Lorenzo in Taos*, 27.

253   "I build quite a lot on Taos": Ibid., 35.

253   "Mabel-town": Maddox, *D. H. Lawrence: The Story of a Marriage*, 345.

253   "sub-arty": *DHL Letters* 4, 111.

254   "terrible will to power—woman power": Ibid., 351.

254   "our work together": Luhan, *Lorenzo in Taos*, 66.

254   "a repulsive sight . . . turned it into a brothel . . . that's how powerful he was": Ibid.

254   "surrounded by a shoal . . . some of them less tender": T. S. Eliot wrote the introduction to Father William Tiverton, *D. H. Lawrence and Human Existence* (London: Rockcliff, 1951), vii.

254   a voluminous white cashmere burnous: Luhan, *Lorenzo in Taos*, 66.

254   "so-called flowing lines" . . . "longing to be like a willow": Ibid., 80.

255   "very much wants me to write": *DHL Letters* 4, 310.

255   "Of course it was for this": *Composite* 2, 180.

255   "He said he wanted to write": Ibid.

255   "You have done her . . . She has mothered your books": Luhan, *Lorenzo in Taos*, 71.

255   "She won't let any other woman": Ibid., 72.

255   Mabel also wanted Lawrence to join her crusade: *DHL Letters* 4, 331–32.

255   "tall and full-fleshed": Luhan, *Lorenzo in Taos*, 44.

255   "whole expression . . . extreme fragility": Ibid., 48. Luhan has inserted a long description of Lawrence written by a mutual friend that she seems to accept as representative of her own thoughts about him.

255   "the womb in me": Ibid., 45.

256   Mabel Sterne's "ground" . . . "even by kindness": *DHL Letters* 4, 330.

256   "a big fellow—nice": Ibid., 311–12.

256   "Mabel Sterne has an Indian lover . . . She is pretty rich": Ibid., 313.

256   $1,000 from Hearst for the rights to "The Captain's Doll": Ibid., 302 and 389.

256 "during the hard days": *DHL Letters 4*, 305.
257 "M. Sterne novel of *here*": Ibid., 319.
257 "You've got to remember": Ibid., 318.
257 "your own indubitable voice": Ibid.
257 "sweeping noisily, and singing with a loud defiance": Luhan, *Lorenzo in Taos*, 72.
257 "loneliness that was like a terrible hunger . . . He couldn't admit any rivals": Ibid., 104.
258 "I never even saw the chapter": Ibid., 85.
258 "It's *very* clever at the beginning": *DHL Letters 4*, 319.
258 "exceedingly good and very discussable": Ibid., 301n1.
258 The character based on Mabel: In D. H. Lawrence, *St. Mawr and Other Stories*, ed. Brian Finney (Cambridge: Cambridge University Press, 1983), 202. The untitled fragment was given the title "The Wilful Woman" by Keith Sagar when he published it for the first time in the 1971 Penguin edition of *The Princess, and Other Stories* (see Finney introduction, xxi).
258 "avoided the personal note in life": Forster, *Howards End*, 79.
259 "hates the white world": *DHL Letters 4*, 351.
259 "put it in black and white . . . I don't believe": Ibid., 337.
259 "bullying and Sadish": Ibid.
259 "*antagonistic* to the *living* relation of man and wife": Ibid.
259 "I believe that, at its best": Ibid.
260 "Of course there is no breach": Ibid., 345.
260 "Mabel Sterne's territory": Ibid., 343.
260 "on free territory once more": Ibid., 348.
260 In the mountains: Ibid., 360.
260 He and Frieda went riding: Ibid., 353.
260 beauty of the clouds . . . "so heavy and empty": Merrild, *A Poet and Two Painters*, 105.
261 "full and surcharged with insult": Ibid., 65.
261 "God in Heaven, no": Ibid.
261 "beastly humans": Ibid., 239.
261 "no inside to life: all outside": *DHL Letters 4*, 365.
261 "In *my* country . . . we're *all* Kings and Queens": Ibid.
261 It arrived in Taos on November 6: Ibid., 335.
261 "all very nice, but a terrible wrapper on *Women in Love*": Ibid., 335n2.
261 "F. Wubbenhorst": Ibid., 340.
262 "I do *not* want you to pay": Ibid., 345.
262 "I am sorry, but I am one . . . I am glad I have seen": Ibid., 340.
262 "would look as much askance . . . We make a choice": Ibid.
262 "Do you really want to publish": Ibid., 355.
262 "great thing, a unique thing . . . It is no proof that a man . . . It is absurd for people": John Quinn to Harriet Weaver, October 28, 1922, John Quinn papers, Manuscripts and Archives Division, New York Public Library, Letterbook vol. 26, 305–9.
263 "Why do they read me?": *DHL Letters 4*, 363.
263 Lawrence sent copies of the books . . . as Christmas presents: Ibid., 355 and 362.
263 "You will find it a different": Frieda Lawrence to Adele Selzer, 12-15-22 [postmark], Frieda Lawrence Collection, HRC, Box 5, Folder 6.

16: "Mrs Dalloway Has Branched into a Book"

265 "my first testimony . . . a little uppish": *VW Diary 2*, 205.
265 "two books running side by side": Ibid.
266 "reading with a purpose": Ibid.
266 "Thoughts upon beginning a book": Woolf's sets of notes from autumn 1922, dated October 6 and 16, and November 9 and November 19, are reprinted in Virginia Woolf, *"The Hours": The British Museum Manuscript of Mrs. Dalloway*, ed. Helen M. Wussow (New York: Pace University Press, 1996), 411–19.
266 "make *some* impression . . . cannot be wholly frigid fireworks": *VW Diary 2*, 205.
266 "Book of scraps of J's R.": Woolf, *"The Hours,"* 410.

267   "I must get on with my reading": *VW Diary* 2, 208.
267   "I want to think out Mrs Dalloway": Ibid., 209.
267   "ushers in a host of others": Ibid., 189.
267   "tunnelling" technique: Ibid., 272.
267   "the violent explosion": Woolf, *The Complete Shorter Fiction of Virginia Woolf*, 317.
268   *Jacob's Room* was published . . . in an edition of one thousand copies: *VW Diary* 2, 209 and 209n12.
268   "long, a little tepid"; "Pall Mall [Gazette] passes me over" . . . "an elderly sensualist": Ibid.
268   "the letter I've liked best of all": Ibid.
268   "too highly for it to give me": Ibid., 207.
268   "a great writer or a nincompoop": Ibid., 209.
268   "splash . . . most whole hearted": Ibid., 210.
268   "It's odd how little I mind": Ibid.
268   "At last, I like reading . . . At forty I am beginning": *VW Diary* 2, 205–6.
268   "go on unconcernedly whatever people say": Ibid.
268   a second edition of another thousand: Ibid., 209.
268   "it is superb": Ibid., 209. Garnett himself published his first novel, *Lady into Fox*, in 1922. It was a popular success and won both the Hawthornden Prize and the James Tait Black Memorial Prize, which D. H. Lawrence had won two years before for *The Lost Girl*.
269   "try to get on a step further": *VW Letters* 2, 571.
269   "Septimus Smith?": *VW Diary* 2, 207.
269   But Bunny made another comparison in his letter: David Garnett to VW, October 19, 1922, Monk's House Papers, University of Sussex, SxMs-18/1/D/61/1.
270   "I expect you're rather hard . . . I only have the sound of it": *VW Letters* 2, 572.
270   "foresee this book better . . . get the utmost": *VW Diary* 2, 209.
270   "he said it is like a series of vignettes": VB to CB, October 16, 1922, The Charleston Papers, KCAC, CHA/1/59/1/8.
270   "make my path as I went": *VW Diary* 2, 210.
270   "the 10th of June, or whatever I call it": Ibid., 211.
271   Septimus Smith was mentioned: Woolf, *The Complete Shorter Fiction of Virginia Woolf*, 318–19. The details of Woolf's typescript are on p. 316.
271   "Septimus Smith was utterly different": Ibid., 319.
271   "All the enmities": Ibid., 322.
271   "Mrs Dalloway saw people looking up": Ibid., 323.
272   news of a War Office report on shell shock: Ted Bogacz, "War Neurosis and Cultural Change in England, 1914–22: The Work of the War Office Committee of Enquiry into 'Shell-Shock,'" *Journal of Contemporary History* 24, no. 2 (April 1989): 227–56.
272   "The Anatomy of Fear": *Times*, August 10, 1922, 5.
272   "a document of so great interest": Lord Southborough, G. C. B., "Shell-Shock," *Times*, September 2, 1922, 13.
273   "I was impressed by . . . He is happy": *VW Diary* 2, 204.
274   "I am in excellent form": EMF to SRM, 27-9-22, EMF Papers, KCAC, EMF/18/360/1.
274   "I always intended this": Ibid.
274   "When I began the book": Ibid.
274   "very charming . . . very very minute domestic details": *VW Letters* 2, 573.
275   Morgan wrote to her about the book: *EMF Letters* 2, 32.
275   "the action through the mind of one of the characters": Ibid., 26.
276   "illusion of life may vanish": Ibid.
276   "In the cave it is *either* a man": EMF to GLD, 26-6-24, EMF Papers, KCAC, EMF/18/158.
277   In Forster's 1913–14 draft: Oliver Stallybrass, editor of *The Manuscripts of* A Passage to India (London: Edward Arnold, 1978), argues that in his 1913–14 draft, Forster "got further into the caves episode than appears" in the finished novel, and that he even wrote more of the incident than is evident in the surviving drafts. Stallybrass writes, "My grounds for this belief are, first, the inherent probability that the complexities of this central episode were what brought him to a halt, and, second, the fact that much of the . . . material for this episode . . . [is] written

comparatively neatly, and with very few changes made" in the course of the writing. Stally-brass surmises that Forster destroyed untidy earlier drafts when he resumed work in 1922. See Stallybrass introduction, xiii–xiv, and for Adela's changing names, xvi.

277 "looked up in his face": Ibid., 226.

277 Forster wrote some notes to himself: This is on page B8v of the *Passage to India* holograph with author revisions, in EMF Collection, HRC, Box 2, Folder 3.

277 "got hold of her other hand . . . wrenched a hand free": Forster, *The Manuscripts of* A Passage to India, 243.

277 "She could not push hard": Ibid.

17: "What More Is Necessary to a Great Poem?"

278 "all that I could have desired": *TSE Letters 1 2009*, 763.

278 "You could not have used words": Ibid.

278 "Perhaps not even you": Ibid., 765.

279 "his wretchedly unhealthy wife": Ibid.

279 Tom again left London for the seaside: Ibid., 777.

279 "visit, travel, or stop at hotels": Ibid., 762.

279 "the Supt. . . . not that it will be the most intelligent": *VW Diary 2*, 208.

279 "that rare thing among English periodicals": *Times Literary Supplement*, October 26, 1922, Issue 1084, 688.

280 the *Liverpool Daily Post and Mercury*: *TSE Letters 1 2009*, 789–90n1.

280 "how calamitous these statements": Ibid., 791.

280 "as I have suspected for some time": Ibid., 790. The editors of Eliot's *Letters* indicate that Eliot suspected Aldington himself was the source, but in his November 18 letter to Alding-ton he does not say this explicitly and does not name Aldington to Pound in a letter he wrote on the same day. To Aldington, Eliot wrote, "You should realize as well as I what has made possible the appearance of such a libel and you ought to know as well as I from what source it is like to have emanated. Do not mention this to a single person *until I have seen my solicitor and written you again*. I pledge you to secrecy." He wrote almost exactly the same thing to Pound, though to Pound he wrote of "sources," rather than of one source. Two days later, Eliot wrote to "my dear Richard" in a perfectly friendly tone about *Criterion* editorial matters and closed, "I am seeing my solicitor and have nothing more to add at present except that this libel business is still a *secret* and <u>confidential</u>" (*TSE Letters 1 2009*, 791). It would seem that a more likely source of the "malicious attack from some concealed enemy in London," as Eliot put it (ibid.), was Wyndham Lewis, in whom Eliot had immedi-ately regretted confiding about his doctor's advice to take the three months' leave from Lloyds in September 1921.

281 "protracted and immense strain": Ibid., 798.

281 "The circulation of untrue stories": *TSE Letters 1 2009*, 794.

281 "for my life *or for Vivien's* life": Ibid., 789.

281 "I want to talk about publicity": Gilbert Seldes to Beatrice Kaufman, October 5, 1922, Dial/Scofield Thayer Papers, Beinecke Rare Book and Manuscript Library, YCAL MSS 34, Series I, Box 6, Folder 211.

282 "I sometimes feel as if": Wilson, *The Twenties*, 109.

282 a cheap railroad apartment: Ibid., 29.

282 "bowled over": Lewis M. Dabney, *Edmund Wilson: A Life in Literature* (New York: Farrar, Straus and Giroux, 2005), 3.

282 "It will give you a thrill . . . nothing more or less than": Wilson, *Letters on Literature and Politics, 1912–1972*, 94.

282 "Never have the sufferings": Ibid.

282 reviewed the poem on November 5: T. S. Eliot, *The Annotated Waste Land with Eliot's Contemporary Prose*, ed. Lawrence Rainey (New Haven, CT: Yale University Press, 2005), 34.

283 Wilson often complained that Rascoe: Wilson, *Letters on Literature and Politics, 1912–1972*, 79 and 97.

283 "drew blood": Joost, *Scofield Thayer and The Dial*, 105.

283 "quite beyond words": Scofield Thayer to Gilbert Seldes, November 28, 1922, Dial/Scofield Thayer Papers, Beinecke Rare Book and Manuscript Library, YCAL 34, Series IV, Box 41, Folder 1157.

283 "paragraph by paragraph": Gilbert Seldes to Scofield Thayer, November 5, 1921, Dial/Scofield Thayer Papers, Beinecke Rare Book and Manuscript Library, YCAL 34, Series IV, Box 40, Folder 1129.

284 "in our opinion": Gilbert Seldes to Scofield Thayer, December 14, 1922, Dial/Scofield Thayer Papers, Beinecke Rare Book and Manuscript Library, YCAL 34, Series IV, Box 41, Folder 1158.

284 "as to the literary contents too": Joost, *Scofield Thayer and The Dial*, 111.

284 by another thousand, to 7,440: Ibid., 41.

284 the *Dial* soon touted to potential advertisers: Amanda Sigler, "Expanding Woolf's Gift Economy: Consumer Activity Meets Artistic Production in *The Dial*," *Tulsa Studies in Women's Literature* 30, no. 2 (Fall 2011): 322–23.

285 "generally considered the outstanding poem": *New-York Tribune*, December 24, 1922, 17.

285 "probably the most discussed": *New-York Tribune*, January 21, 1923, SM26.

285 ran under the headline "Between Ourselves": *New York Times Book Review*, December 10, 1922, 57.

285 "Dearest darling Wing": *TSE Letters 2*, 8–9.

285 "I think you have understood": Ibid., 11.

286 "imitator . . . extremely ill-focused": Ibid., 11n3.

286 "vast indebtedness . . . there are unquestionably respects": Ibid., 11.

286 "I always envied James Joyce": TSE to Ezra Pound, December 28, 1959, Ezra Pound Papers, Beinecke Rare Book and Manuscript Library, YCAL MSS 43, Box 15, Folder 673.

286 the copy he gave to Pound in January 1923: Ezra Pound's copy of *The Waste Land* is at HRC. Eliot adapted this inscription for the dedication in later editions of *The Waste Land*: For Ezra Pound / il miglior fabbro.

Epilogue

287 "Good bye Mohammed. I meant to review the year": *Pickering 2*, 73.

287 "mark the fact": Ibid.

287 All of the entries: Forster's diary, also known as his "Locked Journal," is in EMF Papers, KCAC, EMF/12/8, vol. 4/4.

288 "I have this moment": EMF to Leonard Woolf, undated, Leonard Woolf Papers, University of Sussex, SxMs 18II.

288 "He is moved, as I am": *VW Diary 2*, 289.

288 "was to be Forster's end": Gardner, *E. M. Forster: The Critical Heritage*, 211.

288 "admirable self-restraint": Ibid., 214.

288 "A little while ago": Ibid., 204.

288 seventeen thousand copies . . . fifty-four thousand: Forster, *The Manuscripts of* A Passage to India, Stallybrass introduction, 19.

288 "A few years ago": Ibid.

289 His income for the year: Harry T. Moore, *The Intelligent Heart: The Story of D. H. Lawrence* (London: Penguin Books, 1960), 386.

289 "Birkendele": Lawrence, *Letters to Thomas and Adele Seltzer*, 189.

289 "very quiet, pretty, peaceful": *DHL Letters 4*, 473.

289 "hateful here . . . It's all the dead hand": Ibid., 552.

289 "sad as ever . . . To me you are": Ibid., 584.

290 Judge John Ford . . . began an attack . . . Seltzer was arrested again: Lawrence, *Letters to Thomas and Adele Seltzer*, 189.

290 "one of the glories": E. M. Forster, *The Creator as Critic and Other Writings by E. M. Forster*, ed. Jeffrey M. Heath (Toronto: Dundurn Press, 2008), 222.

290 "neither of them quite satisfactory . . . improper and scarcely read him": Ibid.

290 "pages and chapters . . . the whole fabric": Ibid., 224.

290 "the most heart-rending account": Ibid., 222.

291 "the promise of a story": Raymond Mortimer to Scofield Thayer, February 22, 1923, Dial/ Scofield Thayer Papers, Beinecke Rare Book and Manuscript Library, YCAL 34, Series IV, Box 36, Folder 998.

291 "which she does not want to print here": Raymond Mortimer to Scofield Thayer, February 26, 1923, ibid.

291 "2 chapters of my Garsington novel": *VW Letters* 2, 543. Not long after "Mrs. Dalloway in Bond Street" had branched into a novel, in the autumn, Woolf learned of the death of an old friend, Kitty Maxse, whom she had not seen in many years. Maxse had fallen on the stairs, and it seemed that her fall was not an accident and may have been suicide. Woolf drew on Maxse and her death as she wrote her novel, but she did not have Maxse in mind when writing her story. See *VW Letters* 2, 573.

291 "I enclose Mrs. Woolf's story": Raymond Mortimer to Scofield Thayer, April 14, 1923, Dial/ Scofield Thayer Papers, Beinecke Rare Book and Manuscript Library, YCAL 34, Series IV, Box 36, Folder 999.

291 "as to the exquisiteness": Scofield Thayer to Raymond Mortimer, April 19, 1923, ibid.

291 Woolf's handwritten note: Dial/Scofield Thayer Papers, Beinecke Rare Book and Manuscript Library, YCAL 34, Series I, Box 8.

291 "putting on a spurt": *VW Diary* 2, 325.

291 "deliver the final blows": Ibid.

291 "so far I have not heard a word": *VW Diary* 3, 12.

292 "floating like an old bottle . . . fresh adventures": Ibid., 15–16.

292 "The only judgment": Ibid., 22.

292 "sparing of words . . . awfully pleased": Ibid., 24.

292 "We are going to build": *VW Letters* 3, 187.

292 "I wonder if this time": *VW Diary* 3, 7.

292 "the utmost sensibility . . . tough as catgut": Ibid.

292 "he will I suppose": Ibid.

292 "to have father's character done complete": Ibid., 18.

293 "lovely gifted aristocrat . . . Not much to my severer taste . . . But could I ever know her": *VW Diary* 2, 216–17.

293 sent her the manuscript of *Mrs. Dalloway*: *LW Letters*, 259–61.

293 "poor Tom": *VW Letters* 2, 593.

293 "as a Trust": *TSE Letters 2 2009*, 6.

293 Faber and Gwyer: Ibid., 823.

293 "he had put so much": Ibid., 124.

294 "an ideal world": Ibid.

294 "Certainly up to the time . . . Since then he has had": Ibid.

294 "Under these circumstances": Ibid.

294 Ezra Pound wrote to H. L. Mencken: Pound, *The Letters of Ezra Pound, 1907–1941*, 174.

294 *For last year's words*: Eliot, *The Poems of T. S. Eliot*, 204.

BIBLIOGRAPHIC NOTE

In *The World Broke in Two* I focus as much as possible on what the people I write about were thinking at the time about their lives and works. For that reason most of my source material has been their diaries and letters, and those of the people who knew them. I have tried to put these contemporaneous thoughts and impressions in context and to make clear where what people thought, or wrote privately, was myopic, mistaken, or false. I consulted many authoritative works about Eliot, Forster, Lawrence, and Woolf that helped shape my understanding of them and their times. Some of these appear in my source notes because I quoted from them directly. I am grateful to the scholarship and insights of other biographers and critics, and to historians of the period who were equally essential as I worked, and I note some key books here.

Barham, Peter. *Forgotten Lunatics of the Great War*. New Haven, CT: Yale University Press, 2004.
Beauman, Nicola. *E. M. Forster: A Biography*. New York: Knopf, 1993.

Briggs, Julia. *Virginia Woolf: An Inner Life*. Orlando, FL: Harcourt, 2005.

Bynner, Witter. *Journey with Genius: Recollections and Reflections Concerning the D. H. Lawrences*. New York: John Day, 1951.

Byrne, Janet. *A Genius for Living: The Life of Frieda Lawrence*. New York: HarperCollins, 1995.

Carter, William C. *Marcel Proust: A Life*. New Haven, CT: Yale University Press, 2000.

Crawford, Robert. *Young Eliot: From St. Louis to* The Waste Land. New York: Farrar, Straus and Giroux, 2015.

Eliot, T. S. *The Waste Land*, ed. Michael North. New York: W. W. Norton, 2001.

Findlay, Jean. *Chasing Lost Time: The Life of C. K. Scott Moncrieff: Soldier, Spy, and Translator*. New York: Farrar, Straus and Giroux, 2015.

Glendinning, Victoria. *Vita: The Life of V. Sackville-West*. New York: Knopf, 1983.

Gordon, Lyndall. *Virginia Woolf: A Writer's Life*. New York: W. W. Norton, 2001 [1984].

Lawrence, Frieda. *The Memoirs and Correspondence*, ed. E. W. Tedlock Jr. New York: Knopf, 1964.

Nicolson, Nigel. *Portrait of a Marriage: Vita Sackville-West and Harold Nicolson*. Chicago: University of Chicago Press, 1998 [1973].

Parker, Peter. *Ackerley: The Life of J. R. Ackerley*. New York: Farrar, Straus and Giroux, 1989.

Walkowitz, Judith R. *Nights Out: Life in Cosmopolitan London*. New Haven, CT: Yale University Press, 2012.

ACKNOWLEDGMENTS

I could not have written *The World Broke in Two* without the support, encouragement, and advice of many friends.

Blake West's love and absolute faith in me made it possible. I love him with all my heart. I dedicate my book to him.

I also dedicate it to my mother, Joanne Goldstein. I think it is a coincidence that she was born in 1922. I am very pleased that on pages 274–75 I was able to quote from a letter that Virginia Woolf wrote to Roger Fry on Sunday, October 22, 1922, the day my mother was born.

I thank my brothers, Lewis, Abbey, and Arnold, and my sisters-in-law Susan, Claire, and Marian, as well as my nieces and nephews, for their continuing interest in my work, and their love.

My father, Harden Goldstein, died in 1969. I inherited his love of books and reading, and I grew up surrounded by his vast book collection, which made me feel close to him and continues to, now that so many of his books, all faithfully kept by my mother through many years and her move from our house to an apartment, are mine. My father collected the works of his contemporaries—Saul Bellow, Norman Mailer, Henry Miller, Philip Roth, and others. But he also had a copy of Thomas Seltzer's trade edition of *Women in Love*, a World War II edition of Eliot's collected poems, and a later edition of Forster's *Pharos and Pharillon*, all of which I treasure. I didn't realize growing up that we had no Woolf in the house, or none, at least, that I've ever found. But a visit to my mother's apartment is also a visit to my father's library, and there are books behind the books on all the shelves, and I will keep looking.

I have many friends whose company kept me going, and many, particularly in publishing and academia, whose advice helped me more than they may have realized. I offer my thanks to Miriam Altshuler, Bobby Berg, Janis Donnaud, Lisa Drew, Deb Futter, Philip Gefter, Peter Gethers, Jay Grossman, Bill Hayes, Daniel Kaizer, Wayne Koestenbaum, Nicholas Latimer, Jeff Masten, Adam Moss, Richard Press, Dan Santow, Christopher Schelling, Michael Seltzer, Tom Spain, Ralph Tachuk, Bob Tuschman, and Paula Whyman. Lorraine Shanley's shoulder and sharp eye were vital. I am grateful that she read a draft of this book and made it better.

Eve Kosofsky Sedgwick, who died in 2009, was my first teacher at the City University of New York Graduate Center. I audited Eve's yearlong seminar on Proust in 1998–99. It was in reading Proust then that I first wondered whether Virginia Woolf had read him and what she thought. *The World Broke in Two* grew from there. I returned to the Graduate Center as a PhD student in 2000, and though Joseph Wittreich trained me to read Milton, and saw me through my dissertation in 2010, he remained a steadfast friend and adviser when I turned my attention to the twentieth century. I thank him and Stuart Curran for their years of friendship and for the high standard their scholarship has set.

Much of this book was written during residencies generously provided by a number of organizations that gave me the time and space—and camaraderie—essential to work. I thank the Norman Mailer Center and Writers Colony, and Greg Curtis for early advice; the MacDowell Colony; the Corporation of Yaddo; Writers Omi; Virginia Center for the Creative Arts; Ucross Foundation; and the Millay Colony for the Arts. It was wonderful to work and play at each place and to meet so many artists whose creativity and friendship continue to inspire me. Thank you especially to Bernhard Brungs, whose gorgeous watercolors of Virginia

Woolf I treasure. Thank you, Steve Meswarb, for driving through an unexpected April snowstorm and for getting us from Denver to Ucross in one piece.

I am indebted as well to the National Humanities Center, Research Triangle, North Carolina, for the research fellowship that provided me a place in its Summer Institute in Literary Studies seminar on T. S. Eliot led by Christopher Ricks and sponsored by the Andrew W. Mellon Foundation; and to the Harry Ransom Center, at the University of Texas, Austin, where the two months I spent researching in their magnificent collections were jointly sponsored by the Frederic D. Weinstein Memorial Fellowship and the Andrew W. Mellon Foundation Research Fellowship Endowment. I am grateful to Jen Tisdale and many Austin friends. I thank Jean Cannon and Pat Fox for all the wonders they made available in the reading room, and I thank Clay Smith for his welcome and for the barbecue.

I am grateful to the English Department at New York University and its chair, Christopher Cannon, and to the dean of the Faculty of Arts and Science, for granting me Visiting Scholar status, and I thank my friend Philip Brian Harper for sponsoring me. I am also grateful to the Funding Exchange, which generously provided a home that made it possible for me to finish writing my book. I give my deepest thanks to my friend Richard Burns for so thoughtfully fostering the arrangement and for making it work so well. Early on, my membership in the Writers Room on Astor Place provided me a desk and many friendships.

I was privileged to research *The World Broke in Two* in many libraries. It is serendipitous that the New York Public Library holds unparalleled collections of papers relating to Eliot, Forster, Lawrence, and Woolf. I am grateful to Isaac Gewirtz and to Rebecca Filner and Anne Garner for making my work in the Henry W. and Albert A. Berg Collection of English and American Literature so enjoyable. Thank you, also, to Rodney Philips, former curator of the Berg, who introduced me to its Woolf collection years ago, and whose friendship unexpectedly set me on my way. I also give my thanks to Tal Nadan and her colleagues in the library's Manuscripts and Archives Division.

My research elsewhere was made more pleasurable—and efficient—by the attentive kindness of many people at each institution I visited. I thank the staffs of the British Library; Columbia University's Rare Book and Manuscript Library; the University of Nottingham Library; the University of Sussex Library; and the Beinecke Rare Book and Manuscript Library at Yale University. Patricia McGuire and her colleagues at the Archive Centre, King's College, Cambridge, were especially hospitable during a long winter's visit. I thank Justine Shaw for her research at the University of Sussex on my behalf and for finding letters written to Virginia Woolf that were of importance to my work. I am especially thankful to two dear friends, Brian Meyer and the late Arnold Markley, whose advice and support helped me achieve my research goals. My thanks also to Loriel Olivier, without whose help the photo insert would not have been possible.

I have been very lucky to work at Roosevelt House, the Public Policy Institute of Hunter College. I am grateful to Fay Rosenfeld for the flexibility in scheduling that made it possible for me to work on this book. I also thank Harold Holzer, the director of Roosevelt House, and Jennifer J. Raab, the president of Hunter College, for their support. The friendship of Pat Battle, Gus Rosendale, Raphael Miranda, and many others at *Weekend Today in New York* has meant a great deal to me as I wrote this book.

When I was just beginning to think through what this book might be, Doris Kearns Goodwin and Lyndall Gordon offered encouragement that inspired me. Thank you, also, to Joy Johannessen, whose early advice proved essential.

Joy Harris is my cherished friend. She is also my literary agent, and I am in her debt professionally and personally. Joy has been my companion and collaborator from our first conversation about *The World Broke in Two* to our most recent. She is a wise reader and discerning adviser, and her devotion has sustained me. Thank you, Joy. I'm grateful to Joy's colleague Adam Reed for arranging so much on my behalf.

Gillian Blake has been an amazing editor at every stage, and her continuing dedication to this book, from conceptual editing at the start to the placement of commas at the end, inspired me. She has been absolutely right all along, careful, surgical, and focused, and frequently at astonishing speed. She patiently and expertly helped shape the narrative from first drafts to last and remained vigilantly alert throughout to the ways in which she could improve the clarity and precision of every sentence, paragraph, and chapter. Her attention to detail is stunning and capacious, and I eagerly incorporated every suggestion she made. She has been a brilliant teacher, and I am grateful for her hard work and her friendship. Muriel Jorgensen's copyediting sharpened the manuscript, and Eleanor Embry facilitated everything with infectious and gratifying enthusiasm. I am grateful to Chris O'Connell for his careful work that made this book better and to Meryl Levavi for making the pages look so good. I thank Rick Pracher for designing a dust jacket so beautiful I will be content if people do judge this book by its cover. I have been fortunate to have many other friends and champions at Henry Holt and Macmillan, including Steve Rubin, Maggie Richards, Pat Eisemann, Carolyn O'Keefe, Jessica Wiener, Jason Liebman, and Robert Allen. I thank them for their commitment to me and this book.

INDEX

ABOUT THE AUTHOR

BILL GOLDSTEIN, the founding editor of the *New York Times* books website, reviews books and interviews authors for NBC's *Weekend Today in New York*. He is also the curator of public programs at Roosevelt House, the public policy institute of New York's Hunter College. A graduate of the University of Chicago, Goldstein received a PhD in English from the City University of New York Graduate Center in 2010. He is the recipient of writing fellowships from the MacDowell Colony, Yaddo, the Ucross Foundation, and elsewhere for his work on *The World Broke in Two*.